D0760535

INSIGHT GUIDES
IN THE SAME SERIES

taiwan

Written by Daniel P. Reid
Edited by Paul Zach
Directed and Designed by Hans Johannes Hoefer

APA PRODUCTIONS

THE INSIGHT GUIDES SERIES RECEIVED SPECIAL AWARDS
FOR EXCELLENCE FROM THE PACIFIC AREA TRAVEL
ASSOCIATION.

TAIWAN
Third Edition Published by:
©APA PRODUCTIONS (HK) LTD, 1986

Printed in Singapore by Nissin Printcraft (Pte) Ltd

Colour Separation in Singapore by Colourscan Pte Ltd

No part of this book may be reproduced, stored in a retrieval system or
transmitted in any form, or means electronic, mechanical, photocopying,
recording or otherwise, without prior written permission of Apa Productions. Brief text quotations with use of photographs are exempted for book
review purposes only.

APA PRODUCTIONS

Publisher and Managing Director: Hans Johannes Hoefer
Financial Controller: Henry Lee
Administrative Manager: Alice Ng
Editorial Manager: Vivien Loo

Project Editors

Helen Abbott, Diana Ackland, Mohamed Amin, Ravindrala Anthonis, Roy
Bailet, Louisa Cambell, Jon Carroll, John Eames, Janie Freeburg, Bikram
Grewal, Virginia Hopkins, Samuel Israel, Jay Itzkowitz, Phil Jaratt, Tracy
Johnson, Ben Kalb, Wilhelm Klein, Saul Lockhart, Slyvia Mayuga, Gordn
McLauchlan, Kal Müller, Eric Oey, Daniel P. Reid, Kim Robinson, Ronn
Ronck, Rolf Steinberg, Harold Stephens, Desmond Tate, Sriyani Tidbal,
Lisa Van Gruisen, Merin Wexler, Made Wijaya.

Contributing Writers

A.D. Aird, Ruth Armstrong, T. Terence Barrow, F. Lisa Beebe, Bruce
Berger, Dor Bahadur Bista, Clinton V. Black, Star Black, Frena Bloomfield,
John Borthwick, Roger Boschman, Tom Brosnahan, Linda Carlock, Jerry
Carroll, Tom Chaffin, Nedra Chung, Tom Cole, Orman Day, Kunda Dixit,
Richard Erdoes, Guillermo Garcia-Oropeza, Ted Giannoulas, Barbara
Gloudon, Harka Gurung, Sharifah Hamzah, Willard A. Hanna, Elizabeth
Hawley, Sir Edmund Hillary, Tony Hillerman, Jerry Hopkins, Peter Hutton,
Neil Jameson, Michael King, Michele Kort, Thomas Lucey, Leonard Lueras,
Michael E. Macmillan, Derek Maitland, Buddy Mays, Craig McGregor,
Reinhold Messner, Julie Michaels, Barbara Mintz, M.R. Priya Rangsit, Al
Read, Elizabeth V. Reyes, Victor Stafford Reid, Harry Rolnick, E.R.
Sarachchandra, Uli Schmetzer, Ilsa Sharp, Norman Sibley, Leslie Marmon
Silko, Peter Spiro, Harold Stephens, Keith Stevens, Michael Stone, Colin
Taylor, Deanna L. Thompson, Randy Udall, James Wade, Mallika
Wanigasundara. William Warren, Cynthia Wee, Tony Wheeler, Linda White,
H. Taft Wireback, Alfred A. Yuson, Paul Zach.

Contributing Photographers

Carole Allen, Ping Amranand, Marcello Bertinetti, Alberto Cassio, Pat
Canova, Alain Compost, Ray Cranbourne, Alain Evrard, Ricard Ferro, Lee
Foster, Manfred Gottschalk, Werner Hahn, Dallas and John Heaton, Brent
Hesselyn, Hans Hoefer, Luca Invernizzi, Ingo Jezierski, Wilhelm Klein,
Dennis Lane, Max Lawrence, Philip Little, Ian Lloyd, Bret Lundberg, Guy
Marche, Antonio Martinelli, David Messent, Ben Nakayama, Vautier de
Nanxe, Kal Müller, Günter Pfannmuller, Van Phillips, Ronni Pinsler, Fritz
Prenzel, G.P. Reichelt, Dan Rocovits, David Ryan, Frank Salmoiraghi,
Thomas Schollhammer, Blair Seitz, David Stahl, Tom Tidball, Paul Van Reil,
Rolf Verres, Joe F. Viesti, Paul Von Stroheim, Bill Wassman, Rendo Yap,
Hisham Youssef.

While contributions to Insight Guides are very welcome, the publisher cannot assume responsibility for the care and return of unsolicited manuscripts
or photographs. Return postage and/or a self-addressed envelope must accompany unsolicited material if it is to be returned. Please address all
editorial contributions to Apa Productions, P. O. Box 219, Killiney Road
Post Office. Singapore 9123.

Distributors:

Australia: Lansdowne Press, 176 South Creek Road, Dee Why, N.S.W.
2099, AUSTRALIA **Benelux:** Uitgeverij Cambium, Naarderstraat 11, 1251
Aw Laren, The Netherlands. **Brazil and Portugal:** Cedibra Editora Brasileira
Ltda, Rua Leonidia, 2-Rio de Janeiro, Brazil. **Denmark:** Copenhagen Book
Centre Aps, Roskildeveji 338, DK-2630 Tastrup, Denmark. **Germany:**
Nelles Verlag, Schleissheimer Str. 371b, 8000 Munich 45. **Hawaii:** Pacific
Trade Group Inc., P.O. Box 1227, Kailua, Oahu, Hawaii 96734, U.S.A. **Hong
Kong:** Far East Media Ltd., Vita Tower, 7th Floor, Block B, 29 Wong Chuk
Hang Road, Hong Kong. **India and Nepal:** India Book Distributors, 107/108
Arcadia Building, 195 Narima Point, Bombay-400-021, India. **Indonesia:**
Jalan Patiunus 47, Pekalongan, Jateng, Indonesia. **Italy:** Via Ganaceto 121,
41100 Modena, Italy. **Jamaica:** Kingston Publishers, 1-A Norwood Avenue,
Kingston 5, Jamaica. **Japan:** Charles E. Tuttle Co. Inc., 2-6 Suido 1-Chome,
Bunkyo-ku, Tokyo, Japan. **Korea:** Korea Britannica Corporation, C.P.O. Box
690, Seoul 100, Korea, 162-1, 2-ga, Jangchung-dong, Jung-gu, Seoul,
Korea. **Mexico:** Distribuidora Britannica S.A., Rio Volga 93, Col
Cuauhtemoc, 06500 Mexico 5 D.F., Mexico. **New Zealand:** Lansdowne
Rigby, Unit 3, 3 Marken Place, Glenfield, Auckland. **Pakistan:** Liberty Book
Stall, Inverarity Road, Karachi 03, Pakistan. **Philippines:** National Book
Store Inc., 701 Rizal Avenue, Manila, Philippines. **Singapore and Malaysia:**
MPH Distributors (S) Pte. Ltd., 601 Sims Drive #03-21 Pan-I Warehouse
and Office Complex, Singapore 1438. **Sri Lanka:** K.V.G. de Silva & Sons
(Colombo) Ltd., 415 Galle Road, Colombo 4, Sri Lanka. **Spain:** Altair, Riera
Alta 8, Barcelona 1, Spain. **Sweden:** Esselte Kartcentrum, Vasagatan 16,
S-111 20 Stockholm, Sweden. **Switzerland:** M.P.A. Agencies-Import SA,
CH. du Bochet 68, CH-1025 ST-Sulpice, Switzerland. **Taiwan:** Caves Books
Ltd., 103 Chungshan N. Road, Sec. 2, Taipei, Taiwan. Republic of China.
Thailand: Book Promotion & Service Ltd., 9/14 Soi Pipat, Silom Road,
Bangkok 10500, Thailand. **United Kingdom:** Harrap Ltd . 19-23 Ludgale
Hill London EC4M 7PD, England. United Kingdom **Mainland United States
and Canada:** Prentice Hall Press. Gulf & Western Building. One Gulf & Western
Plaza, New York, NY 10023.

German editions: Nelles Verlag GmbH, Schleissheimerstrasse 371b,
8000 Munich 45, West Germany. **Italian editions:** Via Ganaceto 121,
41100 Modena, Italy.

Advertising and Special Sales Representatives

Advertising carried in Insight Guides gives readers direct access to quality
merchandise and travel-related services. These advertisements are inserted
in the Guide in Brief section of each book. Advertisers are requested to contact their nearest representatives, listed below.
Special sales, for promotion and educational purposes within the international travel industry, are also available. The advertising representatives
listed here also handle special sales. Alternatively, interested parties can
contact marketing director Yvan Van Outrive directly at Apa Productions,
P.O. Box 219. Orchard Point Post Office, Singapore 9123.

Thailand: Cheney, Tan & Van Outrive, 17th Floor Rajapark Building, 163
Asoke Road, Bangkok 10110, Thailand. Tel: 2583244; Telex: 20666 RA-
JAPAK TH.

Hawaii: Hawaiian Media Sales, 1750 Kalakau Ave., Suite 3-243, Honolulu
Hawaii 96826, U.S.A. Tel: (808) 9464483.

Hong Kong: C Cheney & Associates, 17th Floor, D'Aguilar Place, 1-30
D'Aguilar, Central, Hong Kong. Tel: 5-213671; Telex: 63079 CCAL HX.

India: Dass Media Pvt. Ltd., 207 Bhandari House, 91 Nehru Place, New
Delhi-110 019, India. Tel: 669772/667432; Telex: 315236 PRYA IN.

Singapore and Malaysia: Cheney Tan Associates, 20 McCallum Street,
#17-01/02 Asia Chambers, Singapore 0106. Tel: 2222893/2222725; Telex:
RS 35983 CTAL.

Sri Lanka: Spectrum Lanka Advertising Ltd., 56 1/2 Ward Place, Colombo 7, Sri Lanka. Tel: 5984648/596227; Telex: 21439 SPECTRM CE.

APA PHOTO AGENCY PTE LTD

The Apa Photo Agency is S.E. Asia's leading stock photo archive,
representing the work of professional photographers from all over the
world. More than 150,000 original color transparencies are available for
advertising, editoral and educational uses. We are also linked with Tony
Stone Worldwide, one of Europe's leading stock agencies, and their
associate offices around the world:

Singapore: Apa Photo Agency Pte Ltd 5 Lengkong Satu Singapore 1441.
London: Tony Stone Worldwide 28 Finchley Road St John's Nood London
NW8 6ES. **New York:** Index-Stone International Inc 126 Fifth Avenue New
York NY 10011 USA. **Paris:** Fotogram-Stone Agence Photographique 45
rue de Richelieu 75001 Paris France. **Barcelone:** Fototeca Torre Dels Par-
dais 7 Barcelona 08026 Spain **Johannesburg:** Color Library (Pty) Ltd
P O Box 1659 Johannesburg South Africa 2000 **Sydney:** The Photographic
Library of Australia Pty Ltd 7 Ridge Street North Sydney New South Wales
2050 Australia. **Tokyo:** Orion Press 55-1 Kanda Jimbocho Chiyoda-ku
Tokyo 101 Japan.

An overriding preoccupation with politics has always relegated Taiwan to a shadowy corner of the modern mind. With that realization, the editors of Apa Productions' series of *Insight Guides* had long been on the

sioned as principal photographers for the volume.

Born in San Francisco in 1948, **Daniel Reid** has opted for Taiwan and the Chinese way of life since 1973. He holds a Masters degree in

Reid   *Zach*   *Hoefer*   *Anderson*   *Wassmann*

lookout for a vehicle that would shed light on real Taiwan. The catalyst for such an undertaking came in the form of a manuscript for a guide to the island written by scholar and free-lance writer Daniel P. Reid.

After more than a decade of living in Taiwan, Reid's

Rocovits   *Salmoiraghi*

Chinese language and civilization from the Monterey Institute of International Studies and a Bachelors degree in East Asian studies from the University of California at Berkeley. Reid speaks Mandarin fluently and is proficient in reading and writing Chinese. He

manuscript revealed a fascinating island where more than 18 million industrious people have built a comfortable modern community compatible with their Chinese traditions, complemented by their age-old arts and blessed with the natural beauty of a diverse landscape of fertile fields, green valleys, rugged mountains and sandy beaches.

Reid's work became the backbone of *Insight Guide: Taiwan.* To flesh up the text and the island, additional contributions were provided by Taiwan dramatist Jon-Claire Lee; by a British diplomat and noted China scholar Keith Stevens; and by another American writer resident in Taiwan, Andy Unger. Dan Rocovits, yet another American living in the Taipei area, produced many of the photographic images in this volume while an aspiring Taiwanese photographer, "Smiley" Chyou Su-liang, pitched in with valuable assistance as well as some of her own pictures.

The assortment of words and pictures was assembled into the unique *Insight Guide* format by Apa editors Paul Zach and John Anderson under the creative direction of publisher Hans Hoefer and with help from assistant editor Vivien Loo. Bill Wassman and Frank Salmoiraghi, experienced veterans of other *Insight Guides*, were commis-

dabbles in herbal medicine and acupuncture, practices Taoist deep-breathing and other esoteric Chinese disciplines, and pursues an interest in classical Chinese literature at his cliff-hanging Phoenix Mountain hideaway above Peitou on the outskirts of Taipei. Reid's wife, Michelle, was born in Taiwan of northern Chinese parents.

Reid turned to writing when his triumphs as a Chinese cook and "my more dubious reputation as a wild sybarite who knew all the good places to play at night in Taipei" led him to compose a piece about Taipei's restaurants and nightlife in 1978. Since then, he has written for Asian airline and hotel magazines and has published the *Complete Chinese Cookbook* and *Chinese Herbal Medicine.* His extensive travels on the Chinese mainland resulted in his *Complete Guide to China,* published in 1981, and a contribution to Lansdowne Press' *This Is China.*

Reid's manuscript found its way into the hands of Apa managing editor **John Gottberg Anderson,** who was thrilled to have a thematically thorough and politically sensitive manuscript such as Reid's in his possession. Anderson developed the working structure for creation of the *Insight Guide:*
Continued on page 354

TABLE OF CONTENTS

Cover
  —by Dan Rocovits and Bill Wassman

Cartography
  —by Gunter Nelles and Yong Sock
  Ming

AT RAINBOW'S END

Bao-Dao—"Treasure Island."

A garden of Eden, shimmering in cobalt seas and golden sunshine, rich in resources, fertile, and lush with promise and potential. This was Taiwan to its early settlers.

Tales of the untold riches of this island east of the China coast touched off an endless exodus centuries ago. Pirates and political exiles, traders and adventurers, farmers and fishermen left behind the crowded coastal provinces of mainland China to follow the proverbial rainbow.

Taiwan's rugged beauty, crowned by mountains and carved with valleys, satisfied the Chinese sensitivity to aesthetics and the rhythms of nature. Its forests, thick with camphor, cedar, rattan, oak, fir, pine and other woods were at once beautiful and commercially valuable.

The Chinese also found that food grew abundantly and rapidly in the soils of Taiwan, a significant credential for a people accustomed to the frequent famines and chronic food shortages of the spent and crowded fields of the mainland. Furthermore, the island was fat with mineral resources—coal, sulfur and iron—for building a modern society, and precious stones—jadeite, opal and coral—to fill the Chinese need for creating and savoring works of beauty.

Finally, Taiwan proved to be a safe haven for enterprising émigrés blown to the island by the political storms of the mainland. Disgruntled mandarins and merchants, fed up with the factional vagaries and chronic interference of court politics, made their way to the Treasure Island. The minority Hakka peoples from the Kwangtung coast came to escape persecution and Ming Chinese loyalists came to defy Manchu rule. Most recently, the Nationalists made Taiwan their refuge from the Communist regime on the mainland.

Contemporary Taiwan remains a bastion of traditional Chinese culture, values and life-styles. Its people represent every major mainland province. Its restaurants serve the best of every regional form of Chinese cuisine. Its National Museum houses the world's outstanding collection of works from 5,000 years of Chinese creativity.

The essential features of the world's oldest continuous and most culturally accomplished civilization are all preserved in a compact microcosm of China. And beyond its cultural significance, Taiwan is a dynamic, modern society with a thriving economy, a showcase for the boundless energy, natural entrepreneurial skills and ethusiasm for free enterprise that is inherent in the Chinese character.

Cultural Bonds

The origins of Chinese culture have been traced back as far as the Yellow Emperor who ruled over a loose confederation of clans and tribes in the Middle Kingdom about 2,700 B.C. That puts about 5,000 years of recorded history behind Chinese culture. Other nations and civilizations have come and gone, bursting briefly onto the stage of world history only to fizzle out and disappear forever. China has withstood the good centuries and the bad. Many of her ancient legacies have been preserved in Taiwan right up to the present.

Culture is the glue and varnish that has held the rambling ship of Chinese civilization together for 50 centuries. It has cemented its social systems and traditions into a tough resilient fabric that has withstood history's convulsions. It has produced a written language that has been used with only minor modifications since the time of Egypt's pharaohs. It has prevented China from fragmenting into dozens of distinctly different language and ethnic groups, as did Europe.

In fact, the word Chinese is more of a cultural designation than a racial or political label. There are many ethnic differences between a Manchu and a Cantonese, but both are considered Chinese because they embrace common cultural practices and use the same written language to express their very different spoken dialects.

The ethnic diversity of the peoples of China has precluded any national ethos based on racial purity. The Chinese have developed a more civilized means of measuring men based on social behavior and Confucian ethics.

Religion has also taken a back seat to culture. The Chinese have prevented any religious sect from imposing its arbitrary views

Preceding pages: Maopitou, the coral cape at Taiwan's southern tip: picking tea near Sungpoling; martial arts movie stunt outside Taipei. Left, television actress Jenny Jin in traditional attire at the Grand Hotel.

on the secular state and society. Buddhism, Taoism, Islam, Christianity and other faiths have coexisted peacefully in China for centuries because their proponents — for the most part — have been required to tend to matters of the soul and to stay out of societal and political developments.

Political Schisms

Only in recent history has ideology created a gulf among the Chinese. The Nationalist Republic of China that governs from Taipei and the Communist People's Republic on the mainland both claim to be the sole, rightful government of all China. Even so, neither government disputes the fact that Taiwan is an integral province of China. The Nationalists rule according to the precepts of capitalism and free enterprise. The Communists have opted for the centrally-managed, authoritarian policies of Marx and Lenin. Both governments wish to reunite Taiwan and mainland China — under their own systems.

Despite the political impasse, neither political system has extinguished China's most cherished customs. In fact, classical Chinese culture has become the rallying point of the Nationalists of Taiwan. Its leaders assert the legitimate right to rule all China in the face of political realities, because they say they govern according to fundamental precepts of Chinese tradition. The teachings of Confucius still govern society in Taiwan. Having achieved a comfortable standard of living and a measure of political stability, the Chinese people of Taiwan have returned to the performing arts and made new strides in music, opera, dance, theater and the modern art of filmmaking. They have revived and improved upon the martial arts, medical arts, culinary arts and fine arts. During three busy decades, the Chinese majority that has made a home in Taiwan has engendered a cultural renaissance even as it has astonished the world with its entrepreneurial successes.

Majestic Mountains, Verdant Valleys

The island of Taiwan straddles the Tropic of Cancer roughly 120 miles (193 kilometers) offshore the mainland China province of Fukien, 220 miles (355 kilometers) north of the Philippine island of Luzon and 370 miles

A Taiwanese farmer takes a break from working in *padi* fields near Tainan.

(595 kilometers) southwest of Okinawa. It is anchored in the East China Sea between 21° 45' and 25° 57' North Latitude, and between 119° 18' and 124° 35' East Longitude.

Taiwan is shaped somewhat like a tobacco leaf with its tip pointing toward Japan. It stretches 250 miles (402 kilometers) in length and is about 80 miles (129 kilometers) wide at its broadest point. Its 13,735 square miles (35,571 square kilometers) make the island about the size of Holland. The Penghu archipelago, or Pescadores, and the islands of Kinmen (Quemoy) and Matsu, which are also administered by the Republic of China government in command of Taiwan, add another 230 square land miles (596 square kilometers) to the island province.

Although Taiwan is the smallest of the provinces of China, it exhibits many of the features of the mainland. The central stem of the island is a range of forest-fringed mountains—hard rock formations forged from ancient centuries of volcanic activity. More than 62 of the island's peaks rise 10,000 feet (3,048 meters) or more above the surrounding seas; few passes in the island's central range dip below 8,000 feet (2,438 meters). Taiwan's tallest peak is Mount Morrison at 13,114 feet (3,997 meters). The Chinese call it *Yu-Shan*, the Jade Mountain.

A narrow valley of rich alluvial soil, 100 miles long, separates the middle bulge of mountains from a smaller crest that fronts the east coast. Its cliffs drop sharply to the sea to form the island's most spectacular scenery. The East-West Cross-Island High-way dramatically ribbons its way through the central range to these east coast escarpments. In Taiwan, this highway is aptly called the "Rainbow of Treasure Island."

Primeval volcanoes pushed the island up from under the sea. Evidence can be found in coral from prehistoric seabeds that has lodged in igneous rock formations up to 2,000 feet (610 meters) high in the foothills. While such fiery activity ended eons ago, bubbling pools of hot sulfurous water and hissing steam vents still punctuate the terrain from the health spas of Peitou (outside Taipei) to Szechungchi (in the south).

The broad sea-level plains that spread across the western portion of Taiwan give the island a decided tilt away from the precipitous gray stone cliffs that wall the eastern shores. Short, winding rivers bring

A representative of Taiwan's revered older generation at home in Taitung.

rain water and alluvium from the mountains to the west, making the plains extremely fertile. Taiwan boasts more agriculturally useful and level land than all the myriad islands of the Philippines and Japan. Most of the island's population, numbering more than 18.2 million, lives on the western plains.

The Lady's Moods

An island proverb warns that "Taiwan's weather is like the mood of a woman"—in other words, subject to sudden change. The climate is as diverse as the island's endlessly fascinating landscapes: semi-tropical in the north and at mountain altitudes, totally tropical in the flatlands of the south.

There are two distinct seasons: hot (May through October)—and cold (November through March). Unfortunately, the island's excessive humidity exaggerates these seasonal changes. Although the temperature rarely exceeds 90 degrees Fahrenheit (32° Centigrade) in the summer, humidity seldom drops below 80 percent, turning the entire island into a kind of giant sauna. Likewise, winter temperatures do not usually fall below 40°F (5°C), but the dampness that hangs in the air can chill the bones.

The most pleasant times of the year are the brief spells of spring and fall that can occur during April-May and October-November. Skies are generally clear, nights are cool and days moderate.

But at any time of year, Taiwan's weather may change dramatically. No one is surprised to wake up to hot days in January or fierce thunderstorms in July. Rain and shine can alternate in the course of a single day. High and low temperatures can vary as much as 15°F from one day to the next.

Nature wrings an average annual rainfall of more than 40 inches (1,000 milliliters) from the cloak of humidity that hangs over Taiwan. In higher elevations, the average rainfall can exceed five times that figure. Much of the island was drenched by 45 consecutive days of steady rain in early 1983.

The northeast winter monsoon and the southwest summer monsoon provide the moisture. The northeast monsoon moves in from late October to late March, causing rain in the windward reaches of northeast Taiwan. The southwest monsoon takes its turn from early May until late September and can cause wet weather in the south while the north enjoys drier spells. The thirstiest spots are Huwei in Yunlin County and the island of Yuweng Tao in the Penghu archipelago.

The most feared aberrations in Taiwan's moody weather are typhoons. These *chufeng*, as the Chinese call them, are also known as the "supreme winds." They swell up in the Indonesian archipelago, sweep through the Philippines and storm toward Japan—via Taiwan. The season lasts from mid August until early October. During that time, no less than a half-dozen typhoons each year may cross or skirt Taiwan. At three to four-year intervals, a typhoon of major proportion crashes into Taiwan with wind speeds of 100 miles (160 kilometers) per hour or more. Such storms can capsize enormous ships, flood low-lying cities, trigger massive landslides, uproot trees and blow down dwellings.

In 1968, a typhoon drowned downtown Taipei in 13 feet (four meters) of water and made rowboats the only plausible means of transportation. One of the worst typhoons to hit Taiwan occurred in August of 1911. Barometric pressure at the southern port city of Kaohsiung fell below 28 inches, reportedly the lowest reading ever recorded in Taiwan. Winds of 156 miles (251 kilometers) per hour battered the island.

Visitors caught in Taiwan during a typhoon need not panic, however. In fact, it can prove to be an experience as exhilarating as any island adventure. Taiwan's new steel-and-concrete structures and modern hotels are generally immune to serious damage. It's safe to watch from the windows, but risky to walk the streets. Old-time Taiwan hands take advantage of the halt in normal activities to gather with friends and relatives in homes and hotels. They stock up on food and drink and hold typhoon parties.

Taiwan's landscapes, seascapes and seasons are varied enough to provide diversions for the most peculiar of interests. Offshore islands and shallows teem with fish and sparkle with coral formations for scuba and snorkeling enthusiasts. Backpackers and hikers can lose themselves in the foothills, while the taller peaks and sheer cliffs provide limitless challenges for mountain climbers and goats. Rainy days are perfect for exploring the National Palace Museum, the restaurants or the shopping extravaganzas. From its bustling cities to rugged countryside, Taiwan is as enticing to the modern traveler as it has been for centuries to multitudes of overseas Chinese.

Right, a military guard at Taipei's National Revolutionary Martyrs Shrine. Following pages: portrait of Lukai tribe members.

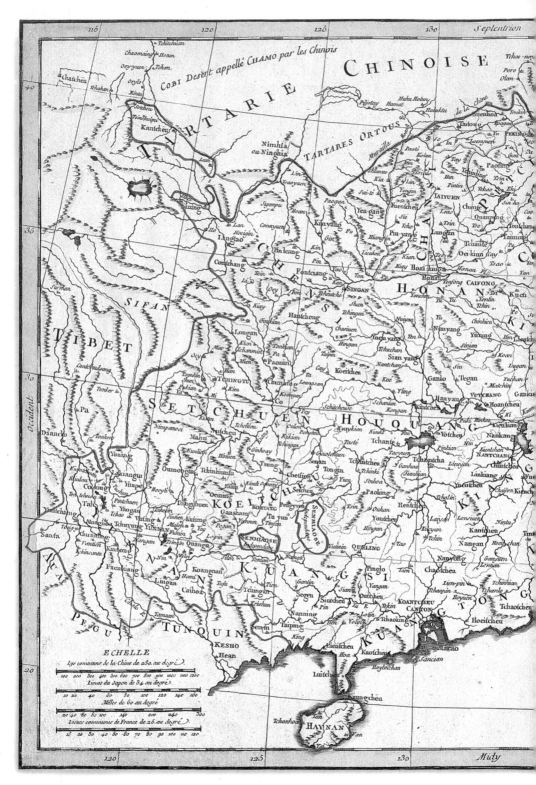

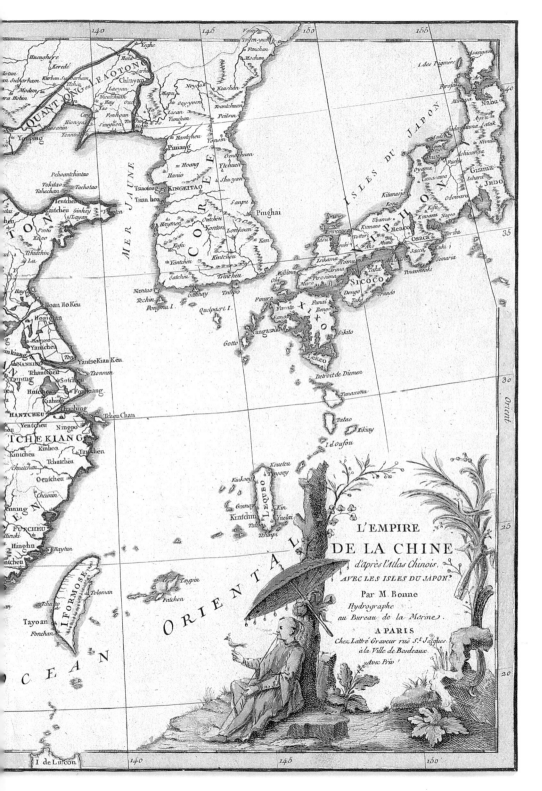

DIARY OF AN ISLAND ENCHANTRESS

"Isla formosa. Isla formosa!" Portuguese sailors used to shout with admiration from the decks of their ships as they sailed past Taiwan, en route to Japan, during the 16th Century. The island thus became known to the West by the Portuguese word *formosa*, "beautiful." And like many a beautiful woman, Taiwan's history has been both tranquil and tempestuous, peaceful and passionate, scandalous and dramatic.

This enchantress of the East China Sea has lured successive waves of Chinese immigrants from the mainland, explorers and

at least 10,000 years ago. Archaeologists believe Taiwan's links with mainland China may be just as old. They have identified four stages of prehistoric tool development that match those of the mainland, plus two later stages indicating that prehistoric Southeast Asian culture somehow spread to the southern and eastern coasts of the island. The early aborigines, whose descendants now form a colorful part of Taiwan's cultural spectrum, are believed to have come from Malaysian and ancient southern Chinese Miao stock.

exploiters from the West, and aggressive imperialists from Japan. All desired to possess her, and her diary of intrigue reveals that each in turn did. But of all her suitors, China proved to be the best match for the feisty, fecund island. The marriage of China's highly sophisticated, aesthetically oriented culture with Taiwan's bountiful beauty and rich natural endowments has produced one of the most dynamic lands in the Far East. China's ancient heritage and the island's native charms, like *yin* and *yang*, are the inseparable elements that define Taiwan.

Very little is known about Taiwan's earliest history. Radiocarbon dating of primitive utensils found in caves has indicated prehistoric man first appeared on the island

China's Early Courtship

The most ancient Chinese historical record refering to Taiwan indicates that the island was called the "land of Yangchow" before the rise of the Han dynasty in 206 B.C. There even may have been an attempt at that time to explore the island, according to the record, the *Shih Chi*. Compiled by Ssu-ma Ch'ien, it called Taiwan "Yichow." The earliest attempt to establish a Chinese claim to Taiwan apparently occurred in 239

A Taipei museum artist's vision of Taiwan's prehistoric past, above. Right, a bronze pitcher that dates to China's Spring and Autumn period (722-481 B.C.)

A.D. when the Kingdom of Wu sent a 10,000-man expeditionary force, according to the *San Kuo Chi,* the *History of the Three Kingdoms.*

About 1430, the famous eunuch magistrate and navigator from the Ming Court, Cheng Ho, reported his "discovery" of the island to the emperor of China. The name went down in the record books as *Taiwan,* which means "terraced bay." But an imperial prohibition on emigration prevented the Ming empire's populace from emigrating to Taiwan or anyplace else.

Aborigines and Hakkas

Two distinct groups of aborigines occupied Taiwan at the time of the Chinese arriv-

flee south to the Fukien and Kwangtung coasts. There, they successfully engaged in fishing and trading. That brought them to the Pescadores Islands, now known locally as the Peng-Hu,and later to Taiwan. By 1,000 A.D., the Hakkas had probably established themselves in the southern part of Taiwan, driving the native aboriginal tribes off the fertile plains and up into the mountains. The Hakkas grew sugar cane, rice and tea and engaged in active trade with the mainland. Today, the Hakkas rank among Taiwan's most enterprising people.

Other Chinese also set their sights on Taiwan. During the Ming Dynasty (1368-1644), immigrants from Fukien province began to cross the Taiwan Strait in ever-increasing numbers. They pushed the Hak-

al. One group lived sedentary agricultural lives on the rich alluvial plains of the center and southwest. The others were savages who roamed the mountains, fought incessantly among themselves, and continued to practice such primitive customs as ritual tattooing and head-hunting right down to the present century.

Although it is not known exactly when the Chinese first began to settle on the "Beautiful Island," the first mainland immigrants came from an ethnic group called the Hakkas — literally "guests" or "strangers." The Hakkas, a minority group relentlessly persecuted in China since ancient times, were driven from their native home in Honan province about 1,500 years ago and forced to

kas further inland and usurped the rich western plains for themselves. Chinese settlers adopted the term *ben-di-ren,* which literally means "this-place-person" or "native," in order to differentiate themselves from both the Hakkas and the aborigines whom they called "strangers." Even today, the descendants of these early immigrants from Fukien refer to themselves as *ben-di-ren,* thereby distinguishing themselves from the 1949 influx of mainland refugees whom they call *wai-sheng-ren* or "outer-province-people."

Still, the only true natives of Taiwan are the aboriginal tribes. Like the native Indians of America, and aborigines of Australia, they have been shunted off to special reservations. Their delegated homes are in the mountains of central and southern Taiwan. The rest of Taiwan's populace has been descended from various groups of mainland Chinese immigrants. Even the Taiwanese dialect is a direct offshoot of Fukienese.

Pirates, Traders and Foreign Invaders

During the 15th and 16th centuries, Taiwan became a haven for marauding pirates and freewheeling traders from both China and Japan who preyed on the East China coast. The distinction between pirates and traders was largely gratuitous in those days because both groups operated illegally in Taiwan. The island suited their needs. Its industrious inhabitants produced an abundance of food and other vital supplies. Better

Hideyoshi unsuccessfully tried to conquer China by way of Korea. Hideyoshi's designs on Taiwan fared no better. The island proved too unruly to control from afar.

Nevertheless, Europeans next tried to take the island. The Dutch turned to Taiwan after they failed to wrest Macao from their bitter rivals, the Portuguese. In 1624, they established a settlement on the southern coast and built three forts. Fort Zeelandia, near Tainan, is a tourist attraction.

Under the Dutch

In classic colonial fashion, the Dutch imposed heavy taxes and labor requirements on the Chinese residents of Taiwan and imported zealous missionaries to convert them

yet, the populace governed itself along clan and village lines without interference from Peking or elsewhere.

Because it was close to the trading centers and shipping lanes of China, Japan and Hong Kong, yet free from their political control, Taiwan turned into a pirates' paradise. When times were good, they traded. When times were bad, they raided. Now ersatz Rolex and Cartier watches and "pirated" editions of Western best-sellers go for a fraction of their original prices in Taiwan, bolstering the island's reputation as a haven for modern "pirate" manufacturers and publishers. Old habits are hard to break.

The Japanese first attempted to annex Taiwan in 1593 after the warlord Toyotomi

to Christianity. The Dutch East India Company gained the exclusive commercial rights to the island and imported opium from Java in the Dutch East Indies. The Dutch taught the Chinese to mix tobacco with opium and smoke it. The habit rapidly took root in Taiwan, then spread to Amoy and the mainland. Two centuries later, opium would play a notorious role in the terminal decline of the Ching Dynasty, and would become the catalyst for war between China and Britain.

For a while, the Dutch lived in relative

Above, China's Ming Dynasty Emperor Shih-tsung visits the tombs of his ancestors on the mainland while, at right, the Dutch command Fort Zeelandia on Taiwan about 1635.

harmony with the local residents of Taiwan. Their missionaries' religious intolerance ignited a revolt in 1640, but that was easily suppressed. Meanwhile, the Spanish had built two garrisons on the northern end of Taiwan. The jealous Dutch, wishing to maintain complete control over the island's foreign trade, drove the Spanish out of Taiwan in 1642. That same year also marked the beginning of the Manchu conquest of the mainland, an eventuality that exerted lasting impact on Taiwan.

Birth of a Hero

China's Ming Dynasty reigned for 276 years under 16 emperors. The creative arts and sciences flourished. But its glory faded

Cheng, meanwhile, managed to keep the Ming army together. He also took a Japanese wife who bore him a son that he named Cheng Cheng-kung. The son inherited the Ming banner from his father. With it went a new name, Kuo Hsing-yeh, "Lord of the Imperial Surname." He is better known to the West as Koxinga.

With an army of more than 100,000 men and an armada of 3,000 war junks, Koxinga carried on the fight against the Manchus from 1646 until 1658. At one point, he almost recaptured the southern capital of Nanking. But the overwhelming Manchu manpower finally forced Koxinga to retreat to the island bastion of Taiwan, an event that eerily foreshadowed the manner in which Chiang Kai-shek would lead his

under an administration that became increasingly corrupt. At the same time, Manchu leaders built a strong base of support and a huge army in the northeastern provinces. They swept south, easily advancing against the crumbling Ming armies.

Before the Manchus reached Peking, the last Ming emperor, Sze Tsung, named a Taiwan-based pirate, Cheng Chi-lung, to command the remnants of the Ming forces. Nevertheless, large bands of marauding bandits eventually stormed Peking and opened the flood-gates for the Manchu armies to move in and seize control of the government. Emperor Sze Tsung hung himself, a humiliating final act in the saga of a glorious era.

Nationalist patriots across the Taiwan Strait 300 years later.

Koxinga's Island

In Taiwan, Koxinga encountered the Dutch, who discounted him as a mere pirate incapable of mounting a serious threat. But Koxinga's spies, aided by Dutch deserters, provided valuable intelligence. In 1661, Koxinga sailed down the coast with 30,000 armed men in a large fleet of war junks and forced 600 Dutch settlers and 2,200 Dutch soldiers to take up arms at the three coastal forts. The seige lasted nearly two years. Koxinga captured Fort Zeelandia and graciously permitted the Dutch governor and

34

his surviving men to leave the island with their remaining possessions. Dutch rule in Taiwan ended a mere 38 years after it began, a trifle by the Chinese calendar.

With the Japanese, Spanish and Dutch all having withdrawn, Taiwan became the personal domain of Koxinga. He gave the island its first formal Chinese government and turned it into a Ming enclave that defied Peking long after the Manchus had established firm control over the entire mainland.

Koxinga's reign was brief but influential. He set up his court and government at Fort Zeelandia near Tainan and developed transportation and educational systems. Great strides were made in agriculture. Tainan became the political and commercial center and Anping grew into a prosperous harbor.

Perhaps Koxinga's greatest and most lasting contribution to Taiwan was his love for things Chinese. He ushered in a renaissance of many ancient Chinese laws, institutions, traditional customs and lifestyles. His entourage included more than 1,000 carefully chosen scholars, artists, monks and masters of every branch of Chinese culture.

Koxinga died at the age of 38 only a year after his conquest of Taiwan. He was later named a national hero and is venerated in Taiwan as a *chun tzu*, "perfect man."

The Manchus Take Over

Koxinga's son and grandson maintained rule over Taiwan until 1684 when the Manchus finally succeeded in imposing sovereignty over the island, snuffing out the last pocket of Ming patriotism. Taiwan officially became an integral part of the Chinese empire as the Ching court of the Manchus conferred the status of *fu* (prefecture) on the island. But Ching rule remained nominal at best. The Manchu magistrates sent to govern Taiwan usually succumbed to intrigues and self-indulgent decadence.

Despite strict prohibitions against further emigration to Taiwan, colonists continued to pour across the Strait from the mainland. During the first 150 years of Manchu rule, the island's population increased seven-fold. Karl Gutzlaff, a Prussian missionary who visited Taiwan in 1831, observed:

The island has flourished greatly since it has been in the possession of the Chinese...The rapidity with which this island has been colonized, and the advan-

tages it affords for the colonists to throw off their allegiance, have induced the Chinese to adopt strict measures... The colonists are wealthy and unruly...

One early bone of contention between China and the West concerned the fate of shipwrecked sailors washed ashore on Taiwan. These hopelessly involuntary visitors were routinely beaten, imprisoned and often beheaded, either by the Chinese authorities or by aboriginal savages. Whenever the Western powers sued the court of Peking to intervene in such incidents, they discovered that Peking had little real authority over island affairs, and even less interest. So Western nations resorted to "gunboat diplomacy" to rescue their crews from

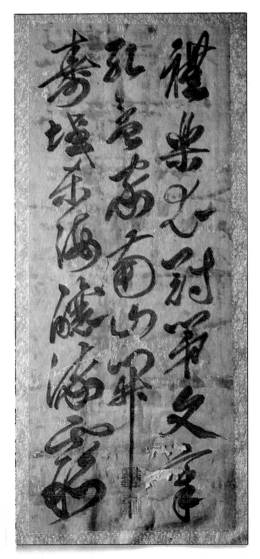

A portrait of Taiwan's first Chinese ruler, Koxinga, as rendered by one of his island descendants, left; and a sample of Koxinga's actual calligraphy from about 1660, right.

Taiwan, and dealt with the islanders rather than with the Manchus in Peking.

War With the West

One of the first foreigners to recognize Taiwan's economic potential and to advocate its outright annexation was Dr. William Jardine, co-founder of the powerful British trading firm Jardine, Matheson, and Co. Jardine became alarmed when China took up arms in 1839 to suppress the British opium trade in Canton. He informed British Foreign Secretary Lord Palmerston: "We, must proceed to take possession of three or four islands, say Formosa, Quemoy and Amoy, in order to secure new markets and new footholds in China."

When the first Anglo-Chinese conflict, or "Opium War," broke out, it further antagonized the strained relations between China and the West. Crews of British vessels subsequently shipwrecked off the coast of Taiwan met with even harsher treatment. The ships were plundered, then broken to pieces and burned. The crews were stripped naked and forced to walk painful distances to captivity.

The British were not the only foreign power that showed interest in Taiwan during the 19th Century. Several American traders and diplomats also advocated annexation of the island. They included Commodore Matthew C. Perry, who realized Taiwan's strategic importance in the Far East. Gideon Nye, a wealthy American merchant and a leading member of his country's expatriate community in Canton, proposed in 1857 that "Formosa's eastern shores and southern point ... in the direct route of commerce between China and California and Japan, and between Shanghai and Canton, should be protected by the United States of America." Nye also had personal reasons for his proposal: he suspected that his brother Thomas, who mysteriously disappeared on the opium clipper *Kelpie* in 1849, had been captured and killed in Taiwan.

The Treaty of Tientsin, which ended the first Opium War in 1860, opened four Taiwanese ports to foreign trade: Keelung and Suao in the north; Taiwanfoo (Tainan) and Takao (Kaohsiung) in the south. During the ensuing decade, foreign trade in Formosa grew by leaps and bounds. Most of the activity involved British and American firms. Primary export products included camphor, tea, rice, sugar, lumber and coal.

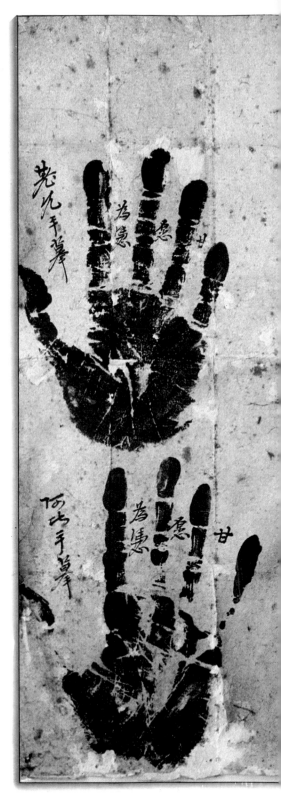

An early aborigine used his handprint to authorize his transfer of property to Chinese settlers in Tung Shih, Ilan County, in 1866.

36

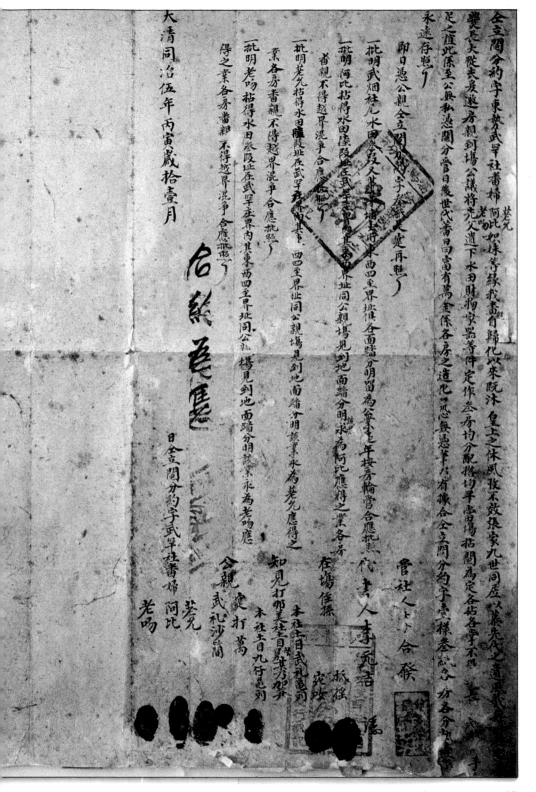

全立闔分約字東勢武平社蕃婦阿比妚妹等緣我蕃有歸化以來沐　皇上之休風浴采效張家九世同居以暴先代之遺風矣　荛兄

變惡大熾夫爰邀房親到場公議將先父遺下水田財物家器等件定作叁房均分配撥切平當場扷闔為定各扷各掌不混　其

足之道此係至公與私悉闔分當日後世代蕃日同高南有萬金係各房之遺化一惢無憑芔八有讓合全立闔分約字壹樣叁紙各房各執

永遠存照　

即日憑公親全立闔分約字叁紙是寔再照　

一批明武烟社尼水田尽叁文人建坲土坪水西四至界批慎各面踏分明留為公粜壹年按房輪當合應批照　　　　　代書人李元結　為

一批明阿比扷得水田淥段地在武平叁　界址同公親場見到地面踏分明永為阿比應得之業各房　　　　　　　　　　嘗社人上户合候

　親不得越界混爭合應批照　　　　　　　　　　　　　　　　　　　　　在場佳孫

一批明荛兄扷得水田瞳段址在武平产　其東　四至界址同公親場見到地面踏分明該業永為荛兄應得之　　　知見打邪美娃打邪

　業各房　親不得越界混爭合應批照　　　　　　　　　　　　　　　　本社十目武礼蔑剌

一批明老吻扷得水田叁段址在武平至界内其東西四至界址同公親場見到地面踏分明該業永為老吻應　本社十目九行邑列

　得之業各房嘗親不得越界混爭合應批照　　　　　合親武礼沙鎮闌

大清同治伍年丙寅歲拾壹月　　　　　　　　　　　　日全立闔分約字武平社蕃婦阿比　荛兄

　　　　　　　　　　　　　　　　　　　　　　　　　　　　　　　老吻

The sole import, which sometimes exceeded exports in value, remained opium.

By 1867, 25 foreign traders lived in northern Taiwan at Tanshui and Keelung, and another dozen lived in the south at Taiwanfoo. Trade boomed, doubling in volume in 1869 and doubling again in 1870. Colorful expatriate communities flourished around the ports. They maintained close ties with their counterparts in Hong Kong, Canton and Amoy. Unfortunately, the perennial problems of legal responsibility and political authority continued to plague Taiwan's foreign relations much as they do today.

A negative aspect of the trade boom was the increased frequency of violent incidents, corresponding to the greater number of foreign trading vessels that called at the island's ports. Brawls between drunken European and American merchant marines and the local Chinese usually ignited the violence. The inevitable vendettas followed. Local magistrates refused to take action in such cases, insisting that the foreigners petition authorities in Peking. But because of Peking's lack of influence and interest in the island's affairs, nothing ever got done through such "legal channels."

The situation was further aggravated by the arrival of foreign missionaries in the early 1870s. Zealous missionaries from the various sects of Christianity fanned out over the island and staked out exclusive "territorial domain." That created more confusion than the tenets of their conflicting religious doctrines. The missionaries, backed by their native countries, competed for exclusive domains in much the way traders competed for monopolies of major exports. The periodic attacks on foreign missionaries and their Chinese converts led to the same futile wrangling between local magistrates and foreign officials as did the incidents in the commercial sector. Only displays of force produced settlements.

Yet one thing was clear to all the squabbling parties. Taiwan was indeed an alluring beauty. It was rich in resources and strategically located. But it was also untamed. There was a need for law and order that Peking could not provide. Expatriates clamored for the home governments to step in. The Japanese did just that.

Tokyo's Triumph

In 1872, a Japanese ship foundered and sank off the coast of Taiwan. Three of its crew drowned. But only 12 of its 69 men survived. The other 54 were slaughtered by Botan aborigines. When the news of the killings reached Tokyo, Japanese military circles immediately prepared to launch a punitive expedition against the Botan tribe. Only Foreign Minister Soyeshima Taneomi held back the impending attack. He decided to first try to work out a diplomatic resolution in Peking.

Soyeshima was accompanied by Charles Le Gendre, who resigned as U.S. Consul to Amoy in 1872 in order to enter the service of Japan's Meiji Emperor as an advisor to the planned military expedition to Taiwan. Le Gendre had extensive experience in the island. He had negotiated settlements involving several American ships wrecked there, in some cases dealing directly with Formosan aboriginal tribes. But Washington always ignored Le Gendre's calls for greater American vigilance in Taiwan. Now he advised Tokyo it should prepare for war if its foreign minister's mission to Peking failed.

Soyeshima managed to obtain a formal audience with the Chinese Emperor, in itself a significant accomplishment. The Emperor tacitly admitted that the aboriginal tribes inhabiting parts of eastern Taiwan were beyond his political control. All Japan hailed that disclosure as a diplomatic victory, but Soyeshima's return to Tokyo was marred by factional infighting over the military's long postponement of plans to intervene in neighboring Korea, another Chinese protectorate. The disgusted foreign minister wiped his hands of the Formosa affair and Le Gendre stepped in. A violent revolt of samurai protesting Meiji reforms in February 1874 impressed upon the Japanese government the urgent need for a "foreign adventure" that would vent the pent-up energies of dissatisfied samurai. So on April 27 that year, 2,500 troops, 1,000 coolies and several foreign advisors led by Le Gendre boarded warships bound for Taiwan.

The military expedition landed at two points in southern Taiwan, one clearly within Chinese jurisdiction. Japanese troops made a few forays into the mountains to punish the offending aborigines. But their continued presence in the south prompted strong Chinese protests and a willingness to negotiate. After protracted talks in Peking, the Chinese government agreed to pay Japan 100,000 taels of silver to compensate the families of the dead crewmen and 400,000 taels for the expenses incurred by the military expedition. In return, Japanese forces withdrew from Taiwan and returned to Tokyo in triumph.

China continued to run Taiwan as a prefecture of Fukien province for more than a decade after the departure of the Japanese.

It was declared a province of China in 1886. The population had surpassed 2.5 million.

But the repercussions of the Japanese occupation continued to resound through Taiwan. For one thing, Japan's bold military move for the first time in history had created a semblance of law and order on the island. In fact, some foreign traders even seemed to welcome the Japanese occupation of 1874 because it forced Chinese authorities to take greater interest in the island's affairs and virtually eliminated attacks on its foreign settlements. Meanwhile, militarists back in Tokyo soon began rattling their swords and demanded outright annexation of Taiwan, Korea and the Ryukyu Islands.

Full scale war between the two oriental

ferior and barbaric. Vast sums that had been earmarked for modernizing China's navy had been diverted by the Empress Dowager Tze-Hsi to restore and redecorate her elaborate Summer Palace north of Peking. Thus, the decimated Chinese navy was no match for Japan's.

Japan literally dictated the terms of the notorious Treaty of Shimonoseki which ceded outright possession of both the Ryukyu Islands and Taiwan, the start of half a century of Japanese rule over the Beautiful Island. It also gave Japan a decisive role in Korea that would culminate in annexation 15 years later in the wake of the Russo-Japanese War.

Taiwan moved rapidly into the modern age under the tutelage of Japan. A domestic

Japanese flags and soldiers in the streets of Lukang in Central Taiwan in 1934. The Japanese occupation lasted from 1895 to 1945.

superpowers again broke out in 1895 when the Japanese invaded Korea, long a loyal ally of China. China sent armed and manned ships to Korea's aid, but the Japanese sunk them in a blatant effort to fuel hostilities. China had managed to buy off Japan before to avert war but this time the Japanese were not for sale. Nothing short of territorial gains would satisfy Japan's burning desire for an overseas empire that would surpass the colonial conquests of Britain.

China suffered total and ignoble defeat at the hands of a nation it had considered in-

network of railways and roads was constructed, connecting important points of the island for the first time. The Japanese also built modern schools, hospitals and industries and updated agricultural methods. Most importantly, strict Japanese rule ended the factional bickering and futile debates that had always marked island politics.

Still, occupation proved oppressive and ultimately unpopular. The Japanese required everyone to adopt Japanese names and speak the Japanese language. They exploited Taiwan's rich natural resources exclusively for the benefit of Japan. And resident Japanese officers and magistrates enjoyed elite privileges denied to local citizens. In effect, Japan tried to remold Taiwan in its

民國十三年，總理督率三軍，指揮義師，於桂林誓師北伐，先生膺隨侍之職，並兼任大本營參軍。此為十二年孫中山先生與蔣中正先生攝於廣州以留紀念。

中華民國二十五年十月

42

own image by forcing the island to sever her connections with her ancient Chinese cultural roots. Taiwan toiled under Japanese rule until Allied forces won World War II. After Japan surrendered, Taiwan was restored to Chinese rule on Oct. 25, 1945, an event still celebrated annually on the island as "Restoration Day."

During the following years, Taiwan suffered the same kind of "carpetbagger" treatment accorded the American South after the Civil War. Hordes of adventurers from mainland China stormed across the Taiwan Strait and systematically dismantled the extensive industrial infrastructure left by Japan, shipping everything of value back to Shanghai for sale.

Meanwhile, civil war had broken out in earnest on the mainland. The struggle for control of the vast country matched a communist party called the *Kungchandang* against the Nationalist *Kuomintang* (KMT). At the head of the KMT was a fiery leader named Chiang Kai-shek.

The Generalissimo

Chiang Kai-shek's association with the island province of Taiwan bears striking similarities to the saga of Koxinga. Both men fought to preserve the traditional order in China and both established a bastion of that order in Taiwan in defiance of their enemies on the mainland. Most significantly, both men successfully launched a renaissance of classical Chinese culture which has made Taiwan a living repository of China's most ancient and cherished traditions.

Chiang Kai-shek was born on Oct. 31, 1887, in Chekiang province. His mother was a devout Buddhist and his father a salt merchant who died when Chiang was only eight. At the tender age of 14, Chiang's mother arranged for him to marry Mao Fu-mei. In 1908, she gave birth to Chiang's first son, the man who today heads the Republic of China government in Taiwan, Chiang Ching-kuo.

At that time, the Chinese monarchy was disintegrating. Nationalism became the dominant force and revolution was in the air. Caught up in the rapidly changing swirl of events, young Chiang took up military studies in Japan. It was there that he first met a dynamic revolutionary, Sun Yat-sen.

Chiang participated in Sun's revolutionary forays into China and completed his military.

Preceding pages, the statue of Chiang Kai-shek that overlooks Sun Moon Lake. Left, Chiang with Dr. Sun Yat-sen (seated) in 1924. Right, the "Generalissimo" in 1930.

studies in 1912. That same year, Dr. Sun Yat-sen became the first provisional president of the Republic of China. Henry Pu Yi abdicated as emperor, ending the Ching Dynasty and closing the history books on China's 50 centuries of rule by monarchy. Chiang returned to China shortly after his second son, Chiang Wei-kuo, was born.

Two episodes left permanent imprints on the character of young Chiang after his return to China. For 10 years, he resided in Shanghai, where he cultivated relationships with the fabulously wealthy merchant and banker families of that great city. Those contacts helped him to forge a political power base that would ultimately carry Chiang through two decades of warfare and provide the backbone for Nationalist successes on

Taiwan. Chiang loved Shanghai and Taipei was largely built in its image.

The second influential episode occurred in 1923 when Sun Yat-sen sent Chiang to Moscow as his personal emissary. Chiang returned with a deep distrust of the Russians and a profound hatred of communism.

Chiang Kai-shek could be labeled a "conservative revolutionary." His concept of changing China was to foster nationalism, overthrow the hated Manchu regime in Peking and end China's humiliation at the hands of foreign powers. But his vision of a modern China remained grounded in traditional Confucian social values. He believed that the rebirth rather than the destruction of traditional culture was the answer to China's woes. A born and bred Confucian, he cherished values like loyalty and obedience.

After the successful "Northern Expedition" against the warlords who had partitioned China into personal fiefdoms, Chiang triumphantly rode into Shanghai preparing to consolidate his power. In 1927, Soong Mei-ling became his second wife. She was the daughter of Shanghai's most powerful banking family and younger sister of Sun Yat-sen's widow. Dr. Sun had died in Peking at the age of 59.

"Madame Chiang," as she became known in the West, was an American-educated Christian. Prior to their marriage, Chiang Kai-shek converted to Christianity. His new wife and his conversion were important influences on the rest of his life.

With the help of Allied armies, Japan surrendered in 1945. But Chiang's problems continued. The Communists seized the opportunity and abandoned Japanese arms to turn against his Nationalist army. Civil war raged across the vast Chinese landscape for four long years.

Chiang was personally honest and as incorruptible as the severest Confucian scholar. But his administration was plagued by corrupt and incompetent subordinates. Their greatest disservice to China was not graft, however, but their failure to report the truth to their leader.

Chiang was not insensitive to the sufferings of his people, but was rarely exposed to it. While taking his habitual stroll one summer afternoon in 1944, he stumbled upon an

The story of Chiang Kai-shek's campaigns against the Chinese Communists, and his war against the invading Japanese, is well documented. The Japanese occupied Manchuria in 1932. In 1937, they took Tientsin and Peking, captured Chiang's beloved Shanghai and overran the Nationalists' capital city of Nanking. Their advance was bolstered by bombing raids conducted from Japanese airfields in Taiwan.

In 1943, the Generalissimo, as Chiang came to be called, met with U.S. President Franklin D. Roosevelt and Britain's Prime Minister Winston Churchill at the Cairo Conference. The trio pledged the return of Manchuria, Taiwan and the Pescadores to China after the war.

officer leading a row of fresh recruits through the woods roped together like animals. Infuriated, Chiang beat the officer. Only the intervention of an aide prevented Chiang from killing the man outright. The following spring, after continued reports of the roping practice, Chiang had the general in charge of conscription summarily shot.

Chiang Kai-shek was elected president of the Republic of China in 1948. But by then the war had swung in favor of the Commu-

Above, Chiang Kai-shek and Madame Chiang (far left and right) with Franklin D. Roosevelt and Winston Churchill at the Cairo Conference in 1943; and right, Chiang broadcasts news of his government's move to Taiwan in 1949.

nists. Hsuchow, Tientsin and Peking fell to the enemies. On Jan. 21, 1949, facing imminent defeat, Chiang Kai-shek resigned the presidency.

Exodus to Taiwan

Chiang had resigned leadership positions several times before. Each time he bounced back to power by virtue of the sheer vacuum his departure left. This time proved no different. Soon he emerged from solitude to lead the best two divisions of his army and a rambling entourage of scholars, merchants, monks and masters of classical arts across the Taiwan Strait to the island bastion. On Dec. 7, 1949, the Republic's government moved its headquarters to Taipei. The

helped launch the industrial revolution that was the catalyst for the island's phenomenal economic growth. Overnight, Taiwan found itself with an entrepreneurial elite of former landlords who had the money and the motivation to invest in Taiwan's future.

Other reforms followed. The educational system was overhauled and thousands of students were sent abroad to absorb new technology and scientific training. Although national affairs remained firmly in the hands of the Nationalists, democratic institutions were established at local levels.

Chiang governed the island according to Sun Yat-sen's "Three Principles of the People." Known as the *San Min Chu-i* in Chinese, Dr. Sun built his framework for sensible government on *min tsu*, national-

Nationalists defeated pursuing Communists in a devastating "last-stand" battle on the island of Quemoy and have held that island ever since.

Chastened by defeat on the mainland, Chiang was determined to reform Nationalist policies on Taiwan. One of his first acts was to execute the rapacious governor-general responsible for the looting of Taiwan's wealth and the bullying of its people since 1945. Next, Chiang initiated a land-reform policy as sweeping as the one instituted by the Communists but with one vital difference. Instead of villifying and killing landlords, the Nationalist government paid them well for their land, then offered them matching funds and tax breaks. That move

ism, or the liberation of China from foreigners; *min chuan*, democracy, or government by the people and for the people; and *min sheng*, livelihood, or economic security for all the people. Of the three principles, Dr. Sun considered nationalism the primary goal and that the fastest way to that goal was through a democratic system that provided for the livelihood of the people.

Chiang amplified on his interpretations of Dr. Sun's Three Principles in his book *China's Destiny,* published in 1943. Chiang faced turbulence and difficulties that Dr. Sun had not encountered and had to adapt the philosophy to cope with problems on the mainland, then in Taiwan, in order to reach his mentor's goals.

In Taiwan Chiang maintained strict political discipline and social order, but gave the island's industrious populace free reign in the economic sphere. The Chinese enthusiasm for capitalism propelled the private sector from 44 percent of Taiwan's economy in 1953 to 75 percent in 1974, at the expense of state monopolies. At the same time, the island's population more than doubled from 8 million to more than 18 million.

The year 1965 proved a particularly critical test of strength for Taiwan and its leadership. Financial aid from the United States that had provided a cushion for Taiwan's economic leaps was terminated. Yet industrialization, modernization and economic progress accelerated.

that helped him fulfill part of his dream of a free, prosperous China. But the diary also reflected a humble man acutely aware of his own shortcomings and profoundly dedicated to his people, in sharp contrast to his common portrayal in the Western press as an arrogant, stubborn man. His last testament written on March 29, 1975, one week before his death, reveals his concern:

Just at the time when we are getting stronger, my colleagues and countrymen, you should not forget our sorrow and our hope because of my death. My spirit will always be with my colleagues and countrymen to fulfill the Three People's Principles, to recover the mainland, and to restore our national culture.

The passage ends with a line that modestly

The Generalissimo's Passing

Throughout his later life, Chiang Kai-shek maintained strict Confucian decorum and an austere personal lifestyle. He never smoked, drank or gambled. Even at formal banquets with their obligatory "bottoms-up" drinking, Chiang ordered his toasting cup to be filled with water from a liquor decanter. At home he favored the long gowns and Mandarin collars of traditional Chinese scholars, and every evening he and his wife knelt together in Christian prayer. His only recreational indulgences were long leisurely walks in the mountains.

Chiang kept a diary all his life that was as filled with color as the island enchantress

summarizes Chiang's career and reflects his enigmatic character: "I have always regarded myself as a disciple of Dr. Sun Yat-sen, and also of Jesus Christ."

Chiang passed away shortly after midnight, on April 5. A spontaneous outpouring of grief erupted throughout Taiwan that testified to the Generalissimo's popularity. A sudden cloudburst rained on Taipei and cleared just as abruptly, prompting speculation that even "heaven wept" at Chiang's passing. In May 1978, there was an orderly

Above, National "Double Ten" Day festivities fill Taipei's Presidential Plaza with color and pageantry. President Chiang Ching-kuo signals his optimism about the future, right.

transfer of power to Chiang Kai-shek's son, Chiang Ching-kuo.

Growth Despite Setbacks

Despite well-publicized political setbacks — such as its expulsion from the United Nations in 1971 and severance of diplomatic ties by the United States in 1979, Taiwan continues to thrive and survive. Its Gross National Product has steadily grown and foreign trade has flourished through cultural contacts and trade associations, a remarkable achievement in the wake of political adversity.

Officially, the Nationalist government describes Taiwan as "the island province of the Republic of China," and Taipei as the na-

Taiwan's insistence on maintaining the Republic of China label lies at the heart of many of its diplomatic problems today. There are strong indications that the island's athletes would be permitted to participate in the Olympic Games and other major international sporting events, and that many Western capitals would reopen diplomatic relations, if the Nationalist government would simply substitute the Taiwan label for that of Republic of China.

But neither the Nationalists nor the Communists would accept such a change. Both governments agree that Taiwan is part and parcel of China proper, and an integral province of China. Both consider reunification a must — on their own terms. Taipei's prerequisite for opening formal negotiations with

tion's provisional capital. Peking ("northern capital"), the seat of the Communist's People's Republic of China, is called Peiping ("northern peace") by the people of Taiwan, inferring that it is *not*, in fact, a capital.

The Nationalist government of Taiwan regards the mainland Communists as interlopers who have no business in China. Textbooks and government posters — even the national anthem trailers that precede the showing of movies in theaters — still use maps that depict Taiwan together with the mainland as indivisible as parts of the Republic of China. On the other hand, the Communists consider Taiwan a "renegade province."

the mainland is that Peking abandon communism and accept the Three Principles of the People as the foundation of a modern Chinese state.

With the exception of matters affecting national politics and internal security, the leaders in Taiwan continue to operate the island as one of the least restrictive, most *laissez-faire* societies in the world. They believe mainland China could also enjoy economic success if freed from the restraints of communism. The leaders in Taiwan believe it is the government's responsibility to maintain secure borders, law and order, and a generous dose of *ren-ching-wei*, "the flavor of human feeling." The people of Taiwan have done the rest.

TAIWAN, INC.

Among the most curious components of the anabatic skyline of Taipei are the big, brightly colored balloons that bob above the rooftops. Moored to new construction projects, the balloons serve as beacons that beckon buyers to the city's newest condominium complexes.

These balconied skyscrapers bear a strong resemblance to the airborne abodes that clutter the skies of Taipei's favorite foreign cities, Los Angeles and Miami. It's in price that they differ. Condominiums generally cost more in Taipei, anywhere from a cool US$100,000 for the barest of closet-sized dwellings to US$500,000 or more for standard Western-style units. The buyers here barely blink at such prices.

In 1972, the Taipei Hilton Hotel was the tallest building in town, looming like a lighthouse over a sea of squat dwellings and tiled roofs. Today, the Hilton is barely discernible in the forest of new skyscrapers that has sprouted during the building boom of the last decade. The dense skyline rises above equally congested streets where enormous gas-gulping Cadillacs and Oldsmobiles and sleek Mercedes-Benzes wade like whales through a sea of sardine-sized cars and motorcycles. Such limousines retail for about US$75,000. Added to that price is a small fortune in annual road and license taxes calculated according to the market value of the car. On a more modest level, the most conspicuous vehicles (other than buses and motorcycles) are taxis, most of them locally manufactured by Yue-Loong. Prices start at about US$7,500.

As in the other newly prosperous cities of Asia, shopping and eating are popular pastimes in Taiwan. The stores of the city are as crammed full of merchandise as the restaurants are crowded with customers. Taiwan's eateries never seem to lack business, even though tens of thousands of establishments vie to attract the island's discriminating diners. In fact, the government has expressed concern that the people of Taiwan spend enough money in restaurants each year to finance the construction of two full length north-south expressways from Keelung to Kaohsiung.

Preceding pages, award-winning student poster from Taichung. Left, futuristic atrium of a Taipei hotel. Right, a high-flying ham beckons buyers to a new apartment venture.

The Capitalism of Consumption

Of course, expensive condominiums and limousines are still beyond the means of the average resident of Taiwan. But the average person does enjoy a level of living well above that of most of the world. It is estimated that 99.7 percent of Taiwan's homes have electricity and that there are 103 televisions for every 100 homes on the island. With 50.8 cars and 236 telephones for every 1,000 persons, Taiwan's standard of living is higher than every other Asian country ex-

cept Japan. And, in at least two respects, the people of Taiwan live better than the Japanese: they enjoy greater average living space, 188 square feet per household; and they consume more average calories (2,729) of food per day, including 75 grams of protein. That makes the people here the best fed of anyone living in any country between Tel Aviv and Tokyo.

Taiwan's comforts and wealth corroborate what many economists and observers have called the economic "miracle" that has occurred here since World War II. The Nationalist government parlayed enlightened economic policies into pure profit. It nurtured the Chinese penchant for the potent motive forces of capitalism. The populace responded resoundingly, working long hours to make the dream come true. Indeed, Taiwan's brand of capitalism makes the West's version seem sluggish and restrictive.

The prescription for the island's economic health is foreign trade. In 1983, total world trade with Taiwan exceeded $45 billion. More than a third of that, about $15 billion, involved the United States. Despite political differences, Taiwan remains the fifth largest trading partner of the U.S. The island is only a fraction of the size of its American partner, but it enjoys a US$4.5 billion trade surplus over the Western giant. In order to redress that advantage, Taiwan's government since 1976 has been sending an annual "Buy American" mission to the United States to purchase up to $600 million

worth of grains, machinery and other products. It's an East Asia largesse that is eagerly anticipated each year by American farmers and factories.

Trade has been Taiwan's biggest business since Chinese and Western merchants first discovered the island's wealth of resources. During the 18th and 19th centuries, its major exports included sugar, coal, rice, tea, lumber and tobacco. But the most lucrative product was camphor which grew abundantly in Taiwan's dense mountain forests. By 1870, five British, two German and two American trading companies were firmly established in Taiwan and business boomed. Today, more than 2,000 manufacturers supply products for export.

From Farms to Factories

While foreign trade has been Taiwan's principal moneymaker, agriculture historically has been the primary occupation of its people. Even today, Taiwan remains one of the world's richest culinary cornucopias. Each day, ships and cargo jets take containers of fresh fruits and vegetables to markets throughout the Far East.

Taiwan is also the world's major supplier of such luxury foods as canned asparagus, mushrooms and pineapple and of a wide range of traditional Chinese food items. The escargot served in fancy French restaurants is as likely to come from Taiwan as it is from France. At the other end of the dining spectrum, the food-processing industries of Taiwan are so renowned that the international fast-food giant, McDonald's, has recently begun to test Chinese tastes for foreign fast-food with several franchise outlets in Taipei, but it remains to be seen whether beefburgers will replace beef-noodles on the chinese palate.

Fishing is another traditional occupation that has contributed significantly to the island's prosperity. Currently, fishermen haul in nearly 1 million metric tons of seafood each year from the waters around Taiwan. Most goes to local markets and restaurants, but exports of frozen seafood earns the island about US$400 million annually. The frozen-food industry is highly developed, yet some of the seafood is shipped live. Each day, jumbo cargo jets lift off from Taipei bound for Tokyo, packed solid with wriggling live eels individually sealed in plastic bags of water. Taiwan has also been a pioneer in the field of "fish farming."

Yet the trading emphasis has rapidly changed. Modern industrial products are replacing agricultural products and natural resources as Taiwan's primary exports. For example, in 1960 sugar accounted for 43 percent of Taiwan's exports. By 1981, it represented less than 3 percent.

The island's broad industrial base and foreign exchange reserves were cultivated during the 1950s and 1960s by emphasizing one major industry—textiles. With strong government support, Taiwan surpassed Japan and England as the world's major supplier of textile goods. Since the beginning of the 1970s, strict textile import quotas in

Workers paint enormous chains at China Shipbuilding Corporation in Kaohsiung, left. Right, Cow-powered plow meets his modern match in Taiwan's agricultural countryside.

Europe and the United States, and competition from labor-intensive neighbors like Korea and Indonesia, have put a dent in the economic contribution of the textile industry. But it continues to be important and progressive.

In 1982, Taiwan's top three exporting companies were RCA Taiwan (which shipped US$164.6 million worth of electronics products), Far Eastern Textiles (with foreign sales of US$157.3 million) and Nan-Ya Plastics (with US$152.1 million in export earnings). The significant words here are electronics and plastics. The latest wave of economic progress has carried technology-intensive companies to greater significance than labor-intensive textile industries.

After the United States and Japan, the countries of the Association of Southeast Asian Nations (Singapore, the Philippines, Thailand, Malaysia, Indonesia and Brunei), and Europe are its major trading partners. And it maintains a surplus with all except Japan.

The hiking boots and tents, jogging shoes and warm-up suits, radios and televisions, toys and trinkets, Christmas lights and plastic pine trees, and untold other products sold in many foreign countries often are branded with the "Made in Taiwan" label. The strict requirements of foreign markets have forced Taiwan to greatly improve quality control over its products. As a result, there are increasingly satisfied customers overseas.

For the average resident of Taiwan, economic indicators have combined to provide a

'Made in Taiwan'

A few facts and figures put Taiwan's economic might into a world and regional perspective. During the 1970s, Taiwan's economy grew at an average annual rate of 10 percent, a figure most Western economies rarely achieve in the best of times. The gross national product continues to grow at 5 percent each year in defiance of the world recession of the early 1980s.

Taiwan currently ranks 14th among the world's "Top 20" exporters. Textiles, clothing and footwear account for 28 percent of exports, electrical and electronic machinery 25 percent, miscellaneous manufactured products 23 percent, and metal products 7 percent.

per capita income of nearly US$2,500, 10 times greater than that of the mainland. In Asia, only the people of Japan, Hong Kong and Singapore earn more. The government predicts per capita income will surpass US$4,000 by 1990.

Of course, the society has countless rags-to-riches stories. The man considered the richest in Taiwan, Wang Yung-chin, chairman of Formosa Plastics, began his career delivering rice door to door. Former farmers now sit in cushy leather chairs directing dynastic industrial empires that span the globe. Small-time traders become millionaires overnight by marketing the right product to the right Western market at the right time. Many of the island's greatest enterprises are still operated in the family style so often preferred by the Chinese.

Taiwan's workforce numbers about 7 million. There is virtually no unemployment. The greatest percentage of the population works in commercial and service sectors which employ 39 percent of the work force. Another 33 percent work in the manufacturing fields. By comparison, the number of workers in agriculture has fallen to just 19 percent of the total employed.

Laissez-faire, not to mention *savoir-faire*, can be credited for Taiwan's continuing economic successes. Virtually any citizen can open a shop, factory, restaurant or trading company simply by filling out the appropriate government forms and hanging a sign over the door. There is very little—some

That's because these products are made in Taiwan by underground factories that pirate foreign designs.

After a few years, the gold-plating of the "Rolex" may wear off and the seams of the "Gucci" shoes may come apart, but such pirate products sell as well or better than their genuine counterparts. They even last long enough to attract status-conscious consumers. Western tourists tend to be more easily fooled by these pirate products because they come to Asia with the expectation of buying expensive items at low prices. The Chinese, on the other hand, are well aware they are buying pirated products and do so only because prices are reasonable.

Many of the manufacturers of the pirate products have never even heard the words

say too little—government interference or regulation in the freewheeling business sphere. That has created a degree of chaos and fraud, but it has also prompted intense competition in the marketplace and has enabled the cream of the competitive crop to rise to the top of the system.

Modern Piracy

One area in which Taiwan businessmen take the words "free enterprise" too literally is the realm of trademarks and copyrights. In Taiwan, it's possible to buy "Rolex" watches, "Gucci" shoes, "Cartier" lighters and other brand-name products for a mere fraction of the prices they bring in the West.

"copyright" or "trademark." But pressure exerted by the original manufacturers of such items is beginning to change that.

Taiwan is one of the four booming Asian islands which have been dubbed "The Gang of Four" by some jealous Western nations. Along with Japan, Hong Kong and Singapore, Taiwan has been turning economic tables against the West for the past two decades.

The irony is obvious. Only 100 years

Above, women fuel Taiwan's labor-intensive garment industry. Right, women also provide the "manpower" for computer industries like the manufacture of silicon chips. Following pages: secretaries, in a coffee shop and at the Sun Yat-sen Memorial.

ago, Western traders believed that China formed a vast, infinite marketplace for Western-manufactured goods. "If every Chinese added one inch of cloth to his robes," they claimed, "Western textile mills would reap immense fortunes." Today, Chinese traders in Taiwan toast each other at banquets with a twist on that old phrase: "The American market is inexhaustible!"

One of the Asian "Gang of Four" is ailing, however, and Taiwan has set her sights on inheriting its wealth. The Communist Chinese government has insisted that it will "regain sovereignty" over Hong Kong when Great Britain's lease on the Crown Colony expires in 1997. As a result, the Hong Kong dollar has plummeted, real-estate prices have tumbled, and many ty-

drives Hong Kong's millionaires into the arms of Taiwan.

The only possible stumbling block to continuing economic health for Taiwan is its overdependency on foreign trade. Taiwan has a trade dependency factor of 110 percent. That figure represents the ratio of total two-way trade against gross national product. By comparison, South Korea's trade dependency is 80 percent and Japan's only 31 percent. Its trade dependency was underlined in 1982 when the government reached only half of its targeted GNP growth rate. If the economies of the island's major trading partners suffer as they did during the recession that year, Taiwan can also suffer.

Nevertheless, Taiwan's economic future appears bright. The political setbacks of the

coons have started moving their fortunes elsewhere.

Taiwan is making bids to attract the fortune, fame and following that Hong Kong has enjoyed as East Asia's economic leader for more than 100 years. Banking laws are being reviewed to facilitate international transactions. The government also has plans to establish several "free-trade economic zones" at ports including Kaohsiung, Keelung and Taichung

If Taiwan succeeds in luring the jittery Chinese fortunes and economic expertise of Hong Kong to her own shores, it will represent an economic coup of major proportions in the Far East. Ironically, it is the aggressive attitude of the Peking government that

1970s only redoubled the determination of Taiwan to prosper economically. The island remains completely self-sufficient in food production. Social life in Taiwan is remarkably stable; wealth is distributed far more evenly than ever before; and abject poverty is virtually non-existent. Most importantly, the island is run by a team of economic experts, not professional politicians whose primary concern is their own re-election. In fact, so many professional bankers hold portfolios in the current administration, that the local press has dubbed it "The Financial Cabinet."

In light of these facts, Taiwan's economic success is not the least bit "miraculous." It is logical, well-planned and inevitable.

'THE FLAVOR OF HUMAN FEELING'

The unique social trait the Chinese call *ren-ching-wei*, "the flavor of human feeling," permeates all social relationships in Taiwan and inevitably spills over into the island's politics and economics. In effect, it simply means that no matter what the occasion—whether business or pleasure, public or private, important or trivial—human considerations always take precedence. In personal relationships feelings are more important than logic or legality. The Chinese refuse to allow human values to be swallowed up by the growing concerns of modern science, industrial technology and the fast pace of contemporary life.

Ren-ching-wei encompasses the bitter as well as the sweet. It explains the courtesies and rudeness of everyday life in Taiwan, the spirit of compromise and the stubborn demands of maintaining "face," the emotional outbursts that produce torrents of colored language, private hospitality and public indifference. Indeed, every human element intimately associated with the daily give-and-take of Chinese social life has its roots in *ren-ching-wei*. These elements have been woven into a social fabric in contemporary Taiwan that is as tough and resilient as it is vibrant and appealing.

In the following pages, the warp and woof of *ren-ching-wei* is made clearly visible in essays on the influence of Confucian thought and the importance of traditional religious practices in modern Taiwan.

THE LEGACY OF CONFUCIUS

When friends visit from afar,
Is this not indeed a pleasure?
  — *The Analects of Confucius*

For more than 2,000 years, Chinese scholars aspiring to government office were required to memorize *The Analects* or *Lun Yu*, the most hallowed of all classics penned by Confucius. Today, authorities in the offices of Taiwan's tourism bureau often borrow the opening lines of the *Lun Yu*, for obvious reasons.

The fact that Confucius began his great work with such a disarmingly simple and welcoming maxim emphasized the importance the philosopher placed on friendship and social etiquette. Confucius believed that true pleasure cannot be found in selfish sensual abandon or in personal gain, but rather in generosity to friends and in social intercourse. Hospitality has been one of China's most consummate arts ever since.

Confucius, also known to the Chinese as Kung Fu-dze or "Master Kung," was born in the kingdom of Lu near modern Shantung in the year 551 B.C. As a child, he demonstrated profound interests in ancient rites and rituals and often would dress up in formal robes to perform traditional ceremonies that had been all but discarded by the people of his time. People who knew Confucius admired him for his erudition and his sincerity. But because he lived in a time of internecine chaos known as the "Warring States Period," few men of influence were willing to adopt his pacific ideas, much less appoint Confucius to positions of influence.

Without a platform from which to address the masses, Confucius set out to peddle his ideas on his own. He set forth from Lu while still a young man and traveled throughout the empire taking his message of peace, friendship and reform to the various petty princes. Most received him with great interest and hospitality, but few showed intentions of changing their warring ways in deference to Confucius' philosophy of social harmony.

While traveling, Confucius also gathered and studied authentic materials that re-vealed the secrets of the earlier Golden Age of Chinese culture—the Hsia, Shang and Chou dynasties. One of the men who assisted him in that task was Lee Dan, known to posterity as Lao-tze, "The Old One." Lao-tze was the founder of the school of Taoism and composer of the beguiling doctrines of the *Tao Te Ching*. He was also in charge of the imperial archives of the Chou Dynasty which housed all the surviving documents detailing events from the 23rd Century B.C. to Confucius' day. The records were preserved in archaic script on

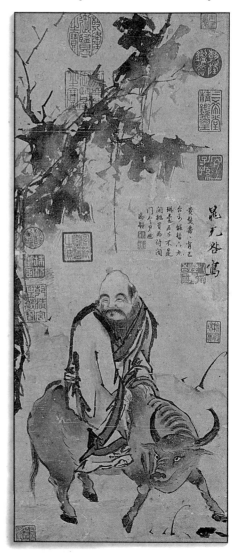

Preceding pages, worshippers reflect Taiwan's Confucian traditions by conducting rites honoring the local God of Agriculture. Portraits of Confucius (left) and Lao-tze (right).

tiles, bamboo and tortoise shells. Lao-tze permitted Confucius to use the archives and copy as many records as he wished. The ancient documents formed the basis for his so-called "Confucian Classics."

The Fires of Chin

"I never created or wrote anything original," Confucius claimed. Instead, he considered himself an interpreter and transmitter of the profound ideas and deeds of the ancient sage kings of China's Golden Age dynasties. Confucius admired seven venerables—Yao, Shun, Yu, Tang, Wen-Wang, Wu-Wang and the Duke of Chou. And his own interests in these men won for them a continued following among the Chinese.

Although some modern scholars question the attribution of certain works to Confucius, the great sage is generally credited with putting the documents of the imperial archives into a common, contemporary language and with publishing them. The Five Classics of Confucianism, known as the *Wu Ching*, consist of the *I Ching* (Book of Changes), *Shi Ching* (Book of Poetry), *Shu Ching* (Book of History), *Li Chi* (Book of Proprieties) and *Chun Chiu* (Spring and Autumn Annals). Later, lesser works published by Confucius or his disciples and believed to contain the original philosophies of the Master were the *Ta Hsueh* (The Great Learning), *Chung Yung* (Doctrine of the Mean) and *Hsiao Ching* (Classic of Filial Piety).

The *Lun Yu* consists of a collection of the notes and journals of the Master's conversations, teachings and journeys told in some 496 chapters. Believed to have been compiled by the disciples of his school, it is often regarded as the basic "scripture" of Confucianism.

Publication in itself was a bold move for Confucius. Never before in Chinese history had anyone but kings and ministers published books. But Confucius was a commoner, or at most a member of an impoverished family of nobility. His years of writing and interpretation of hallowed doctrines were followed by 44 years of teaching, yet another revolutionary course. Before he arrived on the scene, only aristocrats and royalty received formal education. Confucius, however, welcomed to his school of thought anyone who demonstrated a keen intellect and a sincere desire to learn.

By the time of his death at the age of 72, some 3,000 students had been attracted to the teachings of Confucius. About 70 disci-ples are believed to have carried on his work and further expounded upon his ideas during the period of great intellectual fervor known as the "100 Schools Period." Thousands of books were published and tens of thousands of students educated as a direct result of the example set by Confucius.

Among them were Meng-tze, better known as Mencius. Considered second only to Confucius among the great sages of ancient China, Mencius further advanced the concepts of his predecessor and reaffirmed basic Confucian principles, particularly the notion that government should be for the good of the people and not the ruler, and that human nature was basically good.

In 221 B.C., the enlightened age of Confucius and Mencius was buried under the militant Chins who swept down from the northwest. Led by founding emperor Chin Shih-Hwang-ti, China was united for the first time under a bureaucratic government. But Chin was contemptuous of learning. "I conquered the empire from the saddle of a horse, what need have I for books," he said.

Chin viewed the contending schools of philosophy as potential sources of sedition and a threat to his empire. So he ordered the executions of hundreds of scholars. They were buried alive or sent to slave on the Great Wall of China. He also ordered most books in China to be burned. Only tomes on agriculture, divination and medicine were spared from the infamous "Fires of Chin."

It is a testimony to the strength and endurance of Confucius' doctrines that his works somehow survived the conflagration. Private editions of his works were secreted in walls and underground vaults. After the demise of the Chins, the ensuing Han Dynasty collected the hidden works of Confucius during the 2nd Century B.C. and declared the official canons of a new state philosophy called *Ru-Hsueh* or "Confucian Studies." From then until Confucian studies were formally abandoned in 1905, the Confucian classics remained the most sacrosanct source of knowledge and moral authority for every ruler and bureaucrat of China.

Li and Ren

Confucian philosophy is far too complex to cover in detail here. But a few highlights reveal the wisdom of Confucius. His most celebrated concepts were those of *li*, illustrated by the Chinese character 禮, and *ren*, represented by the character 仁.

Li has been translated by various scholars as "rites," "ceremonies," "etiquette" and "propriety." Its combined implications underline all social behavior in the Chinese system. It provides the appropriate behavior for every single situation a person may face in life. If *li* conflicts with the law, a "superior man" will not hesitate to follow the dictates of *li*. Such a concept has driven many of mankind's subsequent greatest leaders from Jesus Christ to Gandhi. *Li* also incorporates the many formal rituals by which a person symbolically expresses propriety and confirms his commitment to it, like the sacrificial rites that honor deceased ancestors.

Even more important is Confucius' concept of *ren*. Its character consists of the symbols for "man" (人) and the number

and benevolent and the sources of friction among people would be eliminated. In his utopian prescription for humanity, Confucius promoted peace and social harmony.

Confucius established the "Five Cardinal Relationships" as a guide to the social behavior that would motivate followers to his utopia. These rules governed relations between subject and ruler, husband and wife, parent and child, elder sibling and younger sibling, and between friends. The last is the only social relationship of equality possible in a Confucian society. The rest demand the absolute obedience of inferior to superior.

Such common and continuing traits of

"two" (二). *Ren*, thus, dictates social relations. It can be roughly interpreted by the English words "benevolence," "kindness" or "human-heartedness." Confucius advised his followers: "Be strict with yourself, but be benevolent towards others." He emphasized a blend of the virtues of self-discipline and generosity. If all mankind conducted itself according to the virtues of *ren* and *li*, all social behavior would become appropriate

Above, life in Confucius' China. A "Knick-Knack Peddler" as painted by Li Sung about 1200 A.D.

Chinese society as authoritarian government, filial piety, patriarchal family structure, primogeniture and the importance of personal friendships—all of which endure in the social life of Taiwan today—can be traced to the Five Cardinal Relationships of Confucius. For example, a Chinese woman in Taiwan who gets divorced automatically forfeits custody of all her children to her former husband, regardless of the grounds for divorce. That practice follows Confucius' rules for the patriarchal pattern of family structures.

Sun Yat-sen—known as "Gwo Fu," or

"Father of the Country," to Taiwan's people—was well aware of the influence of these teachings of Confucius. In the early years of the 20th Century, he was concerned with developing a nationalistic spirit among the Chinese, to enable them to band together for the overthrow of the decadent Ching dynasty. "The Chinese people have shown the greatest loyalty to family and clan, with the result that in China there have been 'family-ism' and 'clan-ism' but no real nationalism," Dr. Sun lamented. The great statesman believed that while loyalty to family and clan should be preserved, the traditional loyalty that a subject held for his emperor should be redirected to the best interests of the state in general.

Confucius also formulated a version of the

man." Confucius stressed that the superior man was not necessarily an aristocrat or powerful politician, but simply a person of virtue. He taught that anyone aspiring to become a gentleman must strive for virtue and cultivate it. Learning was the key to that process. "The superior man makes demands on himself; the inferior man makes demands on others," Confucius said.

In practice, this concept led to the system of appointing learned Confucian scholars to administrate China on behalf of the emperor and diminished the role of hereditary princes and royal relatives. The system was later bolstered by civil service examinations which, at least in theory, were open even to the humblest peasant. Rule by men of knowledge and virtue managed to hold the un-

"Golden Rule." But like many things Chinese, it takes an opposite tack from the Western concept. "Do not do unto others what you would not have them do unto you," is a reasonably accurate translation of Confucius' version. To "do unto others," as the West does, would be far too aggressive and presumptuous for the Confucian gentleman. The practice of actively performing good deeds is considered a form of social interference in Chinese society. Instead, the Chinese prefer to simply refrain from doing bad deeds.

Any individual who successfully followed the precepts of Confucian teaching could attain the goal of the Master's philosophy— that of becoming the 君子 or "superior

wieldy empire together from the 2nd Century B.C. until the birth of the republican form of government in 1912. The Confucian concept of the superior man also explains the respect that the Chinese have always had for men of scholarly accomplishment.

Spiritual Spheres

Confucianism as practiced by the Chinese is not a religion in the strict sense of the word. Technically, it is not even a philoso-

Above, modern rituals in Taichung pay homage to the life and precepts of Confucius. Right, youths perform classical music during festival honoring Confucius.

phy. It is a way of life that puts equal importance on theory and practice.

Confucius himself rarely expounded on religious subjects, despite repeated inquiries from his disciples. "Not yet having understood life, how can we possibly understand death?" was his simple retort. Confucius did not deny the existence of gods and lesser spirits. He obviously felt that there was some universal force on the side of right. But he felt man should steer away from spiritual concerns and concentrate on creating a harmonious society in this world.

The Chinese of Confucius' day were extremely superstitious people who spent an inordinate amount of time and energy on formal sacrifices that invoked myriad spirits. They practiced divination, prayed for rain

a religion, temples to the great sage abound. Each of the 2,000 counties of China built a temple in his honor after his death. In Taiwan, September 28 each year has been designated Teachers' Day, a national holiday honoring Confucius. Elaborate ceremonies are held at Taipei's Confucian Temple. Taiwan's other testament to the Confucian tradition is Kung Teh-cheng, a teacher of philosophy at a Taipei university. He is the 77th direct descendant of Confucius.

Contemporary Influences

The most lasting of the legacies of Confucius has been the perseverance of the primacy of family and friends. This legacy

and pursued other quasi-religious activities. When Confucius insisted that man's most pressing concerns lay in this life, religious matters receded and social issues moved to the forefront. Since Confucius' time, the Chinese have never felt the need for a single omnipotent god or an exclusive, all-embracing religion. They have simply referred to the powers above as "heaven," an impersonal and inscrutable force which drives the universe. Meanwhile, they have welcomed any and all religious faiths to their land—as long as they did not interfere with social concerns. Still, to be on the "safe side," many Chinese continue to pay homage to a variety of gods,

Although Confucianism is not considered

persists in Taiwan, mainland China and far-flung Chinese communities throughout the world. Family and friends provide the individual with many of the social and economic services performed by courts, police, banks, lawyers and the other impersonal institutions of the West.

It is the family, not the individual, that has been the basic unit of social organization in China since the Duke of Chou established the system of *bao-jia* by law during the 12th Century B.C. The Duke divided society into units of 10, 100, 1,000 and 10,000 families according to neighborhoods and districts. Each unit chose a leader from its ranks who was responsible for the behavior and welfare of all the families under his jurisdiction. This leader reported directly to the leader of the next highest *bao-jia* unit. If a man committed a crime, the head of his own household initially would be held accountable, followed by the head of his 10-family unit, then the leader of the 100-family group and so on. Thus, minor crimes rarely got reported beyond the *bao-jia* organization which retained the authority to settle such matters internally. A 20th Century version of the *bao-jia* system persists in contemporary Taiwan; the "street committees" and "work units" of the Communist government on the mainland are but variations of the ancient social organization.

In Taiwan, the entire family commands collective responsibility for the behavior and welfare of each of its members. When a man

Such ancient precepts have produced some bizarre results in modern courts. In a case in Taipei, a younger cousin of a man convicted of a serious offense was exonerated of complicity in harboring his criminal cousin. The judge reasoned that because the two men were cousins and the criminal was the eldest of the pair, the young man had no choice but to protect his lawbreaking relative. Confucius' *li* demanded the filial act and superceded the law. Ironically, if the young man had protected a good friend under similar circumstances, he would have been convicted and punished for complicity in the crime because of the absence of family ties. The same logic decrees more serious penalties against people who commit crimes against members of their own family than for

became a high-ranking official in dynastic China, his whole family was honored with gifts and titles, but if he committed treason or other serious crimes, his whole family shared the punishment, whether it was death, mutilation or distant exile.

Today, the laws of the Republic of China government in Taiwan hold families responsible for the welfare of their elderly. That law has created an effective social security system that does not burden the state or society at large. A family loses "face" if its elderly members are forced to rely on government welfare payments or other handouts. Likewise, certain consequences can fall on a family if its young people get into trouble.

any similar offenses perpetrated against strangers.

Getting it Done
With Guan-hsi

In Chinese society, family comes first, state and occupation second. Close connections are maintained with all family members, even those who move halfway around the world. Such extended networks provide sources of warmth and comfort as well as a

Above, old men imitate art at Confucian temple in Lukang. Right, a ritual of contemporary life in Taiwan: the daily morning flag-raising ceremony at Tainan's city hall.

secure form of social welfare.

One example of the significance of these ties is built right into the Chinese language. The Chinese have distinct words for elder brother (*geh-geh*), younger brother (*di-di*), elder sister (*jie-jie*) and younger sister (*mei-mei*). There are different words for grandparents, cousins, uncles and aunts depending upon their age and the side of the family that they represent. Talk to a Chinese person about your Aunt Sarah and he will undoubtedly inquire whether she's *gu-ma*, your father's sister, or mother's, *ah-yi*. There are words for "classmates," *tung sywe*, implying that two people attended the same school no matter how many years apart; and "colleagues," *tung shih*, for people who work in the same office. There is

owed, and are always repaid in kind. Years of experience have taught the Chinese to trust personal friends and relatives to get things done, but they feel uneasy asking favors of strangers.

The Chinese do not make friends easily. But when they do, the friendship lasts for life and is constantly reinforced by the ritual exchange of gifts and favors. The betrayal of a personal friend is regarded as a heinous social offense which can have serious repercussions throughout the offender's network of *guan-hsi*. That network is only as strong as its weakest link, so each new relationship is given careful consideration before being taken on.

The Chinese forms of Confucian-style relationships proliferate in the Chinese busi-

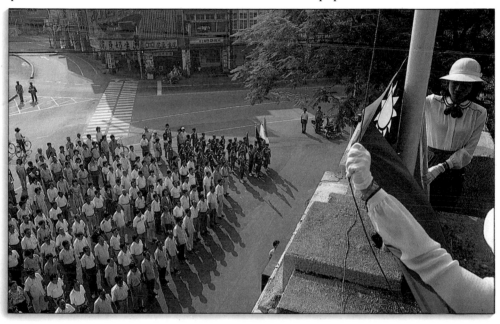

even a term—*tung ren*—for "people with whom you have something in common."

Friends form the other half of the Chinese social equation. Every Chinese person has a network of carefully cultivated friendships, his *guan-hsi*, or "connections." Good *guan-hsi* in the right places often helps get things accomplished on both sides of the Taiwan Strait. It can magically produce a last-minute reservation on a "fully-booked" airline flight and can open doors and help cut through red tape in government offices.

Westerners often view the cultivation of such connections as a discriminating form of "cronyism," but the Chinese believe it is perfectly natural to perform favors for friends. Favors are never requested unless

ness world—and virtually keep it from unraveling. The Chinese routinely select business associates from among established family members and friends, unlike Westerners who tend to choose their friends from among business associates or professional groups.

An American or European who loses his job often loses most of his friends as well—until he finds a new position among new acquaintances. A Chinese businessman who loses his job or goes bankrupt has his family and friends to rally to his support in helping him obtain new employment or build a new business. Afterwards, he continues to deal almost exclusively with the same group of people rather than with new associates.

Likewise a Chinese businessman can invoke the social pressures of his *guan-hsi* network whenever an associate defaults on payments and contracts. That practice eliminates the need for expensive, protracted court actions that can exhaust participants and clog the legal system.

Courts of Last Resort

Indeed, courts of law are another social institution that are largely co-opted by the Confucian ethics of Chinese societies. Since the Duke of Chou created the *bao-jia* system, the Chinese have been encouraged to settle personal disputes within their own families, neighborhoods and occupational groups, rather than impose their problems

on the public. The court is always the last resort.

By the time a case gets that far, both parties are automatically considered guilty of failing to solve their conflict according to the precepts of *li*. Chinese judges, incensed by the imposition of private squabbles upon the public domain, have been known to render decisions unfavorable to both parties—regardless of whom is the plaintiff and whom is the defendant.

The Chinese believe that their family and friends are in a much better position to understand a member's behavior and motivations than a court. And since the family holds collective responsibility for a member's misdeeds, it has a pressing reason

to resolve disputes quickly, to the full satisfaction of all parties involved. In the end, the family also avoids having its problems broadcast to the public and losing "face."

Taiwan and the many Chinese communities overseas often appear to be paradigms of peace and lawfulness. In truth, they suffer their share of criminal activities. The peaceful appearances are in part a result of the Chinese preference to settle matters among themselves and to avoid police involvement and the accompanying press coverage. Even cases of assault and involuntary manslaughter frequently have been settled in Taiwan directly between families of the victim and the perpetrator, with the police acting as mediators and with the absence of court involvement. When the two families agree on a financial settlement to compensate for the victim's injuries or death, the case is closed.

Banks are another Western innovation frequently bypassed by the *guan-hsi* system. In fact, banks were unknown in China until the 20th Century. In Taiwan, most people participate in private small "investment associations" called *biao-hui*. A group of friends, relatives and colleagues pool their money to form a mutual fund from which each member may take turns borrowing. The borrower has access to large loans from the group once or twice a year. As with commercial banks or loan institutions, they must be repaid over a period of time with interest. The Chinese rely on the personal closeness of the group to inhibit fraud or default. Such private loans occasionally involve millions of dollars

Taiwan is among the most densely populated pieces of real estate in the world. But had it 50 times the land, the Chinese would still live close to each other. *Re nau*, they say, which literally is something like "noisy warm." They are easily appalled at the enormous spaces a single foreigner may live in. In the first place, it is not frugal. But probably more important, it must be very lonely.

The systems of *bao-jia*, *guan hsi* and *biao-hui* are just a few of the idiosyncratic reminders of the enduring dominance of Confucius in contemporary Chinese life. Rule by *li* rather than law and the emphasis on personal relationships instead of legal ones fuel the "flavor of human feeling" that moves modern Taiwan.

Modern evidence of Confucius' influence on the Chinese of Taiwan takes the form of friendly morning foxtrots in Taipei, left, and right, an impromptu performance of traditional music.

TEMPLES AND DEITIES: RELIGION

The clatter of wooden divining blocks tossed upon stone floors punctuates murmured prayers. White wisps of fragrant smoke curl from hundreds of incense sticks and disappear among the aged beams above. Offerings of fresh fruits and cakes adorn the altars under the tranquil gaze of ornate images. Little children frolic while their mothers pray for another son. Old men in T-shirts smoke cigarettes and engage in animated conversation. These are all part of the timeless scene one encounters upon entering a Chinese temple in Taiwan.

Paradoxically, despite the remarkably rapid development of Taiwan from a rural agricultural society to an industrialized complex of urban enclaves, traditional religion has flourished. Indeed, the ubiquitous temples of Taiwan are as much a feature of its skylines as are factories.

Popular Chinese folk religion consists of a blend of practices and beliefs that have developed out of animism, ancestor worship, Confucian custom, Taoist thought, Buddhist ideas of salvation, and various folk beliefs. In Taiwan, these forms of worship are generally similar to those still practiced by other Chinese communities in Southeast Asia, Hong Kong and Macau. But despite the common thread that runs through traditional beliefs and rituals, and the fact that the island is comparatively small with good communications, local practices in Taiwan differ considerably from region to region, even within a few miles.

Although Taiwan has separate Buddhist, Taoist and Confucian temples, the common man blends the practices of all three with a measure of superstition and ancestor worship. To further confuse matters, most peasant devotees refer to this religious hodgepodge by the umbrella term "Buddhism," even as they regularly visit local folk-religion temples to worship heroes and deities unknown to Buddhism. There is little concern for logic in folk religion.

Where Two Worlds Meet

Many traditional temples, particularly the smaller ones, appear deserted except on

Preceding pages, the classic lines of Tainan's Temple of the Holy Mother at Deer Ear Gate. Left, the awesome altar of Ma Tsu's main shrine at Deer Ear Gate. Right, a devotee.

festival days. Then they are alive with activity from dawn to dusk. While incense is burned, the reservoirs of the temple's oil lamps are constantly topped up to the tolling of a bell, providing devotees with a flame to light their paper offerings. Larger temples are almost always bustling with devotees who present offerings of incense to the deities, or who seek advice through the use of divining blocks or sticks.

Religious solemnity is not one of the earmarks of these temples. Some village temples even double as schools, stores and

recreation centers. Temples are often cool spots where ladies and elderly folks meet and chat with acquaintances, relax or play cards.

Because the supernatural and human worlds coexist in the popular folk religion of Taiwan, temples represent the place where the two worlds can meet and communicate. The living devotees provide the resident deities with incense, oil and food offerings; in exchange, they receive advice and protection against demonic influences responsible for such earthly sorrows as plagues, disasters and illnesses.

There are any number of requests that might be put to a deity. Devotees may ask for something as minor as assistance for a child in passing a school examination, or as dire as a cure for a terminally ill family member. An unemployed man might ask for a job, a pregnant woman may request an easy delivery. These problems can be put to "specialists" like the goddess of fertility, or to "general practitioners" who can hear any requests. Although devotees do not always leave the altar satisfied, most do feel renewed hope and comfort. Even many Chinese who are skeptical about the gods' powers perfunctorily carry out rituals, just to stay on the safe side of the mysterious heavenly powers.

The inquisitive visitor's first insight into the nature of Chinese folk religion comes from the architecture and decor of the temple buildings themselves.

which is said to capture and trap evil spirits; or the Three Star Gods of Longevity, Wealth and Posterity. These roof symbols usually reflect the role of the temple's main deity. Often one of these symbols tops the main gate while another crowns the main hall.

Below this central symbolic image are the fantastic and often gaudy assortment of figures so much associated with Chinese temples. The eaves slope down, then rise again in sudden curves, with multicolored dragons and phoenixes, fish and flowers flying from the tips. The phoenix, a mythical bird said to appear only in times of extreme peace and prosperity, and the dragon, symbol of strength, wisdom and good luck, are the two most auspicious symbols in Chinese

Dragons and Phoenixes

One important element of architecture is the temple roof. This is where one finds the most ornate decor and skilled craftsmanship. Indeed, temple roofs are alive with images of deities, immortals, legendary heroes and fantastic mythological animals, all of which serve to attract good fortune to and repel evil from the temple and surrounding community.

The center ridge of a temple roof usually is crowned with one of four symbols: a pagoda, which represents a staircase to heaven; a flaming pearl, which symbolizes the beneficial *yang* spirit, the sun, and usually is flanked by two dragons; a magic gourd,

mythology.

These exterior features, however, are at first glimpse very much the same in Buddhist and folk-religion temples alike. Inside the difference is much more obvious. Buddhist temples and monasteries in general contain few images, with one to three major gilded Buddhas on a main altar. Confucian temples, severe by comparison, do not contain any images. The image of Confucius can be found on one or two of the altars of a few folk-religion temples, however.

Above, one of the ubiquitous old temples in the Penghu (Pescadores) Islands. Right, a pig and pineapple meal for the spirits that roam during the Feast of the Hungry Ghosts.

Home of the Gods

In the eyes of devotees, folk-religion temples are the public residences of the deities. Taiwan's temples were originally built in the 18th and 19th centuries by Chinese craftsmen. They range in size from small, dog kennel-size shrines containing one or two images or tablets to large establishments with several main halls flanked by minor ones, each holding separate altars and murals. As a rule, a temple is named after the chief deity on the main altar. Even if the temple has a literary label or is home to a score of other gods, the locals still usually refer to it by the name of its principal deity.

Once drab with age and lack of maintenance, many of these old temples have been

and civil mandarins, or even young learned scholars.

The main altar of a typical folk-religion temple bears the image of its major deity attended by minor aides, officials or servants. Fronting the principal deity is a smaller image of the same god; this miniature is borne from the temple precincts to bless devotees as they stand in their doorways, or is carried during festivals to other neighboring temples.

In addition to the main altar, most temples also have two secondary altars flanking the main one on either side; in some larger temples, there are further altars down the side walls. Beneath the main altar, at ground level, are one of two forms of small altar. One contains a tablet dedicated to the tu-

renovated in recent years. In some cases, their colorful new ornamentation has transformed them into exotic curiosities that may appear garish to the Western eye. Modern folk-religion temples have also been built, especially in central and southern Taiwan. These are invariably large and costly buildings with only one or two images.

The interior decoration of folk-religion temples varies considerably. Many of them contain fascinating murals depicting scenes from Chinese mythology and history. Pillars and balustrades may be intricately carved works of art. Most temples have guardians painted on the outside faces of the main doors; these pairs can vary from ferocious generals to more benign-looking military

telary or protective spirit of the temple itself; the other contains stone or wooden "white tigers," the bringers or destroyers of luck. A common offering for these tigers is a slab of fatty pork.

Incense and Other Offerings

There are always five items on the table before a temple's main altar. A large incense pot is flanked by two decorative vases and two candlesticks. The incense pot itself is a primary religious object—in some temples it is regarded as the most sacred. It is filled with ash accumulated by years of worship, and is the repository for the spirit of the venerated Jade Emperor. Ash is taken from one existing temple to start the main pot in a new temple. In some temples, the main incense pot is situated just outside or inside the main entrance; it is here that devotees begin their round of prayers and offerings. They place one or three sticks of incense in each pot throughout the temple, depending upon the seniority of the deity before whom the pot stands.

In addition to incense, offerings include food and drink, oil and objects made of paper. The type of food provided depends upon the season, the appetite of the particular deity, and the pocketbook of the devotee. Food is normally left at the temple only long enough for the deity to partake of its aroma, a period often defined as the length of time it takes for an incense stick to burn

down. Afterwards, the food is taken home to the dinner table of the devotee and his or her family. Any leftovers are later "disposed of" by the temple keepers.

In some temples, only fruit and vegetables are offered to the gods. One particular cult prohibits offerings of duck. In season, boxes of mooncakes—baked pastries stuffed with sweet bean paste—are placed on temple altars. Bowls of cold cooked rice are often left before minor deities, including underworld gods. Tea or wine, in rows of three or five small cups, is occasionally offered. Nothing is ever presented in groups of four; that is regarded as the number of death.

Another form of offering is paper money, tied in bundles and placed under the image

or on the altar table. This "hell money" represents either large sums of cash drawn on the "Bank of the Underworld," or else lumps of gold or silver taels, the currency used in Chinese imperial times.

Hungry Ghosts

In addition to the gods, ancestors are also commonly at the receiving end of offerings and tokens of respect in temples. Traditionally, ancestral tablets were kept in family homes, and respects were paid at a living-room altar. Increasingly, however, families have paid temples to house the ancestral tablets on a special altar and assume the responsibility for offering and prayers, especially if there is a possibility of neglect at home. These tablets bear the ancestors' names and (in recent times) photographs. It is important that they be given regular offerings, lest they become "hungry ghosts."

According to Chinese folk religion, a soul upon death is hastened through the various courts and punishments of purgatory in order to be reborn again. At the same time, there is the contradictory belief that the underworld is remarkably similar to the human world, and that its inhabitants require food, money, clothes and a house. Thus when a family member dies, the living relatives do their best to see that the spirit of the deceased enters the underworld in comfort. They provide food offerings in the hope that the aroma will give sustenance. They offer spirit money and paper artifacts—elaborately designed like the real things—to represent houses, cars, clothes and often servants. These "substitutes" are transported to the underworld by burning. Relatives who fail to care for the spirit of a deceased family member set another "hungry ghost" loose in the world.

Once every year, for 15 days in the seventh lunar month (August and/or September), the needs of these ghosts are met in the Festival of the Hungry Ghosts. At this time, when hungry souls are released from the underworld to roam the human world in search of sustenance, Chinese families take steps to propitiate these spirits. Fearing the depradations this rampaging band of ghosts might inflict, they burn paper money and leave food on the edges of streets just outside their homes.

Most towns in Taiwan also hold a large

Left, urns of ashes are marked by photographs of the dead in Taiwan. Right, the visage of an icon of Kuan Kung peers through neon light reflections in a Tainan temple.

parade. Images of the tutelary City God and his two generals are carried around the streets, patrolling to monitor the ghosts' behavior. At the end of the 15-day festival period, local temples hold banquets for the ghosts. Temporarily appeased and gratified, the spirits return to the underworld for another year.

The Chinese Pantheon

A huge pantheon of gods and goddesses colors traditional Chinese religion. Most are the heroes and worthies of Chinese myth, legend and history, deified either by imperial order or popular choice. Some can even be equated with the saints of Christianity. Some of these deities are so well known that their

calamities as floods, drought, accidents, sickness and crop failure.

The fascinating origins and legends that surround these deities go deep into Chinese history. They reach devotees through street-opera themes, tales related by professional storytellers in tea houses, or at mother's or grandmother's knee in much the same way as the legends of King Arthur and Robin Hood have survived in the West.

It is generally believed that the altar images of deities are temporary residences for those gods, and that the spirit is only present in the image when required. Many devotees consider incense to be a lure to entice a spirit into an image. Others maintain that a deity's spirit is omniscient, and is contained within each and every image portraying him (or

images are found in many or most temples; others are unique to a single temple. Some communities have cult followings that have grown up around a particular historical figure believed to have protected or guided the town, or to have worked a miracle there. The best-known deities have proven their reputed powers to generations of Chinese over the centuries.

Dozens of identical images may be lined up on altars beside the statues of some deities. These represent the god's armies complete with infantry and calvary. Such supernatural soldiers command offerings of food from temple worshipers. In return, they protect their territory from the hungry ghosts and demons which threaten with such

her) from the time the statue is consecrated until it is retired.

Some devotees believe that the power of a deity in any particular statue deteriorates with increasing age and eventually loses its efficacy completely. When this happens, the temple's following must either obtain a new image or have the old one recharged at another temple whose deity is still powerful. The Chinese, being pragmatists, will only pray to those deities whose supernatural power has been proven by answered petitions.

Kuan Yin and Kuan Kung

The two deities most frequently seen on altars in Taiwan's temples are Kuan Yin and

Kuan Kung. Kuan Yin, regarded by the Chinese as the Goddess of Mercy, has evolved and transformed through centuries from its prototype, Avalokitesvara, an Indian *bodhisattva* who foreswore *nirvana* in order to save mortals.

Kuan Yin is a shortened form of a title which means "One Who Sees and Hears the Cry From the Human World." Worshipped especially by women, this goddess comforts the troubled, the sick, the lost, the senile and the unfortunate. Her popularity has grown through the centuries so that she is now also regarded as the protector of seafarers, farmers and travelers. She cares for souls in the underworld, and is invoked during post-burial rituals to free the soul of the deceased from the anguished torments of purgatory.

No other figure in the Chinese pantheon appears in a greater variety of images. Kuan Yin's standard image depicts her as a barefoot woman carrying a small upturned vase of holy dew. She may be seated on an elephant, standing on a fish, nursing a baby, holding a basket, with six arms or a thousand, one head or eight, one atop the next. The main identifying factor is her bare feet. On public altars, Kuan Yin is frequently flanked by two aides: a barefoot, shirtless youth with his hands clasped in prayer, and a maid demurely holding her hands together inside her sleeves. Her principal feast occurs yearly on the 19th day of the second lunar month.

Kuan Kung is the second most popular of deities in Taiwan. A historical soldier of the 3rd Century A.D., he fought with two sworn companions to try to save a disintegrating dynasty. When captured by the enemy in 220 A.D., he refused an offer to defect and was decapitated, proving his loyalty. The courage of the three heroes has been chronicled in one of China's most famous novels, *The Romance of the Three Kingdoms.*

Today, Kuan Kung is the patron deity of such disciplined groups as soldiers and policemen and of merchants and businessmen but he is often incorrectly referred to as the God of War. In Buddhist temples, he is one of two guardians on the main altar. Also known as Kuan Ti and by a score of other titles, his image is easily recognized by the severe puce or red face. Often he is accompanied by his two cohorts—Chou Tsang, a tall, black-faced sword bearer, and Kuan Ping, his scholarly adopted son. Kuan Kung may be standing or seated, astride a red horse or holding his black beard in one hand and a book in the other. His

festival is held on the 13th day of the fifth lunar month.

The Jade Emperor And Other Deities

Among the most important of other deities worshipped by the people of Taiwan are the following:

● Yu Huang Shang Ti, the Jade Emperor. Also known as Tien Kung, he is the supreme deity of folk religion. His rule was traditionally conceived of as equal to that of the reigning emperor of China. His special concern is meting out justice to men through his subordinate deities. He is ultimately responsible for the deification of other gods, or for their dismissal from the pantheon as and

when necessary.

On the Jade Emperor's birthday (the ninth day of the first lunar month), special sacrifices of pork, chicken, duck and occasionally goat are placed before his image. Although the emperor himself is considered a vegetarian, he is believed to feast with meat-eating friends.

The emperor is usually depicted with two servants who hold fans above his head. In a few temples, he is flanked by civil and

Above, a wooden image of the Jade Emperor on the altar of the Holy Hall of the Martial and Literary Arts in Kaohsiung. Right, Lu Tung-pin, the main deity on a secondary altar of the Chinan Temple near Taipei.

military aides. Tien Kung's wife is rarely depicted on the altar.

Images of the Jade Emperor normally show him seated in imperial robes, his flat-topped crown notable for the short strings of pearls that dangle from the front. He holds a short, flat tablet in both hands before his chest. Historically, he did not come into prominence until the 9th Century A.D., considered fairly late by Chinese historical standards.

● The San Kuan Ta Ti, "Three Great Rulers." This trinity rules Heaven, Earth and the Waters, and is regarded as second only to the Jade Emperor in the pantheon's hierarchy, which bears important similarity to the imperial Chinese bureaucratic structure.

Devotees look to the San Kuan to deliver them from evil and calamity. Originally worshipped throughout China, they are the main deities at about 60 temples in Taiwan, especially in Taoyuan and Hsinchu counties. They are depicted as a trio of identical images who sit on side-by-side thrones, three bearded mandarins with scholars' bonnets, each holding a tablet in front of his chest.

The Demon Slayer, the Doctor And the Goddess of Sailors

● Hsuan Tien Shang Ti, the "Supreme Lord of the Dark Heavens." He is also known as Shang Ti Kung and to foreigners

as the Northern Emperor. Hsuan Tien, a famous exorcist and slayer of demons, is depicted on altars as a fierce soldier, dressed in armor and usually seated. He has bare feet that rest on a tortoise and snake, makes a magical sign with the fingers of his left hand, has unkempt hair, and is often accompanied by two aides, General Kang and General Tien. He is also the patron deity of butchers and of people setting up businesses.

● Pao Sheng Ta Ti, the "Great Emperor Who Protects Life." Also called Ta Tao Kung, he is revered for his ability to cure the sick. Regarded by the people of Taiwan as the patron deity of native medicine, Pao Sheng was a legendary physician of the 10th Century A.D. His fame spread after he healed an ailing empress.

Pao Sheng's image, easily confused with that of other deities, usually depicts him as a seated, benign, bearded mandarin accompanied by two of his 36 warrior aides, or occasionally by youths each carrying a box of medicinal herbs. Pao Sheng is the main deity in about 140 of Taiwan's temples, chiefly in Fukienese communities around Yunlin and Tainan. He does not appear in temples of the Cantonese ethnic minority. His birthday is celebrated on the 15th day of the third lunar month.

● Ma Tsu, also known as Tien Shang Sheng Mu or Tien Hou, is an exceedingly popular figure throughout Taiwan. Legend claims that she was the daughter of a 9th Century Fukien fisherman named Lin. One day, her father and two brothers were caught in a typhoon at sea. The girl, asleep at home, left her body during a dream and appeared from out of the clouds above the boat. She grasped her two brothers with her hands and her father with her teeth. Unfortunately, the mother at home kept asking the body of the sleeping girl what was happening. In desperation, Miss Lin answered, but in doing so lost her grip of her father.

Miss Lin died at the early age of 20 and some believe she was deified by the Emperor of China. She became the patron deity of sailors, but evolved into a goddess to whom any problem could be put. Her image is usually that of a seated dowager wearing a flat-topped crown with a bead screen similar to that of the Jade Emperor. She normally holds a scepter in her right arm or a tablet before her chest. Her two assistants are demons that she subdued and turned into loyal servants: the green Chien Li Yen, "Eyes Which See for One Thousand Li (about 300 miles)," and the red Shun Feng Erh, "Ears Which Listen for a Favorable Wind."

There are about 375 temples in Taiwan in which Ma Tsu is the principal deity. Among the most important are those at Lukang and Tainan. Her birthday is celebrated on the 23rd day of the third lunar month. There are large parades in all the major ancient port towns, with special theater performances in Peikang and Lukang.

Gods of City, Earth and Kitchen

● Cheng Huang, the City God appointed by the Jade Emperor to protect a specific town and its inhabitants. In some cities, there might be two or even three City God temples—one each for the city, the county and the prefecture. The City God is the final judge on what should be recorded in the report on each soul of those who die within his parish. He also acts as a link between mankind and the higher gods.

In some City God temples, a large abacus is suspended from a ceiling or wall with the inscription: "Beyond human calculations." In other words, man's life is ordained by fate.

Among the City God's retinue are two generals known as the "harbingers of death," Hsieh and Fan. Legend says they were friends on a military campaign. Fan was drowned during torrential rain by a flash flood when Hsieh had gone for an umbrella. Filled with remorse, Hsieh hanged himself. Their images now tell the story: Hsieh wears white sackcloth for mourning, carries an umbrella, and is depicted with his tongue hanging out. Fan, the shorter of the two, has a black face indicative of drowning. In City God temples, they can be seen with black smeared around their mouths. This is said by some to be opium, by others sweets; either way, it is a bribe to beseech them to be light on punishments.

The image of the City God himself is almost identical with that of the Jade Emperor. It is best differentiated by the images of the attendants around him, like Hsieh and Fan.

● Chu Sheng Niangniang, the "Matron Who Registers Births" and the goddess of fertility. She receives the souls of the deceased after they have been purified in purgatory, and decides into which human body the soul will be reborn. Her image characteristically holds an open book in one hand and a writing brush in the other.

● Kai Tai Sheng Wang, the "Saintly King Who Settled Taiwan," better known to history as Koxinga. His story is told elsewhere in this volume. His image is approached by devotees for advice and guidance; his festi-

val is celebrated on the 16th day of the first lunar month.

● Fu Te Cheng Shen, the Earth God. Every community has an Earth God who protects the parish. In return, all births, deaths and marriages must be reported to this god. Among his responsibilities are controlling ghosts and protecting crops from pests and disease. He rarely has a temple to himself, and in rural areas frequently resides in a small roadside shrine. His standard image is that of a smiling elderly man, seated, dressed in blue robes and carrying a stick. His festival falls on the second day of the second lunar month.

● Tsao Chun, the "Kitchen God." His crude likeness on a cheap print or a tablet rather than a wooden image is found over the stove in most traditional Chinese homes. From this location, he sees and hears the family's domestic affairs. Thus the week before Chinese New Year, when he reports directly to the Jade Emperor on the family's activities of the past year, he is given a proper festive send-off by the family. By the time he returns on New Year's Day, a new print has been pasted up over the stove.

● Wang Yeh, also known as Wen Shen, the "Gods of Pestilence." Varying in number, according to legend, from 36 to 360, these deities destroy demons which cause plague and other pestilence. Many small temples are built to them throughout Taiwan.

● San Tai Tzu, "the Third Prince," a mythological deity also known as Na Cha, and patron saint of spirit mediums. Easily recognizable in images, he has a white or pink face and highly decorated robes. In one hand is a jade bracelet; in the other, a sword or javelin; and beneath one bare foot is a fire-wheel said to be able to carry him through the skies.

● Wu Ying Chiang Chun, the "Five Spirit Generals." Their images take the unusual form of a rack containing five sharp spikes, each topped by the carved head of a general.

Local Heroes Deified

There are hundreds of additional deities. Among them are unique local heroes, like the Japanese policeman who saved members of one local Chinese community, and earned deification. Another temple is dedicated to the spirit of a buffalo.

Right, a tantric Buddhist image that symbolizes a spirit quelling evil adorns a traditional piece of tapestry from the Ching Dynasty.

There are some extremely popular deities. One of them is the so-called Monkey God—Sun, the Great Saint—about whom legends abound and whose mischievous acts are retold with great glee. Another is Chi Kung, a Buddhist monk well known to folk religion, whose ribald exploits were said to include frolics in nunneries and a love for dogmeat despite his vegetarian vows.

There is also a small group of temples in Taiwan that contain wooden memorial tablets to the spirits of those killed while resisting bandits or who died for the common good in clan wars.

With the multitude of deities to be found in Taiwan, it should perhaps not be surprising that many devotees know neither the name nor the function of the local deity to

Take-out Temple Images

The images of deities are carved in specialty shops like those that line the road east of Taipei's Lung-Shan Temple. Images brought to Taiwan from the mainland before 1949 are prized for quality workmanship, as are those fashioned by the artists of Amoy in Fukien province. In contemporary Taiwan, Lukang is generally reputed to turn out the finest master carvers.

Even with the increasing numbers of modern assembly lines on the island, the traditional carvers of temple images have an ample market for their craft. In fact, some temples stock quantities of images of their major deity. These statues line the walls or the altar table and are loaned or rented out

whom they pay reverence. In a majority of temples, there are individual altars dedicated to a theme—fertility, health, agriculture, crafts and trades, or the like—rather than to a particular deity.

Buddhist images also occasionally turn up on the altars of folk-religion temples. In addition to Kuan Yin, these include the historical Buddha, Sakyamuni or Gautama; the Buddha of the future, known as Milofu or Maitreya; and Northern Buddhism's, Omitofu. Others might include Wei To, the guardian of the Buddhist law (Dharma), and Ti Tsang Wang, the savior of souls. The 18 Lohan, disciples of the Buddha, are often represented in temple murals for convention rather than for worship.

for personal devotions. One rural temple south of Taichung, for instance, stocks about 50 small images of Shen Nung, the agricultural god, standing in serried rows down the sides of the main hall. Farmers with crop problems borrow the images, and return them with an offering after the harvest season.

Communication between a devotee and a deity can take several forms. One of the

Above, devotees carry an icon of the sea goddess Ma Tsu in a wooden palanquin during festivities in Peikang. Right, a religious medium enters a trance during a Taipei puppet show in a temple.

most common methods involves the use of two kidney-shaped divining blocks with flat and round surfaces. Worshippers hold these in incense smoke before an image while putting their petitions to the deity. Then they drop the blocks on the ground. Depending upon how the blocks come to rest on their flat and round surfaces, the god is believed to have replied, "Yes," "No" . . . or "Try" again."

Another method of getting messages from the spirit world is through the use of divining spills. Sixty to 100 of these numbered sticks stand upright in a tube. The devotee rattles the container in front of the deity while whispering his wish. Eventually, one stick works its way up and out of the container and falls to the floor. The number on the spill

speaking and acting in the manner of the deities that are believed to have possessed them. In particular, the Monkey God, San Tai Tzu and General Chao are the deities most commonly thought to provide advice and to cure ailments through human mediums.

In the case of the Monkey God, a special device known onomatopoeically as a "ping-pong bottle" indicates when the deity's spirit is present in his image. The device consists of a long, narrow-necked bottle with a flat base that is upturned into a second bottle containing water. The base of the upturned bottle is made of paper-thin glass. Devotees believe that when the base "pings," the spirit of the Monkey God has entered its

corresponds with a printed fortune slip—the deity's response—kept in a rack behind the counter of the temple keeper.

Some devotees favor the use of a forked stick and sand table. Two worshippers, possessed by the deity, hold the stick while it automatically races through the sand, writing characters that can only be deciphered by the temple keeper. Each character is smoothed away after reading to make space for the next.

Spirit mediums also act as intermediaries between the living and the super-natural world. Most mediums, known as *dangki*, hail from southern Fukienese and Chaochow communities of Taiwan. They operate in many of the traditional temples,

image, regardless of whatever changes in atmospheric pressure may have caused the sound.

A spirit medium possessed by the Monkey God may actually crouch, leap, scratch and walk like a monkey before settling down in a chair to write prescriptions for worshipers' problems.

A regular practice of entranced mediums is nicking their tongues with knives, broken pottery or skewers, and wiping the blood onto papers that are then burned by devotees. The ash is taken in water as a kind of medicine.

During festival celebrations, mediums often stick skewers through their cheeks and tongues or pierce their backs with tiny fish hooks weighted down with objects that pull against the skin. The mediums appear to feel no pain in their trance——much in the same manner as Hindus in several overseas communities who endure the tortures of their faith's Thaipusam festival.

Other than these dramatic displays of religious fervor, certain temples in Taiwan perform various rituals throughout each and every day. Temple staff members are always on call in case a devotee requires some form of ritual assistance. As many as a dozen different rituals may be performed simultaneously, in small groups each with a different member of the temple staff, and with other devotees lining the walls awaiting their turns. Usually, these are purification or exorcism rites. Staff members, who routinely oversee them, are dressed in street clothes — but they are clad also in a ceremonial red hat and carry a whip and buffalo-horn trumpet, or a handbell and sword. The practices of these "Red Heads" include spitting a fine spray of rice wine over hot coals to produce spurts of flames.

These temple attendants also preside over rites that involve small wooden palanquins, carried in the temple by pairs of youths or older men. As the chair begins to shake, faster and faster, it is believed that the spirit of a deity has descended into the palanquin. The deity then uses one of the bearers' poles to scratch messages into the ground. Such rites are aimed at strengthening the armies of the supernatural to drive off invading demons and hungry ghosts. They frequently involve talismans, magical signs chalked on benches set over trays of lighted candles, as well as food offerings. Human figures move in designated patterns amid clouds of incense smoke in the dimly lit temple halls. The extraordinary sounds of buffalo horns and the steady throb of drums can give a very eerie feeling to casual onlookers and demons alike.

Visitors are generally welcomed to temples so long as they do not intrude upon devotees engaged in prayers or rituals. It is customary to place a small monetary contribution in the large box that usually commands the center of the temple court, or on the temple keeper's counter. This represents *hsiang yow*, an oil and incense offering for the deities. Images of the deities should not be touched.

At right, children don colorful costumes to ride in parades and processions during a Taoist festival in Tainan.

DANCING TO DIFFERENT DRUMS: ABORIGINES

With their bold handicrafts, stunning red-on-black ceremonial costumes, and animated dance and music, Taiwan's aborigines have woven their own distinctive thread into the fabric of the island's human tapestry. More than 250,000 aborigines, the remnants of 19 tribes, live in Taiwan, mostly in the remote valleys and on the rugged slopes of the central mountain range. About nine of the tribes have maintained sufficient numbers to keep their colorful cultures alive.

Inevitably, many aborigines have been absorbed into the boom and bustle of the Chinese commercial and industrial development. But some tribes still cling to the primitive techniques of slash-and-burn agriculture, moving on to virgin forests every few years. Their primary crops include millet for brewing liquor, sweet potatoes and taro. Cash crops like wild mountain mushrooms, pears, peaches and plums for the gourmet markets of the island have also become a popular and lucrative form of income for sedentary tribes.

Other aborigines still make their livings by hunting. They track deer, mountain goats, bears, civet cats, wild boars and monkeys. Some of their take is sold to commercial markets, some used locally. Until the 20th Century, one of the most prized trophies of some aboriginal hunters was the human head. The Japanese stamped out that primitive custom during their 50-year occupation of Taiwan. But the days of head-hunting are still recalled in the motif of a three-headed figure that appears in the woodcarving and handicraft designs of some tribes.

Uncertain Origins

The dispute surrounding the origin of Taiwan's aborigines still heats up discussions in anthropological circles. The only point on which most scholars agree is that the tribes arrived in the island long before the Chinese and have probably been here for about 10,000 years. Human artifacts at least that old were discovered recently on the banks of the Peinan River near Taitung, lending further credence to estimates of the length of aboriginal habitation of Taiwan.

Preceding pages, Ami tribesmen dance at a harvest festival near Hwalien. Left, young Ami women in traditional dress. Right, ancient aboriginal shield with ornamentation.

The artifact discoveries may also help anthropologists pinpoint the original homelands of these peoples. Some schools of thought believe the tribes are proto-Malays who migrated to Taiwan from the Malay peninsula and Indonesian archipelago. Another theory places their origins in Mongolia. A third theory is that the aborigines represent the northernmost outpost of Polynesian culture and sailed here from the islands of the South Pacific. In light of the diversity that exists even between individual tribes, some scholars have speculated that

Taiwan's aborigines may have roots in all three regions.

The nine tribes that prevail in Taiwan are the Ami, Atayal, Paiwan, Pingpu, Yami, Lukai, Peinan, Saihsia and Taiyu. The largest group is the Ami, which boasts more than 60,000 members. They populate the scenic mountains and valleys near Hwalien on the east coast. Travelers can taste their traditions at the Ami Culture Center in Hwalien. The Ami are mainly farmers; their annual Harvest Festival, held during the last weeks of July and early August, brings out the best of their traditional dance forms, music, costumes and customs.

The group of aborigines most accessible to Taipei vistors is the Atayal, who live in the lush valleys of Wu-lai only an hour's drive away from the capital. Unfortunately, their proximity to Taipei has driven them out of the hunting trade and into the tourism business. They even charge a fee to have their pictures taken.

A more authentic enclave of aborigines are the Paiwan, who inhabit the mountains of eastern Pingtung near Kaohsiung in the south. The snake-worshipping cult of the "hundred-pacer" still remains strong in Paiwan tradition.

Death Dance
Of the 'Hundred-pacer'

The "hundred-pacer" snake revered by the Paiwan and other aborigines takes its

name from its deadly abilities. The aborigines say that victims of the snake drop dead before they can run 100 steps. Venerated as the "spiritual elder" of the tribe, the "hundred-pacer" is the embodiment of its ancestors. The snake's visage appears in abstract form on almost all aboriginal arts and crafts.

The Paiwan, in particular, are master woodcarvers. They whittle magnificent totems, doors, eaves, beams, smoking pipes and other masterpieces from the trees of Taiwan's alpine forests. They also weave, sculpt stone and fashion beadwork using ancient designs and techniques. The faithfulness of this tribe to its ancestral heritage has even inspired a Chinese scholar and anthro-

pologist to research and record their ways at close range. Professor Kao Yeh-rong has lived among the tribe for more than 10 years.

Another culturally interesting tribe, the Lukai, occupies a cluster of hamlets called Wutai Village in lofty Pingtung County. The 200 households of the tribe include a small inn with six rooms that welcomes visitors. The entire town is constructed from stone slabs that have been quarried in the surrounding mountains. The architecture of the dwellings resembles the piled slate homes that dot the Himalayan highlands of western China, northern India and Nepal. The Lukai love remote, inaccessible cliffside habitats — the higher the better—and regard 10-hour treks to neighboring villages as simple strolls.

The strong attachment of the Lukai to their tribal traditions blossoms in the beautiful tunics and robes that they wear on special occasions. These garments are intricately embroidered in black and silver. Members of the tribe are also renowned throughout Taiwan for their athletic abilities, particularly in archery and in marathon running.

One fascinating display of Lukai prowess occurs in their unique "swing contest," one of the most entertaining rituals in the island. Prospective brides mount an enormous swing, with their legs bound to prevent them from flailing. Then big, brawny tribesmen in full ceremonial attire swing the ladies until they sail like kites to dizzying heights. Afterwards, the girls are carried from their swings and dropped into the arms of their most ardent admirers.

The Peinan, Pingpu and Yami

The Peinan tribe shares traditions similar to those of the Lukai. They live mainly in the foothills of the central mountain range near Taitung and occasionally congregate on the city's outskirts for major festivals that include swing contests.

Another Taiwan island tribe of note is the Pingpu of Tainan County. It still practices a ritual form of night worship that remains essentially unchanged from ancient times— with two exceptions. Severed pig's heads have replaced disembodied human heads as the sacrificial offerings, and electricity has replaced torches for lighting. Another curious facet of the ritual is that many of the

Left, wooden carving of hunters capturing a wild boar crafted by Paiwan tribe artists of southern Taiwan. Right, an elderly member of Orchid Island's primitive Yami tribe.

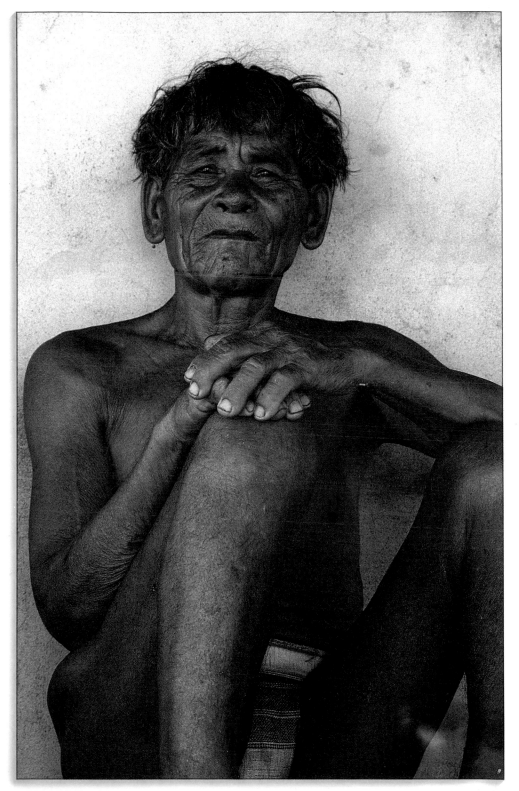

current participants are ethnic Chinese rather than Pingpu tribesmen. A large percentage of the tribe has abandoned its traditional form of worship for Christianity.

The aboriginal tribe that has been least affected by Taiwan's headlong lunge into the modern world is the Yami. They live on Orchid Island off the southeast coast and are the only seafaring aborigines. For half a century, the Japanese deliberately isolated Orchid Island as a kind of living anthropological museum. And until recent years, Yami men and women wore little more than loincloths. Their fishing boats, each hewn from a single giant tree, are beautiful vessels that glide over the waters of the southern Pacific.

Of particular interest in the modern world

of women's rights and sexual equality are the marriage customs of the Yami. Women significantly outnumber the men of the island and have parlayed their numbers into a potent social force. Upon engagement, the male moves into the family home of the female for a one-month "trial marriage." During that time, the prospective groom must constantly prove his prowess in hunting and fishing, exhibit his ability to design and build boats, and demonstrate other requisite skills. If he fails the tests, he is sent packing in disgrace and another suitor is brought in for the bride's consideration. Even the man who successfully completes the trial period and wins the bride is expected to continually prove his worth to his wife and her family.

Otherwise, the typical Yami woman is liable to exercise her most prized right—the power to unilaterally divorce a husband at any time on any grounds and seek new mates.

All in all, aboriginal society throughout Taiwan remains highly matriarchal. Women often tend the fields and orchards while men stay home to tend to the children and the housework. The increasing exposure of the younger generation of aborigines to Chinese and Western ways, through television and school contacts, has begun to erode some of these traditions. Yet, the younger generation has remained on good terms with the more conservative older tribal elements. There are signs of a renaissance of native culture as the young renew their understanding and appreciation of their roots.

The remarkable vitality of these dwindling races is best reflected in the creative arts. The dazzling costumes and headgear of all aboriginal ceremonial tribal attire remains the most distinctive feature. The costumes are usually woven by the women, who turn out bold primitive patterns in neon colors for capes, shawls, shirts, vests, shoes and sandals. The weaving of red on a black background is a dominant style, though motifs incorporate elements of all three regions from which anthropologists believe their ancestors may hail.

The creative drive of the aborigines also finds eloquent expression in primitive woodcarving, particularly tribal totems. The totems stress three motifs—faces, snakes and sex. Human heads and sexual organs are depicted with such bold, basic strokes of the chisel that they turn out as abstracts of highly artistic sophistication.

In the performing arts, aboriginal musicians and dancers move to the rhythms of nature. They perform their traditional steps with an agility and enthusiasm that can infect spectators. In fact, many aborigines have gone on to become popular contemporary singers and dancers. Ami tribeswoman Wen Mei-kui, known as the "Empress of Mountain Song," performed at the White House in the United States at the invitation of President Ronald Reagan after winning an all-island singing contest sponsored by Taiwan Television.

Left, a potential Lukai bride is lashed to a rope swing during harvest festivites near Taitung, while other Lukai women lock arms in dance, right. Following pages, the Pagoda of Filial Virtue above the mists of Sun Moon Lake; a tourist coach emerges from a tunnel in the Taroko Gorge; and the Spring and Autumn pavilion on Lotus Lake.

PLACES

Having washed off the dusty provocations of modern travel in the shower and left your bags in the room, you leave your hotel to get some feeling for this island they call Taiwan. If you have come here through normal travel channels, you arrived at the sparkling new Chiang Kai-shek International Airport and are spending your first few days in Taipei, the nerve center of the island.

Stepping out the door and skillfully dodging various offers of assistance, you step out onto the street and are met by a blast of wind which takes your breath away. A stray sheet of newsprint scurries with the intensity of a sprinter over the hot black asphalt, lifting then, in a dance with dust devils, settling languorously back onto the street. Oriental figures move, tight packages of arms and legs, through the uncertainties of the brilliant weather. The sky is a technicolor blue, sucked clean by the gusts and breezes, while billowing cumulus clouds, stacked deep, define the horizon. White tendrils of cloud scud across the sky, reflected in the bronzed glass of a skyscraper, fragmenting the scene like a photograph taken by some distant satellite. The air in Taipei occasionally blows a curious mist into your face, like raindrops that have been beaten senseless by a storm then brushed off as inconsequentially and unwanted as lint.

You step off the curb to flag down one of the ubiquitous cabs that make it so easy to get around Taipei. Barely acknowledging your entrance, the driver dives into the rapids of Taipei traffic. Weaving around cars, motorcycles and pedestrians, dodging large growling buses, riding bumpers and cutting in front of madcap thrusts of traffic, he slices a path through the anarchic jungle of city streets. This is done without the rage or frenzy which you might assume to be the only possible motivation for such a driving style. Indeed, he remains calm and cheerful throughout the entire nightmare journey, alternately the perpetrator or victim of pranks which would certainly provoke a fistfight if they occurred on the streets of some other nation.

You catch your breath and discover that you have found one of the rare drivers who speaks a fair amount of English and is eager to use it. He introduces himself as Chen Chung-kuang, which translates badly as "Renewed Brilliance Chen," a routinely auspicious name that jolts you back to the days of ancient China. But the appointments of Mr. Chen's taxi are a stark contrast to the traditional implications of his name. Thick pile imitation leopard skin seats are bound in a tight skin of PVC. Small diamonds of reflective tape—orange, yellow, green—outline the doors. A deep flower-like ashtray of rose-pink glass sits between the two front seats. Donald Duck, bug-eyed with culture shock, stares in plastic disbelief as he dangles from the rear-view mirror.

Kitsch, you reflect, is hardly what you expected to see here in the Republic of China. What then? Certainly not sinewy bodies pulling rickshaws. Pagodas and temples? Of course. But bearded figures in flowing robes, crooked staff in hand? No. Save that for the movies and museums. For now, the driver knows where to take you—and what you want to know.

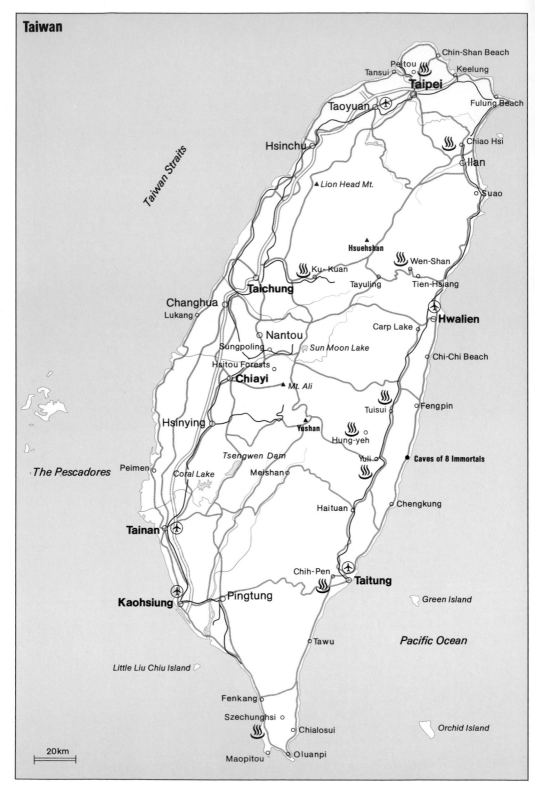

Taiwan

Chin-Shan Beach
Peitou
Tansui
Keelung
Taipei
Taoyuan ✈
Fulung Beach
Hsinchu
Chiao Hsi
Ilan
Lion Head Mt.
Suao

Hsuehshan
Ku-Kuan
Wen-Shan
Taichung
Tayuling
Tien-Hsiang
Changhua
Lukang
Carp Lake
Hwalien ✈
Nantou
Sungpoling
Sun Moon Lake
Chi-Chi Beach
Hsitou Forests
Chiayi
Mt. Ali
Tuisui
Fengpin
Hsinying
Yushan
Hung-yeh
Tsengwen Dam
Yuli
The Pescadores
Peimen
Coral Lake
Meishan
• Caves of 8 Immortals
Haituan
Chengkung
Tainan ✈

Chih-Pen ✈
Taitung
Kaohsiung ✈
Pingtung
Green Island

Tawu
Pacific Ocean

Little Liu Chiu Island

Fenkang
Szechunghsi
Chialosui
Orchid Island
Maopitou
Oluanpi

Taiwan Straits

20km

102

Note: Numbers in brackets
indicate the page where the
places are described in the text

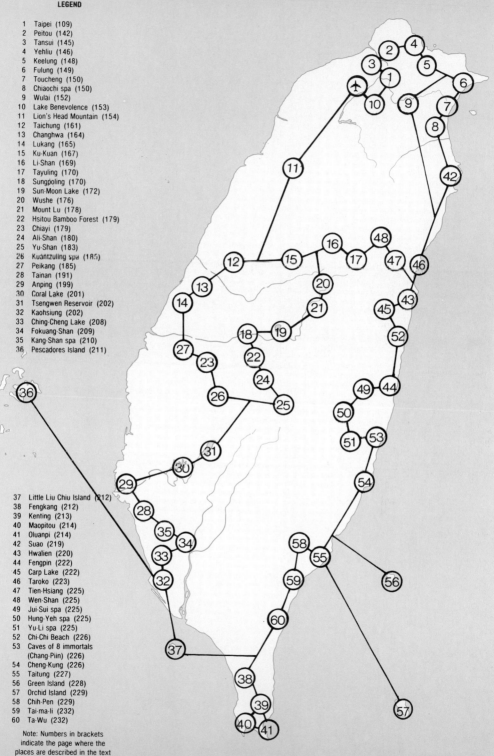

TAIPEI: MODERN HUB WITH AN OLD HEART

When the Nationalist government of the Republic of China established its center of operations in northern Taiwan in 1949, Taipei was little more than a sleepy backwater town, a moist blanket of rice fields and mudflats. As late as the middle of the 1960s, the city had few paved roads and pedicabs were the primary means of public transportation.

The change that forever altered the face of Taipei during the 1970s was truly dramatic. All the blessings and evils of modernization gripped the city in a frenzy of growth that continues today to push Taipei upward and outward. The clatter of pedicabs has given way to the clunk of pile-drivers, the clang of railway trains and the click of taxi meters. Tens of thousands of taxis, buses, private automobiles and lorries, and hundreds of thousands of motorcycles clog the concrete underpasses, overpasses, roundabouts and flyovers of modern roads and freeways. The drab, gray compartments of concrete that once characterized Taipei architecture now squat in the shadows of sparkling glass and metal sky-rises.

The remarkable change that has swept Taipei has also affected the city's nearly 3 million residents. The utilitarian fashions of the '50s have finally been put into mothballs in favor of the latest trends and designs from Paris, Hong Kong and Tokyo. Young people patronize cafes that serve Blue Mountain Coffee from Jamaica and pastries from France, and dance in discos to the latest sounds from New York and London. Businessmen carry Pierre Cardin briefcases, lunch in British pubs and regularly jet to overseas appointments. Housewives drive their Honda Accords to air-conditioned markets.

Yet this veneer of 20th Century sophistication does not mask one implacable fact. Taipei remains one of the most staunchly traditional cities of the Orient. For all its modern appointments, Taipei has not succumbed to the creeping Westernization that has infected the very social fabric of such cities as Hong Kong and Singapore. In their headlong lunge into the future, neither the city nor its people have left behind their glorious heritage. The heart that keeps Taipei ticking is unquestionably Chinese. And it is that unfaltering beat that makes Taipei endlessly fascinating.

A High-rise Explosion

Taipei's stylish new facade can be attributed in part to a pair of changes in governmental policy that occurred in 1978. That year, the ruling powers rescinded a longstanding ban on the construction of new hotels and other highrises in Taiwan. Permits to build scores of skyscrapers were quickly issued. Taipei absorbed the bulk of the buildings. Hotels and office buildings mushroomed, each offering more luxurious appointments than the next. Well-heeled residents donned the latest fashions and rushed to the new atrium lobbies, revolving bars and chic boutiques to see and be seen.

The second administrative move that proved to be a catalyst for the introduction of international trends in Taipei was a relaxation of restrictions on overseas travel. Prior to 1978, residents of Taiwan were prohibited from leaving the country except to visit relatives or

aipei
北市

receding ages, aipei's kyline, and he Chiang ai-shek Memorial. eft, ancient nd modern ashions. ight, statue f sage ronting Asiaworld omplex.

for business or educational purposes. The new policy permitted people to receive passports and exit visas purely for pleasure trips. Applications poured in faster than they could be processed. Many residents of Taipei had been saving for decades for the chance to taste foreign flavors first-hand. They flocked to Tokyo, Hong Kong, Singapore and Seoul. Some ventured as far as Europe and the United States. Along with new tastes in food, fashion and recreation, they brought back modern problems.

The new construction laws have resulted in many ill-conceived buildings thrown up with little concern for zoning laws or architectural aesthetics. In addition, road construction has been unable to keep pace with the ever-increasing numbers of motor vehicles: there are now nearly a half million registered motorcycles, about one per household, in Taipei. The resulting traffic congestion has made it difficult to enforce traffic codes. In order to cope with the chaos, Chinese drivers have coined an expression that accounts for their wreckless road habits: "Fight to be first, fear to be last!" Exhaust from the vehicles, combined with smoke from the

industrial complexes that ring the city, has added another modern malaise to Taipei. A veil of smog hangs over the city much of the year.

Even more problematic has been the constant flow of newcomers seeking their fortunes in the big city. The economic boom attracts thousands of new residents from the countryside each month. By 1981, 8,300 people were crammed into each of Taipei's 272 square kilometers (105 square miles), making it one of the world's most densely populated cities. Despite their earthy philosophy and love of nature, the Chinese have traditionally favored city life to rural life, especially during healthy economic times.

Yet for all its newly acquired ills, the underlying current of traditional Chinese culture and lifestyle continues to make Taipei an extremely attractive destination for travelers. Not unexpectedly, the greatest source of visitors to Taiwan annually are the overseas Chinese communities of the world, particularly Hong Kong. Taiwan also remains a magnet for the Japanese who have idolized classical Chinese culture and borrowed heavily from it during the

Dusty Heng Yang Road, circa 1910.

past 1,000 years. The overseas Chinese and foreigners alike find another irresistible facet to Taipei—its people. In the end, *ren-ching-wei*, "the flavor of human feelings," leaves every visitor with the urge to return.

A Historical Blueprint

Historically, the outskirts of Taipei have attracted more interest than its current metropolitan center. When Koxinga drove the Dutch from Taiwan in 1661, he appointed a general named Huang An to command army and naval forces stationed at Tansui on the mouth of the Tansui River, northwest of modern Taipei. New farming methods were introduced along the river banks and soldiers were sent as far as Chihlan-sanpo to reclaim land.

Early in the 18th Century, reclaimed lands were extended from Hsin-chuang to the area of modern Wanhua, now the heart of Old Taipei. Wanhua, then known as Mengchia, eventually became a major port that reached the peak of its activity in 1853. Port activity later shifted to Tataocheng.

Emperor Kuang Hsu of the Ching Dynasty was the first to designate the area as an administrative center. In 1875, he set up the district of Taipei Fu at the site of modern Chengchung. He also completed a five-kilometer (3.1-mile) protective wall around the city.

The Japanese furthered the area's administrative reputation when they occupied Taiwan in 1895. They changed Taipei Fu into Taipei Chou, then merged suburban areas into an administrative district known as Taipei Ting.

In 1920, 23 years after plans had been drawn, Taipei was formally recognized as a city. During the next dozen years, its population soared from 150,000 to 600,000. The area it occupied expanded from 19 to 67 square kilometers (7½ to 26 square miles).

When the Republic of China regained Taiwan in 1945, Taipei was made the capital of the nation's provisional government and was divided into 10 administrative districts. It became a special municipality by decree in 1966, confirming it as Taiwan's political, cultural, economic and military center. The towns of Chingmei, Mucha, Neihu, Nankang, Peitou and Shihlin were incorporated into Taipei in 1968.

Busy West Gate district, circa 1983.

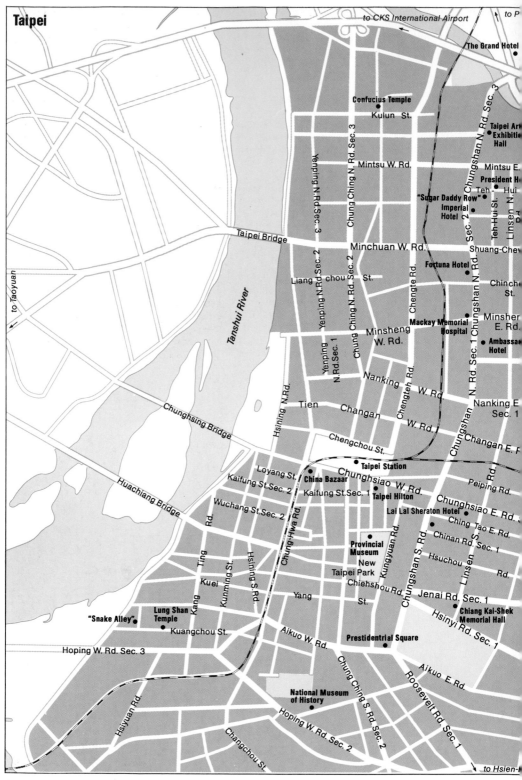

Taipei

to CKS International Airport

to P

The Grand Hotel

Confucius Temple

Kulun St.

Taipei Art
Exhibitie
Hall

Mintsu W. Rd.

Mintsu E.

President H

Teh · Hui

"Sugar Daddy Row"

Imperial
Hotel

Teh-Hui St.

Linsen N.

Yenping N.Rd.Sec. 3

Chung Ching N. Rd. Sec. 3

Chungshan N. Rd. Sec. 3

Chungshan N. Rd. Sec. 2

Sec. 2

Taipei Bridge

Minchuan W. Rd.

Shuang-Chev

Liang · chou

St.

Chengte Rd.

Fortuna Hotel

Chinch
St.

Yenping N.Rd.Sec. 2

Chung Ching N. Rd. Sec. 2

Tanshui River

Mackay Memorial
Hospital

Minsher
E. Rd.

Chungshan N. Rd. Sec. 1

Minsheng
W. Rd.

Ambassa
Hotel

Yenping
N.Rd.Sec. 1

Chungshan

Chunghsing Bridge

Nanking

Chengteh Rd.

W. Rd.

Nanking E
Sec. 1

Hsining N.Rd.

Tien

Changan

Changan E. F

W. Rd.

Chungshan

Chengchou St.

Taipei Station

Peiping Rd.

Huachiang Bridge

Loyang St.

Chunghsiao W. Rd.

Kaifung St.Sec. 2

China Bazaar

Kaifung St.Sec. 1

Taipei Hilton

Chunghsiao E. Rd.

Rd.

Wuchang St.Sec. 2

Lai Lai Sheraton Hotel

Ching Tao E. Rd.

Linsen

Chung-Hwa Rd.

Chinan Rd. Sec. 1

S. Rd.

Chungshan S. Rd.

Hsuchou

Rd.

Ting

Rd.

Provincial
Museum

Kungyuan Rd.

New
Taipei Park

Kuei

Kunming St.

Hsining S. Rd.

Yang

Chiehshou Rd.

Jenai Rd. Sec. 1

Kang

St.

Chiang Kai-Shek
Memorial Hall

"Snake Alley"

Lung Shan
Temple

Kuangchou St.

Aikuo W. Rd.

Presidentrial Square

Hsinyi Rd. Sec. 1

Hoping W. Rd. Sec. 3

Chung Ching S. Rd. Sec. 2

Aikuo E. Rd.

Roosevelt Rd Sec. 1

Hsiyuan Rd

National Museum
of History

Hoping W. Rd. Sec. 2

to Hsien-

Changchou St.

112

Shrine of Martyrs

ing Mt.

The Ritz
an Rd

Rongshin Garden

Hotel Miramar

China External Trade
Development Council

Domestic Airport Terminal

Limousine Bus Stop to &
From CKS Airport

Expressway to Keelung

Sung Chiang Rd.

Chienkuo N. Rd.

Hsingan St.

Chang Chun Rd

Chienkuo N. Rd.

Ling Chiang St.

Fuhsing N. Rd.

Turhua N. Rd.

ing E. Rd. Sec. 2

Nanking E. Rd. Sec. 3

Brother Hotel

Nanking E. Rd. Sec. 4

Nanking E. Rd. Sec. 5

Asiaworld Plaza Hotel

Kuangfu N. Rd.

Yitung St.

Changan E. Rd. Sec. 2

Ling St.

Pate Rd.

Fuhsing S. Rd.

insheng
Rd. Sec. 1

Sung Chiang Rd.

Chunghsiao E. Rd.

Tunhua S. Rd.

Tourism Bureau

Sun Yat-Sen

Kuangfu N. Rd.

Keelung Rd. Sec. 1

Sec. 2

E. Rd. Sec. 1

Chinan Rd. Sec. 3

Memorial Hall

Taipei Regency Hotel

Jenai Rd. Sec. 2

Jenai Rd. Sec. 3

Jenai Rd.
Sec. 4

Hsinsheng

sinyi
Sec. 2

Hsinyi Rd. Sec. 3

Hsinyi Rd. Sec. 4

Howard Plaza Hotel

Kuangfu S. Rd.

Keelung Rd. Sec. 2

American Institute
in Taiwan

Beverly Plaza

Antung St.

Chienkuo N. Rd.

Antung St.

Tunhua S. Rd.

Lin Chiang St.

St.

Tunghua

Hsinsheng S. Rd. Sec. 2

500 m

CITY SIGHTS

Modern visitors to Taipei, like the settlers of old, experience the outskirts of the city first. The new **Chiang Kaishek International Airport** is located in **Taoyuan**, about 40 kilometers (25 miles) southwest of the capital. The modern glass-and-concrete terminal building is one of Asia's largest and has been designed to facilitate immigration and customs procedures. Buses or taxis whisk new arrivals along the fast, clean North-South Expressway that links the airport (and points north) to Taipei.

The first order of business upon arriving in Taipei is selecting accommodations from the bewildering array of hotels that has sprouted since 1978. Taipei once had a notorious reputation among travelers and tour operators as a place of insufficient, inadequate hotel space. The government suspiciously viewed the hotel business as a "special industry" intimately connected with the pursuit of wine, women and song, a view that was perhaps a mental hang-over from the infamous days of pre-war Shanghai. Existing hotels were subjected to relentless inspection, taxation, regulation and other officially sanctioned torment.

The relaxation of building rules coincided with a general easing of sanctions against the hotel industry. Now the dearth of accommodations has given way to a glut of hotels that range from inexpensive but coarse small establishments to posh palaces of comfort. To contend with the competition, most hotels upon request offer a discount as high as 50 percent off published rates.

The granddaddy of the international standard hotels, and still the most highly regarded, is the **Taipei Hilton**. Its standard of professional services has remained consistently high despite increasing competition from flashier new neighbors like the Lai-Lai Sheraton. The management of the Hilton showcases traditional Chinese courtesy and ambience within the framework of a modern hotel. It has done so by fielding an all-Chinese staff that is professionally trained and that has earned it international food and beverage awards three times. A multimillion dollar re-

Flyovers and underpasses in government district.

novation has smoothed out some of the rough edges that have appeared over the years.

Newer hotels that have earned followings include **The Ritz** and the **Beverly Plaza**. Opened in 1978, The Ritz has only 218 rooms, which enables it to provide intimate, personalized service. It prohibits tour groups, making it popular among businessmen. The Beverly Plaza is even smaller with 118 rooms. Located in the newly developed southeastern section of the city, it is fronted by a tree-lined boulevard.

The **Lai-Lai Sheraton**, by contrast, has 705 rooms and covers a full city block. It goes for superlatives—the biggest rooms, the most restaurants and the most bars in a single hotel in Taipei. Another newcomer, the **Fortuna Hotel**, has opened at the site of the former Central Hotel on Chung Shan North Road, and the US$60 million **Howard Plaza** boasts a fortune in original artwork and traditional Chinese furnishings.

By far the most famous hotel and, indeed, one of the most imposing landmarks of Taipei is the **Grand Hotel**. Located atop a ridge at the north end of the city, it looks like an ancient Chinese palace. It was built in the classical imperial style of old China under the watchful eye of Madame Chiang Kai-shek. An older, original wing is built into the hillside behind the massive multi-storied new wing, crowned by the largest classical Chinese roof on earth. Sculpted gardens and shaded walkways make it a good place for a stroll which will provide excellent views of the city. Somehow, the Grand Hotel manages to maintain an air of dignity and peace in the midst of the tumult of the city. Guests are permitted use of the swank Yuan Shan Club next door. A more comprehensive list of accommodations is included in the Appendix.

Taipei was once described as the "ugly duckling" of Asian cities. That impression took root during the 1960s of drab buildings, dusty streets, open gutters and battered pedicabs. The modern look that Taipei has fostered during the past decade has all but erased its old reputation. Spacious six-lane boulevards shaded by islands of tropical trees have helped provide breathing space between the walls of

Majestic eaves of Grand Hotel on a misty morning.

new buildings. In these modern features, Taipei differs little from other burgeoning 20th Century cities of Asia. It is its traditional nooks and crannies that have the most to offer the visitor.

The sights covered in this cursory look at the city attempt to provide a satisfying blend of the old and the new. To facilitate travel, the names and addresses of each site are included in Chinese characters in the margin for easy reference for taxi drivers.

The Grand Hotel and its north-area neighbors are as good a spot as any to begin touring Taipei. Within a short distance of the Grand are several other attractions. East of the hotel is the **National Revolutionary Martyrs Shrine** on Pei-An Road. Open from 9 a.m. to 5 p.m. daily, the entire complex is built in the palace style of the Ming Dynasty. Each structure attempts to reproduce a similar hall or pavilion in Peking.

National
Revolutionary
Martyrs
Shrine

國民革命忠烈祠

Dedicated to the fallen heroes of China's wars, the arched portals of the main gate open onto a vast courtyard past guest pavilions, drums and bell towers. Two gigantic brass-studded doors open onto the main shrine where the names of the heroes are inscribed beside murals depicting their feats. The late President Chiang Kai-shek considered this a favorite retreat and frequently spent entire afternoons strolling through the grounds and halls. A changing of the guard occurs every hour.

National
Palace
Museum

古宮博物院

From Tranquillity to Gaudiness

Only a short taxi ride to the west of the Grand Hotel, behind the Zoological Gardens, is the **Temple of Confucius**, 275 Talung Street. It is tranquil compared to the city's other bustling places of worship. Absent are the throngs of worshippers supplicating their gods with prayer and offerings, the cacophony of gongs and drums and the gaudy idols. Absent too are images of Confucius. The tranquility is fitting: Confucius preached the virtues of peace and quiet. The architecture of the temple is subtle yet exquisite, and highlighted by magnificent roofs.

Temple of
Confucius

孔子廟

By contrast, the **Bao-An Temple** at 61 Ha-Mi Street, not far from the Confucian Temple, is a gaudy monument to traditional Chinese folk religion. This 230-year-old Taoist temple sports carved dragons writhing in solid rock on the main support columns and an in-

Left, the
changing of
the guard at
National
Revolutionary
Martyrs
Shrine.
Right, young
and
fashionable.

terior crowded with the icons of many deities. Buddhist elements are also apparent in the architecture, in testimony to the syncretic nature of Chinese religion.

The **Municipal Zoological Garden** at 66 Chung-Shan North Road is primarily of interest to Taiwan residents, although it does exhibit creatures indigenous to the island like the rare Formosan spotted deer. The zoo was built by the Japanese in 1914 on a site that has yielded some 5,000 stone tools, artifacts, skeletal remains and pottery shards of archaeological importance.

Saga of Imperial Treasure

Nestled in the foothills behind the Grand Hotel is the most popular and important attraction in Taipei and probably in all of Taiwan. An imposing complex of beige brick buildings, topped with green and imperial-yellow slate roofs, houses the collection of the **National Palace Museum**. It is located in the suburb of **Wai-Shuang-Hsi**, about 20 minutes by taxi from the Grand Hotel area. The building is impressive, but the treasures within are unimaginable.

Here, in enormous chambers with carefully controlled climatic conditions, are displayed some 11,000 works of art representing the zenith of 5,000 years of Chinese creativity. And these are just a fraction of the more than 600,000 paintings, porcelains, bronzes, rubbings, tapestries, books and other art objects stored in nearly 4,000 crates in burglar-proof vaults tunneled into the mountain behind the museum.

Taipei's National Palace Museum opened in 1965. But the history of its treasures, which reads like a John le Carre thriller, can be traced back more than a thousand years to the beginning of the Sung Dynasty (960-1279 A.D.) The founder of that dynasty, Emperor Tai-tzu, established the Hanlin Academy to encourage literature and the arts. His brother and successor, Emperor Tai-tsung, later opened the Tai Ching Gallery, where some of the items in the collection were first housed. Emperor Tai-tsung then established the Imperial Gallery as a government department for the preservation of rare books, old paintings and calligraphy. The Imperial Gallery, the prototype for Taipei's collection, was the Northern Sung's Palace Museum.

The Sung collection was transported from Peking to Nanking during the Ming Dynasty, then back again, foreshadowing the collection's many moves of the 20th Century. The major period of collecting occurred during the Ching Dynasty (1644-1911). The Ching emperors, particularly Kao-tsung (1736-1795), were avid art collectors. The majority of the items in the present collection are the result of their effort to seek out China's most important treasures.

But the real intrigues began in 1924. In November of that year, the provisional Nationalist government in Peking gave the last surviving Manchu emperor, Pu-Yi, and his entourage of 2,000 eunuchs and ladies two hours to evacuate the fabulous Forbidden City. Then the government sent 30 young Chinese scholars and art experts to identify and inventory the overwhelming collection of art treasures that had been hoarded there for more than 500 years by Chinese emperors.

It took the scholars two years just to sort out and organize the collection. In the meantime, the government formally established the National Peiping Palace

The National Palace Museum.

Museum and began displaying some of the treasures.

End of an Odyssey

By the time the task of identifying all the priceless objects was completed in 1931, the Japanese had attacked Manchuria and threatened Peking. The art collection had, and still has, enormous symbolic value to whomever possesses it because it bestows a measure of political legitimacy upon its owners. To prevent the Japanese from seizing the collection, the Nationalists carefully packed everything in 20,000 cases and shipped it in five train loads south to Nanking.

That began a 16-year odyssey. The priceless treasures were shuttled back and forth across the war-torn face of China by rail, truck, oxcart, raft and foot, always just a few steps ahead of pursuing Japanese and, later, communist Chinese troops. Incredibly, not a single item was lost or damaged.

A representative selection of the best items was shipped to London for a major art exhibition in 1936—prompting an uproar among China's intellec-

The 79 carved wooden cups, Ching Dynasty.

tuals who feared the foreigners would never return the works. But all was returned. The following year, the Japanese occupied Peking and threatened Nanking. Once again the precious collection was loaded aboard lorries and transported over hills, rivers and streams in three shipments to China's rugged western mountains.

After World War II, the Nationalist government brought the art objects back to Nanking. But when communist control of the mainland appeared imminent in 1948, 4,800 cases of the most valuable art objects were culled from the original 20,000 cases and sent for safekeeping to the Nationalist bastion on Taiwan. They were stored temporarily in a sugar warehouse in Taichung where they remained until the Chung-Shan (Sun Yat-sen) Museum Building in Wai-Shuang-Hsi opened in 1965.

Among the items cached are 4,389 ancient bronzes, 23,863 pieces of immaculate porcelain, 13,175 paintings, 14,223 works of calligraphy, 4,636 pieces of jade, 153,094 rare books from the imperial library and 389,712 documents, diaries and palace records. Many of the items are still locked in

their original storage cases and have yet to be displayed. Massive red steel doors lead to the catacombs in the mountain where the steel trunks are stacked one atop the other. One semicircular corridor is 186 meters (610 feet) long, the other 150 meters (492 feet). The temperature is kept at a constant 64 degrees Fahrenheit (17.8°C) and dehumidifiers are situated all along the corridors.

Jade Vegetables
And Ivory Boats

Little by little, the Palace Museum has been revealing most of the secrets of its security vaults. Paintings are rotated in special exhibitions every three months and other objects, like Hindustan jades and *ting* bronzes, are rotated at two-year intervals. The museum's permanent collection includes artifacts from Tomb 1001 (excavated in Honan province) on the second floor, along with bronzes, oracle bones, ceramics, porcelains and paintings. Enamels, jade, small carvings, lacquers and more paintings are displayed on the third floor. A typical Chinese scholar's studio

has been recreated on the fourth floor. New museum administrative headquarters under construction will open up more space for displays in the main building by 1984.

Of particular interest are the paintings. They include many of the most important landscape masterpieces and portraits painted during the Sung, Yuan, Ming and Ching dynasties from the 10th to the 17th centuries. The exquisite porcelain artistry of the Yuan, Ming and Ching dynasties includes all forms of the famous Sung ware—Ju, Kuan, Ko, Ting, Chun, Chien-yang and others. Bronze artifacts cast between the 17th and 5th centuries B.C., calligraphy by such notables as Wang Hsi-chi and Lu Chi, and priceless works of jade—much of it created under the discerning eye of the Chien-Lung Emperor of the Ching dynasty—are also part of the collection.

There are such famous pieces as the *fei-tsui* jade cabbage stock, carved during the Ching dynasty, complete with camouflaged grasshopper; and a unique set of 79 wooden cups, carved paper-thin so that all can be held in a single large cup. There's an amazing collection

Left, archaic Jade cup, Sung Dynasty. Right, porcelain jar, Ching Dynasty.

of miniatures carved from wood and ivory. One tiny cruising yacht, only 5.3 centimeters long and three centimeters high, has a full compliment of crew and guests carved into its interior cabin.

Tour guides who speak a variety of languages leave the ground-floor lobby at regular intervals with groups. Self-guiding pamphlets and books are also available. A good approach to the overwhelming collection is to take a cursory tour of the galleries and their objects in the morning, break for lunch at the museum restaurant, then return for a more intensive look at items of particular interest in the afternoon.

Photography is prohibited in the museum. However, satisfactory transparencies of most objects are available in the museum souvenir shops along with reproductions of paintings, porcelain and other items. The museum is open daily from 9 a.m. to 5 p.m.

More Museums

Visitors who enjoy touring museums may wish to take a breather after a day at the National Palace galleries. But Taipei offers a number of other museums. Military enthusiasts will find some 10,000 items representing China's 20th Century war ammunition at the **Chinese Armed Forces Museum**. It is located in the city center at 243 Kuei Yang Street, Section 1. The **National Museum of History** at 49 Nan Hai Road contains another 10,000 Chinese art objects that date from 2,000 B.C. to modern times, including a fine sampling of Chinese currency. After touring its exhibits, visitors can stroll the grounds of the **Taiwan Botanical Gardens** next door. It contains hundreds of species of trees, shrubs, palms and bamboo.

The **Taiwan Provincial Museum** at 2 Hsiang Yang Road is less interesting than the others, but offers important displays of the island's aboriginal tribes; including samples of their handicrafts, clothes and household articles. Behind the museum is **New Taipei Park** which features several pagodas and pavilions. It also has the only statue on the island dedicated to a non-Chinese—U.S. Air Force General Claire Chennault, decorated with the nation's highest honors for his air-war assistance in World War II and still a popular figure in Taiwan history.

Left, carved lacquer plate, Chien-lung Ware, circa 1736-1795. Right, National Palace Museum vault.

The best time to walk the grounds of New Park is at the break of dawn, when thousands of the city's residents stretch, dance, aerobicise, exercise and move through various forms of *tai-chi, shaolin* and other martial arts. Visitors are welcome to join in with the groups for an invigorating start to a day in Taipei.

Memorial Halls of National Heroes

In addition to museums, Taipei boasts two more memorials of interest. The most impressive is the massive monument to the late president, the **Chiang Kai-shek Memorial Hall**, located on Chung-Shan South Road, south of the Taipei Hilton and not far from New Park. Dedicated on April 5, 1980, the fifth anniversary of Chiang's death, the enormous hall dominates the landscaped grounds and soars to a height of 76 meters (250 feet). Inside is an imposing 25-ton bronze statue of the late president.

The main entrance to the memorial is a magnificent arch in traditional Ming style that towers 30 meters (100 feet) high and stretches 76 meters (250 feet)

across. One charming feature of the memorial are the 18 different styles of traditional Chinese windows built at eye-level along the entire length of the wall surrounding the memorial. Under construction on the lovely 62-acre grounds is a modern National Opera House and Concert Hall. The memorial itself closes at 5 p.m., but the park grounds remain open for evening jaunts or jogs.

The other major memorial is dedicated to Chiang's mentor and the founder of the Republic of China, Dr. Sun Yat-sen. Located in the far eastern recesses of town at Section 4 of Jenai Road, the main building of the **Sun Yat-sen Memorial** boasts a sweeping, gracefully curved Chinese roof of glazed yellow tile. A bronze statue of Dr. Sun is in the main lobby. He remains the only common denominator between the rival Communist and Nationalist regimes of China. Both revere him as the founder of modern China. In recent years, even communist China has begun to display Dr. Sun's portrait prominently in Peking's historic Tien-An-Men Plaza during national celebrations.

The administrative nerve center of

Chiang Kai-shek Memorial Hall
中正紀念堂

Sun Yat-sen Memorial Hall
國父紀念舘

The Chiang Kai-shek Memorial.

the Nationalist government, most prominently the **Presidential Building**, is located at the north end of Po-Ai Road. The plaza fronting this building is the site of enormous, colorful celebrations during the "Double Tens"—that is, October 10, National Day each year. Both the Presidential Building and the Grand Hotel shine with the lights of thousands of bulbs and decorations during the festive events.

Under 'Dragon Mountain'

Also in the plaza in front of the Presidential Building is the massive **East Gate**, the biggest of five built as part of the 19th Century city wall. Most were torn down by the Japanese during an urban renewal program.

The oldest and most famous of Taipei's myriad temples is **Lung-Shan** or "Dragon Mountain." The name is a reference to the large collection of toothsome creatures on its busy roof. The temple is at 211 Kuang-Chou Street in the heart of Old Taipei, southwest of the city's contemporary center. It was built in the first half of the 18th Century to honor the island's patron deities,

Kuan Yin and Ma Tsu.

The building was inadvertently hit by an Allied air raid on June 8, 1945. So intense were the flames from the incendiary bomb, they melted the iron railings surrounding the large camphor-wood statue of Kuan Yin. The hall was totally destroyed—yet the wooden statue somehow withstood the searing flame, except for a bit of ash and debris around its feet. The main hall was rebuilt in 1957 around the statue which gazes with unceasing equanimity at worshippers from its spot on the main altar. Devotees attribute the survival of the statue to the supernatural powers of the deity herself.

In addition to the miraculous carving of Kuan Yin, the temple is renowned for its fine stone sculpture, wood carving and bronze work. Only the top winners in annual island-wide carving competitions are permitted to perform maintenance and restoration work at Lung-Shan. Especially striking are the 12 main support columns that hold up the central hall. They appear to come alive with their dragons hewn from solid stone. Open from 7 a.m. to 10 p.m., Lung-Shan is usually packed with wor-

Lung-Shan Temple
龍山寺

Lung-Shan Temple courtyard.

shippers and is a perfect place to witness traditional Chinese rites.

Another temple of note is **Hsing-Tien** at 261 Min-Chuan East Road in the northeast quadrant of the city. Dedicated to the red-faced, blackbearded Kuan Kung, this Taoist temple is also filled with throngs of worshippers most times of the day or night. On either side of the main prayer hall is a miniature garden alcove built around a tiny pond, perfect examples of how the Chinese symbolically incorporate elements of nature into temple architecture.

This temple and others around the island employ dozens of elderly women wearing blue smocks who busy themselves cleaning the premises, maintaining the icons, and assisting the faithful with their offerings. These women have all experienced incidents of extreme mental or emotional trauma during their lives and enter temple service as a form of spiritual and psychological therapy. The system has worked so well that most of the women eventually recover their mental balance, then continue to serve in the temples out of gratitude or devotion.

Night in 'Snake Alley'

Taipei is divided into northern and southern sections by Chung-Hsiao Road, site of the Hilton and Sheraton hotels and the Taipei Railway Station. Chung-Shan North and South roads slice the city into eastern and western portions. This should make it easy to find one's way around the city. But problems are compounded for foreign visitors by the fact that most street signs contain only Chinese characters. What's more, major roads are separated into sections that can be several blocks long.

Despite the confusion, wandering aimlessly through Taipei's streets is a good way to familiarize oneself with the city and its inhabitants. It will uncover many surprises that could never be duplicated on guided tours around the main tourist attractions.

Another way to absorb the traditional color that drips from the city's pores is to take in the public markets. Most are open from dawn until midnight. All sell an amazing variety of fresh vegetables, fragrant fruits, meats, fish, poultry, spices and condiments. At night, the fresh-produce vendors retire from the

Hsing-Tien Temple

行天宮

Snake Alley fortune teller

scene, to be replaced by scores of food stalls on wheels. These instant cafes serve every conceivable kind of Chinese snack food at miniscule prices.

The most exotic night market of all is the two-block lane in the Wanhua district called "Snake Alley" by Western visitors. It is only a few minutes' walk from the Lung-Shan temple. Chinese know this alley's main thoroughfare as Hwa-Hsi Street.

The Western sobriquet stems from the nature of business conducted by some of the street's vendors. Their shops have stacks of cages filled with deadly hissing snakes. The vendors flip open the cage tops and deftly fish out snakes that they try to sell to onlookers. Customers watch as the snake they choose is strung live on a wire, stretched taut and literally "zipped" open before their eyes with a small knife.

Blood and bile from the squirming snake are squeezed into a glass containing potent spirits and Chinese herbs. For customers who seek an additional "kick," the vendor will even add a few drops of poison venom to the mixture. The carcasses of the gutted snakes are left to hang and twist in the night, while the concoction is drunk by men who believe the potion strengthens the eyes and lower spine, eliminates fatigue and, inevitably, promotes male sexual vitality. Later, the meat is taken back to the kitchen to slice into snake soup, a tasty and nourishing dish.

Other than the gruesome snake shows, the alley offers countless Chinese fortune-tellers, vendors of herbal potions, tattoo parlors, fresh fruit stalls and hawkers of baubles and bangles. It also has several excellent restaurants specializing in fresh seafood.

Another convenient market, **Ching-Kuang**, is located near the intersection of Nung-An and Shuang-Cheng streets in the vicinity of the President Hotel. This is strictly for night owls in search of "munchies" when the pubs and nightclubs begin closing at the midnight hour. Farther afield is the **Shih-lin Market**, one of Taipei's largest and most complete. It sprawls across several acres north of the Grand Hotel in the suburb of Shih-lin. Despite the occasionally appalling appearances of these markets, the food is uniformly safe for consumption. Culinary cleanliness is an ancient Chinese tradition.

AN EMPORIUM WITHOUT END

Taipei offers many arresting attractions, but most are overshadowed by its biggest draw—shopping. Every Asian country boasts its indigenous arts and crafts, souvenirs and gifts, traditional handmade and modern manufactured products. But it seems that Taiwan has more to offer than most of its neighbors. So crammed with merchandise are its shops that most storefronts spill out into the streets and sidewalks, making it difficult to walk or drive through some popular shopping areas.

China
Ceramics
Factory

中華陶瓷公司

The key to shopping in the Orient is to know what to look for in each country and where to find it. In Taipei, the key to a rewarding shopping experience is to buy only local products, whether one is in the market for handicrafts or calculators. Brand-name manufactured products imported from abroad are not only heavily taxed and expensive, they often turn out to be no more than clever copies of the genuine articles. Of course, there *are* visitors who are looking for less expensive imitations.

As for arts and crafts, the Chinese are renowned throughout the world for their charming natural themes and exquisite workmanship. The traditional arts of China have been well preserved in Taiwan. The capital city sells everything imaginable, from classical landscape paintings to elegant calligraphy to finely-carved jade and antique hardwood, most at comparatively reasonable prices. Dozens of shops on either side of Chung-Shan North Road, Taipei's main commercial artery, specialize in Chinese porcelain, woodcarving, brasswork, marble products, gold, lacquerware, antiques, furniture and jewelry. Most will claim to have "set prices," but it is possible to bargain when making large purchases. The following survey provides pointers for browsers and buyers alike.

porcelain
陶瓷

Perusing the Porcelain

The art of firing and glazing fine porcelain was invented in China, thus giving rise to a word that has entered English vocabulary—chinaware. Taipei is an international center for the production and sales of porcelain.

Left, old
shops and,
right, modern
department
store plaza in
Taipei's West
Gate district.

Stores also carry a generous supply of antique porcelain, but uneducated buyers should beware of such claims. Even some experts have difficulty distinguishing genuine museum pieces from "instant" antiques that have been finely crafted by modern artisans right down to the last nick and crack.

It is safest and easiest to go for reproductions that are advertised as such. The shapes, patterns, colors and glazes of every era of Chinese history have been faithfully reproduced in Taiwan's ceramics factories. Many of them are truly striking. Department stores as well as specialty gift shops offer a selection of Chinese porcelain.

At the **China Ceramics Factory** in suburban Peitou, visitors can tour the vast workshop and watch as a piece of porcelain is slowly worked through the various stages of production. After the factory tour, visitors can purchase finished products from the enormous collection in the show room. Packing and mailing services are available to customers.

Visitors spellbound by the misty landscapes of Chinese painting and the elegant, expressive swirls of Chinese calli-

graphy will also find Taipei a shopper's paradise. Contemporary artists in Taiwan produce copies of the most renowned masterpieces from the past, as well as original works of their own. Regardless of expert advice, the only real criterion for selecting a painting or piece of calligraphy is whether it appeals to your senses or not.

By Brush and Ink

The prices for antique creations of brush and ink will discourage most buyers. And, often because of the wear of centuries, they do not look as attractive as today's recreations. The **National Palace Museum** offers a superb selection of reproductions of antique paintings and calligraphy. For contemporary originals, there are fine gift shops on Chung-Shan North Road or the galleries listed in the Guide in Brief. Visitors who take a more active interest in these ancient arts will find the beautiful brushes, molded ink blocks, carved ink stones, water pots and other accessories at the **China Bazaar** on Chung-Hwa Road or · at other specialty shops throughout the city.

Wooden Wonders

The Chinese magic touch with wood stems from their age-old romance with things of nature. Woodcarving has been the favorite medium of Chinese craftsmen and architects who seem to instinctively understand how to mold each swirl in a stick of wood.

Most woodcarvings take their themes from Chinese folklore, mythology and religious traditions. They can be extraordinarily alive with detail. Whether gilded, lacquered or simply polished, Chinese woodcarvings make excellent household decorations that never cease to delight the eye. A range of traditional and contemporary carvings is on sale at the government-sponsored **Chinese Handicraft Mart**, 1 Hsu-Chow Road.

Coral and Jade

Taiwan's jewelers have capitalized on the increasing popularity of resources right from their own watery backyard to become the world's largest producers of coral jewelry. Pink, red and black coral are fashioned into rings, bracelets,

woodcarvings
木刻

calligraphy
書畫

jade and gems
寶石

Left, contemporary calligraphy and, right, exquisite carving.

130

necklaces and a variety of carved decorative pendants and figures. Coral varies in price according to quality and color, but is less expensive than gemstones. At the same time, it makes for an attractive fashion accessory.

Another reasonably priced material used in local jewelry creations is Taiwan jade. This dark green stone is indigenous to the island, but does not compare in quality or delicacy to antique jade from the mainland. The latter can also be purchased in local antique and curio shops.

All That Glitters

Opals are also a good buy in Taipei. Merchants sell the raw stones and craftsmen can place them into any setting. Cloisonné fashioned into rings, bracelets, pendants and other jewelry, as well as vases, plates, containers and other items, is another specialty of island craftsmen. Dozens of good jewelry stores are located on Chung-Shan North and Heng-Yang roads, as well as in most hotel shopping arcades.

Gold has long been popular in Asia as an investment as well as a fashion accessory. When shopping in Taipei or any city in Asia, look for stores specializing in locally-crafted gold items. The Chinese usually spurn the 14 karat items imported from Europe in favor of local items that have a gold content ranging from 18 karats to pure 24 karat gold.

Despite the higher gold content, bracelets, pendants, rings, earrings and other jewelry fashioned locally usually cost less than European gold jewelry. That's because Chinese jewelers base their prices on the international price of gold with only a slight mark up added for the craftsmanship that goes into the pieces. Make sure you are aware of the daily rate per gram of gold before making your rounds in order to bargain for the best possible price.

When buying jewelry made from gold remember that the higher the gold content, the softer and more delicate the jewelry. Solid gold bars that double as pendants are particularly popular items.

The Magic of Marble

Among Taiwan's natural resources, only marble seems to exist in inex-

Marble merchandise.

haustible abundance. Most is quarried and processed in and near the east coast town of Hwalien, where there is an enormous factory and showroom operated by the Retired-Servicemen's Engineering Agency (RSEA). Plant tours are conducted, demonstrating how marble is processed. The craftsmen have a knack for utilizing the stone's natural grains and patterns to suggest such images as lofty mountain peaks, billowy clouds, misty valleys and thick forests. Natural patterns are magically worked into lamp stands, plaques, desk-pen sets, ashtrays, lighter holders, cigarette boxes, candlesticks, bowls, plates, cups, chessboards and more. The Hwalien factory has a branch in Taipei called the **RSEA Display Center** at 32 Chung-Shan North Road, Section 2. Most gift and souvenir shops carry marble products.

Lovely Lacquer,
Brash Brass

Ever since the artisans of China pioneered the creation of lacquerware, the end products have been popular throughout the Far East. Especially attractive are lacquered screens, carved chests and boxes, bowls and plates inlaid with decorative patterns, and small lacquered carvings. The **China Bazaar** and shops along Chung-Shan North, Sections 2 and 3, carry healthy helpings of lacquerware.

Taipei is also a fitting place to buy brass fittings. Even shiny brass bed frames can be purchased for a fraction of their cost in the West, disassembled and shipped home. Items salvaged from old ships make excellent decorations for the home as well as the yacht. Taiwan operates the world's biggest ship demolition and salvage center in Kaohsiung; classic pieces from old luxury lines can be found in the nautical brassware specialty shops along Chung-Shan North Road.

Furnishing the Home

Traditional Chinese furniture is as handsome as it is functional. With its ornately carved arms and legs, panels inlaid with mother-of-pearl, marble or other precious materials, layers of lacquer or gilt and perfectly proportioned lines, Chinese furniture never fails to catch the eye or spark conversation. It

marble
大理石

lacquerware
漆器

brassware
銅器

antique and
contemporary
furniture
古董傢俱

Gold gapers.

Bai-Win
Mercantile
House

白銀公司

kitchen items

廚具

electrical
goods

電器

books

書

Gobs of
Garments.

also makes a valuable addition to any household.

Recommended shops for genuine antique furniture or decorative artifacts, beautifully restored and refinished, include **Bai-Win Mercantile House** in the suburb of Tien-Mou and the **Unicorn**, further north in suburban Peitou. For contemporary furniture fashioned from wood, rattan, bamboo and metal, try the cluster of shops in Section 5 of Chung-Shan North Road in Shih-lin, just before the Tien-Mou bridge.

To add a touch of China to the kitchen, amateur cooks and connoisseurs of local cuisine will find a full range of traditional culinary supplies on sale in Taipei. The China Bazaar sells chopsticks, woks, bamboo steamers, ladles, rice bowls, vegetable baskets and anything else needed to prepare Chinese meals. Fancy dried mushrooms, black and white fungus (also known as "tree ears"), preserved eggs, dried fruits, lotus seeds, chrysanthemum buds, dried beef and pork, and canned condiments that add the perfect touch to the finished banquet, are all available in the food sections of Taipei's modern de-

partment stores. Some stores also specialize in fancy foods. Look for the windows filled with rows of hams, stacks of colorful cans and bins of dried foods.

Finally, electrical items of all kinds are available in Taiwan. Quality control has improved immensely since the days when the "Made in Taiwan" label meant careless work and a lack of durability. Today, Taiwan produces watches, calculators, automobiles and motorcycles, toys and sporting goods, kitchen appliances and other contemporary gadgets under strict supervision to meet the exacting demands of tough international markets.

The Bristling Book Business

Taipei is a bookworm's dream and an international publisher's nightmare. Because of increasing pressure from outside the country, Taiwan has recognized international copyright laws. But local publishers still "pirate" anything and everything in the English language, then sell it for about a quarter of its original market price. However, the fact is that most of these publications would not even be imported into

Taiwan because of their high costs, so the practice technically does not affect the fortunes of the original publishers. But it does prove a boon to local readers—and to visitors in the market for an inexpensive literary trip.

Everything from expensive reference books, dictionaries, cookbooks, novels, even encyclopedias can be purchased in Taipei for a fraction of the cost overseas. Collectors of books that are difficult to find at any price in the West will be surprised to find the pirated versions in Taipei. Technically, pirated books may not be taken outside the island. But the ban does not apply to books which the original publishers have copyrighted in the Republic of China. The same applies to records and tapes.

Book dealers abound along Chung-Shan North Road. The most complete selection of English works can be found at **Caves Books**, 107 Chung-Shan North, Section 2.

Silks and Satins

The custom tailor is still a familiar sight in Taipei, as in most Chinese communities in the Far East. The difference here is that Taiwan produces most of the textiles that go into the tailored products, making them even less expensive than in places where the material must be imported. There are complete lines of modern manufactured fabrics produced primarily for export, as well as traditional Chinese patterns.

Among the venerable fabrics fashioned into fine clothing in Taipei and other cities on the island are silks, satins and fine brocades. Silk brocades are especially beautiful and constitute a major bargain by international standards. For a truly alluring outfit of classical Chinese style, ladies should try the *chipao*, better known by the Cantonese word *cheongsam*. The *chipao* is made to fit snugly and requires at least two fittings for it to turn out well. The sexy slit up the sides can be made as low—or as high—as is wished.

The best textile retailers in Taipei line Heng Yang and Po-Ai roads, just a few blocks from the Hilton. For bargains on ready-made clothing, the overstocked shops, department stores and boutiques at West Gate and Chung-Shan North Road are worth a look.

Caves Books
敦煌書局

silks and satins
絲綢

A Taipei
"tea-totaler."

The Semantics
of Chinese Tea

Tea is an intrinsic part of Chinese culture. Subtly fragrant yet physically fortifying, delicate but bracing, aesthetically pleasing while medically beneficial, tea reflects the cosmic balance and spiritual harmony that is such an important part of the Chinese mind.

A few cups of good Chinese tea, taken after a heavy meal, help emulsify and break down fats and proteins. Tea promotes digestion and eases the metabolic strain on the liver which otherwise must bear the burden of digesting the fats and protein. At the same time, tea stimulates the mind. It's this refreshing blend of physical and spiritual benefits that has made tea the most popular beverage in the Orient.

The Chinese drink tea in a manner considerably different from the Westerners. They never add milk and sugar. They prefer to savor the subtle bouquet and unique flavor without distraction or interference from foreign substances. That's why the quality and vintage of the leaf are so important. Chinese connoisseurs approach tea much as West-

ern gourmets approach wine. They take several probing sniffs and sips so they can identify the type and origin of the leaf. Sometimes, they pay fortunes for a few ounces of especially fine vintage tea.

Taiwan specializes in three types of tea leaves. Those used for green tea are steamed immediately after picking to arrest bacterial growth. Then they are rolled by hand to squeeze out excess moisture and release flavor enzymes. The leaves are finally dried and packed. When brewed, they turn a light green color and have a flavor that is delicate and somewhat tangy.

Green teas are rich in Vitamin C. Connoisseurs contend that they stimulate the spirit better than any other blend. Green tea is particularly popular among monks and scholars who claim that it improves their abilities to think and meditate for prolonged periods without fatigue. Lung-Ching or "Dragon Well" is considered one of Taiwan's best green teas.

Oolung or "Black Dragon" teas are fermented to varying degrees after picking. That accounts for their darker color and more robust flavor. The taste is

somewhat fruity with a bouquet that has a spicy hint. In Taiwan, Oolung is considered the top blend, and Tung-Ting Oolung ranks as the best of the crop. This prized variety, grown on Tung-Ting Mountain in Taiwan's massive central range, is renowned throughout the world for its fragrance and body. A gift of top quality Tung-Ting Oolung Tea is comparable to giving a friend a bottle of the best French cognac.

Another popular Oolung tea favored by foreigners is Tieh Kuan-Yin or "Iron Goddess of Mercy." This tea is 50 percent fermented, giving it a sterner constitution than Tung-Ting. It benefits digestion; the elderly have attributed other medicinal benefits to its use.

The third type of leaf produced in Taiwan is Black Tea, inexplicably known to the Chinese as "Red Tea." It is more commonly drunk in the West than by the Chinese. Black teas are 100 percent fermented, giving them a very dark color and strong taste when brewed. They lack the subtle bouquet and delicate balance of flavors which Chinese connoisseurs favor. Black teas are often used to make specialty blends. They are mixed with dried fruits like *lichee* or orange peel, with fragrant additives like jasmine blossoms or spice, or simply with other varieties of tea. Taiwan produces excellent black teas, but the best blends come from India.

Taipei has many fine tea shops. They carry a wide range of local leaves including the "straight leaf" for orthodox purists and fragrant, flavorful melanges for the more adventurous. In addition to bulk tea sold by weight, the shops offer teas packed in decorative containers for gift-giving.

In the traditional Chinese tea ceremony, a miniature red-clay pot is stuffed with leaves, filled with boiling water and steeped for a few minutes. Then the brew is poured into thimble-sized cups and sipped while very hot. The process is repeated five or six times, always producing a subtly different flavor, until the leaves are spent. Then the pot is stuffed with fresh leaves and the process is repeated. In Taipei, the traditional "tea art" manner of drinking the brew can be sampled at several excellent tea houses. They include **Lu Yu Tea Center** at 64 Heng-Yang Road, 2nd Floor; the **Cha Tao Tea Shop** at 229 Min-Chuan East Road; and **Wisteria**

Tea House, #1 Hsin-Sheng South Road, Lane 1b, Section 3. The former offers classes in tea ceremony and the Chao Tao boasts traditional decor in private tea rooms.

Spirits and Smokes

Chinese wines and spirits generally do not appeal to Western palates. But samples for gifts or souvenirs can be purchased from the **Taiwan Tobacco and Wine Monopoly Bureau** at 83 Chung-Shan North Road, Section 2. It is open from 8:30 to 11:45 a.m. and 1:30 to 4:30 p.m. Monday through Friday. During the major national holidays, the bureau sells Chinese spirits in lovely decorative decanters.

Smokers will find that the most popular local cigarette is one with the unlikely name of Long Life. The best quality brand comes in a round tin of 50 cigarettes called Prosperity Island. Taiwan also produces Liberty pipe tobacco and Gentleman cigars. In addition to local wines and tobaccos, the Monopoly Bureau regulates the importation and sale of all foreign alcoholic beverages in Taiwan.

Tieh Kuan
Yin tea
鐵觀音茶

tobacco
and wine
烟酒

Top Shop Stops

West Gate
西門町

Two of Taipei's top shopping, dining and recreation areas are located only a few blocks from the silk and satin district. The one called **West Gate** ranks as the local equivalent of New York's Times Square and London's Piccadilly Circus. Movie theaters, department stores and hundreds of little boutiques and specialty shops dominate this bustling district. Here one can become immersed in local color as well as shop. At peak hours, the area teems with people and visitors may find themselves literally swept down streets and back alleys that they may not have intended exploring. The district is named for the massive brick gate that protrudes incongruously amid the tangle of freeway fly-overs at the north end of the area.

Nearby, Chung Hua Road runs through the heart of the **China Bazaar** district. Walkways leading to overhead bridges connect two to three levels of shops and more shops that dominate the area. The walkways also provide excellent views of the railway system which parallels the street. The China Bazaar occupies four long blocks of this road

Chinese fan
factory.

and is also known as "Haggler's Alley." It is one of the few places in towns where bargaining is not only possible, but is expected.

Even so, department stores remain the best places to buy manufactured consumer products in Taipei at set prices. Those officially approved by the government for patronage by foreign travelers are **Far Eastern**, **Sesame**, **Shin Shin**, **Evergreen**, **Cathay**, **Jen Jen**, **Hsinkuang**, **The First**, **Lai Lai** and **Today's**.

One of the most luxurious department stores of recent vintage is **Asiaworld** on Nanking East Road in the business part of town. In addition to ultra-modern shopping complex with the usual range of merchandise goods, it is linked to a dining complex that boasts dozens of restaurants that claim to have a seating capacity of 10,000 at any one time.

Travelers interest in trade with Taiwan's manufacturers and suppliers should pay a visit to the Export Product Display Center and Mart at the Sungshan Domestic Airport in the northeast part of Taipei.

NORTHERN SOJOURNS

Taipei's sights, shopping and amusements monopolize most of the time travelers spend in the northern part of Taiwan. But a brief jaunt beyond the big city will provide glimpses of the resort and rural life of the island. This topmost tip is a microcosm of Taiwan with its mountains, hot springs, beaches, paddy fields, villages and temples. Within a day's sojourn from Taipei, visitors on tight schedules can even get a look at the colorful culture of the island's aboriginal tribes.

A Mountain Escape

The fastest route of escape from Taipei's sea of humanity and humidity lies up nearby **Yangming Mountain**. About 30 minutes' drive via winding roads north of the city, Yangming Mountain is known as the local "Beverly Hills." Large numbers of wealthy industrial tycoons, movie stars and entrepreneurs, as well as expatriate businessmen, live here in luxurious villas that cling to the cliffs in the cool clear climes above Taipei. Originally called "Grass Mountain," the name was changed to honor philosopher Wang Yangming (1472-1529). Wang was the personal favorite of late President Chiang Kai-shek, who also kept a villa here.

Halfway up the main road, a sign points left toward **White Cloud Villa**, the world's second largest supplier of orchids. Visitors are permitted to wander through the greenhouses and gardens that brim with more than 1 million plants. It's also possible to snack at the Villa's mountaintop restaurant which provides panoramic views of Taipei. White Cloud orchids can be purchased in the departure lounge of the Chiang Kai-shek International Airport, fully fumigated and officially approved for export to the United States or European countries.

The peak is crowned by **Yangming National Park**. This well-maintained park features walkways that wind

Preceding pages, serene lakeside scene. Left, Taoist ascetic meditates on Taipei's Phoenix Mountain.

through colorful gardens of trees, bushes, fragrant flowers and grottos. From the middle of February to the end of March, the annual "Spring Flower Festival" is held in the park. At that time, the entire mountain is awash with cherry blossoms and carpeted with bright flowering azaleas.

For a small fee, visitors can enter Yangming Moutain Park on foot. People in automobiles pay more. There's a restaurant for people who arrive at lunch or dinner time. The worst time to visit the park is on Sundays and holidays, especially during spring and summer, when the crowds from the lower elevations crowd the place.

Hot Springs
In the Hills

A less lofty but equally entrancing retreat a few minutes from Taipei is the suburb of **Peitou** (pronounced "baytow"). It nestles snugly in lush green hills north of the city and can be reached by winding back mountain roads from Yangming Mountain, or from Taipei via a much-less-scenic route that passes through the suburb of Tien-Mou.

Peitou literally means "Northern Sojourn." It has a Japanese feel that has lingered since the Japanese turned the town into a charming resort for their officers and magistrates at the turn of the century. More recently, Peitou became notorious as a getaway for large groups of male tourists from Tokyo and other locales. The attractions were Peitou's therapeutic hot springs—and women.

Peitou lured the men because prostitution was legal here. That ended (in theory) in 1979 when the Taipei City Council finally passed an often-shelved resolution prohibiting the practice of the world's oldest profession. Although this measure has not entirely succeeded in sweeping the "fallen flowers" from the scene, it has improved Peitou's overall ambience and reputation and has put an end to the all-male tour groups that once dominated the scene. Now families and couples enjoy the unequaled delights of this unique village as well.

The old-world charm of Peitou is best sampled in its older inns with their distinctively Japanese flavor and ser-

Peitou
北投

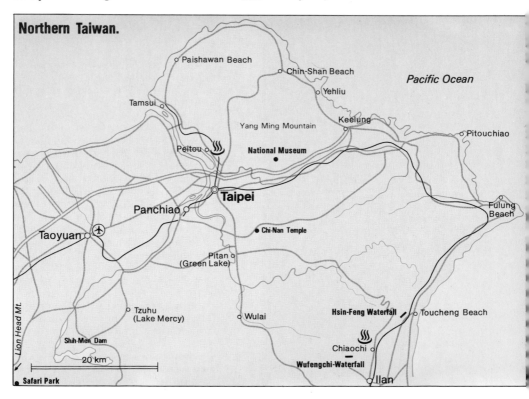

Northern Taiwan.

Paishawan Beach

Chin-Shan Beach

Pacific Ocean

Yehliu

Tamsui

Keelung

Yang Ming Mountain

Pitouchiao

Peitou

National Museum

Taipei

Panchiao

Fulung Beach

Taoyuan

● Chi-Nan Temple

Pitan
(Green Lake)

Tzuhu
(Lake Mercy)

Wulai

Hsin-Feng Waterfall

Toucheng Beach

Lion Head Mt.

Shih-Men Dam

Chiaochi

20 km

Wufengchi-Waterfall

Ilan

● **Safari Park**

vice. The modern high-rises were hastily slapped together to accommodate the convoys of male Japanese during the 1970s. Among the traditional inns, one standout is **In-Song-Ger**, known to Westerners as the Whispering Pines Inn, at 21 Yu-Ya Road.

Proprietor Johnny Wu woos customers to the In-Song-Ger with a combination of hospitality and personalized service. Visitors can party here for an evening or spend several days relaxing in the rooms. Once shoes are left at the door, guests enter a world of tatami mats, low Japanese-style tables, garden views, and traditional alcove displays of fresh seasonal blossoms and scrolls of terse verse in elegant calligraphy. The original inn was constructed nearly a century ago and has since been renovated and expanded into the current style.

The In-Song-Ger and several other hotels in the area feature hot sulfur spring water that runs directly from the tap into private tiled tubs, sunken or inclined above-ground. Some also have large *furo*-style pools for large groups. After a stint in these hot tubs, a professional massage provides revival. This is one of the traditional occupations of the blind in China. A good rubdown from a blind masseuse costs about NT$400 for 45 minutes.

Exploring Peitou

Peitou is easy to explore on foot. A right turn at a bridge just beyond the **Dragon Gate Hotel** leads directly to **Hell's Valley**. The steamy, open sulfur pits here offer a first-hand look at the natural activity responsible for the area's hot springs. Local people boil fresh eggs in the medicinal waters that gurgle through the sulfur-stained rocks. Such specially-prepared eggs and other snacks are on sale at the hawker stands that flank Hell's Valley.

After walking through the center of town, with its quaint city park and Chinese pavilion, strollers will come to a traffic island near the **Kyoto Hotel**. The left-hand fork leads uphill toward the Whispering Pines Inn. The right-hand fork proceeds past the **New Angel** and **Hilite** hotels. At the latter, Chi Yen Road offers access to a challenging diversion: a climb up tranquil **Phoenix Mountain**.

Those who venture up Chi Yen Road come eventually to a large double staircase guarded by two enormous "lucky dogs." The stairs lead to the **Chen Memorial Garden**, whose chief attraction is its tranquility. The paved pathway behind the garden is the start of the exhausting mountain ascent. From the summit, there are sweeping views of Taipei, Peitou and the surrounding countryside. Trekkers find well-marked hiking paths leading in four directions from the top of Phoenix Mountain; all lead to main roads so you cannot get lost.

Beyond the Chen Memorial Garden is the **Monastery of Central Harmony**, a complex of pavilions, halls, arcades, shrines, statues and gardens. Buddhist monasteries like this one are peaceful retreats set in nature's lap. It's possible to arrange for the nuns at this monastery to prepare an elaborate, delicious luncheon of traditional Buddhist vegetarian cuisine. A guide or acquaintance who speaks Taiwanese must call ahead, however, a day or two in advance. Guests must arrive promptly between 11:30 a.m. and 12 noon so as not to interfere with the meditation and service schedules of the nuns who are inclined to be not too polite with such "intruders."

If you follow the road up and around the Whispering Pines Inn to 32 Yu-Ya Road (directly behind Insular Hotel), you'll come to the **Taiwan Folk Art and Antique House**, a rambling museum-shop built into the halls and colonnades of an old Japanese villa. Here you'll find artwork and antiques for sale, a charming traditional tea-house, several classical Chinese gardens, and hot mineral baths.

Attractions within easy reach of Peitou central include another impressive temple and mountain. **Hsing-Tien Temple** lies across from the Chung Yi train depot, high on the road that runs between Peitou and the coastal town of Tansui. It has the same name as its sister temple in downtown Taipei, but the setting is considerably more scenic, with a landscaped garden covering the entire hill behind the temple. The main hall and subsidiary shrines are as lavishly decorated as any in Taiwan, but better maintained than most. The ruling deity here is the red-faced Kuan Kung.

The western horizon of northern Taiwan is dominated by a 475-meter

Temple
Soaring
to the Clouds
凌雲寺

Goddess of
Mercy
Mountain
觀音山

Tansui
淡水

Hanging
around Hell's
Valley.

(1,557-foot) mountain. It is called the **Goddess of Mercy Mountain** because from a distance its profile resembles that of Kuan Yin. Visitors who take the time to make the steep climb to its peak will be rewarded by breath-taking views of the island's northern coastline and the Taiwan Strait as well as all of Taipei County.

Goddess of Mercy Mountain can be reached by taxi or bus from Taipei. The climbing path starts at a small town at the foot of the mountain. Plantings of tea, tangerines and bamboo mark the lower slopes. About halfway up the mountain are two Buddhist temples, both called **Temple Soaring to the Clouds**. The upper temple's staff offers good vegetarian meals.

Northern Circle Routes

The drive along Taiwan's northern coastline rewards visitors with its scenic natural sights, charming farm towns and fishing villages. The entire route can be covered comfortably in a single day of driving from Taipei.

Two major roads skirt this coastline. They meet in Keelung to form a wide semicircle around Taipei. A recommended route is to proceed northwest from Taipei to Tansui, then northeast through Paishawan, Chin-Shan, Wanli and Yehliu to Keelung. From this harbor town, travelers have the option of taking a quick freeway ride back to Taipei. From Keelung, it is also possible to continue on a southeast coastal course to Pitou-chiao, Fulung and its excellent beach, and Toucheng, then return north to Taipei past waterfalls and via Pitan.

The terminus of the North Coast Highway is a town with a rich historical heritage. **Tansui** was the main point of contact in northern Taiwan between Chinese and foreign traders during its heyday as the island's major port in the 19th Century. Even before that, the Spanish—who had occupied Keelung—extended their claim to Tansui, where they built a castle called **Fort San Domingo** on one of its hills. Local residents had another name for the fort: Hung Mao Cheng, "Fort of the Red-Haired Barbarians."

Today, the old British headquarters, built in 1876, stand on the same lofty site. The British presence was headed

by a celebrated naturalist, Robert Swinhoe, who lived on the grounds of the old fort. The Chinese regained possession of the site when the British closed their consular compound in 1972. Remnants of the fort's cannon and eight-foot-thick walls still stand, but the location is off-bounds to visitors.

In addition to the Spanish and British presences, Tansui was occupied by the Dutch in the 17th Century, bombarded by French warships in 1884, and claimed by the Japanese in 1895. Before they left in 1945, the Japanese built the island's first golf course here, the **Taiwan Golf and Country Club**. Opened in 1919, the club remains popular among many of the visitors and residents alike.

Today, Tansui's biggest draw is its fresh seafood. Strategically located at the confluence of the Tansui River and the Taiwan Strait, fishermen make a prosperous living here. Seafood stalls and small restaurants abound.

A short drive north from Tansui is **Paishawan Beach**, or White Sands Bay. Because of its proximity to Taipei, it draws huge crowds on summer weekends. Otherwise, it is a convenient spot to swim and sunbathe. The beach has snack bars, changing rooms and a nearby hotel.

Queen's Heads And Serpent's Eggs

The North Coast Highway rounds the northernmost nib of Taiwan north of Paishawan, then turns in a gentle southeasterly direction toward **Chin-Shan**, site of a once-popular beach that has been reduced to nothing by fierce storms and tidal action.

Even more evidence of the forces of nature are on display at **Yehliu**, literally "Wild Willows." The coral promontories here have been etched into all manner of artistic shapes by weather and erosion. The terrain now resembles the surface of another planet, a feature that attracts overwhelming crowds of curious onlookers from the big city.

In fits of poetic fancy, the Chinese have given appropriate names to some of the rock formations over the years. There's a "queen's head" rock that could pass for the profile of the ancient Egyptian sovereign, Nefertiti. There's a dinosaur, griffin and fish, and even the

Paishawan Beach
白沙灣海濱

Chin-Shan Beach
金山海濱

Yehliu
野柳

Seascape (below) and Queen's Head at Yehliu.

146

famous lost shoe of Cinderella. Some of the swirls and bumps in the rock faces look a lot like eggs that may have been left here to hatch by some ancient sea serpents.

To cope with the crush of visitors and to attract even more, **Ocean Park** has recently opened at the parking lot near the entrance to Yehliu. Here, the usual contingent of dolphins, seals and other aquatic performers strut their stuff much as they do at sea parks around the world.

The highway runs through **Wanli** and on to the port of Keelung. En route, there's a modern recreation park with full facilities called **Green Bay Seashore Recreation Club**. The club is open to the public for a nominal fee. The main attraction are its beaches. The bay itself provides the venue for para-sailing, hang-gliding and sailing. Equipment for these activities can be rented at the clubhouse. The Green Bay Club also provides an amusement park for children and several dozen beachside bungalows. These expensive overnight accommodations must be booked well in advance.

Cruising into Keelung

Taiwan's northernmost city and second largest port is **Keelung**, junction for the North Coast and Northeast Coast highways and the northern terminus of the North-South Expressway. Its natural harbor has 33 deep-water wharves and four mooring buoys that can handle vessels up to the 30,000-ton class. About 34 million tons of freight is handled here annually. Only Kaohsiung in the south has more extensive port facilities.

Like Tansui, Keelung has long been a crossroads for Taiwan's contacts with the rest of the world. Local brigands, Japanese pirates, Spanish conquistadors, Dutch soldiers, American traders and Japanese imperialists have all made Keelung their base of operations at various times during the past three centuries. Keelung's population of nearly 350,000 are basically a blue-collar lot wedded to the port trade and its offspring industries. But its setting and history make it an interesting stop for the visitor.

Keelung's main point of interest is an enormous white **statue of Kuan Yin**.

Ocean Park
海洋公園

Green Bay
Seashore
Recreation
Club
翡翠灣遊樂區

Keelung
基隆

Green Bay
Beach.

Chung-Cheng
Park

中正公園

Cruising into
Keelung
Harbor.

The 22.5-meter (74-foot) statue is propped up on a 4.3-meter (14-foot) pedestal that enables the deity to watch over the entire city. Her stature is increased by her placement high on a hill in **Chung-Cheng Park**. Two finely proportioned pavilions grace a knoll next to the statue. Stairs inside the statue of the goddess of mercy lead to a wonderful perch for panoramic photos.

On the wild side of town, there are numerous **seamen's bars** near the corners of Chung-Yi and Hsiao-San roads, by the harbor and railway depot. Salty seamen and wanton women mingle here from dawn to dusk when the "fleet's in." Among the favorite hangouts are the Hollywood, New York and Hong Kong bars. Most of these spots open for business at 9 a.m. to cater to those seeking an "eye-opener" rather than a "nightcap."

An alternate return route to Taipei, instead of the expressway, is a narrow but scenic road which winds from Chin-Shan to Seven Star and Yangming mountains.

The Northeast Coast Highway moves out from Keelung to coastal enclaves like **Juipin** and **Pitouchiao**. The latter site is located on a stone bluff overlooking the Pacific Ocean. Like Yehliu west of Keelung, its exotic rock formations make for spectacular blends of land and sea.

A few minutes' drive south of Pitouchiao lies **Yenliao**. A historical monument here was erected in honor of the Chinese soldiers and civilians who died resisting the 1895 invasion which led to Japan's colonial occupation of Taiwan.

Fulung, the next stop on the Northeast Coast Road, belies the notion that Taiwan's best beaches lie only in the southern reaches of the island. The white sand beach here hugs the northern shore of a cape that juts into the Pacific Ocean. Because of its location, the sun rises on one's right and sets on one's left as one looks out to sea. To further enhance the setting, the cove is entirely surrounded by rolling green hills. Enthusiastic strollers will find that the shoreline stretches for miles in both directions.

About 100 meters inland, a river runs parallel to Fulung Beach, in effect forming a secondary beach. There's a bridge that leads to the seashore proper. Small

sailboats and sailboards for windsurfing can be rented.

A hostel at Fulung offers simple rooms as well as rustic beach bungalows at reasonable rates. Reservations can be made by calling the Railway Information and Service Center (tel. 311-0221 or 371-3358 in Taipei).

The route south from Fulung to **Toucheng** passes a wonderfully ornate Taoist temple that faces the sea. It is called the **Celestial Palace Temple**. Toucheng itself is a tiny coastal village with a modest beach resort that is usually less crowded than Fulung or other northern beaches. As the road skirts the shore, travelers get a look at an offshore island called **Kueishan**—"Turtle Mountain"—for obvious reasons.

The area's main attraction, however, lies not along the sea, but in the hills behind Toucheng. About five kilometers (three miles) behind the village is **New Peak Falls**. This swimming resort is one of the few spots on the entire island where it is possible to swim and dip in the cool mountain waters of a natural waterfall.

The falls—known locally as **Hsin-Feng**—are 500 meters beyond the main

entrance to the resort, inside a canyon. A bridge and a rocky path lead to a knoll overlooking the idyllic pool. By stepping carefully down the rocky ledge, swimmers can slide into the refreshing water which cascades 50 meters (over 160 feet) down a stone chute. Conventional swimming pools, snack bars and changing facilities are nearer to the main gate, as well as a half-dozen modern family bungalows for overnight stays.

Spa of "Fallen Flowers'

The other principal attraction of this lovely region is the **Chiaochi spa**. This spa has a long-standing reputation among local libertines as "a great place to pick wild flowers." Rumor has it that the spa served as a training ground for young country girls bound for Peitou during that town's heyday as one of Asia's greatest "gardens of delight." Today, Chiaochi and Peitou still share a similar ambience. Although the "garden" has mostly gone to seed, a few hardy "perennials" still blossom.

Dozens of hotels and inns here have hot mineral water piped directly into

Toucheng
頭城海

Chiaochi Spa
礁溪溫泉

New Peak Falls
新峯瀑布

Keelung.

Temple of
Heavenly
Accord

協天廟

Kueishan,
the "Turtle
Mountain."

the bathtubs of the private guest rooms. The water is clear, but contains concentrations of boric acid, calcium carbonate, sodium bicarbonate, silicon, magnesium and other minerals. Not only does it offer external healing powers; one can drink it to alleviate stomach and gastrointestinal ailments. Comfortable hotels include the **Hill Garden**, **Jen-I** and **Lucky Star**. Numerous small restaurants scattered about the town specialize in fresh seafood and other authentic Chinese dishes.

Two temples cater to the faithful in Chiaochi. The curved eaves and golden tiles of one of them fill the skyline in front of the Hill Garden Hotel. Further down the main road, the **Temple of Heavenly Accord** is rising. When completed, it will include a magnificent seven-story temple hall.

Less than 10 minutes' drive into the hills behind the Chiaochi is Taiwan's **Five Peaks Flag Scenic Region**, or **Wu-Feng-Chi**. Vendors around the parking lot sell the area's most sought-after products: dried mushrooms, preserved plums, loquats and other fruits, fresh ginger and medicinal herbs. Among the latter is a furry little doll with four

"legs" formed by roots and two "eyes" made with buttons. The vendors call it "Golden Dog Fur." It's actually a plant which roots in stone and grows from remote cliffsides. When rubbed into cuts, scrapes, lacerations, sores and other festering skin wounds, it stops the bleeding immediately and promotes rapid healing with a minimum of unsightly scarring.

The trail from the parking lot leads to **Wu-Feng-Chi Falls**, a lovely vine-and-fern-spangled waterfall that cascades musically in sprays and sheets down a 60-meter (197-foot) slab of cliff. A viewing spot faces the falls from across the stream. Cement steps lead up along one side of the canyon, enabling one to get close enough to cool off in its stinging spray.

Route 9 continues south from Chiaochi to the bright little country town of **Ilan**. In this community, in the city, the route becomes "Main Street;" a quaint row of temples, shops and such. A half-hour south of Ilan lies the international seaport of Suao, southern terminus of the Northeast Coastal Highway and the northern terminus of the even more spectacular Suao-Hwalien

Highway. It is covered in detail in this book's pages on "East Coast: A change of Pace."

Wide Awake in Dreamland

A lovely ride back toward Taipei is in store for travelers who double back up the Northeast Coast Highway to **Erh-Cheng**. Route 9 twists and turns through the spectacular Central Mountain Range, revealing vistas of spellbinding beauty as it zigzags back to Taipei.

Near the city of **Pitan** is the **Chih-Nan Temple**, one of the most important landmarks in the north. This "Temple of the Immortals" has been under constant construction and expansion for nearly 100 years. Perched on a lush green hillside, it exemplifies the concept of a temple as a magic mountain peak. There are supposedly 1,000 steps along the winding approach to the temple. The temple provides housing for about 50 Buddhist monks.

South from Pitan, the mountainous retreat of **Wulai** is the best place in northern Taiwan to witness genuine aboriginal culture. Beyond the town, a suspension bridge hangs across a river. From here, a walking path and mini-trains take visitors to the **Clear Flowing Garden**, where a beautiful waterfall cascades into a deep gorge. Local aborigines perform traditional music and folk dances in the garden.

A cablecar carries visitors across the gorge to a place in the mountains appropriately called **Dreamland**. Dreamland has more aboriginal performances, a lake for rowing and fishing, plenty of places to eat, and an amusement park for children. Nearby hot springs also provide therapeutic bathing.

Traditional aboriginal arts and crafts, wild mountain mushrooms, Chinese herbs and spices and other souvenirs are available in the parks and in stores in Wulai village. Wu-Lai's many restaurants offer such exotic local fare as wild boar, deer, pheasant, snake and freshwater eel.

South of Taipei

Several other attractions within hailing distance of Taipei beckon the casual traveler. All lie south of Taipei. Fifty kilometers (31 miles) away, down the

Chih-Nan Temple
指南宮

Wulai
烏來

Wulai's Dreamland.

provincial Route 3 near the town of Ta-Hsi, is **Lake Benevolence**, temporary resting place of the late President Chiang Kai-shek. His body rests above ground in a heavy granite sarcophagus in his former country villa, awaiting the day when political conditions permit a return to his birthplace in mainland Chekiang Province.

The location, thick with camphor forests and bamboo groves, reflects the bucolic beauty of Taiwan's countryside. Some 6,000 people visit Lake Benevolence each day to pay their respects to the late president. The villa and grounds are open only by prior arrangement but visitors are free to wander around the lake and its surrounding at any time.

The **Shihmen Reservoir** in the same vicinity offers motorboat rides and a restaurant. Its **Stone Mountain Dam**, begun in 1955 and completed in 1964, was built with the aid of consulting engineers and experts from the United States.

Further south, 75-hectare (185-acre) **Safari Park**, with all that the label im-

plies, has been opened at **Leofoo** village, about 60 kilometers (37 miles) from Taipei. With its stock of wild animals from Africa, Asia and the Americas, it has turned into one of the finest animal parks in Asia. The surrounding scenery is spectacular and suited to a "safari." Park staff drive visitors in a fleet of zebra-striped vehicles. The park attracts more than a million visitors a year.

Unlike some wildlife parks which have had trouble getting animals to mate, the denizens of Leofoo have been keeping the park well-stocked. In fact, the lion population jumped from 25 to 84 animals in a single year, all by natural reproduction. Taiwan's climate and diet seem to suit the park's creatures better than most places; the variety and number of animals is expected to continue to increase. With natural wildlife habitats disappearing all over the world at alarming rates, parks such as this may soon be the only places where the creatures can survive and reproduce. The park also features a Pet Corner which permits visitors to fondle lion cubs and baby animals of all kinds.

Lake
Benevolence

慈湖

Leofoo Village

六福動物園

Bus "safari"
at Leofoo.

The Lion's Head

Also bearing a beast's name, but some distance south of the safari park, is **Lion's Head Mountain**. When viewed from the proper angle, the peak does bear a resemblance to the king of beasts. But the mountain's main significance is as a center of Buddhism. Most of the temples here were built directly into natural caves during the past 75 years.

Beginning at the arched entrance above the parking lot, it is possible to hike up to the lion's "head," then back down along its "spine," visiting the temples and other sights along the way. The round-trip walk takes about two hours. The first main temple on the path is the **Chung-Hwa Tang**. Hearty, healthy vegetarian meals cooked by Buddhist nuns are available in the dining room adjoining the temple for about NT$80. The main shrine hall of the temple, just above the dining room, rises on beautifully sculpted stone columns that depict celestial animals and ancient Buddhist legends. The massive multi-storied structure just beyond the temple is the **Kai-Shan Monastery**, a

different kind of study and activities center for resident monks and nuns.

Another steep path winds up around the lion's "mane" to the **Moon-Gazing Pavilion**. It serves its purpose on dark starry nights, as well as on bright nights lit by the full moon. From there, the paved trail cuts down past several more cave-temples, the **Pagoda of Inspiration**, monastic quarters, bridges and viewing terraces. The charming rustic cave-shrines of the **Water Screen Nunnery** are the last major sights on the trail which deposits hikers back on the road near the parking lot.

Four of the temples along the trail provide food and lodging. Accommodations are simple but adequate with tatami floors, quilts for bedding and washing facilities. The nominal fee runs only about NT$200 per person, but most visitors donate more to express their appreciation.

Lion's Head Mountain is 20 kilometers (12½ miles) east of the North-South Expressway, about halfway between Taipei and Taichung. It is a pleasant excursion for travelers heading from the capital city to central and southern Taiwan.

Lion's Head Mountain 獅頭山

Crypt of Chiang Kai-shek at Lake Benevolence, left. An image of the Buddha (below) and a pagoda (right) on Lion Head Mountain.

CENTRAL TAIWAN: PEAKS AND PLAINS

Less than an hour out of Taipei, travelers on the southbound expressway begin to see dramatic changes in the surrounding countryside. Factories become fewer, lush farmland more prevalent. The gray tones of the capital give way to Kelly green patchworks of ripening rice, fruit plantations and vegetable plots. The modern urban facade of 20th Century Taiwan fades into the eternal patterns of rural China.

Central Taiwan, roughly covering the region from Miaoli to Chiayi west of the Central Mountain Range, boasts the most varied terrain on the island. From the summit of snow-capped Yu-Shan, the Jade Mountain, the landscape drops 3,997 meters (13,114 feet) to the major new seaport at Taichung Harbor. The alluvial plain that divides the highlands from the Taiwan Strait is filled by vast green rice fields and plantations of bananas, pineapples, papayas, sugar cane, tea and other crops. The region features major industrial centers like Taichung and Chiayi, ancient port and temple towns like Lukang, the lovely holiday resort of Sun Moon Lake, the alpine wonderland of Ali-Shan, bamboo forests, hot springs, and numerous other attractions.

Easy-going Taichung

The urban center of Central Taiwan is **Taichung**—whose name means, not coincidentally, "Taiwan Central." The pace and pressure of modern metropolitan Taipei are replaced here by a far more mellow approach to life. Taichung is what Taipei looked and felt like 15 years ago, before the big boom of the 1970s.

Taiwan's third largest city, Taichung has a population approaching 700,000. Located on the plain about 17 kilometers (10 miles) from the coast and 100 kilometers (62 miles) south of Taipei, it enjoys the island's best year-round climate, without the seasonal extremes of heat and cold which mark the north and south.

Taichung was founded in 1721 by immigrants from the Chinese mainland. They originally named it "Ta-Tun," or "Big Mound." Today, 50-acre **Chung-Shan Park** occupies the hillock on which the original settlement was built. The city's current name was adopted by the Japanese after they took possession of Taiwan in 1895.

The most recent milestone in Taichung's history was the opening in 1976 of **Taichung Harbor**. This event has opened Central Taiwan to international export markets and suppliers of natural resources. A 10-lane expressway connects downtown Taichung with its coastal harbor.

Although Taichung is neither as scenic nor as diverse as Taipei, it has numerous points of interest. The **Taichung Martyrs Shrine** on Li-Hsing Road was erected only in 1970. But it nevertheless provides a superb example of the harmony and balance inherent in classical Chinese architecture. Many locals claim it is even more outstanding than the martyr's shrines in Hwalien or Taipei. Protected by two bronze guardian lions, the Martyrs Shrine commemorates the sacrifice of 72 Chinese patriots beheaded in 1911 by the tottering Manchu court, on the eve of the republican revolution. It is open daily from 9 a.m. to 5 p.m.

Taichung
台中

Chung Shan Park
中山公園

Taichung Martyrs Shrine
忠烈祠

Preceding pages, butterfly hunters in central mountains; Wen-Wu Temple roofs, Sun Moon Lake. Left, East-West Cross Island Highway view.

The Great Sage
And the Happy Buddha

Next to the Martyrs Shrine is Taichung's tranquil **Confucian Shrine**. While every major city in Taiwan has a shrine hall dedicated to the great sage Confucius, this one is notable for the constrained design of its roofs. True, Confucian temples are normally free from the pervasive din, garish decor and constant foot traffic which mark Buddhist and Taoist temples. But in this shrine, the eaves—rather than flaring audaciously heavenward—curve gently downward, cleaving close to the earth. Indeed, earth, not heaven, was the sage's prime concern.

On the altar of the shrine is a simple blackstone stele with the name of Confucius engraved in gold on its smooth, otherwise unadorned surface. Although he believed in the existence of spirits and deities, Confucius insisted that man should steer as clear of them as possible.

Every year on Sept. 28, Confucius' birthday, this temple hosts a colorful spectacle of ancient rites and rituals, archaic costumes, and 2,000-year-old music played on equally antique instruments.

The **Pao-Chueh Temple**, on the northern edge of the city at 140 Chien-Hsing Road, contains one of the largest and fattest Buddha images in all Taiwan. This is the proverbial "Happy Buddha," Milofo. (In other Buddhist traditions, he is known as Maitreya, the Buddha of the future.) Milofo sits laughing on a massive pedestal in one corner of the temple compound, towering 31 meters (101 feet) above the ground. Smaller statues of the same Buddha are scattered around adjacent courtyards, along with other interesting Buddhist iconography. In the main shrine hall are three Buddha images, protected at the gate by a brace of fierce guardians. Within the hollow pedestal of the giant pot-bellied Happy Buddha is a simple folkcraft museum.

A 20-minute drive from downtown Taichung is **Tunghai University**. The entire wooded 345-acre campus was built according to the architectural style of the Tang Dynasty, the period regarded as China's "Golden Age" of culture and the arts. This subtle and restrained style differs radically from

Confucian
Shrine
孔子廟

Pao-Chueh
Temple
寶覺寺

Tunghai
University
東海大學

Left, East-
West Cross
Island
Highway
view.

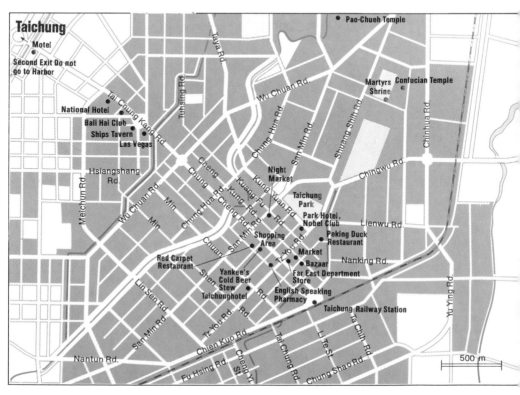

the sometimes-garish style that prevailed in China after the Ming period. Almost all campus buildings are constructed in the square, squat, colonnaded Tang style, with plain tile roofs. The one modern departure is the abstract **Christian Chapel**, designed by the famous Chinese architect I. M. Pei (now a resident of the United States) to symbolize a pair of hands touching in prayer.

Shopping for 'The Works'

Taichung's main **shopping district** is located along Chung-Cheng Road between the railway station and Wu-Chuan Road. There are silk and satin shops, fresh produce markets, and a number of interesting herb shops, redolent with the pungent aromas of potent medicinal plants. Tsu-Yu Road, which crosses Chung-Cheng Road, is the city's principal artery for restaurants and coffee shops. The central **open-air market** is located along the lanes one block toward the train station from Tsu-Yu. In the evening, a colorful **night market** is open for business around the corners of San-Min and Kuang-Fu

roads.

Throughout this district, also, are scores of barber shops and beauty parlors. Visitors should permit themselves to be pampered in these places at least once while in Taichung. "The works," which includes a shampoo, trim and good massage, run about NT$450 (US$12) for about two hours of exotic treatment.

Taichung's nightlife is not as colorful as that of Taipei, but there are several popular watering holes. Just down Taichung-Kang Road from the popular **National Hotel** are the Polynesian-style **Bali Hai**, the **Ship's Tavern**, **E. Lisa's Pub**, and the **Las Vegas Club**. In the basement of the National Hotel, there is live piano music in the **VIP Lounge**. Around the corner from the **Park Hotel** is the **Nobel Club**, noted for the city's prettiest hostesses, the best band, and the highest minimum charge—NT$400 per person.

Local gourmands report that the best Chinese food in all of Central Taiwan is served at the **Pond-Garden Spring**, a multi-storied Shanghai-style restaurant at 71 Chung-Cheng Road. Prawn, eel, chicken and duck dishes are superb.

San-Min Road
三民路

Chung-Cheng
Road
中正路

Tsu-Yu Road
自由路

Taichung
Martyrs
Shrine.

Also recommended are the **Peking Duck** on Kung-Yuan Road near Chung Shan Park; the dim-sum lunches at the **National Glory Pavilion** next door to the Park Hotel; and the night market for snacks. The **Red Carpet** on Ping-Teng Road specializes in Western-style steaks and seafood.

The 'Eight-Trigram' Mountain

Thirty minutes by road southwest of Taichung is the typical country town of **Changhwa**, notable for the impressive Buddha image atop its so-called "**Eight-Trigram Mountain**," Pa Kua Shan.

The 30-meter (98-foot) concrete Buddha image meditates serenely atop a five-meter (16-foot) lotus dais. It took five years to complete, and required 300 tons of concrete. Surrounding it is a veritable "Buddhaland" of shrine halls, pavilions, pagodas and statues displaying every aspect of Mahayana Buddhist history and thought. A complete amusement gallery for children is built into the red-enameled colonnades of the complex.

The concrete Buddha itself is hollow—and six stories high. Life-size dioramas of Sakyamuni Buddha's life are built into the walls. The second floor features the story of his birth, the third his enlightenment under the *bodhi* tree, the fourth his discourses and teachings, and the fifth his death and entry into *nirvana*.

Behind the Buddha image is a palatial three-story temple, one of the largest in Taiwan. Within is an impressive host of gilt icons. In the shrine hall on the top floor is a large golden statue of the Buddha, attended by two disciples. Beside this main hall are a traditional octagonal pagoda of eight tiers and an ornate three-tiered pavilion of classical design.

"Eight Trigram Mountain" gets its name from the combinations of broken and unbroken sticks used by the Chinese in traditional divining procedures, as prescribed in the *I Ching*.

Lukang: Ancient Ports and Temples

Beyond Changhwa, about 21 kilometers (13 miles) from Taichung, the ancient harbor of **Lukang** ("Deer Port") lies sleepily on the shores of the Taiwan Strait. The most popular port of

Changhwa
Eight-Trigram
Mountain

彰化八卦山

Confucian
Shrine,
Taichung.

Lukang
鹿港

Phoenix

Mountain
Temple
（鳳山寺）

Ma Tsu
Temple
（媽祖廟）

Eight-Trigram
Mountain.

entry during the Ching Dynasty (1644-1911) for waves of Chinese immigrants from Fukien province, Lukang was abruptly closed down by the Japanese in 1895. Thereafter, silt and sand rendered the harbor useless for commercial shipping, and fishing has become the major activity.

Tradition is at its best in Lukang. Narrow residential lanes have changed little since the Ching Dynasty days. Artisans can still be seen fashioning furniture with ancient tools and techniques in open-front shops. Old temples and their artisans are alive and well. Altar tables, shelves, ornaments, beams, eaves and other furnishings and fixtures are hewn into shape and finished with elaborate detail at the numerous workshops which line the main street. The fragrance of freshly sawn camphor and wet lacquer wafts everywhere. Incense is also produced in Lukang, and it is interesting to view the creation of the enormous coils which hang from temple ceilings and burn for days.

The oldest temple in Lukang, and one of the oldest in Taiwan, is the **Dragon Mountain Temple**, dating from

the 18th Century. It is located on San-Min Road, just off the main avenue, Chung-Shan Road. The Dragon Mountain Temple was constructed by early Chinese settlers as an expression of gratitude of Kuan Yin, the goddess of mercy, for their safe passage from the mainland. Kuan Yin is enshrined in the main hall. The temple structure reflects a classical mainland style of a design that differs markedly from the style which subsequently developed in Taiwan.

A 200-meter stroll through quaint Oriental lanes brings one to the **Phoenix Mountain Temple**, a small structure built in the early 19th Century by immigrants from Chuen-Chou prefecture in Fukien province. The painted guardians on the main doors are particularly excellent.

Down Chung-Shan Road from the Dragon Mountain Temple is an impressive old **Ma Tsu temple**. The image of Ma Tsu on the main altar is said to have been carried here in 1684 from the original Ma Tsu shrine on Mei Chou Island by Admiral Shih, who captured Taiwan for the Ching emperor. If true, this story substantiates the claim of

Lukang's people that this was the first center of the Ma Tsu cult in Taiwan. There is a host of other exotic icons here. Among them is the magnificent Jade Emperor in a temple of his own in the same compound.

Many more temples and shrines are tucked away among Lukang's lanes. Signs to them are posted throughout the residential maze. Also worth a visit is the **Lukang Native Culture Museum**, a 30-room villa that is itself a collector's item. Designed as a private residence by a Japanese architect in orientalized Edwardian style, it is one of the most unusual mansions on the island. Within is an interesting collection of old furniture and household fixtures, vintage photos and paintings, personal effects and costumes, books and musical instruments, and other knickknacks which reflect original lifestyles of Taiwan's people.

There are a few local inns in Lukang for those who wish to stay, although the town is usually regarded as a day excursion from Taichung. One restaurant merits a stop, however: this is the **New Lukang Seafood House** at the junction of routes 142 and 143. As its name suggests, seafood—fresh and excellent—is served. Nobody speaks English here but there is no need to fret; stand before the iced tanks and use the "pick and point" method.

Return taxi fare from Taichung is about NT$1,000, and half that from Chunghwa. Buses and trains also ply the Taichung-Chunghwa-Lukang route.

The Rainbow of Treasure Island

North and east of Taichung, the **East-West Cross-Island Highway** (Route 8) stretches from Tung-Shih for 200 scenic kilometers (124 miles) through the Taroko Gorge to the east coast. The Chinese claim no visit to Taiwan is complete without a trip across this road, for it displays with striking beauty the full gamut of the island's rainbow hues: lush tropical valleys and winter snow-capped peaks, alpine forests and rocky ravines, steamy hot springs and roaring rivers, mountain lakes and the shimmering sea.

The East-West Cross-Island Highway was completed in 1960 at the cost of US$11 million and 450 lives. Ten thousand laborers, most of them retired

Lukang Native Culture Museum
鹿港 文物館

East-West Cross-Island Highway
東西橫貫公路

Changhwa.

servicemen who had fought on the mainland in the 1940s, struggled four years to complete it. It has become known as "the rainbow of Treasure Island." In two places, the highway forks: at Li-Shan, "Pear Mountain," it traverses the upper spine of the Central Range to reach Ilan and the Northeast Coastal Highway 112 kilometers (70 miles) away; and at Tayuling, it cuts south around Hohuan-Shan, the "Mountain of Harmonious Happiness," to Wushe and Mount Lu spa, a distance of 42 kilometers (26 miles). The latter route eventually leads back to Taichung or on to Sun-Moon Lake.

The western half of the Central Range, between Ku-Kuan and Li-Shan, sometimes resembles Switzerland more than subtropical Taiwan. Visitors should let the terrain guide their choice of clothes: a sweater or jacket is often a welcomed encumbrance at these altitudes, even in mid summer.

Transiting 'Valley Pass'

The first 20 or so kilometers from **Tung-Shih** lead past a series of alternating rice fields and vineyards. The first

hill station is **Ku-Kuan**, "Valley Pass," a hot-springs resort lying at about 1,000 meters (3,280 feet) altitude, about an hour's drive off the North/South Expressway. Undergoing major tourist development in mid 1983, Ku-Kuan features numerous hotels and inns, restaurants and handicraft shops. A roaring river careens in an aquatic symphony over a boulder-strewn bed right through the village. Hot mineral waters is piped directly into the private baths of hotel rooms, but there are no big communal or outdoor pools. Though this water is not as hot as the springs on the east coast, a soak in or a shower with it is therapeutically effective and relaxing.

Rather than mineral water, however, Ku-Kuan's major attraction is the 1.7-kilometer (1.1-mile) walk through **Dragon Valley** to the impressive 76-meter (250-foot) Dragon Valley Falls. The stroll begins with the crossing of a teak suspension bridge over the river. The path weaves past a cave-pen of Himalayan black bears, a house-sized cage of acrobatic monkeys, a pair of dignified Manchurian cranes, and numerous other denizens of an outdoor zoo. It proceeds through sculpted

shrubbery and brilliant bougainvillea to the **Mahjong Terrace of the Eight Immortals**, high atop a crag overlooking the river, and the **Goddess of Mercy Grotto**, a shrine set in a bend in the gorge. A serene white ceramic statue of Kuan Yin rests within. Here you'll find her in her usual meditation posture— sitting in repose on a lip protruding from the rocky face of the gorge across the river, with her hands held in a benevolent *mudra* (gesture), the deep rumble of the river for her *mantra* (holy chant), and the phantasmagoric face of the gorge as her *mandala* (mystical meditation scroll). A shrine gate and altar are set just beneath her kindly gaze by the path for anybody who cares to burn an incense stick before departing with her blessings. Look for the small bridge nearby; across this bridge are two small wooden pavilions hugging the cliffside provide *the* place to rest and be lost in the roar of the river.

Around the next bend, the gorge terminates in a narrow canyon strewn with automobile-sized boulders. Here, the **Dragon Valley Falls** cascade into the stream. Even on sunny, windless days it is always "raining" with a fine mist created by the upward deflection of the waterfall's sheer force and volume by the pool and boulders at its foot. Viewing terraces are staggered 30 meters (about 100 feet) up the side of the gorge opposite the falls. This is the most easily accessible of Taiwan's major waterfalls.

En route back to the village, the trail forks left to the riverside where you'll find a spacious pen full of proud peacocks and other large gay-feathered birds. Standing next to this is a charming Chinese garden grotto with pools, fountains and mountains as its backdrop. Then make your way to an open pavilion set on top of a small stone bluff and see how the Dragon Valley stream courses into the main river. Dragon Valley merits at least half a day of meanderings and musings if you enjoy Nature's sights and sounds, and if time permits.

Restaurants along the main highway through Ku-Kuan specialize in steamed fresh rainbow trout. The **Mountain River Live Trout Shop**, almost directly across the street from the new **Dragon Valley Hotel**, is especially recommended for authentic specialties like

Mahjong Terrace of the Eight Immortals
八仙台

Dragon Valley Falls
龍谷瀑布

Mountain River Live Trout Shop

山江活鱒魚

Ku-Kuan's hot-springs spa.

fresh beef, mountain mushrooms, carp and other fish.

The Climb to Pear Mountain

Beyond Ku-Kuan, the highway climbs steeply into the Central Range. At the **Teh-Chi Dam**, a pleasant hostel clings to steep green hillsides overlooking a lake below. Tons of water gush into this reservoir beneath the impressive hydroelectric plant.

A two-hour drive from Ku-Kuan, is **Li-Shan**, "Pear Mountain," on the crest of the Central Range near the Cross-Island Highway's halfway point. The spur route to Ilan begins here. Continually swept by fresh alpine breezes and drifting mists, numerous lodges and restaurants dot the slopes of this mountain village. Most impressive is the **Li-Shan Guest House**, a sort of alpine version of Taipei's Grand Hotel. Terraces, pavilions and sculpted shrubbery grace the spacious grounds. The best place to eat is the **Pear Garden Restaurant**, a Szechuan eatery near the village center.

An interesting side trip from Li-Shan is the **Fortunate Longevity Mountain Farm**, better known locally as Fushou-Shan. Essentially a large fruit orchard spread across a hilltop, Fushou-Shan appears more European than Asian. The entrance to the farm is through an arched gate less than one kilometer east of Li-Shan village. From there, a pine-lined drive leads past a Christian church and steeple in a persistent five-kilometer ascent. Bamboo and palm vegetation is left far behind. Terraced acres of apple and pear orchards surround Western-style farm houses. Trees are braced against the stiff mountain wind by elaborate bamboo scaffolding. Individual fruits are protected in bags from insects and birds. These fruits are on sale (in season) on the farm. At the entrance to the farm is a small museum of local artifacts and illustrations. Along the Fushou-Shan drive is the **Celestial Pond**, where President Chiang Kai-shek kept a private holiday bungalow. The road ends at **Hwa Gang**, a grassy knoll guarded by giant wind-torn trees.

Li-Shan is the staging point for mountaineering expeditions to **Hsinglung-Shan**, also known as Mount Sylvia, Taiwan's second highest peak at 3,884

Teh-Chi Dam
德基水庫

Li-Shan
梨山

Pear Garden
Restaurant
梨園餐廳

Fushou-Shan
福壽山

Pine Snow
Hostel Ski
Resort.

meters (12,743 feet). Climbers normally stay overnight at the **Wuling Farm** before making the final summit ascent. The four-day round-trip expedition requires a police permit and prior permission from the Alpine Association in Taipei.

'Harmonious Happiness'

Thirty kilometers (19 miles) beyond Pear Mountain, the village of **Tayuling** straddles the crest of the highway at an elevation of 2,600 meters (8,530 feet). East of here, the highway descends rapidly past Wen-Shan Hot Springs and through the Taroko Gorge to Hwalien on the east coast. This passage is described in detail in the Eastern Taiwan section of this book.

Tayuling is the junction for Route 14, which cuts south around **Hohuan-Shan**, the "Mountain of Harmonious Happiness," and continues to Mount Lu Hot Springs and Wushe. Hohuan-Shan, looming 3,420 meters (11,220 feet) above sea level just nine kilometers (5½ miles) south of Tayuling, is Taiwan's only winter ski resort. For about two months, from early January to early

March, heavy snowfall turns the mountain white. A 400-meter (1,300-foot) lift carries skiers up the slopes. The **Pine Snow Hostel** provides accommodation; equipment rentals and ski instruction are available. Even in the heat of summer in the lowland plains, temperatures here rarely rise above 60°F. Hiking and hot-springs bathing are the most attractive recreational activities at that time of the year.

South of Taichung

The most scenic road south from Taichung is Route 3 along the foothills. Ten kilometers (six miles) from the urban center, a "Happy Buddha" sits atop the **Wufeng Temple** hall on a wooded hilltop. Long, colorful dragons, hewn from solid stone, are mounted along the railings on the steps leading to the Buddha.

In **Tsaotun** town, about 20 kilometers (12½ miles) from Taichung, the **Taiwan Provincial Handicraft Exhibit Hall** contains an extensive display of local handicrafts and modern manufactured goods. The four-story air-conditioned building houses bamboo and rattan furniture, Chinese lanterns, lacquerware, ceramics, stonecraft, woodcraft, curios, jewelry, cloisonne, textiles and other traditional items.

Another two kilometers from Tsaotun is **Chung-Hsing** village, seat of Taiwan's provincial government. Taipei, while regarded as the provisional national capital by the Republic of China government, is not the center of provincial affairs.

Sungpoling Tea

About eight kilometers (five miles) past the county seat of **Nantou**, at the village of **Ming-Chien**, Route 16 conjuncts Route 3 and cuts east in the direction of Sun Moon Lake. Seven kilometers further, the **Sungpoling** ("Pine Bluff") tea-producing region spreads across a hilly plateau. Despite the label, there aren't many pines on this bluff. Instead, groves of areca palm and giant bamboo shelter large tea plantations. At most times of day, girls wearing straw hats and bandannas can be seen plucking the tender leaves and buds from these green shrubs and dropping them into huge baskets carried on their backs. Interspersed between the

Hsinglung-Shan

興隆山

Tayuling

大禹嶺

Wufeng

霧峯廟

Hohuan-Shan

合歡山

Taiwan Provincial Handicraft Exhibit Hall

台灣省手工業陳列舘

Nantou

南投

Ming-Chien

名間

Sungpoling

松柏嶺

Goddess of Mercy Grotto, Dragon Valley, left. Sungpoling city showers, right.

tea plantations are fields of pineapples and banana trees, giving the entire plateau a shimmering green glow.

The main street of Sungpoling village is lined with tea shops offering a service known locally as "Old Folks' Tea"— because only old folks (and travelers) seem to have the time to enjoy it. Samples of many varieties of tea are brewed in tiny clay pots and poured into thimble-sized cups, with constant infusions of fresh hot water to keep the flavor strong and fragrant. Bulk teas are available for purchase, along with traditional paraphernalia for brewing. Tea connoisseurs are guaranteed to fall in love with Pine Bluff.

Tungting, a young leaf from the highest fields above Sungpoling, is regarded as Taiwan's best tea. It has a superb flavor, subtle fragrance and practically no "bite." Those who buy bulk tea in Sungpoling get the same wholesale price as major Taipei retailers: NT$300 to $2,400 per catty (1.3 pounds), depending upon quality. The more expensive the blend, the better the bargain.

In addition to its famous tea, Sungpoling has one other attraction worth the diversion: a Taoist temple known as the **Palace of Celestial Mandate**. Some of the most exquisite stone sculpture in Central Taiwan, depicting Taoist legends and Chinese folklore, comprises the portico. Of special interest, carved in full relief from solid stone, are the two enormous round windows which brace the temple—one depicting the celestial dragon and the other the tiger, a duo found in all Taoist temples. The intricate ceiling work inside the hall and the finely painted 15-foot solid-wood doors are also impressive.

Sun Moon Lake: Honeymoon Heaven

Taiwan's most enduringly popular honeymoon resort is **Sun Moon Lake**, 762 meters (2,500 feet) above sea level in the western foothills of the Central Range. Entirely enfolded in mountains and dense tropical foliage, the lake takes the shape of a round sun when viewed from some of the surrounding hills, or of a crescent moon when seen from other heights.

Under sunny skies, the dreamy landscapes of turquoise waters, jade-green hills and drifting mountain mists lend

Palace of Celestial Mandate

受天宮

Sun Moon Lake

日月潭

Sun Moon Lake.

Wen-Wu
Temple
文武廟

Arch at Wen
Wu Temple.

themselves well to the moods and passions of honeymooners and other amorous couples. Once one of the favorite get-aways of President Chiang Kai-shek, the lake was formed in the early 20th Century when the Japanese built a dam for hydroelectric purposes. Prior to that, there was a major aboriginal settlement in this area. Traces remain at the aboriginal village on the south shore of the lake.

Its beauty notwithstanding, Sun Moon Lake's popularity often leaves it crawling with busloads of package tourists from Taipei and abroad. Some of the most interesting sites around the lake can be more crowded than the museums of Taipei. But there are a number of hillside trails and shoreside walks for hikers in search of privacy.

The best way to enjoy the scenic beauty of Sun Moon Lake is to rise at daybreak and walk, drive or take a cab along the road that winds around the lake. Bus service commences at 8 a.m. At dawn, however, the crowds are still snoozing, and early birds have the whole lake to themselves.

A good starting point for an exploration of the lake precincts is the **Sun Moon Lake Hotel**, perched on a high embankment overlooking the lake. Heading east and south, the road leads first to the majestic **Wen-Wu Temple**, the Temple of Martial and Literary Arts. This Taoist shrine, dedicated to Confucius and the two great warrior deities Kuan Kung and Yueh Fei, is built into the hillside in three ascending levels. The two largest stone lions in Asia stand sentry at the entrance, and the portico is graced by two full-relief windows of carved stone, depicting the celestial dragon and tiger. A viewing terrace at the rear of the temple allows unimpeded vistas of the lake. The sea of golden tiles on the temple roofs is indicative of the scale and ambition of Chinese temple architecture.

The shrine to Confucius occupies the upper rear hall. The decorative motifs have been drawn from Chinese folklore that antedates by centuries the arrival of Buddhism in China. Symbolic of the ultimate subservience of the sword to the pen, the temple's martial shrine sits slightly below the literary shrine. Within are the red-faced Kuan Kung, sometimes incorrectly referred to as the god of war, and the white-faced Yueh Fei, a

Sung Dynasty patriot and military hero who attempted without success to recover the empire from the barbarian tribes.

The temple complex is interesting for its complicated layout, with various pavilions and side halls connected by ornate passages and stairways. Throughout the grounds stand potted *bonsai* trees, tropical flowers, and shrubs sculpted to resemble animals. The 15-foot door gods at the entrance, carved from solid camphorwood, colorfully painted and gilt, rank among the best in Taiwan.

Further along the road, a bronze **statue of Chiang Kai-shek** gazes across the lake to the Pagoda of Filial Virtue. Preening peafowl scream from a **Peacock Garden**. A considerable distance further on, the drab and commercial **Aboriginal Village** sits by the lakeshore.

Relics of the Buddha

High on a hill near the southern end of the lake, the **Hsuan-Tsang Temple** houses some of China's most precious Buddhist relics. Chiang Kai-shek himself ordered that this temple be built for safekeeping and preservation of the relics, known as *ssu li-tze*.

Devout Buddhists believe that small kernels of this type—found among the ashes of highly accomplished Buddhist monks and Taoist adepts after their cremations—are formed by the forging of spirit and energy after a lifetime of intensive meditation and other spiritual disciplines. The ashes of the historical Buddha, Sakyamuni, yielded 12 cups of these tiny black-and-white pebbles, some of which are enshrined in the Hsuan-Tsang Temple. Flames will not consume them. Steel sledgehammers cannot crack them. Of course, Western science thumbs its nose at the Buddhist explanation, insisting that they are kidney or gall stones. But one Chinese monk cremated in Taiwan in the early 1950s left more than 10,000 of these tiny nuggets in his ashes, enough to fill a flour sack. Another monk's body refused to decay after his death, and his hair continued to grow. He was encased in solid gold and placed in his own shrine hall.

The *ssu-li-tze* nuggets have other unusual properties. The two that were

Pagoda of Filial Virtue.

Sun-Moon Lake (日月潭)

Toward Puli and Mt. Lu 往埔里/蒼山

日月潭大酒店
Sun Moon Lake Hotel

文武廟
Wen-Wu Temple

孔雀園
Peacock Garden

朝霧碼頭
Harbor

涵碧樓大飯店
Hotel

慈恩堂
T'zu En Church

光華島
Kuang Hua Island

玄光寺
Hsuan Kuang Temple

地山文化中心
Taiwan Aboriginal Culture Centre

玄奘寺
Hsuan-Tsang Temple

德文村
Aboriginal Village

慈恩塔
T'zu En Tower

Toward Shui-Li and Hsitou Forest 往水里/溪頭

carried to this site by monks during the National Exodus of 1949 have not remained static over the centuries. They have expanded, contracted, or even generated new kernels depending upon how much prayer and offering is performed. There are now seven little nuggets enshrined at the temple, but an attendant reports that one of them is beginning to shrink and disappear due to insufficient visits by the faithful.

The relics are kept within a miniature jewel-encrusted pagoda of solid gold on the altar of the main shrine hall. A tiny lightbulb illuminates the small nuggets inside the pagoda.

Also in the main shrine hall are a gilt reclining image of the Buddha and a handsome statue of Hsuan Tsang himself. This Tang Dynasty monk made a pilgrimage to India that was immortalized in the classical Chinese novel, *Journey to the West.* After 17 years of Buddhist study, lecturing and travel in India, Hsuan Tsang returned to the imperial Chinese capital of Chang-An in 645 A.D. Over the next two decades, he translated, 1,335 sutras from the Sanskrit language into classical Chinese thus playing a major part in bringing the Buddhist religion to the Chinese masses.

On the second floor of the Hsuan-Tsang Temple is a shrine to Kuan Yin, the goddess of mercy. On the third floor, another small golden pagoda protects a shard of Hsuan Tsang's skullbone, looted from China by the Japanese during World War II. In 1955, a Japanese monk was dispatched to return the relic at Chiang Kai-shek's request. Upon handing over the relic, the monk-messenger died; his ashes are kept in a wooden pagoda behind Hsuan Tsang's bone. The age and authenticity of the skullbone have been verified.

Virtue and Mystery

Atop a hill beyond the Hsuan-Tsang Temple stands the ornate nine-tiered Tzu-En, the **Pagoda of Filial Virtue**. It was erected by Chiang Kai-shek in memory of his mother; hence, the name. An uphill walk through cool green glades of bamboo and fern, maple and pine leads to the foot of the pagoda. From here, there are spectacular views of the entire lake and surrounding

Wusne Reservoir.

scenery.

Last stop on the lakeside jaunt is the **Glory of Mystery Temple**, a minor shoreside shrine. Below this temple is a dock from which rowboats or motor launches can be hired for short cruises to **Kuang-Hua (Glory of China) Island**. This lovely wooded islet has an open pavilion on it.

The best restaurants at Sun Moon Lake are the **Moon Terrace** at the Sun Moon Lake Hotel, and the dining room of the Evergreen Hotel. These Hunan style restaurants have delicious food, great lake views, and tasteful ambience. The specialty is fresh lake carp, either braised, steamed or highly spiced. Sun Moon Lake produces a unique carp called the "President Fish"; it is delicious but quite bony.

Buses from Taichung depart from Sun Moon Lake every half-hour or so between 7 a.m. to 2 p.m. Taxis from Taichung run about NT$1,000 one-way; a good deal if you can fill the cab with four persons.

Enlightened Souls and Fungi

A picturesque two-hour drive from Sun Moon Lake is another favored honeymoon resort, the Mount Lu spa. The road to the spa passes through **Pu-Li**, a village known as "the exact geographical center of Taiwan." On its outskirts, the **Monastery of Enlightened Souls** founded in 1924, stands in a grove of palms. A short distance further, a marked turnoff leads three kilometers up a pretty valley to **Carp Lake**, a pleasant picnic spot devoid of people except straw-hatted local farmers. These horticulturalists specialize in growing edible and medicinal fungi on wooden planks in shaded arbors.

Twenty-four kilometers (15 miles) from Pu-Li, past exotic landscapes reminiscent of the mountain scenery of Kuilin in mainland China, the settlement of **Wushe** is embraced by the tall peaks of the Central Range. Although its name means "Foggy Community," it is renowned for its crystal-clear alpine air, as well as the profusion of wild cherry and plum blossoms which shower the village in early spring. Far below, the green mirror of Wushe Reservoir is surrounded by abrupt mountain escarpments. The Chinese word for landscape is *shan-shui*—literally, "mountains and water"—and this lake is a perfect *yin-*

Pu-Li
埔里

Monastery of Enlightened Souls
醒靈寺

Carp Lake
鯉魚池

Wushe Dam
霧社水庫

Pu-li area padis, left, and field worker fashion, right.

yang example. A trail leads from the village to the lake, where only shore-fishing is permitted. In Wushe village are a few local inns and aboriginal handicraft shops.

Wushe made its mark on Taiwan's history in 1930, when primitive aboriginal tribes residing there staged a bloody but futile uprising against Japanese occupation forces. The Japanese, with modern weaponry, mowed down 1,000 of the tribesmen, but not before losing 200 of their own number. A memorial plaque in the village commemorates the conflict.

A Hidden Shangri-La

Mount Lu spa nestles in the valley below Wushe. The final stretch of Route 14 leads across a swaying automobile suspension bridge, strung high over a roaring river, then through a dripping tunnel to a fork in the road. The left-hand fork climbs to the peak of Lu-Shan, but prior permission is required for this ascent. The right-hand fork drops another kilometer to the spa. Mount Lu village straddles a turbulent stream traversed by a pedestrian sus-pension bridge. Hot-springs inns lie along the banks of both sides of the river.

On the far side of the river, just beyond the last hotel, a trail leads past a pair of waterfalls to the smoldering source of the spa's hot water. The simmering puddles which have formed in crevices around the source are hot enough to boil eggs. Many visitors do just that. The water lends flavor and vital minerals and trace elements to the eggs, making them highly nutritive.

Mount Lu village is famous for its tea, medicinal herbs, and other mountain products such as venison, petrified-wood canes, wild blossom honey and dried wild mushrooms. Potent medicinal deer-horn shavings, tanned deerskins and other products that are either very expensive or unavailable in Taipei are common purchases here. The best place to stay here is the Mount Lu Garden Guest-House, the last inn on the left across the river. This is the only establishment with large old-fashioned Japanese style *furo*-tubs, ideal for lengthy soaks and big enough for a whole family.

There are three important experimental forests in the mountains of

Mount Lu Hot Springs

廬山溫泉

Mount Lu spa.

Hueisun Forest
惠蓀林場

Hsitou Bamboo Forest
溪頭

Chiayi
嘉義

Hsitou Bamboo Forest.

Central Taiwan. The **Hueisun Forest**, with its towering trees and flowering shrubs managed by Chung Hsing University, is in the highlands north of Pu-Li. The Ali-Shan forest of cypress, cedar and pine is accessible from Chiayi. But the **Hsitou Bamboo Forest**, a 22-kilometer (14-mile) side trip off Route 3 between Taichung and Chiayi, may be the most interesting of the trio.

Forty percent of Taiwan's supply of raw bamboo and bamboo products come from this 6,150-acre forest research station operated by National Taiwan University. (The experimental center was first established in 1903 by Tokyo University.) There are dozens of varieties of bamboo in this cool green forest, along with vast tracts of cypress, cedar, pine and other evergreens. The station cultivates and distributes more than 1 million tree shoots annually for Taiwan's various extensive reforestation projects.

Visitors to Hsitou can stroll at leisure along paved footpaths shaded by leafy canopies. At 1,150 meters (3,773 feet) above sea level, this is a favorite spot for hikers and campers. Motor vehicles are strictly prohibited within the recreation areas.

One of the most popular walks leads to the **Sacred Tree**, 3,000 years old and 46 meters (150 feet) high. **University Pond** features a bamboo bridge arching gracefully over carp-filled waters. A seven-kilometer trek leads to a remote ravine with a lovely waterfall. For the most hardy, Mount Ali is a full day away by foot; but this excursion requires a permit and proper equipment.

Souvenir shops in Hsitou village sell bamboo products and other mountain goods like mushrooms, tea and herbs. There are two guest houses operated by the Taiwan Forestry Bureau and an alpine hostel, managed by the China Youth Corps, built entirely of bamboo and local woods. Bamboo shoots are, of course, the specialty of the resort's single restaurant.

Sunrise on Mount Ali

The city of **Chiayi** straddles Route 3 about halfway between Taichung and Tainan. In itself, this manufacturing center on the fertile western plain is not of special interest to the casual traveler. It is a springboard to numerous impor-

tant attractions, however, including the Peikang and Wufeng temples, Kuantzuling spa and Mount Ali.

East of Chiayi, **Mount Ali** (Ali-Shan) and the **Jade Mountain** (Yu-Shan) rise from the mists of the Central Range. The latter, at 3,997 meters (13,114 feet), is the highest mountain in Asia east of the Himalaya, south of the Soviet Kamchatka Peninsula and north of Sabah's Mount Kinabalu. The former is far more visited, however. In fact, statistics has it that it is Taiwan's favorite alpine resort.

Ali-Shan's popularity is due primarily to the famous sunrise view from **Celebration Peak**. Indeed, it is a spectacular event. As visitors stand shivering in their jackets 2,490 meters (8,169 feet) above sea level, gazing into the graying mist, the sun suddenly peers over the horizon. Golden shafts of light pierce the night, scudding across the thick carpet of clouds which cover the valleys to the east. This famous Sea of Clouds springs to life like a silver screen the moment sunbeams glance across it, undulating in vivid hues of gold and silver, red and orange. Then the sun embarks on its daily journey across the sky, the clouds disperse, the sea fades, and the day begins. It's all over in a matter of minutes.

More often than not, however, fog and mist are so thick atop Celebration Peak that sunrise watchers find themselves floating in the Sea of Clouds rather than hovering in clear skies above it. Then, although sunrise itself is a mere hazy blur, the spectacle is yet to come. As the sun climbs higher, distant valleys begin to light up like a bright green tapestry beneath the sun, while Celebration Peak remains shrouded in fog. It's an eerie sight to see day breaking below while night still reigns above.

Ali-Shan
阿里山

Yu-Shan
玉山

The Legend of Clouds and Rain

At 4:15 every morning, a tour bus leaves the **Alishan House** packed with visitors from Taipei, Hong Kong, Japan, and American Chinese communities. Hundreds of people already stand in eager anticipation of the sunrise by the time the bus reaches the top of Celebration Peak an hour later. Before 7 a.m., most of them will be back at the hotel for breakfast, and by noon

Sunrise over Ali-Shan.

they'll be on their way home. And if the weather at Ali-Shan is terrible—if there are rain and clouds through the entire excursion—many of them will be happy rather than disappointed.

There are two explanations, both founded in legend, for this seeming paradox. In very ancient times, long before even the concepts of *yin* and *yang* had been formalized, clouds and rain symbolized the mating of heaven and earth. It is said that a king of Szechuan made an excursion to Mount Wu, "Sorcery Mountain," where he grew tired in the middle of the day and fell asleep. He dreamed that a woman approached, identified herself as the Lady of Mount Wu, and said: "Having heard that you have come here, I wish to share pillow and couch with you."

As the lovers parted, the woman told the king: "I live on the southern slope of Mount Wu, on top of a high hill. At dawn I am the morning clouds; in the evening I am the pouring rain. Every morning and night I hover about these hills."

The legend of the Fairy Maiden of Mount Wu established a standard for Chinese writers, who ever since have used "clouds and rain" as a poetic metaphor for the sexual act. Clouds symbolize the vital essence of the woman, rain that of the man. Colorful thematic variations have enriched centuries of Chinese literature with phrases like: "After the rain had come, the clouds dispersed," and "The clouds grew thick but the rain never came."

Essence of the Mist

But there is one other reason, even more compelling than the sensual imagery, that draws Chinese to mountain retreats several times a year. Drifting mountain mists are regarded as possessing extraordinary curative powers, due to their high concentration of *chi*.

Chi (pronounced "chee") means "life force" or "vital energy." It is the most fundamental of all Chinese medical concepts. *Chi* is considered the basic force which animates all forms of life. The most potent *chi*, it is believed, rises in the atmosphere and clings as mist to the mountaintops, like cream rising to the top of milk. The legend of Mount Wu further reinforces this concept, suggesting that mountain mists are the vital

Shivering spectators at Ali-Shan sunrise.

essence emitted during the mating of heaven and earth on high mountain peaks.

From time immemorial, Chinese have cultivated the custom of *deng-gao*—"ascending high places." They believe the *chi* found in the mist strengthens their longevity and virtue. One of the most ancient of all Chinese characters, *hsien* for "immortal," combines the symbols for "man" and "mountain." And while the practical and urban Chinese are not likely to become mountaintop ascetics, they do remain absolutely convinced of the restorative powers of high-altitude mists.

Rain and mist, however, may not hold the same delight for foreign visitors as for the Chinese. Not to worry; there are other reasons to visit Ali-Shan. The entire mountain is blanketed with thick forests of red cypress, cedar and pine, some of them thousands of years old. When these ancient plants finally fall to rest, the Chinese let sleeping logs lie. The great gnarled stumps and petrified logs form some of Ali-Shan's most exotic sights. Some of these natural phenomena suggest romantic images and have been named accordingly—"Heavenly Couple" and "Forever United in Love" are two of them. The strolling paths and garden grottoes behind Alishan House incorporate several of these formations, and there are many more on the trails to and from the **Sisters Ponds**.

By Train to Ali-Shan

Perhaps Ali-Shan's greatest attraction for nostalgic Western travelers is the long train ride to the mountain resort from Chiayi. Antique narrow-gauge diesels, especially restored for this route, cover the zigzagging 72-kilometer (45-mile) distance in about three hours. The rails cross 114 bridges and pass through 49 tunnels, one of them 769 meters (2,523 feet) long. At the mountaintop depot are several coal-burning locomotives—original "choo-choo" trains—that still haul passengers and lumber through the mountains, all the while belching smoke and piercing the still air with shrill whistles.

It is best to book train tickets in Taipei and reserve a room at the Yu-Shan area hostel.

182

Alishan House hotel one full week prior to the excursion. The **Taiwan Forestry Tourism Corporation** office, across the street from the main railway station, can make all arrangements. There are other inns at Ali-Shan, but the Alishan House, under the aegis of the Forestry Tourism people, is the oldest, most charming and picturesque. Its Shanghainese dining room has the best food at the resort.

Two-day package tours are marketed by many travel agents in Taipei. There is also a five-hour express bus connecting Taipei with Ali-Shan; it departs the capital twice every morning.

Climbing Jade Mountain

Ali-Shan is the billeting post for mountaineering expeditions to **Yu-Shan**, the Jade Mountain. Even higher than Japan's majestic Mount Fuji, this peak was called "New High Mountain" during the 50 years of Japanese occupation. Its original name was restored by the Chinese in 1945. Westerners often refer to it as Mount Morrison.

Prior permission to climb this peak,

Tung-Pu
東埔

Monastery of the Great Immortals near Kuantzuling.

now a national park, is required from the Alpine Association, whose offices are at 30 Lan-Chou Street in Taipei. Police permits are also necessary; they can be obtained by visitors to Taiwan at the Provincial Police Department, Foreign Affairs Section, directly across the street from the Lai-Lai Sheraton in Taipei. Treks to Yu-Shan of course require proper alpine clothing, hiking shoes, backpacks and standard mountaineering gear.

From Ali-Shan village, an alpine logging train shuttles climbers 20 kilometers (12½ miles) to **Tung-Pu**, a remote hot spring nestled in the mountains at 2,600 meters (8,530 feet) above sea level. There is a rustic hostel there for overnight stays; another hostel is high on the mountain slopes at about 3,300 meters (10,800 feet) elevation. Four full days should be allotted for this breathtakingly beautiful round-trip

After the excursion into the mountains, other trips might seem anticlimactic. But temple lovers, especially those proceding south from Chiayi, or heading to or from Ali-Shan by road, may want to stop at the Chinese shrine

known as **Wufeng Temple** to pay respects to the "Loyal Lord of Mount Ali."

Wu Feng's Sacrifice

Wu Feng, perhaps the only historical personage revered by both the Chinese and the Taiwan aborigines, was an 18th Century Chinese official. Born in 1699 to a merchant family in mainland Fukien province, he emigrated to Taiwan as a youth and studied in great detail the aboriginal customs and dialects. Appointed official interpreter and liaison between Chinese settlers on the plains and recalcitrant aboriginal tribes in the mountains, he worked tirelessly to end feuding between the two camps.

The aborigines followed the disturbing practice of invading the plains every year, after reaping the bounty of their mountains, to harvest Chinese heads as sacrifices to their gods. At the age of 71, Wu Feng devised a courageous scheme to once and for all end the barbarism.

On a certain day and at a certain place, he told his aboriginal friends, they would see "a man wearing a red hood and cape, and riding a white horse. Take his head. It will appease your gods." The tribal warriors followed his instructions, lopping off the head of the mysterious rider. Only after removing the red cowl did the aborigines discover that the man they had killed was none other than their old friend Wu Feng This act of self-sacrifice so moved and terrified the local aboriginal chief that he called a conclave of all 48 tribal headmen in the Mount Ali region. They agreed to ban the practice of headhunting once and for all.

This "cowboys-and-Indians" story is given more depth by a visit to the Wufeng Temple. Within it is a small museum of artifacts and a series of large oil paintings, with English-language captions, recalling the life and times of Wu Feng. Nineteenth Century aboriginal lifestyles are depicted in a collection of vintage photographs.

Scheduled for completion in June 1984 is an enormous memorial garden commemorating the peace established between Chinese and aborigines through Wu Feng's efforts. This garden will contain clusters of traditional dwellings, garden grottoes, an artificial lake

Kuantzuling
Spa
關子嶺溫泉

Peikang
北港

Ma Tsu
Temple,
Peikang.

and other touches. Wu Feng's birthday is celebrated with elaborate ceremonies on Nov. 12 each year.

Kuantzuling Spa
and "Burning Water"

About 15 kilometers (9½ miles) south of the Wufeng Temple, a short distance off Route 3 to Tainan, is the rustic hot-spring spa of **Kuantzuling**. Resting in a low mountain pass between Chiayi and Coral Lake, it has been renowned for its potent therapeutic mineral waters since the Japanese occupation. Chronic skin ailments find rapid relief in these waters. Taken internally, the potion is said to relieve chronic stomach and gastrointestinal problems. The Japanese-style **Kuantzuling Inn** and the old **Eastern Emperor Inn** are among the better hostelries.

The road that runs around the mountains behind Kuantzuling village has a number of interesting sights. About five kilometers (three miles) from the spa, in close proximity to one another, are the **Exotic Rock** and the **Water-Fire Crevice**. The rock is an enormous fossil-ized boulder the size of a house, part of a prehistoric landslide frozen in place at this spot. Bizarre fossil skeletons can be seen petrified into its sides. The crevice is more astonishing. Boiling hot mineral water bubbles like a cauldron in concert with a constant flickering fire, the flames of which have licked the grotto black. This paradox—fire and water pouring together from the earth—looks literally like "burning water."

Also in the Kuantzuling area are the **Blue Cloud Monastery**, built in 1701; the new **Monastery of the Great Immortals**; and the small, highly ornate **Temple of the Immortal Ancestor**. It is but a short drive to a medicinal **herb farm**, **White River Reservoir** and the **Pillow Mountain Cable Car**. Taxis cover the entire circuit from Kuantzuling for about NT$500 (US$12.50).

Peikang's Ma Tsu Temple

Northwest of Chiayi, via **Hsingang** and its elaborate Taoist temple, is the town of **Peikang** ("Northern Port"). It is a 23-kilometer (14-mile) drive on

Route 159. Peikang's chief claim to fame is its Ma Tsu temple, the most extravagant of the 383 temples on the island dedicated to Taiwan's patron deity, the goddess of the sea. Koxinga attributed the safe passage of his war fleet across the Taiwan Strait to the divine protection of Ma Tsu, and ever since she has been a highly revered deity in Taiwan.

Officially known as the **Palace Facing Heaven**, this is probably the wealthiest temple on the island. More than 3 million pilgrims visit every year, leaving over NT$10 million (US$250,000) in annual donations. During the April or May festival week commemorating Ma Tsu's birth (the 23rd day of the third lunar month), between NT$3 and $4 million is collected.

This festival period is the most exciting time to visit the Peikang temple. Throughout the year, however, the staccato bursts of firecrackers, gongs and drums make it sound like a battlefield. Religious rites are performed with pomp and ceremony that have not changed significantly in 1,000 years. One particularly colorful (and frequent) ritual involves the parading around Peikang town of a holy icon in a gilt, silk-tassled palanquin. When the procession returns to the temple gates, the deity is welcomed back amid thick clouds of incense, exploding firecrackers, and a cacaphonous din of gongs, cymbals, drums and flutes. This is a fascinating and authentic display of ancient Chinese folk religion.

Up On The Roof

Four stone lions and four "Immortals" mounted on dragons guard the front gate of the Ma Tsu temple. But it is the roof that demands serious study. There may not be a livelier, more colorful set of eaves and gables on the island. Hundreds of enameled ceramic figures cavort among miniature mountains, palaces, pagodas and trees, depicting tale after tale from folklore. On the central roof beam are the "Three Star Gods" of Longevity, Prosperity and Posterity, the three most cherished goals of the Chinese people in this life. The pagoda on the main beam of the central shrine hall symbolizes communion of heaven and earth, a kind of "stairway to heaven." The roof beams on the side halls have pairs of gambol-ing dragons pursuing the elusive Pearl of Wisdom. Hours could be spent scrutinizing the roof.

Within the temple courtyard stands a three-tiered pagoda where paper offerings are burned. Pilgrims pay real money to temple vendors for ersatz paper money, incense and other gifts for the gods. Thus the temple fills its coffers with legal tender, the gods benefit from the symbolic offerings, and the pilgrim is blessed by both.

There are many tall image cones (known as "Buddha Mountains" in Chinese) bearing the names of the temple's financial patrons, lit like Christmas trees and standing in pairs at the temple's altars. Most temples have only two such cones, but the Peikang temple has 12. This is clear evidence of its immense following and generous patronage. The offering tables are heaped high with meat and fish, chicken and duck, fruit and candy, incense, wine, legitimate cash, even bottles of 7-Up—conveniently uncapped so that the essence might reach the gods.

An extensive open-air market occupies the narrow lanes surrounding the temple.

Ma Tsu Temple

媽祖廟

Festival time, left, and image cone, right, at Peikang's Ma Tsu temple.

THE CULTURAL SOUTHLANDS

Southern Taiwan is the island's oldest settled region and the center of culture. Temples, pagodas, pavilions, forts and other historical and religious sites bear testimony. The Hakka immigrants first arrived on Taiwan's southern shores, as did the Dutch many centuries later. When Koxinga ventured to Taiwan to make his final stand against the Manchus, he established the island's first Chinese government in the south.

The southern seaboard is also the most lushly tropical and humid zone of Taiwan. The hills swell more gently, the sun shines more brightly, and the sea plays ·a bigger role in daily life than elsewhere on the island. What's more, the distinctive "flavor of human feeling" that suffuses Chinese communities everywhere is especially rich in southern Taiwan. People still take time to enjoy the good things in life.

Traditional Tainan

Tainan, the cultural center of Taiwan, was capital of the island from 1663 to 1885. Today the fourth largest city with a population about 650,000, it occupies an area of 175 square kilometers (67.5 square miles). Tainan is to Taiwan what Kyoto is to Japan and Kyongju to Korea: an ancient capital which still commands respect due almost entirely to its cultural status.

Tainan's history, and thus its modern flavor, is inextricably linked with the exploits of Koxinga—known in Taiwan as Cheng Cheng-kung, "The Lord of Imperial Surname." A Ming loyalist, he arrived in 1661 with 30,000 select troops in 8,000 war junks at "Deer Ear Gate" (Lu-Erh-Men) near Tainan. He besieged the Dutch fort at Anping and drove them from the island, establishing a Ming stronghold that lasted three generations until his grandson finally capitulated to the Manchus.

The mighty warrior brought more than troops to Taiwan. He carried a camphor wood icon of Ma Tsu which still sits in the shrine to this goddess at Deer Ear Gate. And his entourage included about 1,000 writers, artists, musicians, craftsmen and master chefs, whose function it was to launch a

Chinese cultural renaissance in Taiwan. A similar select "crème-de-la-crème" of scholars and artisans followed Chiang Kai-shek across the Taiwan Strait in 1949, leading to the current efflorescence of culture in Taiwan.

Today, Tainan remains highly conscious of its rich cultural legacy. For decades a sleepy town of temples and pleasant memories, Tainan currently is rising—like the proverbial phoenix from the ashes—in a concerted effort to restore its former glory. Behind its dynamic and popular mayor, Su Nancheng, Tainan is developing into a tourist mecca. Su encourages light industry, agriculture, fishing and tourism within his domain, but he keeps industrial plants and their accompanying pollution at arm's length. His goal: a clean, cultured city serving as a residential refuge for the industrial center of Kaohsiung, and a showcase destination for foreign tourists. Su is especially determined to protect the scenic beauty and delicate ecological balance of Tainan's extensive tropical coastline. (In 1983, Su won the international Ramon Magsaysay prize for government service.)

Tainan
台南

Preceding pages, visitors visible between small Buddha images) are dwarfed by statues at Light of Buddha Mountain, and (left) scholars stroll through shrine hall at the complex. Right, Koxinga statue at Tainan Shrine.

But while Tainan is Taiwan's most socially progressive city, it is also its most traditional. A maze of narrow lanes, courtyards and garden walls are tucked into hundreds of shrines and temples. Most residents prefer to speak the native Taiwanese dialect instead of Mandarin. Native *pai-pai* religious festivals are observed far more frequently and extravagantly than in the north. Indeed, Tainan has managed to harmonize the demands of classical culture and contemporary economy.

City of Temples

Most of Tainan's chief points of interest are concentrated in the old downtown section, stretching east to west between Chih-Kan Towers and the railway station, north to south between Chung-Shan Park and Koxinga's Shrine. It is a pleasant city to explore by foot, day or night.

Temples are the hallmark of Tainan. The sobriquet "'City of a Hundred Temples" is a modest understatement. There are 220 major temples and countless minor shrines scattered throughout the town and surrounding countryside.

Most are marked by an arched gate or a wall plaque on which the temple's formal name is inscribed.

In Buddhist shrines, four identifying characters are commonly used: 廟 ("temple"), 寺 ("monastery"), 堂 ("hall") and 庵 ("hermitage").

Taoist and folk-religion structures most commonly have three tell-tale characters: 宮 ("palace"), 館 ("building") and 殿 ("court").

Shrine to a Hero

It is perhaps appropriate to begin a tour of Tainan's temples at **Koxinga's Shrine**. Set in a garden compound of tropical trees and breezy pavilions, the shrine was built in 1875 by imperial edict from the Manchu court in Peking. This was a landmark event: it indicated that the former Ming resistance leader had been forgiven, and now had been deified as a national hero.

A statue of Koxinga stands in the central shrine hall, flanked by those of his two most trusted generals. In the colonnades are enshrined the 114 loyal officers who followed him to Taiwan. The rear shrine hall houses an altar to

Koxinga's
Shrine
郡王祠

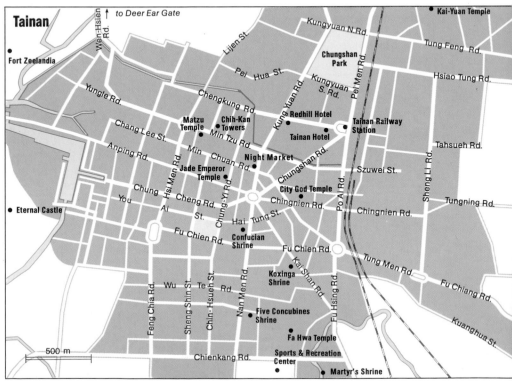

192

Koxinga's mother, accompanied by young princes. An attached museum displays antiques, pottery, paintings, documents and costumes reflecting the life and times of Koxinga.

Left in ruins following the Japanese occupation, the shrine was restored after World War II and again, in 1962. Major memorial festivities for this father of modern Taiwan are held three times a year—on Feb. 12 (the date of the Dutch surrender to Koxinga), April 29 (retrocession day) and Aug. 27 (Koxinga's birthday). The shrine, located at 152 Kai-Shan Road, is open daily from 9 a.m. to 6 p.m.

Confucian Shrine

孔子廟

Three blocks from Koxinga's Shrine is Tainan's **Confucian Shrine**, the oldest temple for the sage in Taiwan. It was built in 1665 by Cheng Ching, Koxinga's son, as a center for the Chinese cultural renaissance in Taiwan. Restored 16 times since then, it still stands out as Taiwan's foremost shrine to Confucius, reflecting a classical architectural style seldom seen on the island.

It is set in a tranquil garden compound. Arched gates and corniced walls divide the complex into a series of courtyards, each with its own halls and

Mayor Su (back row in white jacket) poses with Tainan Boy Scout Troop.

special functions. Originally, these courtyards served as schools for the branches of classical Chinese studies.

Confucius is enshrined in the central "Hall of Great Success" with a simple gilt stele of stone, adorned with fresh flowers and incense. Plaques bearing honorific inscriptions to Confucius from various Ching Dynasty emperors and former President Chiang Kai-shek also hang here. Elsewhere are shrines to Confucius' most distinguished disciples, memorials to a host of historical heroes and famous scholars. Ancient costumes, books and musical instruments—used in annual formal ceremonies marking Confucius' birthday at dawn on Sept. 28—are on display in the temple. (Tickets to the birthday celebration should be booked several days in advance through Tainan hotels.) The shrine is located at 2 Nan-Men Road; it is open 9 a.m. to 6 p.m. daily.

Imperial Concubines And the Happy Buddha

When Koxinga's grandson formally surrendered Taiwan to Manchu forces in 1684, a distant royal relative of the

last Ming emperor was living on the island with his five concubines. Learning of Taiwan's imminent fall, he committed suicide. His concubines—as an act of love and loyalty—hanged themselves on the same day. They were posthumously granted the rank of royal princess, and the **Shrine of the Five Imperial Concubines** (1 Wu-Fei Street) was erected to commemorate the cherished Chinese virtues of loyalty, honor and sacrifice embodied in their action. The small shrine hall houses five doll-like hardwood icons wearing jewels and silken finery. The four maidens painted on the doors represent legendary figures, not the five concubines.

One of Taiwan's oldest Buddhist monasteries is the **Kai-Yuan Monastery**, built during the 17th Century by Koxinga's son and successor, Cheng Ching, in memory of his mother. It is situated on Kai-Yuan Road, about a NT$50 cab ride from the Tainan Railway Station, and is open from 6 a.m. to 7 p.m. daily.

Sitting within the central shrine hall is a smiling, pot-bellied Milofo, the "Happy Buddha." He is guarded by four enormous celestial sentries in fierce poses. The altar table boasts a very old,

intricately carved panel with coiling dragon motifs. Numerous side shrines dedicated to attendant deities contain traditional Chinese temple furnishings of sculpted hardwood. Another shrine hall with altars and image cones sits behind the main hall. And in one corner, visitors may peak into a fully equipped Buddhist vegetarian kitchen, where all the monks' meals are prepared.

Indeed, this is a functioning monastery as well as a public temple. Freshly shaven monks and nuns in robes and sandals can be seen shuffling about the grounds attending to monastic chores, as they have done for century upon century in China. Although this is not the most architecturally impressive temple in Tainan, it does provide fleeting glimpses and insights into the day-to-day life of contemporary Chinese monks and nuns.

Home of the City God

Tainan's residents believe that their behavior is reported to the emperors of heaven and hell by Cheng Huang, the City God. His small, old, and very original temple—**Cheng Huang Miao**—

Temple of the City God

城隍廟

is located on Ching-Nien Road between Chien-Kuo and Po-Ai. It is open daily from 6 a.m. to 11 p.m.

The main shrine is a fascinating jumble of smoke-stained icons, gilt trim, antique hardwood fixtures and intricately hewn beams. Within is a solemn bearded statue of the City God, with life-sized statues of a warrior and a scholar standing guard on either side. In the side-wall niches are two dozen smaller icons of smooth camphorwood, clothed in silk brocade. The facial features and expressive poses are highly individual. Behind the main shrine is a smaller hall and shrine to Cheng Huang. The side walls here are populated by a set of newly painted clay statues, depicting famous monks and masters of the past.

Temple of the Jade Emperor

玉皇廟

The open beam work on the temple ceiling is noteworthy. Unlike other ceilings, this one is varnished rather than painted, its surface etched with fine filigree. Relics and ritual objects hang everywhere, among them two giant abaci, each about five meters by 1½ meters (16½ feet by five feet) in dimension. The hardwood beads of each abacus are the size of melons. One hangs to the

Tainan's Temple of the Jade Emperor.

right of the main shrine, the other from the beams over the front door. These are used by the City God to tally the merits and demerits of each citizen for his annual report to the emperors of heaven and hell.

Temple of the Jade Emperor

An indispensable stop on any Tainan temple tour is the **Temple of the Jade Emperor**, one of the oldest and most authentic Taoist temples in Taiwan. Located at No. 16, Lane 90, Chung-Yi Road, near the corner of Min-Tsu, it is open daily from 6 a.m. to 12 midnight.

A highly detailed facade of stone, carved in deep relief, graces the entrance to the central hall of this gaudy complex. Inside, the Jade Emperor is represented by an austere stone slab engraved with his name. To the right, an elevated shrine called the **Court of the Martial Saint** is dedicated to the red-faced warrior-god, Kuan Kung. It is an exquisite shrine with finely painted door gods and attendant dragons, side panels of sculpted stone depicting animals and Taoist Immortals, a large censer pagoda for burning offerings, and a

circular ceiling inhabited by hundreds of carved gilt gods.

On the left wall is a most significant fresco: a full color reproduction of an ancient painting, depicting the 3rd Century Taoist physician Hwa-To performing surgery on the upper arm of the wounded military hero Guan-kung, who stoically ignores the pain while playing a game of chess with a friend. This is the earliest record of systematic medical surgery in China. Hwa-To is not only revered as one of the fathers of Chinese medicine; he is also renowned as an accomplished Taoist adept and a master practitioner of China's ancient martial arts, and has been deified.

The Temple of the Jade Emperor is one of the most ritually active temples on the island. Exorcisms and other rites are held frequently during the day, many times involving trance mediums. Visitors need merely follow the sound of drums, gongs, cymbals and shouted incantations to the rear courtyard of the temple to find these mediums trying to contact the spirits of deceased friends and relatives on behalf of anxious supplicants, beneath the beatific gaze of the Jade Emperor and his entourage.

Other major temples in Tainan are too numerous to account here. Some of the most important include:

● The **Fa-Hwa Monastery** (100 Fa-Hwa Street). More than 300 years old, it still has about 60 monks and nuns in residence. Beautiful banyans and *bo* trees (*ficus religiosa*) shade the grottos.

● The **Palace of the Empress of Heaven** (18 Yung-Fu Street), Tainan's downtown Ma Tsu shrine. Also known as the Ta Tien Hou Temple, it was built in 1683 to enshrine Taiwan's patron saint. Tall, well-wrought, smoke-stained statues of Ma Tsu and her two "bodyguards"—former demons converted to the side of good—grace the shrine hall. This temple claims to be the oldest Ma Tsu shrine in Taiwan, a claim disputed by the temple in Lukang.

● The **Martial Temple** (229 Yung-Fu Street), dedicated to the warrior deity Kuan Kung. Founded in 1778, it is located directly in front of the Chih-Kan Towers. It boasts particularly fine work on its ceilings and gates.

'Tower of Barbarians'

The **Chih-Kan Towers** themselves were built in Chinese pavilion style during the Ching Dynasty, on the site of the old Dutch Fort Providentia. Little remains today of the original Dutch fortification, once known to local Taiwanese as the "Tower of Red-Haired Barbarians." It was built in 1653 as a Dutch stronghold but was taken over as Koxinga's administrative headquarters in 1662.

The towers (212 Min-Tsu Road; open 9 a.m. to 6 p.m. daily) house visual displays of Koxinga sailing across the Taiwan Strait and ousting the Dutch. Bronze statues in the attached park symbolize the surrender. Nine stone turtles in the park, bearing memorial steles, were inscribed by imperial edict in 1786 and presented to a Chinese magistrate in Taiwan for successfully suppressing an uprising.

Another centrally located park site is **Chung-Shan Park**, only a block from the railway station and the Tainan Hotel. Among the trees and paths is a pleasant landscaped pond with a miniature replica of the "marble boat" built for China's last Manchu empress. The original is at the Summer Palace near Peking.

Also in Tainan city, at 152 Kai-Shan Road, is the **Antiques House of Tainan**. There are four major display rooms. "Nature and Humanities" contains fossils of rhinoceros and elephant found on Taiwan, possible evidence that the island was at one time a geographical part of the mainland. "Politics and Education" houses collections of documents, coins, stamps, seals, books, and other artifacts relating to Taiwan's political and social history. "Literature" reflects Taiwan's colorful history through scrolls, engravings, costumes, porcelain and statuaries. "Customs and Practices of the People" displays household implements and related paraphernalia of daily life. First established on April 1, 1932, at Fort Zeelandia in Anping, the collection was moved three times before finding a permanent home in this former memorial house to Koxinga in 1965. In 1975, the house and collection were expanded.

Temples of Deer Ear Gate

Koxinga landed at **Lu-Erh-Men** ("Deer Ear Gate"), a shallow bay north of Tainan off Route 17. The spot is consecrated by the elaborate new **Ma Tsu Temple**, built upon the site of an

Chung-Shan Park
中山公園

Fa-Hwa Monastery
（法華寺）

Palace of the Empress of Heaven
天後宮

Martial Temple
武廟

Street shrine, Tainan.

older structure. Ma Tsu's shrine, within the main hall, is protected by enough writhing dragons to frighten away a whole army of devils. Her two fierce guardians, one red and one green, stand fully armed in classical martial-arts postures. Sitting serenely before the large central icon of Ma Tsu are a row of smaller, black camphorwood icons bedecked with finery. The one in the center is said to be over 1,000 years old; it was brought to Taiwan from the Chinese mainland by Koxinga. Few icons enjoy greater reverence.

The splendid craftsmanship that went into this temple is indicative of its high regard. In addition to the usual wooden temple doors, there are two magnificent moongates with nine-meter (30-foot) slabs of polished blackstone etched with coiling dragons and flying phoenixes. The six-meter-tall door gods are carved of solid camphorwood and glazed with enamel and gilt. These are said to be the largest temple doors in Taiwan.

A few kilometers beyond the Ma Tsu temple is what Tainan bills as the largest temple structure in this part of Asia: the **Temple of the Holy Mother at Deer Ear Gate**. Visitors can see its golden roof tiles shimmering in the distance long before they actually reach it.

The entry to this temple is formed by an immense two-story facade braced by a pair of large pagodas. The sculpted dragon columns which support the portico were hewn from solid stone by Taiwan's finest temple artisans. The main wall of the double-tiered shrine inside is divided into six ornate niches, each of which enshrines the icons of major deities of Taiwan. The entire shrine area is carved, etched, painted, cast and gilded in incredible oriental detail. The altar table is a triple-length, black-lacquered, gold-gilt fantasy of intricately carved celestial animals, heaped high with offerings to Ma Tsu.

An equally magnificent shrine hall stands behind the first, also with six major shrines in the walls and two intricately carved gilt altar tables. The small black wooden icons are paraded about town on elaborate palanquins during traditional festivals, and they are treated with utmost reverence.

The third hall is a full story taller than the first two. In the ground-floor hall are three well-crafted Buddha images. The central figure is seated on a lotus

Ma Tsu
Temple
媽祖廟

Temple of
the Holy
Mother at
Deer Ear
Gate.

dais; the right one rides a tiger; the left one is mounted on an elephant. On the second floor are three more large gilt Buddhas depicted in various aspects. Housed on the third floor is an ornate triple shrine to the Jade Emperor.

The Holy Mother complex has been under construction for many years and is far from finished. But already it is impressive, with its massive scale and grand ambition, harmoniously blending Buddhism, Taoism and the Ma Tsu cult. Eventually, Tainan plans to develop this entire region for tourism. It can be reached by following Cheng-Kung Road out of Tainan city from the railway station, then bearing right onto Wen-Hsien Road, which becomes Route 17. A left turn on Route 2 leads directly to the temple.

Forts of Anping

In **Anping**, a 20-minute cab ride from downtown Tainan, are more reminders of Tainan's military past. **Fort Zeelandia** was first built by the Dutch in 1623, heavily reinforced between 1627 and 1634. The Europeans held the bricks in place with a mixture of sugar syrup, glutinous rice and crushed oyster shells. This ingenious mixture must have worked, for much of the original foundation is still intact! When Koxinga took possession of Fort Providentia, the Dutch retreated to this bastion, surrendering only after a nine-month siege.

Over the centuries, various additions have been made to Fort Zeelandia. During the Opium Wars of the 1840s, cannons were installed and a lighthouse erected by the Chinese. A Japanese governor constructed the current building to entertain guests.

Not far from Fort Zeelandia is the site of an old Chinese fort once used for Tainan's coastal defenses. Now known as the **Eternal Castle**, silt and sand accumulations have left it far from the shoreline it once guarded. It was constructed in 1875 by Shen Pao-chen, commissioner of naval affairs in Fukien province, after Japanese forces launched a raid against Taiwan on the pretext of avenging shipwrecked Okinawan fishermen killed by aborigines.

The layout of this fort is remarkably secure. The interior ground is set lower than the exterior, and bunkers and arsenals arc placed around the walls. In

Eternal Castle
安平億載金城

Fort
Zeelandia.
安平古堡

Deer Ear
Gate bell-
ringers.

its heyday, the fort could accommodate 1,500 fighting men. Today, no buildings or major artifacts remains. But there is a fine collection of 19th Century cannons on the ramparts.

In the same vicinity as these two forts is one of Tainan's newest atttractions, the **Tainan Wax Museum**. Opened on April 28, 1981, for the 320th anniversary of Taiwan's retrocession to Koxinga from the Dutch, this waxworks hall displays typical scenes in the lives of farmers, fishermen and aborigines during Koxinga's time, as well as events relating to Koxinga's arrival and victory over the Dutch. Costumes, implements, painted backgrounds and other props are authentically recreated. Located at 194 An-Pei Road, it is open daily.

There is so much to see in and around Tainan that side trips seem rather pointless. But those with the time and inclination might wish to take a 45-minute drive north up Route 17 to the village of Kun-Chiang and its **Nan Kun Shen Temple** at Pei-Men. This ornate shrine, built in 1662 and dedicated to five heroes of the early Tang Dynasty, is one of the most frequently visited on the entire island. Images of the five venerables occupy the altar of the shrine hall. They are surrounded by a wealth of excellent woodcarvings. Even the columns are of wood instead of stone. A second hall houses three seated statues of Kuan Yin, the goddess of mercy. In the third is the fearsome emperor of hell.

City Life in Tainan

Tainan does not yet have any large, international-style hotels to accommodate visitors. But the absence of such commercial monoliths is one of the city's charms. The old **Tainan Hotel** typifies local ambiance, and other newer hotels such as the **Redhill** and the **Oriental** are highly satisfactory.

As the most "civilized" city in Taiwan, Tainan naturally excels in that most civilized of all Chinese pursuits— *haute cuisine*. Outstanding Szechuan cooking is presented at the Redhill Hotel and at **Today's Szechuan Restaurant** (62 Chung-Cheng Road). Also recommended are the **Upper Bamboo Grove Seafood Restaurant** (254 An-Ping Road) and the **Korean Restaurant** (175 An-Ping Road). The **night market** on Min-Tsu Road features scores of tiny

Tainan Wax Museum
台南蠟像舘

Ancient Chinese rendering of Fort Zeelandia.

Anping Beach
安平海水浴場

Coral Lake
烏山頭水庫

Modern
Tainan.

eaties where one can feast on Tainan *dan-tze mien*, a local noodle soup speciality. After dinner, many Tainanese retire to sip coffee at the cozy, chic cafes found all over the city. Tainan's favorite coffee house is the romantically moody **Dream Coffee** at 99 Cheng-Kung Road, across from the Redhill.

In terms of nightlife, Tainan is far more sedate than Taipei. Carousers rarely need to worry about waking up with a hangover. The funkiest local scene is at the **Tainan Ballroom**, on the seventh floor of the Tainan Hotel, where girls swing their guests around the floor to the tunes of vintage cha-chas, tangos and jitterbugs.

Thanks to Mayor Su's vision, Tainan has ample recreational facilities for both residents and visitors. On Chien-Kang Road, next to the city's **Martyrs Shrine**, is one of Tainan's showcase projects: an enormous **sports and recreation center** including swimming pools, tennis and squash courts, rugby and soccer fields, running and motorcycle-racing tracks, and much more. There are also food stalls and hotel facilities. Golfers will find the 18-hole, 7,000-yard **Tainan Golf and Country Club** 14 kilometers (nine

miles) north of town at Hsin Hwa. Seaside swimming and sunning can be enjoyed at **Anping Beach**.

Tainan is three hours from Taipei via the North-South Expressway, and 45 minutes north of Kaohsiung on the same highway. There are also regular express buses and trains. Far East Air Transport operates three 40-minute flights between Taipei and Tainan daily.

Coral Lake

Those persons driving the scenic inland route from Chiayi to Tainan are likely to pass the two largest lakes in Taiwan—**Coral Lake** and the **Tsengwen Reservoir**. An underground tunnel three kilometers long feeds Coral Lake from the reservoir. But despite their proximity, the road connecting the lakes winds for 30 kilometers (19 miles) through lovely pastoral landscapes.

Coral Lake derives its name from the countless narrow inlets which probe like fingers into the surrounding hills, making the lake resemble a chunk of raw coral from the air. It is also known as the Wushantou Dam. More than 30 mountain streams flow into this 30-

meter (98-foot) deep body of water. Boats can be rented for fishing or just cruising. Hikers appreciate the network of trails surrounding the lake. Swimming is not permitted, however, because the lake provides drinking water to the region. There is a small resort village, featuring a replica of Peking's Temple of Heaven, and several hostels and inns, including the new **Kuo Min Hotel** on the northern shore of the lake.

Tsengwen Reservoir replaced Coral Lake as Taiwan's largest inland body of water when it was completed in 1971. This enchanting 44-square-kilometer (17-square-mile) reservoir also attracts boaters and hikers. Several tropical fruit plantations in the area provide delicious fresh food to this off-the-beaten-track resort. There is accommodation available at the **Tsengwen Youth Activities Center** operated by the China Youth Corps.

Tsengwen is 60 kilometers (37 miles) northeast of Tainan via Route 3. Ten kilometers nearer to Tainan, via the same route, is the little village of **Yu-Ching**, the western gateway to the **Southern Cross-Island Highway**. This road was completed in 1972 at a cost of US$12.5 million, four years hard labor, and more than 100 lives. Nearly as scenic as its northern cross-island cousin, but lacking the singular attraction of a Taroko Gorge, it can be traversed in a day from Yu-Ching to Hai-Tuan, a small town 60 kilometers due north of Taitung. Those wishing to stay overnight at any of the three rustic hotels en route must obtain prior permission and passes in Taipei.

Kaohsiung: The Industrial Capital

Kaohsiung is Taiwan's economic showcase and a city of superlatives. It is Taiwan's largest international seaport, its major industrial processing center, and the only city besides Taipei with an international airport. The port is the world's second largest dry dock and fifth largest container port.

Kaohsiung 高雄

Kaohsiung is the southern terminus of the North-South Expressway, about a four-hour non-stop drive from Taipei. With more than 1.5 million inhabitants, the city is Taiwan's second largest and the only one besides Taipei to enjoy the status of a "special municipality" — equal to a province, and administered

Tsengwen Reservoir.

202

by the central government.

A city of humble origins, Kaohsiung has experienced meteoric economic growth in expanding to 153 square kilometers (59 square miles) in size. The concentration of heavy industry has caused considerable pollution problems, but Kaohsiung is now trying to attract and develop high-technology industries in its central districts, moving smokestack factories to new suburban industrial zones. Commercial bustle and the cosmopolitan lifestyle of a major seaport characterize the people of Kaohsiung. In contrast with Tainan, most of the city buildings of Kaohsiung are modern steel and glass towers. Streets are broader, and wide-open spaces permit light and air to circulate.

Fishing remains a major enterprise, with over 1,500 vessels plying waters as distant as South Africa for up to a year at a time. Agriculture, however, is glaringly absent in the immediate vicinity, another indication of the city's industrial orientation.

The city is unevenly divided by a canal called the Love River. It bears unfortunate striking similarities to New York's infamous, polluted Love Canal.

A good spot for an overview of the city's layout is **Longevity Mountain Park** (Shou-Shan), which overlooks Kaohsiung harbor near the fishing wharves. It is about a 20-minute walk from the Kingdom Hotel. From the Kaohsiung **Martyrs Shrine** at the top of the mountain, views are impressive either by day or at night. There are several other interesting temples and historical monuments, plus many pavilions and shaded terraces. A cab ride around the park, with a few stops along the way, runs about NT$130, and walkers will find the park open until 1 a.m.

The Temple Circuit

Temple fanciers may want to include three complexes on their rounds in Kaohsiung. The **Three Phoenix Palace** (134 Ho-Pei Road, Section 2; open 5 a.m. to 11 p.m.) is the largest temple in the city. A popular and active temple, it is devoted to the demon suppressor, Li Na-cha. Powerful stone lions stand sentry at the foot of the steps, which lead up to an elaborately carved stone facade. The central shrine hall contains three major icons, exquisite

Longevity
Mountain
Park
壽山公園

Three
Phoenix
Palace
飄宮

North-South
Expressway
road sign,
left. Taiwan
railway
hostess,
right.

gilt altar tables, and 10 large image cones ("Buddha Mountains") that glow warmly like Christmas trees. Faithful Chinese can often be seen practicing divination here.

Behind and above the main hall, a set of steps leads to a smaller shrine with three altars. This is a Buddhist hall: three fine gilt Buddha images—seated respectively on a lotus, an elephant and a lion—share space with statues of warrior guards and the Buddha's disciples.

The **Holy Hall of Martial and Literary Arts**, a three-story Taoist temple dedicated to the warrior deity Kuan Kung and his literary counterpart, Confucius, is open from 5 a.m. to 11 p.m. daily at 114 Fu-Yeh Street. On the ground floor is a triple shrine devoted to the martial deities, with a number of finely crafted hardwood altar tables. The second floor enshrines Confucius, patron of the literary arts, his name simply engraved on characteristically dignified stone steles. The third floor, wherein reside the Jade Emperor and his celestial entourage, is the most magnificent with wall frescoes and detailed ceiling work. Three smaller icons dressed in richly brocaded, jewel encrusted dragon robes sit on a

lacquered table before the shrine.

Not far from the Holy Hall, at 54 Yen-Huang Street, is the **Shrine of the Three Mountain Kings** (open 5 a.m. to 11 p.m.). This three-century-old Buddhist temple is dedicated to three brothers, private tutors to a man who saved the life of the Chinese emperor. When the emperor rewarded the man, the latter gave all credit to his three teachers. The emperor consequently made each brother "King of the Mountain" in three mountainous regions of Fukien province. This beautiful shrine hall houses a dozen deities in an incredibly complex panoply of ornamentation. The huge carved gilt altar table, the solid wood columns and the painted door gods are especially noteworthy.

Little Harbor's Ship Harvest

Kaohsiung is the world's largest scrapper of old ships. Armies of laborers bearing acetylene torches, saws and wrenches break down about 200 steel-hulled ocean-going ships each year. They harvest an enormous quantity of scrap steel, electrical fixtures, nautical devices, copper wire, screws and other parts. Those lucky enough to be in Kaohsiung when a luxury liner is being scrapped can sometimes get great bargains on lanterns, clocks, binnacles and other nautical antiques.

The scrap wharf is located at **Little Harbor**, about 10 kilometers south from downtown. Taxis will run visitors down and back, with an hour to roam about the wharf, for about NT$500.

There are two beaches within the Kaohsiung city limits. **Chi-Chin Beach**, open 7 a.m. to 5:30 p.m. daily, has a black-sand beach that is insulated not only from the bustle of downtown Kaohsiung, but also from the murky waters of the harbor—it is located on the seaward side of a long island which forms a breakwater for the harbor. A four-minute ferry ride, from a small dock next door to the entrance of the Pin-Hai First Road fishing wharf, takes swimmers there. Near the beach are an ornate Taoist temple, dedicated to the god of medicine, and a shop selling a colorful array of seashells.

A bit beyond Longevity Mountain Park, near the northern entrance to the harbor, lies the beach of **Hsi-Tzu Bay**. The water is not as clean as that of Chi-Chin, but it is a pleasant place for

Holy Hall of Martial and Literary Arts

文武聖殿

Kaohsiung Harbor, left. China Steel Corporation, right.

seaside strolls. It is near the new Sun Yat-sen University.

Shopping in Kaohsiung

As Taipei's leading industrial and export city, Kaohsiung is naturally a good place for shopping bargains. Best buys are modern manufactured goods, clothing and other contemporary items, rather than arts and crafts. Most of the interesting shopping areas are located within walking distance of the Kingdom, Major and Ambassador hotels.

A good street for window-shopping and absorbing local color is narrow **Hsin-Le Street**, which runs parallel to Wu-Fu 4th Road between Love River and the harbor area. The street is packed with every imaginable type of contemporary Chinese shops. Side lanes lead to more colorful local markets.

At the foot of Ta-Jen Street, next to the Major Hotel, is an entrance to Kaohsiung's cavernous, three-level, underground **Love River Arcade** of shops and amusement galleries. Each floor of the arcade occupies nine acres of space beneath the canal, making it one of the largest underground centers in Asia. The first level contains endless rows of shops selling ready-made clothing, footwear, household goods, snacks and cold drinks. The second level features more shops, as well as amusement galleries and cinemas. On the third level are a disco roller rink and a bumper-car track.

Taiwan's largest department store, the gargantuan 10-floor **President Department Store**, is on Wu-Fu 3rd Road near Chung-Shan Road. A branch of the **Far Eastern Department Store** is located on Wu-Fu 4th at the corner of Ta-Chih. Good buys in brass ships lanterns, clocks and other nautical paraphernalia can be found at **Henry's** at 9 Wu-Fu 4th Road, near the Kingdom Hotel. A couple of doors down, at No. 6 Wu-Fu 4th, is a well-stocked store with top-quality outdoor camping gear at rock-bottom prices. Several book stores in this area sell popular Western novels and reference books at about a third of their cost in the West. Pharmaceuticals and Western medicines may be found in the tiny, well-organized **Health Pharmacy** on Ta-Jen Street, on the corner across from the Temple of the Three Mountain Kings.

President
Department
Store
大統百貨公司

Hsin-Le
Street
新樂街

Love River
Arcade
愛河商場

Food and Nightlife

As Taiwan's No. 1 fishing port, Kaohsiung naturally offers excellent fresh seafood. The **Sea King** at 2-2 Hsing-Chung 2nd Road (tel. 333-4486) has fresh fish and mollusks heaped high on shaved ice or kept live in tanks.

Two good Szechuan restaurants are conveniently located in the shopping district. The **King's Kitchen** on the second floor at 75 Ta-Jen Street overlooks the municipal plaza, and **Wu's Dumpling Restaurant** is nearby at 148 Chi-Hsien Street, off Ta-Jen. The **Kingdom Hotel** offers Shanghai and Szechuan buffets on alternate evenings, and Cantonese **dim-sum** for lunch.

Very near the Kingdom are two local eateries simply called **Snacks** and **Gruel**. These are typically Taiwanese fast-food cafeterias, offering dozens of different dishes freshly cooked and arrayed on a heated steam table.

After Taipei, Kaohsiung has Taiwan's most active nightlife. The **Chalet Bar** at L'Europe and the **Ship Cabin Bar** on the second floor of the Kingdom Hotel are the most popular Western watering holes in town, and

Sea King
海霸王海產

China
Ship-
building's
mammoth
plant at
Kaohsiung harb
left.

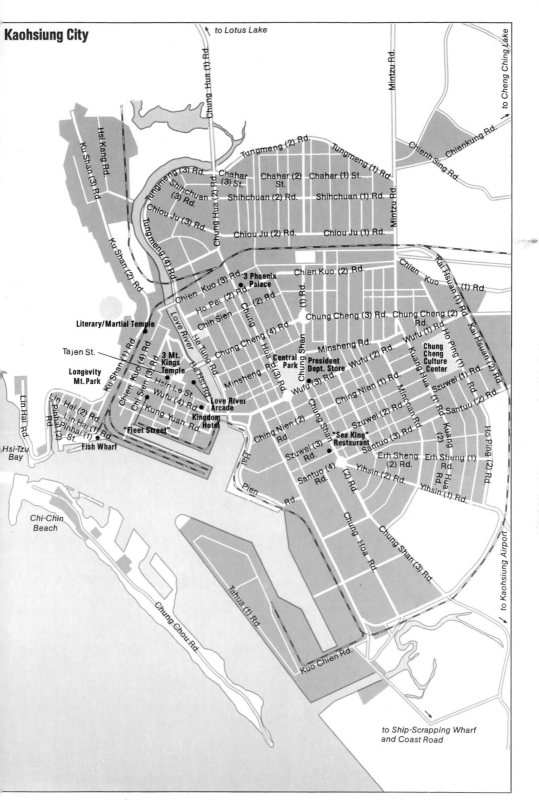

Kaohsiung City

to Lotus Lake

to Cheng Ching Lake

Chung-Hua (1) Rd.

Mintzu Rd.

Chienh Sing Rd.

Chienkung Rd.

Hsi-Kang Rd.

Ku Shan (3) Rd.

Tungmeng (2) Rd.

Tungmeng (1) Rd.

Chahar (3) St.

Chahar (2) St.

Chahar (1) St.

Tungmeng (3) Rd.

Shihchuan (3) Rd.

Shihchuan (2) Rd.

Shihchuan (1) Rd.

Chiou Ju (3) Rd.

Chung Hua (2) Rd.

Mintzu Rd.

Tungmeng (4) Rd.

Chiou Ju (2) Rd.

Chiou Ju (1) Rd.

Ku Shan (2) Rd.

Chien Kuo (3) Rd.

Chien Kuo (2) Rd.

Chien Kuo (1) Rd.

Kai Hsuan (1) Rd.

3 Phoenix Palace

Ho Pei (2) Rd.

Chien Kuo (1) Rd.

Chung Cheng (3) Rd.

Chung Cheng (2) Rd.

Literary/Martial Temple

Chien Kuo (3) Rd.

Chin Sien

Chung (2) Rd.

Ho Ping (2) Rd.

Kai Hsuan (2) Rd.

Love River

Ho Tung Rd.

Chung Cheng (4) Rd.

Minsheng Rd.

Wufu (1) Rd.

Chung Cheng Culture Center

Tajen St.

Ku Shan (1) Rd.

Chien Kuo (4) Rd.

3 Mt. Kings Temple

He Hsi Rd.

Central Park

Chung Shan (3) Rd.

President Dept. Store

Wufu (2) Rd.

Kuang Hua (1) Rd.

Szuwei (1) Rd.

Santuo (2) Rd.

Longevity Mt. Park

Chin Sien (3) Rd.

Hsin Le St.

Wufu (4) Rd.

Minsheng

Wufu (3) Rd.

Ching Nien (1) Rd.

Minchan Rd.

Lin Hai (2) Rd.

Kung Yuan Rd.

Love River Arcade

Ching Nien (2) Rd.

Chung Shan (2)

Szuwei (2) Rd.

Santuo (3) Rd.

Kuang (2)

Lin Hai (1) Rd.

Pinhai (1) St.

Kingdom Hotel

"Fleet Street"

"Sea King" Restaurant

Erh Sheng (2) Rd.

Erh Sheng (1) Rd.

Ho Ping (2) Rd.

Lin Hai Rd.

Pinhai Rd.

Fish Wharf

Hai Pien Rd.

Szuwei (3) Rd.

Santuo (4) Rd.

Yihsin (2) Rd.

Yihsin (1) Rd.

Hsi-Tzu Bay

Chi-Chin Beach

Chung Hoa Rd.

Chung Shan (3) Rd.

to Kaohsiung Airport

Chung Chou Rd.

Tahua (1) Rd.

Kuo Chien Rd.

to Ship-Scrapping Wharf and Coast Road

the top-floor **Sky Lounge** at the Ambassador Hotel is nice for amorous couples. Up the street from the Kingdom, at 97 Wu-Fu 4th Road, is a "'rock-'n'-soul" music club called **The Superstar**, where disc jockeys spin platters of vintage rock at high decibels.

Concerts, symphonies, plays, exhibits and other programs are presented regularly at Kaohsiung's new **Culture Center** for the performing arts.

Midnight ramblers on the prowl find amusement on **Fleet Street**, a one-block section of Chien-Hsin 3rd Road between Wu-Fu 4th and Kung-Yuan. Those who missed Susie Wong in Hong Kong's Wanchai or Taipei's Sugar Daddy Row might find her here, somewhat older and wiser but still smiling and teasing. Fleet Street caters to Kaohsiung's transient merchant seamen, and when the fleet's in, the smoky air of these clubs can grow rowdy. Among the better known bars are the **King's Seamen Club**, the **Cape of Good Hope** and the **Sea Stone**.

Top spots for Chinese-style entertainment include the plush **Mona Lisa Club** in the basement of the Major Hotel and **The Unicorn** wine house at 25 Ta-Jen Street, next door to the Major.

Kaohsiung can be reached from Taipei by train, express bus or plane. China Airlines and Far East Air Transport each operates a half-dozen daily flights between Taipei and Kaohsiung. Both China Airlines and Japan Asia Airways operate international flights to Kaohsiung from Tokyo and Osaka.

Suburban Sights

Within easy driving distance of Kaohsiung are numerous scenic attractions that belie the city's deserved reputation as a center of industry. Lakes, mountains, hot springs and Buddhist refuges are all a short distance away.

A mere 15-minute drive north of downtown Kaohsiung lies lovely **Cheng-Ching (Purity) Lake**. Similarities have been drawn between this body of water and Hangchou's historically renowned West Lake on the Chinese mainland. A broad tree-lined esplanade leads to the Ming-style entry arch of the lake-park. A NT$35 entrance fee gives access to a seven-kilometer road sweeping the circumference of the lake.

A leading attraction at Cheng-Ching Lake is the tall and stately **Restoration Pagoda**. There are islands, towers, bridges, pavilions, an orchid collection and aquariums. Boating, fishing, hiking, horseback riding, golf and swimming (in pools only) are among the activities offered. Just outside the entrance gate to Cheng-Ching Lake, a driveway leads uphill to the **Grand Hotel**, younger sister of the Taipei hotel of the same name. Though smaller than its metropolitan counterpart, the gold-tiled classical Chinese roof here looks even more perfectly proportioned than the one in Taipei.

Twenty minutes' drive north of Kaohsiung in suburban **Tso-Ying** lies another lovely body of water called **Lotus Lake**. The architectural attractions here include Kaohsiung's new **Confucian Shrine**. Divided by corniced walls and moongates into various courtyards and garden grottoes, the entire complex is enclosed within a long, arrow-straight wall enameled in brilliant red and fringed with gold tile.

The **Spring and Autumn Pavilion**, standing on an islet connected to the south shore of Lotus Lake by a causeway, is entered through the jaws of a life-sized dragon sculpture. A stone's

Culture Center
中正文化中心

Tso-Ying
左營

Confucian
Shrine
孔子廟

Dragon and
Tiger
Pagodas at
Lotus Lake.

throw away stand the twin, seven-tiered **Dragon and Tiger Pagodas**. A Taoist temple dedicated to Kuan Kung is located directly opposite the entrance to the Spring and Autumn Pavilion.

Light of Buddha Mountain

Visitors with dual interests in Chinese Buddhism and architecture should not miss a visit to **Fokuang-shan**, an hour's drive northeast of Kaohsiung in lush rolling hills. Better known as Light of Buddha Mountain, this is the center of Buddhist scholarship in Taiwan. The complex consists of several enormous shrine halls surrounded by cool colonnades, pavilions and pagodas, bridges and footpaths, libraries and meditation halls, ponds and grottoes, and exquisite Buddhist statuary.

Near the entrance, the tallest Buddha image on the island—32 meters (105 feet) high—is surrounded by a holy host of 480 life-sized images of disciples.

The major shrine hall is known as the **Precious Hall of Great Heroes**. The size of a large theater, this hall has no artificial lighting. Sunlight enters through windows running the entire cir-

cumference of the hall, along the tops of the walls. Enshrined within are three 20-meter (66-foot) Buddha images, seated in meditation and displaying different *mudras* (hand gestures). Every inch of wall space is neatly compartmentalized into thousands of tiny niches, each containing a small Buddha illuminated by a tiny light bulb. The only other items in this cool, cavernous hall are a huge drum and bell hanging in the corners from wooden frames, and a pair of towering 10-meter image cones bearing the names of the temple's donors. This hall reflects the original purity and tranquility of Buddhism.

The second major shrine is the **Hall of Great Pity**. It houses a white Kuan Yin *bodhisattva* standing on a lotus dais. From a vial in her hand, she pours the sweet nectar of wisdom and compassion. Other sites within the complex include Kuan Yin's Pond for Releasing Living Creatures; the Nine Grades Cave; the Pure Land Cave with colorful dioramas; the Precious Bridge; the Hall of Great Wisdom; and the Pilgrims' Parlor, where inexpensive lodging and vegetarian meals are available.

Fokuang-shan is nestled amidst a

dense bamboo forest. The shortest route there from Kaohsiung is via Route 1 to Feng-Shan, then north on Route 179. It's a one-hour drive. The Buddhist center also operates a shuttle bus from the foot of Longevity Mountain Park in Kaohsiung three times daily, at 9 a.m., 1:30 p.m. and 7 p.m., for NT$100.

Peaches and Butterflies

A further half-hour drive along Route 179 beyond Light of Buddha Mountain, in the direction of Chi-Shan, is a small park called **Three Peach Mountain**. Meandering footpaths lead through a maze of gardens and rock formations. Aviaries display various wild fowl of the island. There is also a deer pen and the Dragon Cloud Temple, a Buddhist shrine.

Beyond the mountain village of **Chi-Shan** on Route 184, another 15 minutes past Three Peach Mountain, exotic **Butterfly Valley** is near the village of **Mei-Nung**. Taiwan is one of the world's most magnificent butterfly kingdoms, and in this valley, on sunny days, the creatures flutter by as thick as snowflakes.

Somewhat off the beaten path is the **Kang-Shan Spa**, also known as Crest Mountain. It lies about an hour's drive north of Kaohsiung in the rolling green foothills of the Central Range. Carbonic hot springs fill the two full-sized swimming pools of the **Kangshan Spa Hotel**, where standard restaurant fare includes turtle stew. Nearby is an exotic rock formation called **Moon World**; it looks like something from another planet, especially under the light of a full moon. This rustic little resort can be reached by exiting the North-South Expressway at Kangshan town, then following Route 177 east in the direction of **Ah-Lien**. The spa lies about five kilometers beyond this small village.

Voyage to the Pescadores

As Taiwan's major port city, Kaohsiung is also the gateway to the various off-shore islands under the jurisdiction of the government in Taipei. Four island groups may be easily visited by foreigners—Peng-Hu (the Pescadores), Little Liu Chiu, Orchid and Green islands. The only restriction is that passports must be presented for travel to these offshore islands.

Kang-Shan Spa
岡山溫泉

Moon World
月世界

Three Peach Mountain
三桃山

Butterfly Valley
蝴蝶谷

Cheng-Ching Lake.

Pescadore
Islands

澎湖羣島

Makung

馬公

Peng-Hu
Islands
scene.

Tight military security measures make it difficult or impossible to approach most offshore islands. Kinmen (Quemoy), for example, is a major military bastion within shouting distance of the Chinese mainland. Small groups of visitors may sometimes visit the fortifications by special permission from various government agencies.

No problem for visits to the **Pescadore Islands**, the "Isles of the Fishermen." Sixteenth Century Portuguese sailors who first put Formosa on European maps also gave these islands their name. Certainly, this 64-island archipelago, with a total land surface area of only 127 square kilometers (49 square miles), has a colorful history.

Nearly every army that has ever launched an attack on Taiwan has used the Pescadores as their springboard. During the Mongol Yuan Dynasty, Chinese pirates used these islands as a base from which to sack ships plying coastal waters. Ming authorities finally suppressed the piracy and established a trading post there, and early Hakka settlers stopped there en route to Taiwan. Then in rapid succession, the Dutch, Koxinga's Ming loyalists,

the forces of the Manchu Ching Dynasty, the French and the Japanese took over the archipelago en route to the main island of Taiwan.

The treacherous coral shoals which surround the Pescadores have claimed countless ships waving flags of all nations. These shipwrecks and foreign occupations help to account for the 147 temples and assorted monuments dotting the otherwise barren Pescadores.

Today, the Pescadores form Taiwan's only island-county. Half of the population of 150,000 live in **Makung**, the county seat. Fishing is the main source of income; the only crops that grow on these flat, windswept islands are peanuts, sweet potatoes, and sorghum for making potent Kaoliang liquor.

The **Peng-Hu Bay Bridge** links Peng-Hu Island via causeways with the chain's second and third largest islands. This 5½-kilometer (3½-mile) line is the longest inter-island bridge in Asia. There are superb swimming beaches near **Lin-Tou Park** and along the shoreline of **Shih-Li**, 14 kilometers (nine miles) south of Makung. Stone grottoes, caves and fishing coves are found all along the shore.

Visitors can make an interesting side trip to the **Isle of the Seven Beauties**, a 20-minute flight from Makung (operated daily by Yung-Hsing Airlines and the Taiwan Aviation Corporation). According to local lore, seven virtuous beauties of the Ming Dynasty period drowned themselves in a well on this island to protect their chastity from marauding pirates. A shrine was subsequently erected to their memory; it is called the **Tomb of the Seven Virgins**.

There are numerous hotels and inns at Makung. Those which provide adequate facilities and services for visitors include the Feng-Kuo, Pao-Hwa and Sheng-Kuo hotels. Excellent fresh seafood is available at small restaurants throughout the Pescadores.

Regular daily round-trip flights operate to Makung from Taipei, Tainan, Chiayi and Kaohsiung. But the most pleasant approach is by boat. A tripledecked luxury ferry operates daily to Makung from the pier at Kaohsiung. The trip takes 4½ hours, and there are daily return runs to Kaohsiung. Boarding time in Kaohsiung is 7:30 a.m.; the ferry departs promptly at 8. Fares vary from NT$200 to NT$400 one way depending upon accommodations.

South of Kaohsiung

Where the North-South Expressway ends, Route 17 proceeds southeasterly along the coast to Taiwan's southernmost tip at Oluanpi.

About 45 minutes' drive south of Kaohsiung, the black-sand beach of **Chung-Yun** lies near the village of **Lin-Yuan**. Those who can ignore the noxious oil refinery nearby find this a delightful beach. A wonderfully ornate Ma Tsu temple called the **Phoenix Palace** faces the sea behind the beach.

From the Chung-Yun wharf, ferries depart sporadically for **Little Liu Chiu Island**, a pleasant wooded islet a few miles to the south. One-way fare on this local ferry—which departs only when the tide is right—is less than NT$200. It takes about an hour to cross, and there are daily return trips. Simple inns on the islet provide possibilities for overnight lodging.

A half-hour further south from Lin-Yuan, on the other side of **Tungkang** town, the village of **Lin-Pien** is renowned for the gourmet seafood banquets served in dozens of roadside restaurants. One place even promises "all you can eat" for NT$100 (about US$2.50).

At **Fang-Liao**, a 1½-hour drive from Kaohsiung, Route 17 merges with scenic Route 1. The latter skirts the coast all the way to the southern tip. Here, the Central Range looms abruptly on the skyline. On the inland side of the road are lush plantations and paddy fields. On the seaward side, fish farmers cultivate all manner of mollusks and ocean fish, their paddle pumps splashing ceaselessly.

At **Feng-Kang**, Route 9 from the east coast joins Route 1. At **Che-Cheng**, another road turns off toward the hot springs of **Szechunghsi** (Four Heavy Streams) Spa.

Che-Cheng
車城

The Sunny Southern Tip

The coastal crescent that occupies Taiwan's southern reaches is known as the **Heng-Chun Peninsula**. Two arms reach into the sea: Oluanpi ("Goose Bell Beak"), longer and to the east, and Maotoupi ("Cat's Nose Cape"), stubbier and more westerly. The broad bay between the two points harbors some of

Heng-Chun
Peninsula
恒春半島

Blessed Spirit
Tortoise.

Kuan-Shan
關山

Kenting
墾丁

Kenting
Beach.

the island's best swimming beaches and many scenic attractions. In the low hills above the two-pronged peninsula sprawls **Kenting National Park**, a lovely haven for exotic flora and strange formations of coral rock. Offshore, the merging of waters of the Pacific Ocean, the Taiwan Strait, the South China Sea and the Bashi Channel creates a pastel tapestry of green and blue swirls.

The town of **Heng-Chun** is situated midway between Che-Cheng and Kenting, about nine kilometers (5½ miles) from each. A short distance south, a turnoff in a westerly direction, toward **Kuan-Shan**, leads to scenic seascapes. The **Palace of Blessed Virtue** is a small temple set in a charming grotto of bizarre rocks and trees. A path leads to **Blessed Spirit Tortoise**, an enormous turtle-shaped rock with a green carapace formed by tenacious vines growing on top.

The roadside resort village of **Kenting** lies between Kenting Park in the hills and Kenting Beach on the shore. The most popular accommodation is the 72-room government-operated **Kenting House**, whose main wing rests at the foot of an abrupt flat-topped mountain.

The peak is vaguely similar to the Devil's Tower landing pad of the movie *Close Encounters of the Third Kind*, and this other-worldly atmosphere is further accentuated by exotic flora and the complete absence of urban blight. Bookings can be made through the Taiwan Forestry Tourism Bureau.

Kenting has been earmarked by the Taiwan government as a site for major urban development, and 125 acres of land have been set aside for the construction of international-class resort hotels.

Kenting National Park was first established by the Japanese in 1906. These Asian aliens combed the earth to find exotic species of plants, and transplanted all that could thrive in this climate to the soils of Kenting. The Chinese have continued to expand the collection: currently there are more than 1,200 species growing in the 48-square-kilometer (18½-square-mile) park. Paved paths and marked scenic routes interlace the park, and most trees and shrubs are identified in Latin as well as in Chinese.

Scenic points include the 100-meter

tunnel-through contorted rock called the **Fairy Cave**; and the deep gorge, opened like a sandwich by an ancient earthquake, known as **One Line Sky**. In the **Valley of Hanging Banyan Roots**, visitors enter a preternatural world where thick banyan roots stretch 20 meters (66 feet) through cliffs of solid stone to reach the earth, their green canopies whistling in the wind high above. From **First Gorge**, confirmed trekkers can enter the dense groves of the **Tropical Tree Preservation Area**. It takes about 1½ hours to make the walk through a wild jungle world of ancient trees, dark ravines, coral-rock formations and shrieking birds.

On the Beach

On the ocean side of Kenting town, **Kenting Beach** features an unspoiled white-sand beach that stretches about 200 meters (some 650 feet). It will soon be extended to a good half-mile in length, with another mile of shoreline beyond for strolling. The clean, clear azure water is warm and gentle, perfect for swimming from April through October. The swimming resort operated by

Kenting House is open to the public.

The Golden Horse bus line has hourly departures to Kenting from Kaohsiung. There is also a special one-day Kenting tour from Kaohsiung, departing from the industrial city at 8 a.m. and returning at about 9 p.m. Full fare is NT$193.

Eight kilometers (five miles) west and south from Kenting, **Maopitou** cape pokes into the sea in a jumble of contorted coral-rock formations, sculpted by eons of wind and water, and entangled in dense patches of seaweed. The sea here shimmers a deep sapphire blue, and the cape provides superb views of the sunswept peninsular crescent. A rocky path cuts roughly through the craggy coral formations.

Among the points of interest is the **South Sea Cave**. A small shrine is maintained here, and elevated sea-viewing terraces make this a fruitful stop for landscape photographers. Roadside stalls offer one of southern Taiwan's most refreshing summer drinks: green coconut water. This clear, cool refreshment, according to Chinese herbalists, has an overall *yin* or "cooling" effect on the internal organs.

Opposite Maopitou, **Oluanpi** arm extends for several kilometers beyond Kenting and boasts Taiwan's best white-sand beaches. Recently declared a seaside park of 160 acres, Oluanpi features a three-kilometer strolling path and fine opportunities for swimming, snorkeling, scuba diving, fishing and sometimes even surfing. Collectors of exotic shells often find a bonanza.

Fifteen minutes by car from Kenting is the **Oluanpi Lighthouse**, a landmark erected at the tip of the cape in the 1880s. It has saved countless vessels from certain peril on the notorious coral shoals which reach into the sea.

Plans have been drawn for modern resort facilities at Oluanpi. Currently, however, the only accommodation is a primitive hostel run by the Taiwan military's foreign affairs department. It is located atop a flat knoll 15 minutes' walk from the lighthouse.

North of Oluanpi cape, 15 kilometers up the east coast, lies an odd geological formation known as **Chialoshui**, "Joyous Waters." A shoreline of strewn boulders and coral cones, riddled like giant sponges with holes drilled by the elements, winds for two kilometers along the coast.

Maopitou
貓鼻頭

Oluanpi
鵝鑾鼻

Kenting
National
Park; left.
Chialoshui,
right.

EASTERN TAIWAN: A CHANGE OF PACE

On the Pacific side of the great Central Mountain Range which bisects Taiwan from north to south lies the island's rugged eastern coast, unsurpassed for scapes of land, sea and sky. Parts of Taiwan's eastern seaboard looks much like California's wild Big Sur coastline and Korea's spectacular east coast drive. Insulated by a sheer wall of mountains from the industrial and commercial developments of the western plains, eastern Taiwan remains a charming enclave of old-fashioned island culture, a refuge where the "flavor of human feelings" retains its natural taste, untainted by modern preservatives.

"East is East and West is West," said Kipling, and in Taiwan seldom do the twain meet. Everything about the east coast is different from the west and north. As if to emphasize this inherent difference, the sun rises over the ocean at around 5 a.m., awakening the east while the west side slumbers in darkness. Then the sun abruptly disappears over the central range in the late afternoon, plunging the east coast into darkness while the rest of the island still basks in sunlight.

The sun and sea have shaped the east's lifestyle. People here are early to bed and early to rise, their skins burnished brown by constant exposure to the strong morning sun and their cheeks rosy from steady ocean winds and mountain mists. Farming and fishing— the fruits of sun and sea—remain the pillars of the east coast economy.

Eastern Taiwan is also "aborigine country." Its rugged mountains and deep inland valleys are home to many of Taiwan's indigenous tribes who still pursue lifestyles far from the mainstream of Chinese culture. The raw beauty and wild terrain here appeal to aboriginal senses, as they do to travelers with wanderlust for remote and unspoiled habitats where nature reigns supreme. On the east coast, the weather is far less predictable, seas are rougher, hot springs hotter, mountains higher, butterflies bigger, and the people more robust than in tamer regions of Taiwan. Travelers here are still welcomed with human hospitality—and curiosity.

Suao Harbor And 'Fisherman's Wharf'

A good place to begin an exploration of the east coast is **Suao**, Taiwan's fifth and newest international harbor. A convenient springboard between northern and eastern Taiwan, Suao is located at the southern terminus of the scenic Northeast Coast Highway, and at the northern end of the breathtaking East Coast Highway. It is also the major link on the spectacular new railway which connects Taipei to Hwalien.

Suao is an orderly Oriental seaport that looks a lot like Hong Kong's fabled harbor did 30 years ago. The new international facility occupies the northern sector of the harbor town. But the local color is concentrated two kilometers south, in the quaint coastal enclave called **Southside Suao**.

Here is the island's most enchanting "Fisherman's Wharf." Timeless Chinese fishing scenes are reflected in the bright pastel paints on vintage high-prowed fishing boats, the hoarse cries of fishmongers, and the heady blend of marine aromas. The marina is lined with seafood restaurants and interesting

Suao harbor
蘇澳

Southside Suao
南方澳

Preceding pages, east coast fishermen, left, Suao-Hwalien Highway. Suao Harbor, right.

souvenir shops. It is highly photogenic, but most of the liveliest action dies down after 9 a.m.

Some of the best seafood in Taiwan can be found in the restaurants along **Fisherman's Wharf Street**, a wharfside lane distinguished by its digital-clock tower (erected by the local Rotary Club) in the shape of a small lighthouse. The entire ground floor of the **Full-Catch Seafood Restaurant** at No. 93 is a big open aquarium, with large tanks displaying live moray eels, lobsters and crabs, turtles, frogs, jumbo prawns, flounder, tuna, shark, swordfish and several species whose names have no English-language equivalents. A specialty of local waters is "oil fish," a rich and tender whitefish.

Cliff-hanging by Motor Convoy

"Breathtaking" is not a cliché when applied to the roller-coaster, 111-kilometer (69-mile) route between Suao and Hwalien. This is literally a cliff-hanger, with the crashing breakers of the Pacific Ocean eroding the rocks 1,000 to 1,500 feet (300 to 450 meters) below the highway. Chiseled into sheer stone cliffs that rise in continual ridges, the road was first built in 1920. It requires constant maintenance to keep it open in the face of frequent rock slides.

As if to add to its interest, this is a one-way stretch of highway—in either direction. Every two hours or so, from dawn to dusk, convoys of private cars, taxis and buses depart from Suao and Hwalien. The Director of Tourism has recently announced plans to widen and expand the Suao-Hwalien highway. By 1988, travelers should be able to traverse this stretch in both directions at all times of day.

In the meantime, the 33 kilometers (20 miles) between Suao and **Tung-Ao**, south along the coast, are not subject to convoy schedules. Visitors can get a foretaste of the fabulous east coast scenery before actually committing themselves to the full trip to Hwalien.

Marble Metropolis of the East

Those who visit **Hwalien** will find it a pleasant, cheery town. With 90 percent of Hwalien County dominated by mountains, the city—the biggest settlement on Taiwan's east coast—entirely

Fisherman's Wharf Street
漁港路

Full-Catch Seafood Restaurant
全滿載

Tung-Ao
東澳

Hwalien
花蓮

Hwalien Martyrs Shrine.

fills the narrow strip of flat land separat-
ing the steep mountains from the sea.

Hwalien's greatest claim to fame is
marble. Billions of tons of pure marble
are contained in the craggy cliffs and
crevices of nearby Taroko Gorge. It is
mined by engineers from the **Retired
Servicemen's Engineering Agency**
(RSEA) headquartered in Hwalien. In
their main factory at 106 Hua-Hsi
Road, near the airport, great bargains
are available on marble lamps, ashtrays,
bookends, vases, goblets and dozens of
other crafted items. These are also
found at most handicraft shops.

Hwalien's finer hotels are notable for
their solid marble waste bins, marble
bathrooms, marble coffee tables, and
entire sidewalks of marble mosaic.
Travelers visiting Hwalien by air for the
first time are startled by the world's only
marble airport terminal.

Hwalien even boasts marble temples.
The **Temple of Eastern Purity**, located
on a hill downtown near the Marshal
Hotel, has floors, walls, columns and
shrines all constructed of local marble.
Within the hall sit three gilt Buddhas.
Behind the hall stands a modest pago-
da, with a small shrine at ground level.

The Hall of Motherly Love

But Hwalien's most renowned temple
predates the discovery of marble here,
and thus is constructed of traditional
materials. This is the Taoist **Hall of
Motherly Love**. The sculpted stonework
on its facade and columns, and its
painted door gods, are its most impressive elements—as in many other major
Taoist temples.

A very ornate shrine devoted to the
Regal Mother of the West occupies the
main hall. Prior to a renovation in 1983,
it was braced by two of the biggest
image cones on the east side of Taiwan,
indicating that this temple is generously
bankrolled by "big wheels" from the
wealthier west, in addition to more
frugal east coast donors. Two very old,
authentic shrines are built into alcoves
on either side of the central altar, each
with its own set of carved dragon columns and a pair of stone guardian lions.

Behind stands a new four-story annex
called the **Palace of the Jade Emperor**.
Here, there is extensive use of marble.
This remarkable building can house
2,000 pilgrims in three floors of dormitories, and can feed them in a huge

ground-floor dining room. A top-floor shrine to the Jade Emperor is surrounded by carved and cast icons representing every major religious tradition of China, a living example of the serene harmony maintained among rival deities in Chinese temples.

The Hall of Motherly Love is located near the end of Chung-Hwa Road, just before it crosses a small canal en route to Carp Lake. Major festivities occur here on the 18th day of the second lunar month, about six weeks after Chinese New Year. At that time, thousands of pilgrims from throughout Taiwan and East Asia converge on the temple to have chronic ills cured through faith and sorcery, receive the blessings of the priests, and leave donations for the temple's maintenance and expansion.

Dancers and Dragon Boats

Hwalien is home to Taiwan's largest aboriginal tribe, the Ami, numbering about 60,000. During the annual Ami Harvest Celebration in late July and August, the town is particularly festive. At other times, authentic performances of traditional tribal dances are staged

for visitors in two places. One is the large marble factory located along the road to Taroko Gorge. The other is the **Ami Culture Village**, located about a 15-minute drive from downtown.

But these centers offer more kitsch than class. Those seeking authentic glimpses of Ami life should try to visit the little coastal town of Feng-Pin, a half-hour drive south of Hwalien. The Harvest Festival's opening ceremonies are especially exciting at Feng-Pin.

The Hwalien **Martyrs Shrine**, built into a hillside on the northern outskirts of town, is an impressive architectural complex which reflects classical Chinese concepts of balance and proportion.

Hwalien's favorite recreational resort is scenic **Carp Lake**, a 30-minute drive by car southwest of the city. Set amid tropical fruit plantations in the foothills of the towering Central Range, this fish-shaped reservoir was created by a nearby dam. In June, the lake hosts colorful Dragon Boat races. Boating and fishing are always the main attractions at Carp Lake. Visitors must carry their own fishing gear, but row-boats, paddle boats and motorboats are all available for rent. Anglers who manage

Ami Culture
Village
阿美文化村

Martyrs
Shrine
忠烈祠

Carp Lake
鯉魚潭

Ami tribe
harvest
festival near
Hwalien.

to reel in one of the lake's famous 50-pound carp can have it cooked at one of the roadside restaurants.

Recently, Hwalien has added a new sport to island itineraries. You may now 'shoot the rapids' here along one of the roaring rivers that cascades down to the sea from the marble gorges of the Central Range.

Fabulous Taroko Gorge

Nine out of 10 people who visit Hwalien do so in order to tour **Taroko Gorge**, one of the most spectacular natural wonders of the world. By car, cab or bus, the route from Hwalien heads north for 15 kilometers (nine miles) through vast green plantations of papaya, banana and sugar cane. When it reaches **Hsin-Cheng**, it cuts west, straight into the cavernous, marble-rich gorge of Taroko.

"Taroko" means "beautiful" in the Ami dialect. Visitors immediately realize that the aboriginals who named the site were not exaggerating. A gorge of sheer marble cliffs, through which flows the torrential Li-Wu (Foggy) River, Taroko winds sinuously for 20 kilo-

meters (12 miles) from the coast to its upper end at Tien-Hsiang.

The first scenic points along the route are the **Light of Zen Monastery** and the **Shrine of Eternal Spring**. The latter is a memorial to the 450 retired servicemen who lost their lives constructing this road, known as the "Rainbow of Treasure Island." The shrine is perched on a cliff overlooking the boulder-strewn river, with a view of a waterfall pouring through a graceful moon bridge.

At **Swallows' Grotto**, the cliffs tower so tall on either side of the road that direct sunlight hits the floor of the gorge only around noon. The **Fuji Cliff** reels visitors' heads as they look up its sheer stone face, echoing the roar of the river below. The **Tunnel of Nine Turns** is a seemingly impossible feat of engineering—it cuts a crooked road of tunnels and half-tunnels through solid marble cliffs. It is difficult to imagine how anyone could have built a road like this.

The **Bridge of Motherly Devotion** is worth a stop to explore the rocky river bed, a jumble of huge marble boulders tossed carelessly down the gully by some ancient convulsion. A small marble pavilion stands on a hillock.

Taroko Gorge
太魯閣

Hsin-Cheng
新城

Fuji Cliff
福磯崖

Shrine of
Eternal Spring
長春祠

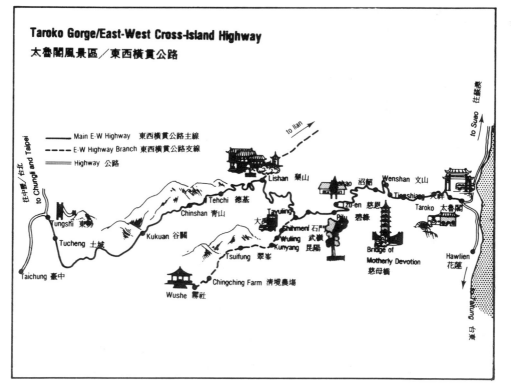

The final stop on the Taroko Gorge tour is **Tien-Hsiang**. Here, in the midst of astounding natural beauty, is the Tien-Hsiang Lodge, Overnight lodging and meals are available. A suspension bridge near the lodge leads across the Foggy River to an exquisite pagoda perched on a peak.

A few minutes' drive beyond Tien-Hsiang, a series of steps at the mouth of a tunnel lead down to the dramatic setting of the **Wen-Shan (Literary Mountain) Hot Springs**. The magnificent walk to the bottom of the gorge is an appetizer for the hot springs themselves. After a swaying suspension bridge crosses the Li-Wu River, steps carved into the cliffside lead to a large hot pool. It lies in an open cave of solid raw marble, directly adjacent to the rocky, rumbling river bed.

The water is crystal clear, despite heavy concentrations of sulfur and other minerals which stain the rocks and waft through the air. A spring lets the hot water seep through a crack in the cave wall; a drain hole empties the pool into the river. Bathers can enjoy the sensation of hot spring and cold river water rushing simultaneously over their limbs. Or they can first immerse in the hot pool, then float on their backs down the river rapids.

There are no showers or vendors to spoil the raw beauty of this spot, and large boulders provide the only cover for bathers changing their clothes. There is a guest house at the top of the gorge at Wen-Shan, however. From here, the East-West Highway continues in the direction of Taichung

Getting to Hwalien and Taroko

Travelers who forego the motor routes to this region have three other options to consider. A new railway links Hwalien with Taipei, with 90 kilometers (56 miles) of steel track that crosses 22 bridges and passes through 16 tunnels, one of them eight kilometers (five miles) long. The trip takes three hours and is usually heavily booked, so tickets should be purchased in advance.

China Airlines and Far East Air Transport offer frequent daily service to and from Hwalien's marble airport. FAT also flies to Hwalien from Kaohsiung. This makes it possible to leave Taipei in the early morning, tour Hwalien and all of Taroko Gorge by bus or

car, and return to Taipei by nightfall.

A sea journey from the northern port of Keelung is another alternative. The 10,000-ton *Hwalien* departs Keelung in the morning and takes five hours to reach the eastern gateway, hugging the scenic coastline all the way. Ordinary and first-class accommodations are available from the Taiwan Car Ferry Co.

The Road to Taitung

South of Hwalien, scenery along the East Coast Highway grows more gentle and pastoral. On one side, the deep blue waters of the Pacific either crash frothily against rocky capes or nuzzle the beaches of quiet coves. Inland, the Central Range forms a massive windscreen, sheltering brilliant green plantations and terraced paddies which cover every patch of arable land.

There are two alternate routes connecting Hwalien with Taitung. Both have their respective attractions. The foot-hill route features three rustic hot springs: **Jui-Sui Spa**, **Hung-Yeh Spa** and **Yu-Li Spa**. It follows the railway and runs parallel to the coast, about 30 kilometers (19 miles) inland. But most

travelers prefer the coastal route for its greater scenic attractions.

A large seated Buddha image, facing the sea some 15 kilometers (nine miles) south of Hwalien, draws the attention of those not "templed out." Another 25 kilometers (16 miles) is **Chi-Chi**, the first good swimming beach south of Hwalien. The small bay here has clear water for swimming, and sometimes the waves break perfectly for body surfing.

Caves and Terraces
Of the Immortals

About 60 kilometers (37 miles) south of Chi-Chi, near **Chang-Pin**, a tall craggy cliff juts into the ocean. This contains the **Caves of the Eight Immortals** and provides superb panoramic views of the east coast. Steps from the parking lot lead to Cave Two, where a shrine hall is built into the mouth of a large cavern facing the ocean, and Cave Three, wherein sit three garish pink Buddha images. The final ascent leads through bamboo thickets to the top of the bluff, Here, the trail splits. The right fork leads to the Sea Lightning Cave, a stone grotto where ascetics once lived and meditated. The left fork ascends to a topmost cave containing a crude shrine with several icons. On a clear day, far-sighted spectators can almost see the southern tip of Taiwan.

After the exertion of the climb, the black-sand beach at the foot of the cliffs is a refreshing place for a dip. There is another beach at **Chu-Hu** (Bamboo Lake) 10 kilometers further south.

Between Chu-Hu and Cheng-Kung, there is an outcropping of contorted coral rock known as the **Terrace of the Three Immortals**. A small islet is just beyond it. According to legend, three of the Eight Immortals stopped here to rest while en route to Peng-Lai, their magic island abode in the Pacific. An asphalt path winds through a maze of bizarre rock formations, with pavilions and picnic tables set up along the way.

A few kilometers further south is the quaint old fishing town of **Cheng-Kung**, whose name means "success." Taitung is still an hour-and-a-half drive from here; tardy travelers will find comfortable if simple accommodation at local inns.

Chi-Chi
磯碕海水浴場

Chu-Hu
竹湖海
水浴場

Terrace of
the Three
Immortals
三仙台

Caves of
the Eight
Immortals
八仙洞

Cheng-Kung
成功

Taitung.

Sleepy Taitung

Palace of the
Empress of
Heaven
天后宮

Carp Hill
鯉魚山

Cheng-Chi
Road
正氣路

Campers tug-
it-out on east
coast.

Perched on a bulge in the map of Taiwan's east coast, at about the same latitude as Kaohsiung, is the sleepy seaside city of **Taitung**. A pleasant, airy town which serves as economic hub for the lower portion of the east coast, Taitung is not much of a travelers' destination in itself. But it makes a convenient springboard for excursions to nearby places such as the Chi-Pen Hot Springs, Green and Orchid islands, and the East Coast Highway.

Within the city limits are a few sites worth visiting. The most popular attraction is **Carp Hill**, with its **Dragon and Phoenix Temple** providing fine views of the city and sea. The temple itself is not particularly noteworthy, except for some interesting icons and a small collection of 3,000 to 5,000-year-old archaeological artifacts recently unearthed in the area. These stone implements include coffin slabs and hand tools, and they prove that man lived in Taiwan long before the dawn of written history. The government plans to house them in a museum which, when completed, will become a major attraction.

On Chung-Hwa Road stands a modest Matsu temple called the **Palace of the Empress of Heaven**. The "Three Star Gods" of longevity, prosperity and posterity smile down from the central roof beam; the ornately enameled and gilt facade is also noteworthy.

Taitung's beach is located at the end of Ta-Tung Road off the main avenue. But the beach is not meant for swimmers. The entire Taitung shoreline froths and churns with rough breakers so turbulent that the water is brown with stirring sands 100 meters from shore. The nearest good swimming beaches are north (toward Hwalien) at Shanyuan, or south (past Chih-Pen) to the wide-open sands of Tai-Ma-Li.

On the plaza in front of the railway station are a half-dozen hotels with adequate facilities for overnight stays. There is good seafood in the eateries along **Cheng-Chi Road**.

Taitung can be reached directly by air from Taipei on Far East Air Transport, which operates two round-trip flights daily. Trains, buses, and the black diesel sedans called "wild-chicken taxis" connect Taitung with Hwalien.

Island Outposts

For the traveler with a taste for off-beat destinations, two islands easily reached from Taitung present worlds far from the mainstream of Chinese civilization.

Within sight of Taitung, about 33 kilometers (19 miles) almost due east, is **Green Island**. Originally called Fire Island because beacons burned there to prevent fishing vessels from wrecking on its coral shoals, it inherited its new name in 1949. The 16-square-kilometer (6.2-square-mile) island has recently been developed for tourism.

Green Island's human history began in 1805, when a fisherman from Little Liuchiu Island (off the southwest coast of Taiwan) was blown off course. Liking what he found, he returned to Liuchiu and persuaded his family and friends to move to this then-uninhabited island. Today, there are about 3,800 permanent residents.

The waters and reefs around Green Island are excellent for swimming, scuba diving, fishing and shell collecting. Trails lead into the hills for day hikers, and a paved 17-kilometer (10.5-mile) road circles the rim of the island.

At the northeast corner of Green Island is the **Kuan Yin Cave**. According to legend, an old fisherman lost his way at sea in a terrible storm about a century ago. Suddenly a fireball appeared in the sky. He let it guide him safely back to shore, where he found safe haven in this cave. Within it he saw a stone that resembled Kuan Yin, the goddess of mercy. Taking this as a divine sign, he prostrated himself before the stone and gave thanks for his safe return. Ever since, the cave has been sacred to the inhabitants of Green Island.

Green Island is accessible by air or sea. Yung-Hsing Airlines and Taiwan Aviation both offer service direct from Taitung. Meanwhile, two local ferries service the island from the fishing port of Fu-Kang, near Taitung. Both make overnight stops at Orchid Island—one of them en route to Green Island on Tuesday, the other after leaving Green Island on Saturday. Those choosing to stay over on Green Island will find a comfortable new hostel on the southern tip of the island.

Kuan Yin Cave
觀音洞

Green Island
綠島

Fu-Kang
富岡

Orchid Island, seashore, below, and Yami tribe resident, right.

Orchid Island
Lan Yu)
蘭嶼

Home of the Yami

Orchid Island is the most unlikely jewel in the waters surrounding Taiwan. An island of 45 square kilometers (17.4 square miles), it is 62 kilometers (39 miles) east of Taiwan's southern tip and 81 kilometers (50 miles) southeast of Taitung.

Also known as Lan Yu, Orchid Island is home to 2,600 Yami, Taiwan's smallest aboriginal tribe. With colorful native costumes and headgear and a strongly matriarchal society, the Yami are often regarded as the northernmost outpost of Polynesia. These people live simply by the sea, supplementing their daily catch with taro and a few fruits. Their boats, built with original hand tools and natural materials, are renowned for their beautiful decoration and perfect crafting.

The government has constructed concrete housing blocks on Orchid Island, but the Yami prefer living in their traditional homes, adapted by centuries of use to their indigenous environment. Built securely underground against hillsides or embankments as protection from the fierce typhoons which rip across the island every year, these homes provide rooms for weaving, ceramics making, storage and other practical functions as well as eating and sleeping. Open pavilions are constructed on stilts, for sultry summer days.

One reason for the relatively pristine condition of Yami culture is that the Japanese, during their occupation of Taiwan in the first half of the 20th Century, isolated the island as a living anthropological museum. Modern appliances were not permitted, and the ancient culture was preserved as much as possible in its original form. The Yami today seem all the happier for it.

The entire beautiful island can be driven around in about two hours. Wild orchids flourish amid the trees, and mangoes and coconuts grow in abundance. Many segments of the shoreline, however, are off-limits to visitors due to military installations.

The best time of year to visit Orchid Island is spring, a festive season when new boats are launched with much fanfare and the Yamis' favorite delicacy— flying fish—literally leaps into their boats.

There are adequate accommodations and meals at the **Yeh Yio Guest House** and the **Orchid Island Inn**. Yung-Hsing Airline flies six times daily between Taitung and Orchid Island. Taiwan Aviation also connects Orchid Island with Taitung, as well as Taipei and Kaohsiung. There is also the ferry service from the port of Fu-Kang.

The 'Source of Wisdom'

Tucked against the mountainside at the mouth of a rugged canyon along the rocky Chih-Pen River is **Chih-Pen Spa**, one of Taiwan's oldest, quaintest and most remote hot-spring resorts. Dubbed the "Source of Wisdom" by the Japanese, it was developed as a resort by these foreign Asian occupants around the turn of the 20th Century.

Chih-Pen village lies along the coast 12 kilometers (7½ miles) south of Taitung. The spa is another two kilometers inland. This is almost as far away as one can get from big, bustling Taipei, both in spirit and in distance, and still be on Taiwan.

The Chih-Pen Valley, which cuts into the steep mountains behind the spa, is highly reminiscent of the gorgeous wild gorges hidden deep within the remote

mountain ranges of western Szechuan province. Here are thick forests and clear streams, steep cliffs and cascading waterfalls, bamboo groves and fruit orchards, robust mountain dwellers and exotic flora and fauna.

The "inn place" to stay at Chih-Pen is the charming **Chih-Pen Hotel**, one of the most amenable hot-springs inns on the entire island. Its bronze fountain and neatly sculpted hedges make it easily distinguishable from the half-dozen or so other hotels lining the roadside at the resort. (If there is any confusion, remember: it is the last one on the left.)

The Chih-Pen Hotel boasts the biggest and best outdoor mineral pools in all of Taiwan. Set against the tangled mountain behind the hotel, the triple pool is canopied by cliff-hanging banyans and swaying palms. It is constructed entirely of smooth cobblestones and oddly shaped rocks. The hottest pool is unbearable for those with tender feet and other extremities. But the medium one is just right for long, soothing soaks. The hot pools are about five meters (16 feet) wide and 1½ meters (five feet) deep, and are fed directly by springs bubbling from the mountain. The adjacent cool pool, fed by a waterfall contrived to drop from an overhanging tree, is big enough to swim laps. Use of these pools is free to Chih-Pen Hotel guests, but anyone may enter and soak there for a nominal gate fee.

Because it is hot and strong, the Chih-Pen mineral water is good for therapeutic bathing. Six soaks of 15 to 20 minutes over a period of two days are guaranteed to alleviate the following ailments: skin irritations and festering sores, rheumatic inflamations, arthritis, lower spine and sciatic pain, weak limbs, poor circulation and sluggish digestion. Non-believers are urged to try the following regimen:

To begin with, soak in one of the hot pools for at least 15 minutes. Slide into the cool pool and swim slowmotion around the rim, using breaststroke or sidestroke. Freestyle swimming is too splashy here; the idea is to reach long and stretch the muscles slowly, rather than pump them full of adrenalin. Stand beneath the waterfall and feel a thousand leathery palms pound your back with a natural water massage, guaranteed to iron the kinks from the most tightly knotted necks, and to

Chih-Pen
Hot Springs
知本溫泉

Chih-Pen
Spa.

loosen the stiffest shoulders. Then drift back to the hot pools and slip in for another long soak, repeating the process at least twice. It's guaranteed to make a new person out of the weariest wayfarer.

The best times to enjoy the pools are at night—when strings of colored lights lend a festive air to the surrounding gardens—and at daybreak—when wild monkeys laugh and chatter as they gather breakfast from the trees above. Sundays and holidays are crowded dates that should be avoided; this is when Chinese customarily pack their families into cars and "head for the hills."

'Clear Awakening'
In the Valley of Wisdom

The **Chih-Pen Valley** is worth a thorough exploration by foot between dips in the spa. A few hundred meters beyond the resort village, a sign points left toward the **White Jade Waterfall**. The falls lie about one kilometer up a winding paved path which echoes loudly with the full-throated calls of strange birds and insects. The waters of White Jade tumble down a jumble of strewn boulders, dense growth of fern and bamboo, and gnarled roots.

A few kilometers up the road from the falls stands the arched entrance to the **Chih-Pen Forest Recreation Area**. A swaying suspension bridge crosses the river to the park area. This wooded world of walking trails, campgrounds, arbors and greenhouses, streams and waterfalls, pavilions and ancient "holy" trees, has few visitors.

The biggest visitor treat in the Chih-Pen Valley is the **Clear Awakening Monastery**, located up a steep hill less than a kilometer from the spa, between the falls and the park. A brace of big male and female elephants in white plaster stand at the foot of the steps to the elegant shrine hall. While Taoist temples display the dragon and tiger, the elephant is strictly a Buddhist motif.

Inside the hall are two of the most exquisite, tranquil and beautifully crafted Buddha images in all of Taiwan. The two statues sit together, one behind the other, gazing in meditative serenity through half-lidded eyes, exuding feelings of sublime harmony. The Brass Buddha, 10 feet tall and 2,500 pounds, was made in Thailand; it occupies the

rear of the shrine. The priceless White Jade Buddha, eight feet tall and 10,000 pounds, is seated in a lotus flower in the foreground. This solid jade image was a gift from Chinese Buddhists in Burma. The presence of such artistically perfect and obviously precious icons is an indication that very powerful monks inhabit this remote monastery.

Along the altar before the White Jade Buddha are arrayed a row of much smaller but equally lovely icons. Visitors should remove their shoes and approach across the carpet for a closer look. To the left of the altar is a small solid-gold, jewel-encrusted pagoda encased in glass. This houses two of the mysterious relics of the Buddha known as *ssu-li-tzu*, tiny hard nuggets extracted from the Buddha's ashes after his cremation over 2,500 years ago. A series of graphic color prints from India are arranged along the upper walls. Captioned in Sanskrit, these illustrate milestone events in the life of the historical Buddha.

On the ground floor is a study hall and lecture room where the monastic community meets to study the sutras. Next to the shrine hall is a dormitory

with communal and private rooms for visitors who wish to stay a night or two, and a dining room which serves good Buddhist vegetarian cuisine. Gangly banyans and lush green mountains surround the monastery, and silence reigns supreme.

Toward the Southern Tip

Perhaps no stretch of major road in Taiwan is as untrammeled as the section between Taitung and Oluanpi at the island's southernmost tip. Trains do not run here. Public buses do, but it is far more convenient and pleasurable to cover this portion by private car or taxi.

Twelve kilometers (7½ miles) south of Chih-Pen lies the town of **Tai-Ma-Li**. A 100-meter-wide beach of gray sand and small smooth pebbles runs for about 15 kilometers (nine miles) along the shoreline. The sparkling blue water is completely free of pollution, the surf is gentle, and privacy is as abundant as the beach itself.

Tai-Ma-Li is principally a fishing town and its fishermen use unique motorized rafts. They are built by lashing together a half-dozen six-meter plastic water pipes, bracing them with bamboo, and binding them with bailing wire. Japanese outboard motors provide the needed power. Fishing and swimming trips can be arranged through the Chih-Pen Hotel.

A few kilometers beyond the village of **Ta-Wu**, some 40 kilometers (25 miles) past Tai-Ma-Li, the main road (Route 9) cuts inland to cross the lower spine of the Central Range. Two hours after leaving Chih-Pen, travelers are deposited at **Feng-Kang** on Taiwan's west coast. From Feng-Kang, highways proceed north to Kaohsiung and south to Kenting and Oluanpi.

Beyond Route 9's cross-island turn-off, the coast road continues south to within 40 kilometers of Oluanpi before it terminates. Eventually this road will complete a circuit right down to Oluanpi, so that one may drive around the southernmost tip without crossing the mountains.

The traveler can go no further from Taipei without leaving the island. It is obvious that the further one travels away from the capital, the more enchanting and unsullied Taiwan becomes.

Tai-Ma-Li
太麻里

Ta-Wu
大武

Feng-Kang
楓港

Left, Clear Awakening Monastery Buddha images. Right, east coast city via bicycle.

232

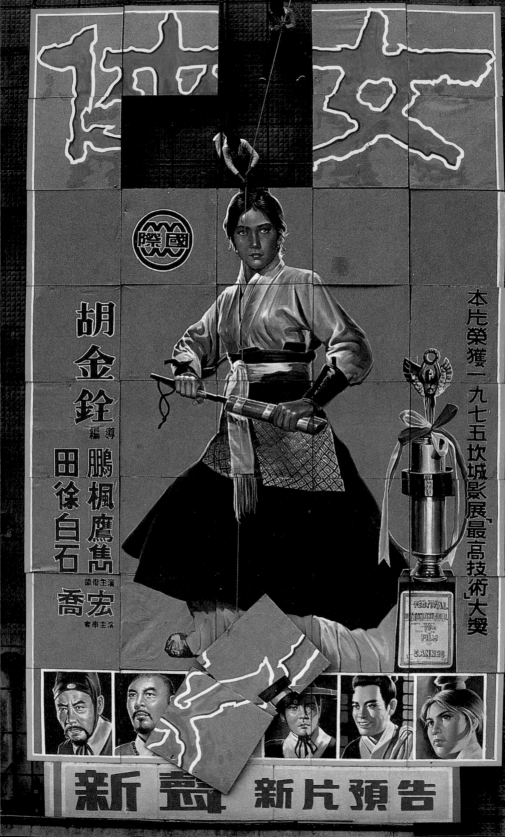

THE TAIWAN TALENT AND VARIETY SHOW

Taiwan has long been a treasure house of talent that has entertained people throughout Asia and many other parts of the world. Its movies, with their emphasis on spectacle and impossible feats of martial artistry, pack theaters every day. Its television dramas, which twist and turn through plots set in the Imperial past and inimical present, command legions of devoted followers. Its entertainers enliven nightclubs overseas, from Singapore to Tokyo.

Taiwan's talents have even overcome the bonds of mass entertainment and made giant strides into the realm of class entertainment. Serious theater, modern dance and classical music have become an increasingly important component of the island's contemporary repertoire. And these arts, like its exports of popular entertainment, are beginning to attract international attention.

Cradle of Kung-fu Films

Taiwan's long romance with the making of motion pictures dates back even before the Republic of China moved its operations to Taipei. The Republic's first film, produced on the mainland, was *The Orphan Who Saved His Grandfather*. It was first screened in 1922.

The film industry enjoyed a "golden age" during the 1930s and 1940s, as Shanghai became the Chinese equivalent of Hollywood. The years of political upheaval and war, however, slowed any great development in the industry until the move to Taiwan. In cooperation with the British colony of Hong Kong, filmmaking entered a period of rehabilitation in 1952. During the next five years, the island's producers began turning out new movies that were marketed in Singapore and Malaysia, as well as locally.

The government spurred the rapid growth of the industry by merging the Taiwan Motion Picture Corporation and the Agricultural Education Motion Picture Corporation into the Central Motion Picture Corporation in 1954. The influx of filmmakers from Hong Kong, who preferred the natural locations and low costs of production in Taiwan, also contributed to the business.

Initially, most of the local movies were dubbed in Amoy, the local dialect often called Taiwanese. The first 35 mm color film produced in Taiwan was the 1957 production of *Liang Hung Yu*, the story of a heroine of the Sung dynasty. It is a tribute to Taiwan's filmmakers and in that same year they captured an award at the Third International Festival of Special Films in Rome for another movie about an ancient heroine, *Hua Mu Lan*.

The first private concern to begin turning out films in the national language, Mandarin, was Kuo Lien Film Company, a joint venture of Taiwan and Hong Kong entrepreneurs. Their first offerings hinged on war themes and literary works. Later, they hit on a formula that was to make Taiwan a motion picture force to be reckoned with throughout the world. Kuo Lien filled its films with action and eventually packed them with martial arts sequences. Soon the sequences were drawn out into entire films full of flying fists, kicking feet, swishing swords, staffs and fans. By the 1970s, the martial arts genre was a firmly-established film form with a passionate international following.

Taiwan's golden age of filmmaking began in 1967. The government, increasingly aware of the cultural and financial benefits of movie exports, put technical and monetary assistance behind the business. Import quotas for foreign films were raised as an incentive for increasing production. Import taxes for overseas Chinese films were rebated to talented studios to encourage local productions. And the Golden Horse Award was established. Like Hollywood's Oscars, it provide recognition to outstanding Mandarin films, actors, actresses and directors.

By the end of the 1970s, the studios of Taiwan, often working with production companies from Hong Kong, were prosperous. The island currently produces more than 150 films each year.

The Movies Grow Up

The cost of the average film made in Taiwan is still a pittance by Hollywood standards. Actors, directors, sets, costumes, publicity and everything else combined

Preceding pages, students perform traditional music at Sun Yat-sen Memorial Hall. Left, workmen piece together massive movie poster in Taipei's West Gate Theater District.

average about US$150,000 per film compared to the multi-million dollar budgets of American movies. But the release of a war extravaganza called *The Longest Night* in 1983 has threatened those low costs. China Film Corporation spent an estimated $1.25 million on that production. If other directors follow the trend toward more expensive productions — and it appears they will — the number of films made in Taiwan each year could be drastically reduced.

Critics have also warned that local audiences as well as the overseas faithful have begun to tire of the formula-action epics and soppy love stories that have been a staple of Taiwan directors for years. On an encouraging note, the Wan Nien Motion Picture Corporation released an unassuming film in

important center of movie production.

Another notable film of recent vintage that held promise of a new artistic trend in Taiwan's filmmaking community was *In Our Time*. Produced by the Central Motion Picture Corporation, it showcased the work of four of Taiwan's most talented young directors in an anthology of four short stories that touched on cerebral concerns rather than exploitative themes. It was composed of Jim Tao's *Sleepwalk*, a tale of childhood innocence coming to grips with the reality of adulthood; Edward Yang's *Expectation*, which looked at the budding sexual desires of a local schoolgirl in the 1960s; Ko I-cheng's *Jumping Frog* a commentary of the anger and idealism of youth that focuses on a nationalistic university

1983 called *Growing Up*. Produced for a mere U.S.$112,500, the movie won audiences as well as critical praise with its endearing story of a young boy who grows up in a traditional, middle-class Taiwan family. There were no established big name stars in the cast and there was little action. But a good script and sensitive acting provided strong emotional impact that found a hungry, new audience.

Growing Up won a special award at a film festival in Spain. But more importantly, the Republic of China government awarded its producers an incentive sum of NT $1.4 million (U.S. $35,000) in recognition of the fact that the direction of its filmmakers must change if the island wishes to remain an

student in the 1970s; and *Your Name Please* by Chang Yi, an ironic slap at the lack of communication in the '80s. *Asiaweek* magazine called the film "an intimate portrait of growing up which stands as much for Taiwan society as any of its members."

Exporting TV Shows and Musical Talent

The world of Mandarin-language television programs, like that of films, has also long been dominated by entertainment spe-

Above, graduation recital of Chinese Cultural University's Department of Dance. Right, popular entertainers on Taiwan television show.

cials and dramas from Taiwan. Television was introduced to the island in 1962 and now consists of three networks all operated as private enterprises that rely on advertising revenues for their income. The industry has its own awards for achievement, the Golden Bell Awards, and a Television Academy of Arts and Sciences with a membership of more than 1,200.

Crews from Hong Kong, Singapore and other Asian nations all look to Taiwan for inspiration and technical training. The result has been the export of a similar look to the shows of those nations including a proliferation of lengthy soap operas and musical variety programs. But Taiwan may also lead the way into new fields of programming. In 1982, a two-hour China Television (CTV)

melancholy lyrical songs have even become hot, black market items on the Chinese mainland. And the name of Tracy Huang, who was born in Taiwan and played the Taipei hotel circuit before taking up residence in Singapore, has become virtually a household word in Chinese communities for her ability to add an oriental touch to popular Western songs.

Yet singers like Teng and Huang have often attracted yawns from critics for their soft, syrupy lends of Western melodies and Mandarin lyrics. It came as a major surprise then that one of the blockbuster albums of 1982 was from a brooding young rock poet of the Bob Dylan/Bruce Springsteen mold. Luo Ta-you, along with singer-songwriter Hou Te-chien, has

dramatic production, *The Homecoming* won a Golden Bell Award for Best Television Drama of the year. Its vivid, realistic portrayal of working mothers in Taiwan proved a marked shift from the traditional, soap opera style presentations of the local networks.

Exports of Taiwan's entertainment specials have been important to the island's talents in other ways. Many entertainers have gotten their first international exposure on such programs, then have gone on to play the nightclub and concert circuits of Asia, and sometimes other regions of the world, and to register hit songs on the Top Ten lists of foreign radio stations.

Cassette tapes of Theresa Teng's most

headed up what Hong Kong Commercial Radio producer Jimmy Fung has called a "breakthrough" on the Taiwan popular music scene.

Luo has taken Western rock and reggae forms and wedded them with incisive observations about life. In "Little Town of Lukang," for instance, from his best-selling first album, he makes the poignant statement "Taipei isn't my home. My home has no neon lights." Inevitably, the candor of Luo's lyrics have met with some frowns from Taiwan's censors. "Chi Hu Che Ye," from a later album was banned from island airwaves, probably because of its cynicism. Yet Luo performed the song at a standing-room only concert in Taipei's Sun Yat-sen

Memorial Hall.

Luo has even taken traditional Chinese folksongs like the popular "Dance of Spring" and given them a fresh contemporary treatment. His popularity has reached beyond the shores of his homeland to Hong Kong and other Asian countries.

Dance, Music and Theater

Taiwan's rise to prominence in the more culturally-oriented entertainment venues is a relatively recent phenomenon. Unlike performances of Peking Opera, Taiwanese Opera and of Chinese folk dance and music, the rise has been led by groups that have blended the best features of Western and

Chinese movement and music.

Probably the most renowned troupe in international circles is Taipei's Cloud Gate Dance Ensemble. Led by the innovative choreography and direction of Lin Hwaimin, the group won worldwide recognition during a tour of Europe in 1981.

The Cloud Gate ensemble has managed to successfully combine traditional Chinese dance techniques with the contemporary choreography of the West. All of its pieces are performed to music written by contemporary Chinese composers, itself an amalgam of local and foreign rhythms.

The success of the Cloud Gate company has sparked the establishment of other ensembles, some private, some attached to educational institutions.

Western classical music, as well as new compositions by local Chinese composers, are performed by groups including the Taiwan Provincial Symphony Orchestra and the Taipei Municipal Symphony Orchestra.

Western-style drama has become a potent force in Taiwan's cultural milieu during the 1980s. In 1982, a short story by Taiwan's renowned author Pai Hsien-yung was transformed into a spectacular stage play that cost more than U.S. $100,000 and sold out an entire eight-day run at the 2,600 seat Sun Yat-sen Memorial Hall in Taipei. Called *Wandering in the Garden/Waking from a Dream* or *WW* for short, the show capitalized on the author's insistence that the play "resemble a Chinese painting which should be patiently observed for its details and enjoyed for its lively colors."

Thus, while using magnificent backdrops, sets and costumes that rivaled those of its own Chinese operas, the Western-style plotting and vehicle proved a hit with Taipei audiences. Even a major film star, Lisa Lu, chose to forsake the security of the movie cameras to appear in the live production.

The *WW* production was quickly followed by another spectacular produced by the Chinese Cultural University. Written by C.Y. Yen, the play called *Black-and-White*, was performed at the National Taiwan Arts Center. Its cast included a crowd of intergalatic beings, dancing pet animals that did a Rockettes kick type number, a pair of comic monks, a Chinese Opera clown and a Chinese-speaking E.T. The show climaxed with the landing of a spaceship over the heads of the audience.

Beneath all the frivolity, Yen insisted his play had a fundamental and universal theme that touched on the meaning of life. The success of the two productions even led the Mong Tai Chi Film Co. to contribute NT $1 million (U.S. $25,000) to the support of stage productions by local universities and schools provided they are performed free of charge for the general public.

The future of serious drama has also been buoyed by the success of the Experimental Drama Festival held at Taipei's National Arts Center in August, 1983. Six locally-produced and written plays were performed ranging from a musical drama to brief comedies. The festival drew a record-breaking audience that pulled the festival out of the red for the first time in its four-year history.

Above, a member of the Cloud Gate Dance Ensemble in performance. Right, mellow sounds from a classical Chinese musical instrument.

CHINESE OPERA: SPECTACLE AS AN ART

Westerners commonly cringe when they first encounter the shrill tones of traditional Chinese Opera. Their ears are unaware such sounds exist.

To the ears of aficionados, however, the high-pitched notes lend emotional strength to the song lyrics, and the prolonged wails accentuate the singers' moods. When added to the traditional accompaniment of thumping drums, clanging gongs, whining flutes and screeching violins, the end result is an ancient sound so abstract it might have been concocted by a modern composer.

The music provides the beat and the backing for a visual spectacle: the electric shades of painted faces, the glittering rainbow of costumes, the exquisite pantomime and the impossible acrobatics. The utterly unique blend of sound and spectacle that results is called *Jing Hsi*, Capital Opera, also known as Peking Opera.

Tea House Theatrics

Peking Opera was formally established in 1790 in the city for which it is named. That was the year the most famous actors from all corners of the Chinese Empire gathered in Peking to present a special variety show for the emperor. The performance proved so successful that the artists remained in the capital city, combining their ancient individual disciplines of theater, music and acrobatics into the form of Peking Opera that inspired contemporary performance styles.

The first venue for these spectaculars were the tea houses of the capital city. With greater popularity and increased complexity of performances, the tea houses evolved into theaters. But the carnival atmosphere persists. Today's Taiwanese audiences eat, drink and gossip their way through the operas in tried-and-true fashion, only to fall silent during famous scenes and solo arias. It may seem rude to Western viewers, but when the Chinese attend an opera, they go intent on enjoying themselves. Since audiences in Taiwan and in other Chinese communities know all the plots of the operas by heart and all the performers by reputation,

they know exactly when to pay undivided attention to the stage action and when to indulge in other pleasures.

The Good, the Bad
And the Green

Chinese Opera has no equivalent in the West. It bears only minor similarities to the classic European style of opera. Thematically, the stories play like high melodrama complete with good guys and bad guys who are clearly defined by their costumes and

face paint. The themes are all drawn from popular folklore, ancient legends and historical events tantamount to Greek mythology or the legends surrounding King Arthur.

It is in terms of technique, however, that Chinese Opera emerges unique among the world's theatrical forms. The vehicles of expression blend singing, dancing, mime and acrobatics and utilize sophisticated symbolism in costumes, make-up and stage props.

Each of the vehicles of Chinese Opera comprises an art form in itself. The use of face paint, for instance, is divided into 16 major categories representing more than 500 distinctive styles. Despite the complexity and enormous array of facial ornamentation, proper application of the paint imparts a

Preceding pages, some fearsome faces of Peking Opera. Right, hitting the high notes during an opera performance. Left, making up for the show.

character with a distinct identity. "The moment we see the face we know exactly who he is and the nature of his character," said a devoted Taipei opera fan.

History credits the invention of the make-up techniques to Prince Lan-Ling, who ruled over the northern Wei Kingdom during the 6th Century A.D. His own features were so effeminate, the prince designed a fierce face-mask to improve his appearance and his chances on the battlefield. The ruse worked wonders. Lan-ling easily defeated enemy forces that far outnumbered his own. His savage mask was later adapted for dramatic use during the ensuing Tang Dynasty. To facilitate the actors' movements and their ability to sing, the design was painted directly onto their faces.

and everything evil.
● Gold is the exclusive color of gods and benevolent spirits.

The extensive use of pantomime in Chinese Opera virtually eliminates the need for elaborate stage sets. And the few backdrops and props that are incorporated in a performance are put to ingenious uses.

The 'Water Sleeve' and Other Inventions

One inventive prop that is actually part of a performer's costume is the "water sleeve," often used to mime emotion and imply environmental conditions. These long, white armlets of pure silk are attached to the

Each color used in painting performers' faces for Chinese Opera has its own basic properties:

● Red is reserved for a good character who is loyal, upright and straight-forward.
● White denotes a crafty, cunning, highly resourceful character like a clown or a criminal.
● Blue represents a vigorous, wild, brave and enterprising character.
● Black is used in honest, upright roles.
● Yellow dominates an intelligent but somewhat reserved character.
● Brown indicates a strong character with stubborn temperament.
● Green is the earmark of ghosts, demons

standard sleeves of the costume and trail down to the floor when loose. Although it is merely an extra length of cloth, the expressive power of the water sleeve can be remarkable when flicked by expert wrists. To express surprise or shock a performer simply throws up his arms. The sleeves fly backwards in an alarming manner. An actor wishing to convey embarrassment or shyness daintily holds one sleeve across the face as if hiding behind it. Determination and bravery can be emphasized by flicking the sleeves

Above, the obligatory family dispute scene in a Chinese opera. Right, a Taipei puppeteer puts his wooden performers through operatic paces.

quickly up around the wrists, then clasping the hands behind the back. A worried character rubs his hands over one another quickly and repeatedly. The furled sleeves tremble on the wrists.

The range of symbolic gestures made possible by the water sleeve is endless. These complement other expressive gestures in mime. Performers dust themselves off to indicate that they have just returned from a long journey. They form the sleeves into a muff around the clasped hands as protection against the cold weather of a winter scene. To cope with hot summer weather, the sleeves are flapped like a fan.

Simple devices like the water sleeve, with its wide range of expression, make stage props generally unnecessary. The few that

Chinese Opera also employs single props for a variety of uses. As simple an item as a chair is exactly what it appears to be when sat upon. But when placed upon a table, a chair is transformed into a mountain. Or it can be used as a throne. If an actor jumps off a chair, he has committed suicide by flinging himself into a well. After that, long strips of paper may be hung from just above his ears to indicate he has become a ghost.

With some basic grounding in the rich symbolism of the costumes, props, face paints and mime gestures, even a spectator who doesn't understand a word of Chinese may be able to follow the plot of a performance of Peking Opera.

While neon-colored costumes and dazzling make-up can enthrall audiences for

are used have obvious connotations. Spears and swords come into play during battle and action scenes. The long, quivering peacock plumes attached to the headgear of some actors identify them as warriors. Ornate riding crops with silk tassels tell any tuned-in Chinese audience that the actors are riding horses. Black pennants carried swiftly across the stage symbolize a thunderstorm, but four long pennants held aloft on poles represent a regiment of troops. A character riding a chariot holds up two yellow banners horizontally about waist high, each painted with a wheel. An actor who appears bearing a banner with the character for *bao*, which means report, is a courier delivering an important message from afar.

hours, the long intervals of song and dialogue can invariably induce bouts of boredom. But just as attention begins to drift, the performances are punctuated by rousing feats of athletics and prestidigitation. In fact, it is often difficult to distinguish the magic tricks from the acrobatics.

Flying Feet, Magic Feats

Chinese Operas don't unfold on a stage. They leap, bound and bounce into action. Performers appear to have an uncanny knack for doing one mid air somersault more than is humanly possible before they return to earth. Hands become feet and upside-down stomachs become grotesque, faces, as two or more acrobats link arms and legs to become one fantastic creature.

The most thrilling portions of Chinese Opera are indisputably the battle scenes. They employ every form of martial art and acrobatic maneuver conceivable—and then some. Sabers, axes and fists fly through the air in a manner that would end in buckets of bloodletting in the hands of novices. The stars of Chinese Opera can fling a sword high in the air—and somehow, quite miraculously, catch it in the razor thin slit of its scabbard.

A famous manuever of the most famous star of 20th Century Peking Opera, Mei Lan-fang, was the celebrated "kite's turn." Mei, a consummate male actor who specialized in playing female roles, is remembered

for his enduring performance as the fickle Yang Gui-fei in an opera called *The Drunken Concubine*. Yang Gui-fei was the favorite consort of the emperor Tang Ming-huang of the Tang Dynasty. In the play, Mei Lan-fang exquisitely portrayed the pampered concubine as she slipped ever deeper into a drunken stupor. The scene culminates with the "kite's turn."

The maneuver began with Mei Lan-fang lifting—with his teeth—a cup of wine from a tray held by trembling eunuchs. He drained the cup dry and made a 180-degree turn. Then Mei arched over backwards and bent almost double to replace the cup on the tray, never once using his hands nor spilling

a drop of wine. Mei is highly revered by Taiwan's opera companies and fans and *The Drunken Concubine* remains a favorite on the island. The emperor Tang Ming-huang, who was eventually obliged by disgruntled troops to execute his beloved but bibulous concubine, was a great patron of the performing arts and has been consecrated as the patron saint of Chinese Opera.

Male Females

Traditionally, female roles in Chinese Opera were performed by impersonators like the incomparable Mei Lan-fang, but modern performances usually employ women as women. Yet the old impersonators perfected such stylized feminine gestures that aspiring actresses find themselves in the odd position of having to learn to imitate a man imitating a woman.

Aside from the introduction of women, Chinese Opera continues to flourish in Taiwan in all the splendor and classical pageantry of its traditional form. The route to becoming an accomplished performer is a grueling one. Most children begin attending classes in opera schools as early as age seven and instruction requires at least eight years. The most noted training center in Taiwan is the Fuhsing Opera School which offers full tuition for Peking Opera, but requires students to take standard educational courses along with the rigorous operatic training.

In addition to Peking Opera, an offshoot simply called "Taiwan Opera" has become popular on the island. Taiwan Opera is usually performed outdoors on elevated stages in public markets. The shows incorporate sparkling costumes and elaborate backdrops.

The innovations in Taiwan Opera range from the use of Taiwanese dialect, instead of the difficult Hu Bei dialect of Peking Opera, to disco-colored robes and western make-up techniques. These changes have expanded the popularity of Chinese Opera to the average man on the street.

Taiwanese Opera's most famous star is Yang Lee Hwa. In a switch on the old custom of having males play the female role, Miss Yang exclusively plays the roles of male characters.

Traditional Chinese puppet shows are also staged frequently throughout Taiwan. They are based on the themes, roles, music and costumery of Peking Opera.

Left, a performer waits his turn in the wings of a Taiwanese Opera. Right, painted puppets sport the familiar costumes of Peking opera.

NIGHTS OF WHITE SATIN

Nights in white satin,
Never reaching the end . . .
— *The Moody Blues*

Day is night in Taipei. Night is day. Darkness and light are petty distractions to its people.

Banks of electric moonbeams pump daylight through the din of a Chinese restaurant, long after dusk. Sparks of brilliance fuel the blaze of a marketplace brimming with diners, shoppers, lovers. The slit in a snake's skin drips blood and bile into a cup of herbal spirits. Shadows beckon. Ivory beauty rustles under its sultry veil of jet black hair, inside a *cheong-sam* of white satin. The slit of the gown exposes a thigh soft as silk. The scent is jasmine. The whispers are warm. The secrets of the Orient tumble out. Or do they?

This is Taipei. Exotic, mysterious, quixotic. A queen of the Far East. Night never ends. And nothing is as it seems.

Something For Everyone

A renowned Confucian philosopher named Ko-dze, who lived in China more than 2,000 years ago, summed it all up: "Food and sex are man's most natural pursuits." Sybarites follow Ko-dze's advice with gourmet refinement and unabashed gusto in Taipei. To satisfy their appetites, thousands of restaurants, bars, clubs, pubs, dance halls, wine houses, even barber shops, conduct business at all hours with a style and variety that overwhelm the novice.

The Chinese of Taiwan are an industrious lot. They pursue the two goals of profit and productivity with relentless drive and genuine enthusiasm. They pursue pleasure with equal determination. By night or day, there is little distinction between hard work and hard play. It's not uncommon for a day of nightlife to begin when the sun is still high in the afternoon sky. All it takes to enjoy a "night" in Taipei is stamina.

It may also take a well-lined wallet. The Chinese are big spenders when it comes to evening entertainment. A big bill earns a Chinese host "big face." Fortunately, many local businessmen are blessed with generous

Left, a Hong Kong song stylist croons in Cantonese at the Sunshine City Restaurant in Taipei.

expenses accounts. They do not flinch when presented a bill for NT $10,000 (US$250) at the end of an evening of fun at their favorite club. In fact, friends often fight over the bill at the end of a banquet or binge—for the privilege of paying it. The Western custom of "going Dutch" by splitting the bill equally is alien and ungracious to the Chinese.

Food and drink go together in Chinese society. A night on the town usually begins with a meal, not after it. The beer, wine and spirits are ordered along with dinner. And the liquid refreshment rarely stops flowing. "When drinking among intimate friends, even a thousand rounds are not enough," proclaims an ancient Chinese proverb. Again, many of the people of Taiwan take that advice to heart. Inebriation is a form of convivial communication here, an opportunity to drop the formal masks of business and reveal the "inner man."

Officially, the stroke of midnight signals the end to nightlife in Taipei. Bars, clubs and discos are supposed to close for business. Indeed, their neon lights punctually blink off. But listen carefully. The sound of laughter still emanates from behind drawn curtains. Knock on a few doors. Nightlife is still beginning. Nothing is as it seems.

Sugar Daddy Row

During Taipei's heyday as a "Rest and Relaxation" haven for weary American soldiers fighting the Vietnam War, nightlife flourished, particularly along "Sugar Daddy Row," the area around Shuang Cheng Street near the President Hotel. It was the equivalent of Bangkok's Patpong district, Manila's Ermita and Seoul's Itaewon.

Those days ended after the Vietnam War, and when the American military abruptly departed Taiwan in the wake of United States "de-recognition" of the Republic of China government in 1979. Taipei's nightlife along Sugar Daddy Row and other areas has since reverted to Chinese-flavored tastes. Pubs and discos have recently made a comeback in Taiwan in their typically tame Western versions, but dedicated night owls prefer the Chinese scene.

Visitors who would rather trod tested paths will find plenty of Western-oriented cocktail lounges, restaurants, entertainment and dancing in Taipei. An evening can begin with "cocktail hour" in the lobby bars of popular hotels like the Hilton and the Lai Lai Sheration. The lobby lounge at the Beverly Plaza exudes a subdued and peaceful ambiance. The Ambassador Hotel's Sky-Lounge offers exactly what it promises— sweeping views of twinkling downtown Taipei with cocktails in cozy booths built for two. Good cocktail bars in leading Western restaurants include those at Europa Haus, Le Corsaire Breton, Chalet Swiss and Zumfass.

The current Western craze in Taipei is the traditional English-style pub, where draught beer and liquors are served in an informal atmosphere complete with dart boards, honeycombed with holes from heavy play. Here, the visitor can socialize with Taipei's

met pizzas baked in a genuine wood-fired brick oven.

Cozy restaurants outside the hotels are led by Le Romantique and Europa Haus. La Lune Vague in Tien Mou on Taipei's outskirts has good food served in an atmosphere of Japanese and Chinese antiques. Mamma Roma, in the lane behind the Sheraton, offers genuine kosher food for people on strict religious diets.

Two Continental restaurants that have music clubs attached for after-dinner entertainment are the Primacy and Royal Audio City. After the American-style broiled steaks, live bands and professional singers serve up music in the lounges.

Otherwise, there are floor shows featuring local talent at the Hoover Theatre Res-

large American and European communities as well as with locals. Popular pubs include The Ploughman's Cottage and Ploughman's Pub, the Hope and Anchor, Sam's Place and the Wooden Nickel Saloon. Most can be found in the Sugar Daddy Row area.

Since the Chinese are food fanatics who appreciate good cuisine of all kinds, Taipei boasts a range of good Western restaurants, many operated by accomplished European chefs. The most luxurious and expensive include the award-winning Trader's Grill at the Taipei Hilton and the elegant Paris 1930 in the Ritz. Fellini's at the Beverly Plaza, stylishly decorated like a Hollywood movie set, is less expensive and specializes in Italian and Continental cuisine including gour-

taurant or the Hillman Theatre Restaurant. These dinner theater-style complexes showcase contemporary Chinese song and dance, acrobatics and stunts, traditional Chinese and aboriginal folk dances and occasional foreign talent. The largest and probably most elaborate of these dinner theaters is the Sunshine City Restaurant at 247 Lin-sen North Road. Its enthusiastic performers and spectacular special effects draw enormous crowds each night.

The Chinese regard Western ballroom

Right, a pretty disc jockey spins Western sounds and left, young dancers respond with the latest moves at the Tiffany Disco in the Taipei Hilton.

dancing as a highly provocative and erotic form of entertainment. That feeling may stem from the old Confucian maxim that "men and women should not touch hands." It may also be a hangover from the notorious pre-war days in Shanghai, when ballrooms were centers for all manner of suspicious nocturnal activity and vice. Consequently, dancing licenses are extremely difficult to obtain in Taipei and can cost proprietors a staggering US $100,000 annually. Much of this cost falls right back on the customer in the form of cover charges and drinks.

Discos and other Diversions

Taipei features two kinds of dance establishments: Chinese-style ballrooms and

The Sugar Daddy Row label hints at the kind of entertainment that is available at many of these clubs. They are staffed with attractive, often charming hostesses, dressed in sexy *cheong-sam* or more modern fashions and coiffed to the hilt. Patrons wishing to sit and chat with the girl of their choice are obliged to buy her a "lady's drink." That usually consists of a glass of tea or colored water that will cost at least NT $200 or about US $5, double the cost of a gentleman's drink. The price of the girl's company is included in her refreshment.

A customer who continues buying the ladies drink after drink is fondly referred to as a "Sugar Daddy" or a "Big Fish." One who refuses to buy more than a drink or two is snubbed as a "Cheap Charlie" and may

discos, the latter replete with loud rock bands or recorded music, flashing strobe lights and lasers, and pint-sized dance floors.

Tiffany's at the Hilton has long been Taipei's leading disco. Newcomers challenging its dominance include the Crystal Palace at the Lai-Lai Sheraton, the elegant Champagne Room in the President Hotel, and the Mabuhay in the Imperial. Unaccompanied guests usually have little trouble finding unattached partners.

Other than discos and floors shows, there are the bars and pubs. One of the easiest places to go bar-hopping is the Sugar Daddy Row area which has numerous establishments within easy walking distance of one another.

find himself without company before long. Sugar Daddy Row has mellowed considerably since the wild days of the U.S. Army "R-and-R" era. But it remains a good place for unattached male visitors to get the feel of Taipei's sensuous evening throb. Among the popular clubs are the Blue Star, Aloha, Sparkle Club, Mayflower and Green Door. While they offer decidedly male-oriented entertainment, clubs with bands and dance floors also welcome couples.

Most of these clubs abide by the midnight curfew. After that, drinking continues at clubs that operate under cover of dark. Other late-night operations are the Hilton's Galleon Pub, the Beverly Plaza's Chinatown Bar and other major hotel piano bars.

Chinese Night Delights

The Chinese diversions of a Taipei night also have a decided male lilt. Banquets, of course, can provide an excellent social and gastronomic experience for mixed groups. But some establishments in the Taipei and Peitou areas cater for all-male groups as well, and include the cost of female companionship and musical entertainment in the banquet bill. The dining begins early by Western standards and many Chinese restaurants close their doors by 8:30 or 9 p.m.

One of the quintessential forms of post-dinner activity for groups of Chinese men is the wine house or *jiou-jia*, occasionally referred to by foreigners as "girlie restaurants." Most serve food and expect

guests to order several dishes, but the main meal is usually taken elsewhere and guests begin flocking to the wine house about 9 p.m. The wine house specialties usually include a variety of "potency foods" like Snake Soup, Turtle Stew, Sauteed Eel or Black-fleshed Chicken. All are ballyhooed as aphrodisiacs.

Wine houses are ancient Chinese institutions that conform to Confucius' own prescription. He said sensual pursuits must always be "delightful but not obscene, fun but not tawdry." So these wine houses harmoniously blend the pleasures of eating, drinking, music and female companionship in a relaxing and luxurious ambiance where—as one anonymous Sung Dynasty poet said—

"wind and rain, heat and cold do not occur and day mingles with night."

Guests entering the gaudy portals of a wine house are greeted by a liveried page or hostess who escorts them through the noisy halls to a private banquet room. At least four persons should participate in a wine house party and at least one should be a Chinese man who is familiar with the routine. Without a sufficient number of guests, the party cannot reach that vital stage of excitement which the Chinese call *reh-nau*, literally "hot and noisy." A Chinese-speaking guest helps translate the nuances of the conversation and activity.

After being seated, guests should advise the waiter of the kinds of drink preferred. Chilled Taiwan Beer and heated Shao-Sing Wine are the common choices. Guests may bring their own bottle but will be charged a nominal corkage fee. Then, some of the renowned virility dishes or a plate of fresh fruit may be ordered.

'Bring On the Girls'

As the waitress leaves the room, the Chinese guest will probably shout for her to "bring on the girls." It is only a matter of seconds before attractive "wine girls" or *jiou-nyu* file into the room, dressed in costly gowns of silk and satin. The party is charged a standard fee for each girl who joins the table during the course of the evening and they usually rotate with other girls every 20 to 30 minutes. This gives guests the opportunity to drink and chat with many different personalities and to feast their eyes on a dazzling variety of pretty faces as the night progresses. It soon becomes impossible to keep track of all the names and faces.

Guests at a wine house should keep one point in mind. A wine house is not a brothel. The wine girls deftly fend off overly vulgar advances. They entertain their guests with charm, chit-chat and jokes, popular songs and toasts. In fact, many can match the male guests glass for glass. Despite their youth and slender shapes, they have a remarkable tolerance for alcohol and find it fun to drink the men under the table.

A popular method of downing liquor other than toasting is a kind of "rock, paper, scissors" finger game in which the loser must drain his glass dry. Chinese men can be seen engaging in this spirited contest in res-

Nightly life in Taipei ranges from a slow dance (left) to the lively toasts, tempos and beauties of the Queen's Restaurant "wine house" (right).

taurants and pubs throughout Taiwan. Any guest who walks out of a wine house sober is considered a cheat or a man with the "capacity of an ocean."

If by the end of an evening, a guest manages to establish a rapport with a particular wine girl, it is possible to arrange to take her out for the proverbial *hsiao-yeh* and even more intimate entertainment. Later meetings may be arranged. Otherwise it costs a standard "take-out" fee paid to the management. That fee can be quite steep, as much as US $75 to $200. The later one leaves, the less the fee. The price includes only the cost of the lady's company. Further activities must be negotiated privately between guest and girl—and in some cases may not be negotiable at all. In this respect,

"cabarets" and "ballrooms." Similar to those of pre-war Shanghai, they differ from wine houses in that there is a large hall rather than private rooms. It usually boasts booths or tables along a vast hardwood dance floor. Tea is served free of charge and beer or soft drinks may also be ordered. Men who enter alone or in groups are soon introduced to "taxi dancers," *wu-nyu*. Like *jiou-nyu* they are dressed to the teeth in the finest silks and satins. Their hair may be coiffed in elegant chignons or brushed out long and straight. For some reason, the dance halls seem to monopolize the prettiest, most sophisticated and most charming girls in Taiwan. The girls are regularly rotated between tables. Before the night is over, a guest may feel like he has talked and

wine houses and the hostess clubs operate in a similar manner, although the latter usually charge a lower "take-out" fee.

A visit to a wine house is a marvelous way for a male to delve into one of the merriest sides of Chinese social pursuits. These establishments always echo with laughter, and crowds. They also reflect the traditional feminine charm of China's lovely women.

Popular wine houses in the Taipei area include the Queens, the Mayflower, the East Cloud, the Apricot and the Jade Pavilion. Costs rarely run less than NT $4,000 (US $100) for a visit of four people for an hour.

Another form of Chinese-style nightlife is the island's dance halls, also known as

danced with a string of contestants in a beauty contest.

Fox Trots and Tangos

Again, the company costs money. A floor manager keeps tabs on the number of girls who visit each table. He also shuffles them around for maximum exposure and earnings. Guests learn to refrain from getting perturbed if a lady they find particularly delightful suddenly departs for another table. She may return if there is a special request to the attendant—or to her.

The main attraction at dance halls, other than the ladies, are big bands that play the full gamut of traditional ballroom dances from waltzes to fox trots, tangos and modern rock. Even a clumsy or totally inept male dancer will feel like Fred Astaire when he takes a turn on the dance floor with an expert *wu-nyu*. These girls manage to lead bumbling partners gracefully around the floor, even giving the illusion that the bumbler is actually leading. As at other such establishments, couples are also welcome at dance halls, and will find their tabs considerably less than those of men who pay for the privilege of being entertained. And unlike wine houses, Chinese dance halls can be enjoyed by foreign visitors who do not have the benefit of a Chinese guide. Conversation generally tends to be quiet and intimate, and there are plenty of English-speaking girls.

Taipei's most popular dance halls are the

Singapore Ballroom, Paris Nights, Overseas Chinese Club, MGM Ballroom and Orient Ballroom.

Imbibing at Bottle Clubs

A more contemporary form of Chinese nightlife is the so-called "bottle club." Customers buy liquor by the bottle; it is stored in special racks for future use. These clubs are generally posh with expensive furnishings, tasteful decor, low lights and "atmosphere." Some provide live entertainment and permit dancing. Wealthy Chinese patrons popularly keep bottles of good French cognac ready and waiting at a hefty NT $4,800 (US $130) per bottle. Scotch, gin

and vodka are also popular and cost from NT $1,800 to $3,000 (US $50 to $80). Again, the cost of atmosphere is included. Customers who bring their own bottle are charged a corkage fee equivalent to the club's least expensive label. Guests who order beer, cocktails and soft drinks by the glass are usually charged a minimum of NT $400 to $550 (US $10 to $15) per person.

Chinese businessmen often choose bottle clubs for entertaining friends and associates on expense accounts. But the clubs are accustomed to accommodating foreign transients and a Chinese guide is unnecessary. As usual, there are plenty of charming ladies available for conversation and dancing—for a price. Again, it is possible to "buy out" a girl for an evening of entertainment outside the club.

Among Taipei's many bottle clubs (the names and management are subject to frequent change) are the Millionaire's Club, the Golden Key, the Golden Diamond, and the National Club.

Males who fail to find satisfaction in the myriad wine houses, dance halls or bottle clubs can work off their frustrations in other ways. Like many of its sister cities of the Orient, Taipei has the usual complement of massage parlors, "health clubs," escort services and then some.

Most people on a Chinese tour of Taipei nightlife opt for the *hsiao-yeh*, the Chinese version of a midnight snack, rather than the nightcap. Chinese revelers believe that hot food will help revive them for further revelry of a more private nature. Restaurants that cater to the midnight snack crowd include The Green Leaf, The Plum Seed and The Happy Leaf. Many working girls from neighborhood Sugar Daddy Row-style clubs head for the Ching-Kuang market at the corner of Shuang Cheng and Nung-An streets.

But the most colorful and atmospheric of all markets is "Snake Alley" with its excellent seafood restaurants and its serpentine blood-and-bile cocktails. These concoctions, guaranteed to be an unusual drinking experience if nothing else, consist of freshly-squeezed blood from the snake of your choice, a dash of bile and strong medicinal spirits. A love potion promising further nocturnal delights? If the drink doesn't deliver, chalk it up to experience. Nothing here is as it seems.

Above, one of the charmers that lights up the Sparkle Club. Putting one in the side pocket at a Taipei pub pool room, right.

TASTING AND TOASTING, THE CHINESE WAY

"Chir-fan le may-yo?"

This common Chinese greeting, heard often in Taiwan, literally translates into "Have you eaten yet?" But the way the Chinese use the words, a more accurate interpretation would be "Hi, how are you?" That's because the phrase carries the implicit cultural assumption that anyone who has eaten recently must be feeling fine. Anyone who is hungry and says so in response to the greeting will without hesitation be offered something to eat before the business at hand can proceed. First things first.

have descended and gleaned the "essence" of these succulent dishes, the practical, living descendants eat the "leftovers."

Chop-chopped Suey

Most Westerners are well aware of the vast variety of Chinese cuisine, but many panic the moment they open an encyclopaedic Chinese menu. Consequently they fall back into ordering familiar, though not necessarily appetizing, dishes like sweet-and-sour pork, chow mein and chop suey. Such meals are poor substitutes for the real

The preparation and consumption of food is a primary preoccupation of the Chinese. Indeed, the typical Chinese considers the quality and quantity of his daily meals as an accurate measure of the overall quality and success of his life.

Even the dead must be fed properly. Most of Taiwan's Chinese families still maintain ancestral altars in their homes where twice each month they make lavish offerings of the best foods they can afford. After the spirits

Preceding pages, midnight snacks and antics at the Shih-lin night market. Left, a Taipei Hilton chef fashions flowers from fruit, and, above, one of the hotel's artistic meat and vegetable platters.

thing. In fact, chop suey is an American invention that few self-respecting Chinese would order, let alone eat. It dates back to the Gold Rush days of the mid 1800s in California when American miners wandered into coolie camps for a bite to eat. Unwilling to share tables with Chinese laborers, they waited for the "second seating." The cooks simply gathered the leftovers from Chinese customers, "chop-chopped" them until they were all "suey" (shredded), and served the mess that resulted to the unsuspecting Americans. They loved it.

Even the obligatory fortune cookie served at Chinese restaurants in the United States and Europe is an item that never turns up on the tables of restaurants in Taipei, Hong

Kong or Singapore. It was invented by a clever Chinese grocer in his attic in San Francisco.

Preparing, ordering and eating authentic Chinese cuisine is an art that requires practice. And Taipei, with its reputation as one of the world's great Chinese culinary centers, is a perfect place in which to develop a degree of expertise.

Northern and Southern Schools

Debate continues to rage among connoisseurs as to the proper classification of China's many regional styles of cooking. Nine distinct styles are officially recognized by Chinese chefs; they can be further subdivided in a regional approach based on commonly shared geographic, historical, climatic and cultural factors.

The Northern school takes in the Peking, Anhui and Shantung cuisines. They are distinguishable by a staple base of wheat rather than rice and an astonishing variety of noodles, steamed buns, baked breads, stuffed dumplings and pancakes. Northern food generally appeals to Western palates because it is heartier and more filling than other forms of Chinese food and incorporates relatively conventional seasonings and ingredients. The Mongol and Muslim influence in northern China has made lamb a favorite meat of that region. The Northerners shy away from chilies and other pungent ingredients, but they love garlic, onions and the smoky saltiness of soy sauce.

One highly recommended restaurant in Taipei that specializes in Northern Chinese cuisine is the **Celestial Kitchen** on the third floor of a building at One Nanking West Road. (See the appendix for a listing of restaurants with their Chinese character names for easy taxi identification). Popular Northern selections include Peking Duck, Mountain Celery in Mustard Sauce, Shredded Lamb Sauteed with Scallions, Baked Bean Curd, Steamed Vegetarian Dumplings and Braised Beef.

The Southern school of Chinese cuisine is based on the culinary traditions of Canton. It embraces all the exotic subtleties of the Cantonese style. An abundance of rainfall, vegetation and wildlife blesses the regions around Canton, producing a cornucopia of ingredients which are cleverly contrived into gourmet delights that please the eye as well as the palate. Cantonese chefs demand fresh ingredients and strive to retain the unique flavor and texture of each one.

The most ubiquitous and original of Canton's specialties are *dim sum*, tasty dumpling snacks stuffed with prawns, beef, pork and other surprises. While other regions of China also produce dumplings and other snacks, the Cantonese surpass all in variety and delicacy. Trolleys laden with steaming *dim sim* of every shape and flavor are wheeled about enormous dining rooms during brunch and lunch hours. Simply point to what you want and you will get it. Favorite venues for gorging on *dim sum* in Taipei are the **Leofoo, Brother** and **Hilton** hotels.

Other renowned Cantonese dishes include Roast Duck, Barbecued Pork, Poached Chicken with Scallion Oil, Steamed Whole Fish and Greens with Oyster Sauce. Hong Kong takes top honors for restaurants in the Cantonese category, but Taipei has its share of fine Southern-style eateries. Try the **Northern Garden** at 63–1 Chang-An East Road, Section 1. Its Cantonese seafood attracts nightly crowds, so make reservations in advance.

Eastern and Western schools

China's Eastern school of cooking evolved in the fertile basin of the lower Yangtze River and along the mainland's eastern seaboard. It usually refers to the cuisines of Chekiang, Fukien and Kiangsu. Seafood, freshwater fish and mollusks are the stars of the menu. Spices and sauces which are rich and slightly sweet, are sparingly applied.

Since most of Taipei's mainland immigrants hail from the Fukien coast and Shanghai, the Eastern school of Chinese cuisine is well represented in the capital. Favorite dishes include the incomparable West Lake Vinegar Fish, River Eel Sauteed with Tender Leeks, Fried Jumbo Prawns, Braised Pork Haunch and Sauteed Sweet-Pea Shoots. These items can be sampled at the **Casual Garden** restaurant in the Lai-Lai Sheraton Hotel or at the **Soo-Hang Eatery** on Chung Hsiao East Road.

The trendiest type of Chinese cooking throughout the world today is the Western school. It includes the meals of Szechuan and Hunan with their red chilies, fresh ginger root, garlic, scallions, and pungent fermented sauces. The flavors are strong and spicy, but not necessarily "red hot," like many of Southeast Asia's cuisines. Traditional Chinese medical theories contend that garlic and ginger have remarkable antiseptic and cleansing properties and drive excess dampness from the human system. That may explain the great popularity of Western

Fresh poultry at one of Taipei's fast food stalls.

264

Chinese cooking in exceedingly humid Taipei.

For Hunan cuisine, the award-winning **Golden China** restaurant on the third floor of the **Taipei Hilton** offers good food and flawless service in attractive surroundings. Memorable delights here and in other Hunan restaurants include Beggar's Chicken, Honey Ham, Steamed Minced Pigeon in Bamboo Cups, Steamed Whole Pomfret and Frog Legs in Hot Chili Sauce.

Szechuan cooking is the single most popular and prevalent style of regional Chinese cooking in Taipei. The **Lucky Star** at 160 Chung Hsiao East Road, Section 4, and the **Glorious Star** at 45 Chi-Lin Road both offer

chefs shine brightly. They blend Chinese, Japanese and local influences in a manner that adds new dimensions to the mouth-watering word seafood.

One of the best and by far the most unusual spot to sample mussels, oysters, prawns, pomfret, carp, fresh sashimi and other seafood is a small restaurant that appears unassuming from the outside and carries the odd name **Flour Meal of Tainan** on its matchboxes. It is located at No. 31 Hwa Hsi Street, in the middle of Taipei's bustling, bizarre "Snake Alley."

Walking out of the murky alley into the "Flour Meal" is like entering one of those small "Arabian Nights" tents which boast palatial interiors in movie comedies. Lights

excellent Szechuan cuisine. A good combination meal could include "Grandma's" Bean Curd, Braised Fragrant Eggplant, Duck Smoked with Camphor and Tea Leaves, Chicken "Kung-Pao," and Whole Carp in Fermented Chili Sauce.

Taiwanese Seafood, Snake Alley Style

Several major restaurants and most night markets in Taipei feature Taiwan's local brand of cuisine. It rarely matches the exquisite flavors and classical presentations of China's great regional styles — with one delicious exception. When it comes to preparing fresh shellfish or whole fish, Taiwan's

blaze from genuine crystal chandeliers on walls decorated by Italian Renaissance-style paintings. Pick your feast from the seafood kept alive on ice-blocks and in tanks. It will be served to you so fresh that some of it still wiggles on the authentic Wedgewood china. In addition to chopsticks, your table will be equipped with silver tableware and a gold-plated teapot full of Chinese rice wine, while waiters speed from table to table with a continuous supply of hot towels.

Notwithstanding the gilt and elegance, the seafood is outstanding. Once a humble noodle stand (hence the name), the restaurant's owner has transformed the place into one of Asia's premier dining experiences. Try the Baby Abalone on the Half-shell, Poached

Fresh Shrimp, Sashimi, Deep-Fried Shrimp Rolls, Steamed Crab and Grilled Teriyaki Eel.

The Yin and Yang
Of Chinese Dining

What the Chinese eat, why they eat it, and the way they prepare it — like all their cultural pursuits — follow a kind of philosophical recipe, with physical and mental well-being as the prime ingredients.'

Back during the Tang Dynasty (618–907 A.D.), Chinese herbal pharmacologists, not cooks or gourmets, determined what could or could not be eaten. They decided when it should be consumed and in what quantities and combinations it should be prepared. An

They also advised gourmands with sluggish digestion to include plenty of *ta-huang*, rhubarb, in their diets.

Most importantly, Chinese culinary experts insisted on maintaining optimum balance in each and every dish as well as in the overall meal. So recipes handed down through the centuries are actually medicinal prescriptions for health. The ingredients and the seasonings used in various dishes were selected to balance the body's vital energies. Any Chinese gourmet worth his salt knows how to harmonize his selections when hosting a banquet: crispy deep-fried items are alternated with moist steamed dishes; meats complement vegetables. The "hot" *yang* foods are balanced with "cool" *yin* items. Winter banquets include "warming" spe-

elaborate system of food pharmacology developed based on the cosmic theories of yin and yang and the Five Elements.

The Tang physicians and pharmacologists divided all foods into three major categories based on their physiological effects. *Yang* or "hot" foods stimulate the body and deplete its energies. *Yin* or "cool" foods calm and nourish the system. "Neutral" foods combined the best features of *yin* and *yang* in perfect balance. Thus the ancient Chinese dieticians recommended that people eat whole barley, rather than milled barley, to benefit from the heating *yang* effects of the meal and the cooling *yin* effects of the bran. They warned people not to eat leeks at the same meal that beef or honey were served.

cialities cooked with lamb, eel, ginger, chicken, chilies and such, while sumptuous summer feasts would favor cabbage, asparagus, spinach, seafood, turnips and other "cooling" dishes.

How to Order
A Chinese Meal

When entering a Chinese restaurant in Taiwan or any country, avoid the pitfalls that await the average foreigner. If you don't

Family-style dining on Taiwan-style Chinese food at a restaurant in Taipei.

get the same menu as Chinese patrons, demand to talk to a waiter or assistant who speaks your language. Pointedly inquire about the freshest items available that day from fish to vegetables and find out about the house specialities. That process will automatically identify you as one who knows his Chinese food and should help prevent the chefs from serving you watered-down versions of their most fiery creations.

The general rule of thumb for ordering a repast from any school of Chinese cooking is to select one main dish for each person in your group, several appetizers, a soup and fresh fruit for dessert. When in Taipei, try a different restaurant and different style of cuisine each day and, if possible, invite along a local acquaintance for invaluable advice.

The quiet, candlelit dinner for two is strictly a Western tradition. Any attempt to recreate one in the chaos and glare of a Chinese restaurant is doomed to failure. The more people in your party, the better. Chinese meals are meant to be festive, often boisterous, occasions.

In the event you find yourself alone and in need of a quick meal, Taiwan also offers the traditional Chinese version of "fast-food." These "one-bowl" meals are the mainstays of any Chinese night market. If you don't speak Chinese, just point to the ingredients you want in your bowl of rice or noodles.

For starters, there is hui-fan. It consists of a large bowl of rice covered with your choice of fish, meats, gizzards, prawns, squid or the like, a savory sauce, and a side bowl of soup. China's famous niu-rou-mien consists of a large bowl of fresh noodles in rich beef broth, covered with chunks of braised beef, green vegetables and your choice of condiments. Such one-man meals are fast and inexpensive.

And if the craving for an occasional taste of Western food strikes your palate, Taipei also offers a wide variety of restaurants specializing in French, Continental, Swiss and British pub meals. The **Trader's Grill** on the second floor of the Taipei Hilton is noted for excellent continental food presented with great professional flare in an intimate candlelit atmosphere. **The Ploughman's Cottage** at 305 Nanking East Road has good British/American meals, excellent pies and cakes, and dart boards. **Europa Haus** on Chang An East Road is renowned for bountiful Continental Buffets.

'The Rapture of Drinking'

No Chinese banquet is complete without beverages, preferably alcoholic. The Chinese never drink on empty stomachs. Dispensing with the formalities of pre-dinner cocktails, they start drinking with appetizing dishes of jiou-tsai ("liquor-food") that start the meal and continue long after dessert has been served. While Chinese pharmacologists consider the overall act of eating a cooling yin activity, drinking warms one with its yang property. In combination, the proper cosmic balance is again attained.

The Chinese first began fermenting grains to produce alcohol during the reign of Yü the Great, about 2,200 B.C. A careless cook set some rice to soak in a covered crock, then promptly forgot about it. Several days later, the cook noticed a powerful aroma coming from the kettle. He tasted it, found the flavor and after-effects to his liking, and soon he and the rest of the cooks and helpers in the kitchen were literally "crocked." The tale undoubtedly comes down through history from the unfortunate master of the house, who went hungry that evening.

On a more convincing note, the most ancient of all artifacts that have been unearthed in China are exquisitely cast bronze drinking vessels dating from the Shang Dynasty, circa 1,500 B.C. Even that paragon of moderation, Confucius, took a tolerant view towards drinking. "There is no limit to drinking, as long as one does not become disorderly," he said.

But Confucius' "Golden Mean" often fell on deaf ears. China's long history tells of many "Drunken Dragons." Most were famous poets and scholars renowned for possessing "the capacity of an ocean" and the ability to down "one hundred cups at a sitting." China's most famous Drunken Dragon was the great Tang poet Li Po. In fact, Li is said to have died a poetically ironic death. Drunken and floating in a boat on a lotus pond, Li Po reached to embrace the image of the moon on the water, fell overboard and drowned. Before that unfortunate end, however, he praised wine as the key to the sublime in an immortal couplet:

The rapture of drinking
and wine's dizzy joy,
No sober man deserves to enjoy.

China has produced a wide variety of fermented wines and distilled spirits for centuries. Most are still available in Taiwan. The most popular dinner beverage is Shao-Hsing Wine, a smoky brew fermented from rice. Dried plums are steeped in the wine, which is served piping hot. The best grade of Shao-Hsing is a fragrant amber vintage called Hua-Diao.

Mao-Tai is a potent spirit distilled from

sorghum and used mainly for the venerable Chinese custom of toasting. For serious drinkers, Kaoliang and Bai-Gar are also made from sorghum but repeatedly distilled until they reach 150-proof. The subtle flavor of bamboo sparks a light green spirit called Chu Yeh-Ching; while five varieties of Chinese medicinal herbs add an extra punch of *yang* energy to a dark viscous liquor called Wu Jia-Pi.

But the overwhelming choice of people who eat Chinese in Taiwan, or anywhere in the Far East, is chilled beer. Although it is a Western import, the adaptable Chinese have found that beer is the perfect beverage for their cuisine. Its carbonation clears the palate and throat of residual oils and flavors between courses and between bites, permitting each dish to be savored for its own unique flavors. In addition, beer is brewed purely from grains, providing an alternate form of cereal — the staple so important to the Chinese diet. Beer promotes digestion, has few rivals as a thirst-quencher and, most importantly, permits frequent toasting without the threat of excessive intoxication.

Taiwan produces its own brand of brew, simply called Taiwan Beer. It has received several international awards and is consumed by the island's sybaritic populace in immeasurable quantities.

Shao-Hsing wine also effectively cleanses the taste buds of lingering oils and spices. It measures in at less than 40-proof, making it another popular toasting potion. The late James Wei, Taipei's master gourmet and consummate banqueteer, insisted that hot Shao-Hsing is the only appropriate beverage for a Chinese meal. His advice invokes the authority of the Sage himself:

You must drink Shao-Hsing at blood temperature. When cold, reject! Drink with full heart and open throat. Remember, also, that while Confucius, a diner of moderation, argued that the meat a man ate should not be enough to make his breath smell of meat rather than rice, he imposed no limit on wine consumption...

Western Whistle-wetters

Diners considering opening a bottle of a fine Western grape wine with a Chinese meal should reconsider. The delicate bouquets of vintage wines from France or California tend to get lost among the strong flavors and potent aromas of Chinese food. Moreover, ordinary grape wine normally is not heavy enough to wash out the mouth after a course of river eel or prawns dipped in pungent mustard sauce.

On the other hand, French cognac has become a favorite alternative among diners in Taiwan and Hong Kong in recent years. Cognac is smoother and less potent than any of the Chinese spirits that are commonly used for toasting at banquets. Since it is extracted from grape wine, it has fragrant flavor but is concentrated enough to cut through the tangy tastes of Chinese cooking. The practice is to serve cognac in small, one-ounce liquor glasses that permit "bottoms-up" toasting. Scotch, rum, vodka and other spirits can be served in the same manner. Chinese restaurants in Taipei allow customers to bring their own bottles of alcoholic beverages without charging a corkage fee. The import of alcoholic beverages is regulated by the Taiwan Tobacco and Wine Monopoly Bureau and some brands of liquor may not be available.

Teetotalers attending a Chinese banquet need not dismay. Delicious blends of Chinese teas are usually served with meals, and many experienced gourmets always keep a cup steaming next to their beer and toasting glasses.

The catalyst for drinking at Chinese banquets is the time-honored tradition of the toast. Rarely do diners raise their glasses to their lips alone. The host customarily starts the bottles tumbling by toasting his guests and the occasion before eating commences. "Gan-bei!" ("Bottoms up!") he will suggest cupping the glass with both hands for courtesy and raising it high in the direction of the guest of honor. From then on, anyone may toast anyone else at anytime for any reason. Even a tasty dish or clever comment may be used as an excuse for a rapturous round of toasts. The prose tends to wax more eloquent as the meal and the drinking progress. It is rude not to respond to a toast, but it is acceptable to resort to a glass of tea or juice instead of alcohol. At some parties, toasting continues until there is no one left still able to raise a glass off the table.

In Chinese society, drinking is an extension of eating and it is pursued in the same spirit of enjoyment and gourmet refinement. The wines and spirits complement the cuisine and facilitate digestion. Furthermore, the drinks elevate the mood of the banquet in comfortable increments, greatly enhancing the warm feeling of camaraderie that is so vital to Chinese eating habits.

Style and class grace Chinese cuisine at a banquet in the cavernous ballroom of Taipei's Grand Hotel.

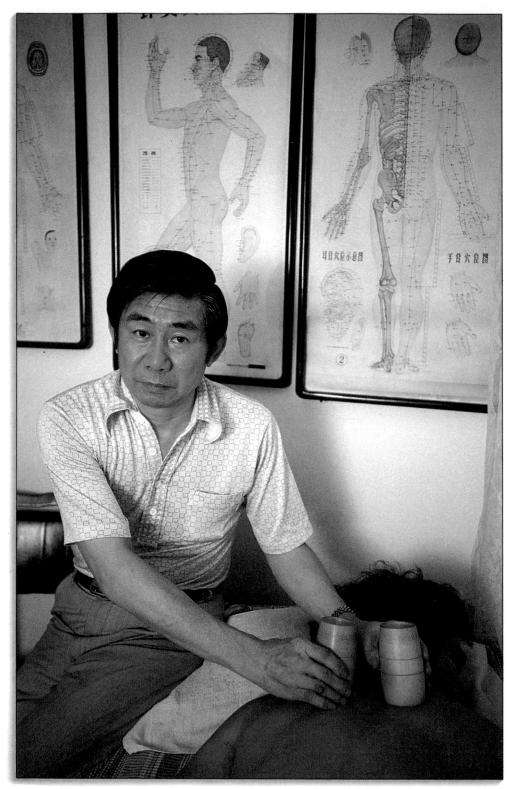

THE MAGIC OF CHINESE MEDICINE

Ancient China's misty past has produced a wealth of stories with bearing on modern concerns. Take, for instance, the case of the curious goatherd who one day noticed that several of his billy goats were behaving in an unusually randy manner, mounting their mates repeatedly in remarkably brief spans of time. Aroused by their amorous behavior, perhaps even a bit envious of their prowess, the goatherd, in time-honored scientific tradition, kept careful watch on his horny herd for a few weeks. He soon detected a pattern. Whenever a billy goat ate from a particular patch of weeds, its promiscuous proclivities peaked. Before long Chinese herbalists had determined what goats had long known: that a plant of the *aceranthus sagittatum* family was one of the most potent male aphrodisiacs in their catalogue of confections. So they called the herb *yin yang-huo* — "horny goat weed."

The World's Oldest M.D.s

Like the martial arts, China's medical arts have come a long way from prehistoric fable to 20th Century fact. The goat story is trite but true. Many of China's most efficacious herbal remedies were gradually discovered in precisely that manner. If a dog nibbled on certain weeds that induced vomiting, the curious Chinese experimented with the emetic properties of those weeds. Thousands of years of such observation and experimentation have provided Chinese medicine with the world's most comprehensive pharmacopoeia of herbal remedies. From the open-faced fronts of garishly lit emporiums in Taipei to dim, closet-sized shops in the back alleys of small Taiwan towns, herbal doctors and dealers do a brisk business providing ancient remedies to contemporary customers.

Historians have traced the beginnings of herbal medicine to Shen Nung, the legendary emperor known as the "Divine Farmer" because he taught his vassals agricultural techniques around 3,500 B.C. "Shen Nung tasted the myriad herbs, and so the art of medicine was born," proclaimed that great Han historian Ssu Ma-chien.

References to various diseases and their herbal remedies first appeared on Shang Dynasty oracle bones, circa 1,500 B.C., that were unearthed this century in China. Their discovery proved that medicine was a formal branch of study in China as long as 3,500 years ago. Books on medicine were among the few tomes spared from destruction during the infamous "Fires of Chin" of 220 B.C.

The first volume that summarized and categorized the cumulative knowledge of disease and herbal cures in China appeared during the early part of the Han Dynasty in the 2nd Century B.C. *The Yellow Emperor's Classic of Internal Medicine* contained the world's first scientific classification of medicinal plants and is still in use by Chinese physicians and scholars today.

The quintessential herbal doctor Sun Ssumo appeared on the scene 800 years later during the Tang Dynasty. He established a pattern of practice still followed by Chinese physicians today. "When people come in for treatment, one does not inquire about their station in life or their wealth. Rich and poor, old and young, high and low are all alike in the clinic," Sun wrote.

Three emperors, all of whom he outlived, invited Sun to be their personal physician. He declined, preferring to pursue his clinical practice among the common people. Previously only the high and mighty had access to professional medical care, but Dr. Sun applied the Confucian virtue of *ren*, "benevolence," to his trade. He established the great tradition of *ren-shu ren-hsin* — benevolent art, benevolent heart — that has guided Chinese physicians ever since.

Sun Ssu-mo was also medical history's first dietary therapist. In his famous study *Precious Recipes*, he wrote:

A truly good physician first finds out the cause of the illness, and having found that, he first tries to cure it by food. Only when food fails does he prescribe medication.

In fact, Dr. Sun diagnosed the vitamin-deficiency disease beriberi 1,000 years before it was identified by European doctors in 1642. Sun prescribed a strict dietary remedy that sounds remarkably modern: calf and lamb liver which are rich in vitamins A and B, wheat germ, almonds, wild pepper and other vitamin-packed edibles.

Another milestone in the history of Chinese herbal medicine was the publication of *Ben Tsao Gang Mu* in the 16th Century. Known to the West as *Treasures of Chinese*

Dr. Tom Huang administers traditional Chinese medical treatment with suction cups at his Taipei office.

Medicine, this authoritative pharmacopeia was compiled over a 27-year period of intensive research and study by the physician Li Shin-chen. He scientifically classified and analyzed 1,892 entries including drugs derived from plants, animals and minerals. The book became popular in Western medical circles during the 18th and 19th centuries and was used by Charles Darwin in the development of his famous system for classifying nature's species. The *Ben Tsao Gang Mu* remains the single most important reference tool for Chinese herbalists today.

East Versus West

The theory and practice of traditional Chinese medicine takes an approach to dis-

In fact, prior to the 20th Century, most Chinese families retained family doctors much as modern corporations retain lawyers. The doctor was paid a set monthly fee and made regular rounds to dispense herbal remedies and medical advice specifically tailored to the individual needs of each family member. When a member of the family fell seriously ill, the doctor was held fully responsible for failing to foresee and prevent the problem. Payments were stopped. Only when he cured the patient at his own expense did his normal fee resume. The system stressed the importance of preventive care. It also served as a powerful deterrent to malpractice because doctors profited by keeping their patients healthy and happy rather than sick and dependent.

ease and therapy that is diametrically different from Western ways. The Chinese prefer preventive techniques; the West concentrates on quick cures. In Chinese countries, medicine is considered an integral part of a comprehensive system of health and longevity called *yang-sheng*, which means "to nurture life." The system includes proper diet, regular exercise, regulated sex and deep breathing, as well as medicinal therapies. Unlike Western medicine, which has become increasingly fragmented into highly specialized branches, Chinese medicine remains syncretic. The various combinations of therapies from different fields in *yang-sheng* must be mastered by every Chinese physician.

Modern families in Taiwan and in other Chinese communities can no longer afford to keep a physician on the payroll, but the precept of prevention prevails. The Chinese trace and treat root causes of weakness and disease rather than their superficial symptoms. The physician draws a medical picture that encompasses everything from the weather and season to a patient's dietary and sexual habits. And true causes are often found far from the symptoms. For instance, Chinese medicine traditionally traces eye

"A Village Doctor Using Acupuncture" painted by Li Tang during the Sung Dynasty, above, and the fine points of modern acupuncture, right.

problems to various liver disorders. Such symptomatic connections are rarely established in the West, where the eyes and liver are treated by two specialists separated by chasms of medical and opthomalogical training.

The Chinese method of probing everywhere for possible causes of disease sometimes raises Western eyebrows. One American women introduced to a Taipei doctor returned from his clinic rather flustered. "He asked me such embarrassing questions!" she said. Everything from diet to elimination and sexual habits is important for the Chinese physician's diagnosis.

The theoretical foundations of Chinese medical arts, like those of the martial arts,

Scorpion Tails And Magic Needles

Herbal Therapy encompasses more than 2,000 organic medicines listed in the Chinese pharmacopeia, but only about 100 are commonly used to treat people. The rest are reserved for only the rarest conditions. Many common ingredients of the herbal pharmacy are standard ingredients of Western kitchens: cinnamon, ginger, licorice, rhubarb, nutmeg, orange peel and other spices and condiments. Herbal prescriptions routinely contain at least a half-dozen ingredients, some added simply to counteract the side-effects of more potent additives.

The old adage "fight poison with poison" originated in this branch of Chinese medi-

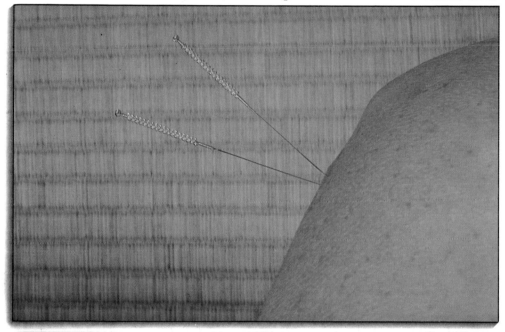

are rooted in the cosmic theories of *yin* and *yang*, the Five Elements (earth, water, metal, wood, fire), and the concept of *chi*, "vital energy." Essentially, Chinese doctors manipulate a patient's internal balance of vital energies by using herbs, acupuncture and other methods to "clear energy stagnation, suppress energy excess, tonify energy deficiency, warm up cold energy, cool down hot energy," and so forth. By reestablishing the optimum internal balance of vital energies and restoring harmony among the body's vital organs, a physician can keep his patient healthy.

Traditional Chinese therapy takes many forms. Some are popular in the West, others confined to Chinese society.

cine. Some of man's most virulent ailments are fought with such potent toxins as jimsonweed *(Datura stramonium)*, centipedes, scorpion tails, and mercury. Herbal prescriptions come in a variety of forms. There are pills formed by blending finely powdered herbs with honey, brews made by boiling and reducing ingredients in water, powders dissolved in juice or water, pastes for external plasters, medicinal wines distilled from herbs steeped in strong spirits for a year or more, serums fermented from herbs using flour and water, and refined concentrates extracted from raw and dried herbs using modern technology.

Acupuncture, probably the most widely used and publicized of Chinese therapies in the West, dates back to the battlefields of ancient China. Soldiers shot by arrows reported that their wounds often eliminated chronic ailments in other parts of their bodies. Physicians refined the technique over the centuries using "needles" fashioned from stone, jade, iron and gold. Today's practitioners of acupuncture stick very thin steel needles into "vital points" along the body's "vital energy" network. More than 800 such points have been identified, but only about 50 major spots are used in common practice.

The insertion of a needle in each point produces a specific therapeutic effect on a specific organ, gland, nerve or other body part. The points are connected to the internal organs and glands by energy channels

points and meridians. With regular application over a period of time, *tui-na* can be effective in relieving and gradually eliminating arthritis, rheumatism, sciatica, slipped discs, nerve paralysis, energy stagnation and related ailments.

Skin-scraping involves the use of a blunt spoon or coin, dipped in wine or salt water, and rubbed repeatedly across vital-points on a patient's skin, usually on the neck or back, until a red welt appears. In cases of heat stroke, colds, fever, colic and painful joints, the practice draws out what Chinese physicians call "heat energy" and releases it through the skin to eliminate the cause of the problem.

Blood-letting requires a sharp, thick needle with a triangular point that is used to

called "meridians." While many of the secrets of acupuncture still mystify physicians in the West today, they acknowledge that it can be effective in treating certain ailments.

Acupuncture has also proven to be effective as a local and general anesthetic. In recent years, patients have undergone painless appendectomies, major operations and even open-heart surgery while remaining alert and wide awake under acupuncture anesthesia. **Acupressure** utilizes the same points and principles as acupuncture, but is applied with deep finger pressure rather than needles.

Massage, called *tui-na* (Chinese for "push and rub"), is applied to joints, tendons, ligaments and nerve centers as well as to vital-

prick open the skin at a vital-point related to the diseased organ. The release of blood induces "evil *chi*" and heat energy to travel along the meridians and escape through the open point.

Suction cups made from bamboo or glass are briefly flamed with a burning wad of alcohol-soaked cotton to create a vacuum, then pressed over a vital-point, usually along the spine. They stick tightly to the flesh by suction. Skin and flesh balloon into the cup, drawing out evil energies by pressure. The

Above, an herbal medicine shop in Lukang and, right, an herbalist displays his cure-alls in Taipei's Snake Alley.

method has been found very effective in the treatment of arthritis, rheumatism, bruises, abscesses, and any ailments related to excessive exposure to wind or dampness.

Moxibustion is the term for a treatment in which a burning stick of *moxa*, made from wormwood and resembling a thick cigar, is held directly over the skin at particular vital-points. The herbal energy radiates from the glowing tip into the vital-point and transmits therapeutic benefits along the meridian network to the diseased organ.

As bizarre as blood-letting, moxibustion and other Chinese medical treatments may sound, all are still utilized with phenomenal success in Taiwan. For many common ailments, the Chinese approach appears to be superior to Western methods. It eliminates

the need for strong chemical drugs, drastic surgery, radiation and other potentially dangerous methods used in the West and puts faith in natural, organic curatives. However, Chinese medicine does not dispute the superiority of Western medicine in the treatment of acute traumatic ailments, injuries and emergency cases.

In fact, physicians in the Far East now blend Chinese theories and Western technology, Chinese therapy and Western diagnosis. Their combination has formed a comprehensive system of medical care called the "New Medicine." Eastern physicians use x-rays, blood and urine analysis, electrocardiograms, biochemical labs and other technology to improve their diagnostic methods,

while at the same time relying on ancient, time-tested Chinese methods of treatment for common ills.

For the traveler who has long suffered from nagging backache, persistent rheumatism, chronic fatigue, throbbing shoulder, "trick" knee, sluggish digestion or other problems, a visit to the right physician during a trip to Taiwan may hold unexpected benefits. Bona fide stories of satisfied customers are common.

In one instance, a Lebanese tycoon visiting Taipei on business was incapacitated by a recurring ailment in his lower spine. Unable to walk, he had to conduct his business from a suite at the Taipei Hilton. A sympathetic Chinese associate enlisted the services of a doctor who specialized in treating spinal injuries. Treated with a combination of *tui-na* massage, external herbal poultices and internal herbal brews, the Lebanese businessman recovered and was back on his feet in two days.

A year later, the condition struck the tycoon again. He called Taipei long-distance and begged the doctor to fly immediately to Beirut, but the physician declined in deference to his obligations to his daily local patients. Undaunted by the refusal, the Lebanese man flew back to Taipei for further therapy. After several long-distance medical visits, his chronic debility was entirely eliminated.

In another case personally witnessed by the author of this book, two petite Chinese women half-carried, half-dragged an elderly New York matron into the clinic of Dr. Tom Huang in Taipei. She was in tears and excruciating pain, but balked at approaching the doctor's couch as if being dragged to sacrificial slaughter on the altar of a tribal witch doctor. She gasped that she suffered from a slipped disc that had plagued her for more than 20 years. "No problem," said Dr. Huang as he rolled up his sleeves, turned the woman over on her stomach and loosened her skirt. With three masterly probes he located the slipped disc, then applied *tui-na* massage for a half-hour, gently but firmly pushing and rubbing the exposed ligament back between the discs. Then he applied a powerful herbal poultice and asked her to return the following day.

By the end of her second treatment, the woman was a convert to Chinese medicine. She actually embraced Dr. Huang and cried: "It's a miracle! For 20 years my doctors back home have given me nothing but pain pills and told me to stay in bed, but you make me feel like a new person in only two days. I can actually walk straight again!"

'MARTIALING' THE ENERGY OF LIFE

It's 3 a.m.

Most of Taipei slumbers after a hard day of work and an equally hard night of play. But from the darkened doors of a candle shop in West Taipei, an ancient man emerges. He strides vigorously up to Round Hill Park on the northern edge of the city as he has for most of his more than 90 years.

There the old man begins the dance that wakes the dawn. His arms arch upward slowly in a giant circle that symbolically splits the primordial unity of the cosmos into *yin* and *yang*. He moves his hips, spine and limbs in a practiced harmony that animates the mystical ballet of *tai-chi*. With his circular movements synchronized to his abdominal breathing, he absorbs the potent *yang* energy that peaks between midnight and dawn.

The sun begins to rise. The old man, looking as spry as the new day, finishes his daily regimen of *kung-fu*. It is time to return home to a light breakfast. There, he sips the first of many cups of an herbal brew containing white ginseng and red jujube sweetened with raw sugar to help maintain the level of vital energy that pulses through his legs, spine and nervous system. Hung Wu-fan has sired another Taipei day as the head of a family household world-renowned for its contribution to the martial arts.

Kung-fu at Dawn

By the time Hung Wu-fan begins breakfast each morning, all Taipei comes alive with the sight of lithe people jogging through the streets, stretching in the parks, shaking off the night's grip and egging their bodies into consciousness with an entertaining array of exercise. New Taipei Park behind the Hilton Hotel is a particularly popular spot for this impressive display of physical culture. From the slow-motion flourishes of *tai-chi* and the graceful thrusts and parries of classical sword-fighting to innovative new fighting techniques and Chinese versions of aerobic dancing, the spirited residents of Taipei display an awesome range of athletic abilities. It's in their blood.

Many of the movements performed in

New Taipei Park, like those of Hung Wu-fan's, hark back to that most noble of Chinese institutions, the martial arts. Contrary to popular misconception, the Chinese martial arts are collectively called *guo-shu*, or "national arts," not *kung-fu*. *Kung-fu* literally translates as "time and energy spent on cultivating an art or skill." It can refer to any skill. A great calligrapher has good *kung-fu*. So does a master chef, master lover or master fighter.

The secrets of the martial arts have been handed down from master to disciple in an

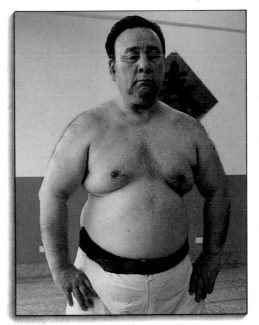

unbroken tradition that reaches across hundreds of centuries to the beginnings of Chinese culture. Many great masters joined the Nationalist exodus to the island of Taiwan in 1949, bringing their secrets and skills with them. Here, they have trained a new generation of adepts. Some of those old masters still appear among the teachers who lead exercise groups in New Taipei Park.

The Dragon Awakens

Two of the greats who came from the mainland were Chang Chun-feng and Cheng Pan-ling. Hung Wu-fan, a native-born Chinese resident of Taiwan, welcomed these homeless and destitute masters to his

Preceding pages, young martial artists in combat: Above, martial arts Master Hung Yi-hsiang and, left, his son, Hung Tze-han, in *hsing yi* stance.

wealthy household, fed them and lavished gifts upon them. In graditude, Master Chang began to school Hung's five sons in the ways of the ancients. Subsequently, Cheng let the Hung family in on the secrets of his mastery of *shao-lin, hsing-yi* and *tai-chi.*

Among Hung's five sons, the two masters discovered a "Sleeping Dragon," a term that describes someone with enormous talent not yet fully developed. Under the tutelage of Cheng, Chang and 15 other renowned masters, the sleeping dragon awoke. Hung Yi-hsiang today is considered one of the greatest living masters of the ancient arts.

Hung Yi-hsiang defies the typical image of a *kung-fu* master. He is neither the wizened old man with flowing robes and knee-length

The Eagle and the Snake

The Chinese originally developed fighting forms by imitating the stances of animals. In fact, martial lore tells that *tai-chi* was invented when a master fighter stumbled upon an eagle and a snake locked in mortal combat. Thus, the Tiger Form, Mantis Form, Bear Form and other classical stances took their shape.

During the 4th Century A.D., the Indian pilgrim Bodhidharma, known to the Chinese as Ta-Mo, introduced Buddhism to China and further enhanced Chinese fighting forms by teaching his recruits the deep-breathing methods of yoga. Ta-Mo also taught the Chinese that martial arts should be cultivated primarily for internal spiritual de-

white beard, nor the brash young Turk of Bruce Lee ilk. Master Hung packs more than 200 pounds of powerful bulk into a compact 5-foot, 6-inch frame. He looks more like a stevedore than a master of the martial, medical and fine arts. He wears baggy, non-descript clothing and rarely shaves. Hair grows over his chest, arms, shoulders and back and he usually answers questions with perfunctory grunts rather than long-winded explanations. But to watch him perform his *tai-chi* forms, or demonstrate the mesmerizing circles of *ba-kua*, is like watching a gentle wind stir willow branches. He breezes through steps that seem impossible. Each move is smooth and fluid yet swift and sudden.

velopment, not for superficial shows of force, and should be used exclusively for defense, never for offense. Ta-Mo has been the patron saint ever since. His blend of external fighting forms derived from animal postures, and internal breathing methods derived from yoga, has been the model for all styles of Chinese martial arts.

These arts are based on the cosmic principles of *yin* and *yang* and the Five Elements of the cosmos: earth, water, metal, wood and fire. The most fundamental concept, a

Above, early risers stretch themselves into shape at New Taipei Park. Right, a Peitou resident musters her *chi.*

280

trait it shares with Chinese medical theories, is *chi* (pronounced "chee"), which translates as "vital-energy" or "life-force." But it also means "air" and "breath." *Chi* is an invisible element contained in air, food, water and every living thing on earth. Martial arts exercises like *tai-chi* cultivate *chi* through rhythmic deep-breathing and direct it around the body with rhythmic motions.

People who deny the existence of anything that cannot be seen and measured have trouble accepting the concept of *chi*, but it is the force that fuels Chinese life and the martial arts. Master Hung Yi-hsiang explained: "Without food we can live for two months, without water for two weeks, but without *chi* we would die in five minutes."

Proper breathing is of central importance in all fighting forms and must be correctly cultivated before a student of the martial arts can move into complex external movements. "Of all forms of exercise, breathing is best," noted Master Hung.

Soft and Round

The essence of classical Chinese martial arts can be defined in two words: softness (*rou*) and roundness (*yüan*). By remaining soft and loose at all times, a person conserves vital energy while an opponent expends his thrashing about. By employing round, circular movements, the master combatant deflects his opponent's direct linear attacks, and all his parries naturally flow "the full circle" to become counter-attacks.

Softness and roundness are maintained and enhanced through rhythmic breathing. Breathing also permeates the body with *chi* during combat. *Chi* cannot flow properly through a hard tense body, and the hard linear movements glorified by the modern Chinese *kung-fu* movies do not promote the circulation of *chi*. Hard styles like Japanese *karate*, Korean *tai-kwon-do* and Chinese *shao-lin* are better known in the West, but the soft, rhythmic Chinese styles like *tai-chi*, *hsing-yi* and *ba-gua* are more traditional.

Hung Yi-hsiang's mastery over his own *chi* came to the forefront under his last and greatest teacher, Master Peng. Peng was a mainlander who had never accepted a single student after fleeing to Taiwan. But his attitude changed when he grew old. He realized he had to reveal his precious secrets to a qualified disciple before his death, or they would be forever lost to posterity. When word of his decision went out, scores of hopeful adepts rushed to his home in the central Taiwan city of Taichung to "be interviewed" for the honor.

Master Peng conducted his audiences in a stark, dark room lit by a single candle. The candle stood on a low table between himself and his visitors. One by one, the eager adepts filed in, spoke briefly with the master, then left. Little did they know that they had been judged before uttering a word!

Only one man passed the silent test. He managed to enter the room, approach the master and pay his respects without once causing the candle flame to flicker. Here was a man in full control of his *chi*. Master Peng had found his disciple. That disciple was Hung Yi-hsiang.

Master Hung not only took up the mantle of his great teachers, he has also developed his own integrated system of martial arts. Hung calls his school *tang-shou-tao*, the

"Way of the Hands of Tang." It blends the finest elements of *hsing-yi*, *ba-kua*, *tai-chi* and the harder *shao-lin*. It takes its name from the Golden Age of Chinese culture and the formative age of Chinese *kung-fu*, the Tang Dynasty of the 6th to 8th centuries A.D. It is Hung's personal attempt to restore the Chinese martial arts to their authentic forms and traditions.

Tang-shou-tao is Chinese *kung-fu* at its classical best — internal, subtle and deeply linked to Taoist philosophy. Master Hung, like Ta-Mo, believes that health and longevity are the true goals of martial arts. He said external self-defense using martial arts can indeed increase longevity and promote health by protecting one from bandits and bullies, but he emphasized that if one's internal powers of *chi* are strong and steady, the bullies will instinctively steer clear.

"The most accomplished martial artists are those who never have to fight. No one dares challenge them," Master Hung said. Quoting Ta-Mo, he advised, "Concentrate on the inner meaning, not the outer strength."

He also elaborated on the apparent contradiction that in softness there is strength. Hung noted that water eventually wears down the hardest rock, that *yin* is ultimately more potent than *yang,* and that properly applied, "four ounces of strength can topple 1,000 pounds."

The most dedicated disciple of *tang-shou-tao* is Hung's second son, Hung Tze-han, who resembles a *kung-fu* movie star. "Ah-han," as friends call him, practices *tang-shou-tao* for long hours each day and spends his spare time poring over ancient Taoist text and martial arts manuals. He even writes and edits scripts for television programs and movies with *kung-fu* themes. Ah-han explained why: "Chinese martial arts make very popular movie themes these days, but most script-writers know nothing whatsoever about the subject. Consequently the public gets a distorted view of Chinese *kung-fu.* By writing some of the scripts myself, and editing others, I try to help correct many common misconceptions held by the public. This is important if we expect the true traditions to survive in the modern world."

Concrete Proof

So what of those "misconceptions"? What of the explosive war-whooping, high-kicking acrobatics of world-famous stars like Jackie Chan and the late Bruce Lee? They do flourish, but masters like Hung take a dim view of such sport. Hung Yi-hsiang acknowledged that *karate* can enable a human being to smash bricks and break boards with bare hands and feet, *tae-kwon-do* can protect a person from common bullies, and modern *shao-lin* forms can vault one into the movies. But he warned that these forms of combat can also bring a premature end to a man's martial arts career. Such hard forms take their physical toll and can exhaust the body's stores of *chi* by the age of 40.

The popular aberrations in traditional forms of modern arts did not appear in China until the 17th Century when the militant Manchus attacked the effete Ming Dynasty. Patriotic Ming loyalists needed to turn out trained fighters as fast as possible, so they eschewed the "soft" Chinese styles that required decades of training. Classical forms were abbreviated and hardened, and training was reduced to three years. That's all it takes for some devoted adepts to become skilled in *karate* or *shao-lin.*

Master Hung said few *karate* or *tae-kwon-do* masters ever live to the ripe old age of Grandpa Hung. And if they do, they are so stiff from a lifetime of beating their bodies against bricks and board they can barely move. However, the soft internal forms taught by tutors like Hung steadily increase stores of vital-energy and gradually improve the tone of muscles, joints and tendons, keeping them pliant and supple for as long as they are practiced.

Hung has been preaching the superiority of soft forms for decades. But his warnings have only begun to be taken seriously in recent years, as scores of fellow artists from opposing schools have hobbled into his studios from all over Asia to try to work themselves back into shape using Hung's soft long-life exercises and abdominal breathing techniques.

Still, given the challenge, Master Hung graphically demonstrates the truths of the Tao and the sudden explosions of power that his theories and training enable him to summon at will. Once challenged by a Japanese artist to prove his might during a tournament in Taipei in the late '60s, the usually modest Hung acquiesced to "save face." With typical Japanese fondness for the drama of crushing boards and bricks, the man dared Master Hung to smash three solid cement cinder-blocks with a single blow, a feat he claimed could not be done.

The blocks were stacked flush against each other. They were placed on a solid flat surface rather than positioned up on blocks to provide space beneath, in the usual manner. Gathering and focusing his *chi* within, Master Hung silently mustered intense concentration. Then he raised his fist high above his head and brought it down with a single devastating blow. He didn't break the cinder blocks. He shattered them. Debris flew in all directions.

The feat was recorded on film. A replay showed that at the moment of impact every hair on Master Hung's right arm and shoulder was standing erect. That was his *chi* running down his arm, he later explained. His reaction to performing the "impossible"?

"Smashing bricks and boards is nothing. Only amateurs are impressed by that!"

Performers strike a threatening posture during filming of a martial arts movie in Peitou.

THE TAO OF CHINESE ART

Writing grew from the need to express ideas, and painting grew from the desire to represent forms. This was the intention and the purpose of nature and of the sages. . .

> —*from a 9th Century treatise on painting by Chang Yen-yuan*

A Chinese painting looks like it does because it was painted by a Chinese artist. He had special tools, a certain training, a somewhat predictable place in society, skill as a calligrapher, and particular philosophic and aesthetic assumptions.

The aesthetics of the undertaking are part of the Chinese cosmogony. The Chinese assign painting and the complimentary art of calligraphy an important place in the natural order of things, as Chang Yen-yuan noted:

> Painting completes culture, helps human relations and explores the mysteries of the universe. Its value is equal to that of the Six Classics (of Confucius), and, like the rotation of the seasons, stems from nature; it is not something handed down by tradition.

Chang described the origins of Chinese painting in almost mystical terms:

> When the ancient rulers received the mandate to rule from heaven, inscriptions on tortoise-shells and drawings presented by dragons appeared. . . . These events have been recorded in jade and gold albums. Fu-hsi obtained the hexagrams from the Yung River, which was the beginning of books and painting; Huang-ti obtained (drawings) from the Wen and Lo rivers, and Shih-huang and Tsang Chieh, who had four eyes, looked up at the celestial phenomena and copied bird footprints and tortoise-shell markings, thus fixing the forms of written characters. Nature could not conceal its secrets, hence it rained millet; the evil spirits could not conceal their forms, therefore the ghosts wailed at night.

In short, Tsang Chieh saw the forms of Chinese characters in nature and recorded them for man's use. In contrast to Western lore where Adam and Eve acquired knowledge, suffering and guilt as a kind of punishment, the Chinese received their culture as a gift or won it through astuteness. The evil spirits that conquered Eden turn up as losers in the Chinese tale. And they still wail at night for their lost secrets.

'Four Treasures'
of Creativity

In historical terms, the earliest Chinese characters were pictographic or ideographic. Indeed, they remain so, though many characters are derived from these originals on a

phonetic basis—according to the sound of the characters rather than the symbols of the sounds.

The original forms of the characters are difficult to discern because they have evolved into new shapes. But the striking fact about Chinese writing is that as the script developed, the older forms were not cast off. They were preserved and used as they are today. The structural evolution of Chinese symbols was essentially completed by the end of the 4th Century A.D.

Almost without exception, the artist of early China was a calligrapher. He was from a privileged class, or he would never have had the endless hours of time on his hands needed to be educated and acquire a mea-

Left, Dr. Wang Shih-I, a noted calligrapher of the Chinese Cultural University, puts the finishing touches on character. Right, Temple etching of an unusual form of ancient calligraphy.

sure of skill with the *maubi*, the Chinese brush which he used to write characters. A degree of competence with the brush was a necessary skill derived from an education in ancient China. If a young man (for there were no women involved, though some were well educated) sought to pass the civil service exam, his road to all posts in government, he might be judged as much for his writing skill as for his ability to produce the rote answers required by the examination.

The *maubi* combined a long straight handle of wood or bamboo with a round tip that came to a point. It was soft, but firm and springy, and was probably made of rabbit, wolf or deer hair. Softer goat hairs were more often used by the painter than the calligrapher.

ink and inkstone, the tools of the calligrapher's and painter's art—were the subject of much discussion and critique. The best brush would be made by famous craftsmen, with hairs from the pelt of an animal captured in the first weeks of March. The best inkstone would grind fine ink quickly and was "cold" enough to keep the fluid wet for long periods. It might come from a famous mountain many hundreds of miles away. The choicest inks were made from the smallest particles of smoke, gathered at the greatest distance from the burning pine wood of *tung* oil and beaten thousands upon thousands of times to improve their quality. The finest papers came from the best houses; they had access to the cleanest water and washed all traces of impurity from the pulp.

The young artist generally wrote on paper which may have been invented as early as the 2nd Century A.D. Lacking paper, he might have chosen silk for his "canvas." Paper, however, provided an extremely sensitive surface which readily betrayed the speed of the brush, the manner of its handling and its charge of ink. Paper permitted no corrections.

The artist's ink came in the form of a dry stick made from lampblack mixed with glue. After adding a little fresh water, the stick was ground in an inkstone. Although grinding the ink was a slow process, it was a part of the painting ritual that quieted the spirit before the art could commence.

These "four treasures"—*maubi*, paper,

The best of the four treasures were held in awe. But even basic stocks were regarded with great respect. The Sui-era calligrapher Chi Yung buried his used brushes in the earth with solemn ritual. Such attitudes were a reflection of the reverence with which the painter-calligrapher approached his art.

A Window on the Soul

The tools of the painter and calligrapher were essentially the same, as was their

"Autumn Colors on the Chiao and Hua Mountains," painted in 1295 by Yuan Dynasty master Chao Meng-fu.

approach to painting and writing. The difference lay in the painter's use of color. Although the aesthetic role of color in Chinese painting never approached the development which occurred in the West, its symbolic role was important. Sze Mai-mai wrote in *The Way of Chinese Painting* that in its use of color, painting "was akin to alchemy, for the simple range of colors in Chinese painting symbolized the Five Elements basic to the thought and practice of alchemy, and the methods of preparing colors resembled and perhaps derived from alchemical brewing and distillation."

Brush handling, by contrast, was all-important. There was never a period of Chinese painting or a particular style in which good brushwork was not regarded as

oracle inscriptions incised on tortoise shells or the scapulae of oxen.

The earliest examples of work by famous calligraphers on display at the museum include the *Ping-fu tieh*—"On Recovering from Illness"—by Lu Chi, who lived from 261 to 303 A.D. Samples of post-Eastern Chin calligraphy are more common. Wang Hsi-chi, who lived during that dynasty, is regarded as the patriarch of the art of calligraphy.

The importance of calligraphic skills grew during the Tang Dynasty. Famous officials who were also renowned calligraphers of that era included Yu Shin-nan, Yen Chen-ching and Liu Kung-chuan. Despite the ancient bars against the role of women in society, one of the preeminent calligraphers

critical. Brush control reaches its acme in the subtle art of calligraphy. Here all is lines and dots, naked, infinitely challenging. The Chinese have always regarded calligraphy as the highest of the arts. With its abstract aesthetic, it is certainly the purest. That is why a man could pass examinations on the strength of his calligraphy. Writing was regarded as a window on the soul.

Historical Calligraphy

Few examples of ancient calligraphy still exist. Most ancient inscriptions were rubbings taken from cast metal vessels. The earliest examples of Chinese writing in Taipei's National Palace Museum are Shang

of the Tang Dynasty was Wu Tsai-luan. She went to work writing copy daily for 10 years to support her ailing husband. Her fame spread so widely that she becamed deified as an immortal who flew to the heavens on the backs of tigers.

The Sung Dynasty saw the rise of calligraphers who carved on wood or stone, took rubbings on paper and compiled their works as copy books, a practice that became a popular method of studying the various artists' styles. Even the short-lived Yuan dynasty produced several important calligraphers. But the 300 years of the Ming Dynasty produced numerous masters and masterpieces. The finest achievement of Ming calligraphy was draft script.

The Ching Dynasty introduced two distinctive styles of calligraphy, one that marked the era from 1796 to 1820, the other from 1851 to 1874. The National Palace Museum's richest examples of the art date from the Yuan, Ming and Ching dynasties.

Nature's Role

The most obvious facet of Chinese painting is its expressions of a quality of life rooted in the Tao—in nature. The concept of Tao existed even before the formal teachings of the school of Taoism. It is a basic term of Chinese cosmology, expressive of the idea that all things have a common original source. The Confucianists and the Taoists differed more in their pre-purpose of ritual was to order the life of the community in harmony with the forces of nature (Tao), on which subsistence and well-being depended. It was not only pious but expedient to perform regularly and properly the rituals of worship, propitiation and celebration. These were acts of reverence. They were also literally attempts to bring heaven down to earth, for they were patterned on the rhythmic transformations in the skies and in nature, in the hope that a like order and harmony might prevail in society.

The Artists' Tao

The painter's preoccupation with the Tao occurred at both the ritual level of the

occupations than on their concept of Tao. The Taoists were concerned with man's direct and mystical relationship with nature, the Confucianists with his role in society. both were aspects of man's oneness with nature's larger harmony, the oneness of Tao.

The Chinese universe was an ordered, harmonic whole. Perceiving this order, the Chinese sought to take their place in and participate in the natural order. Ritual was important because it involved actual participation rather than just symbolic participation. As Sze Mai-mai noted:

 . . . painting and every other phase of Chinese life continued to be governed by the value of the ritual approach. It is worth noting, therefore, that the original Confucianist school and the mystical level of the Taoists. The Chinese painter was often a pillar of society, well-educated, with a responsible government position and considerable duties to his family. He was a man of the world. Chinese literature and poetry abounds with references to this conflict between the weight of responsible citizenship and the withdrawal to relative seclusion that marks the life of artists.

On retirement, the artist was able to devote much more time to Taoist philosophy.

Above, "Enjoying Antiquities by Tu Chin of the Ming Dynasty." Right, "Quails Among the Chrysanthemums" painted about 1131 by Sung Dynasty artist Li-anchung.

As a system, it was better suited to the individual effort of painting because it focused its attention on the relationship between the individual and nature, on the creative act itself; between the painter, his subject and the magical link between the two—his art.

The Tao is not to be understood, it is to be appreciated. To tie it down is to lose it; it is not unknowable but it cannot be explained. To know the Tao is to be at one with it, to operate by its principles, or to allow them to operate through one. As the father of the school of Taoism, Lao-tze, noted in his great treatise, the *Tao Te Ching*:

The Tao (Way) that can be told is not the eternal Tao;

He who deliberates and moves the brush intent upon making a picture, misses to a still greater extent the art of painting, while he who cogitates and moves the brush without such intentions, reaches the art of painting. His hands will not get stiff; his heart will not grow cold. Without knowing how, he accomplishes it."

'Squatting Down Bare-backed'

Taoist thinking had a profound effect not only on what the artist painted but also on how he painted. His spiritual stance while painting was as integral a part of the act as were his tools. The accent on process was all important.

This approach had some bearing on latter-

The name that can be named is not the eternal name.
The Nameless is the origin of Heaven and Earth;
The Named is the mother of all things.

Lao-tze's disciple, Chuang-tzu, elaborated on such mysteries:

Tao has reality and evidence but no action or physical form. It may be transmitted but cannot be received. It may be obtained but cannot be seen.

Such concepts apply equally to the painter, as Chang Yen-yuan later wrote:

day European surrealists who used the process they called "automatism" to give free rein to the unconscious. It is perhaps a measure of the limited success of these surrealists that their iconography came fairly directly from Sigmund Freud. With the Chinese painter, it is not a matter of iconography but of process. The term Tao can be interpreted as "the way," itself connoting process. The painter was a vessel for, or collaborator with, the Tao. And being in tune with the forces of nature, he became the vehicle for their expression.

With its close link to Dada, European surrealism had an extremely anarchic flavor. Freud maintained that creativity sprang from the sublimation of unconscious energies, of restraint exercised by the ego. The Chinese artist seeking oneness with the Tao could hardly be considered an anarchist. Yet his road often shunned social convention, as Chuang-tzu so vividly described:

> When Prince Yuan of Sung was about to have a portrait painted, all official painters came, bowed, and at the royal command stood waiting, licking their brushes and mixing their ink. Half of them were outside the room. One official came late. He sauntered in without hurrying himself, bowed at the royal command and would not remain standing. Thereupon he was given lodging. The prince sent a man to see what he did. He took off his clothes and squatted down bare-backed. The

collection that date from the Tang Dynasty and preceding years.

Flower, birds and landscapes were the favorite subjects of artists who painted during the Five Dynasties and Sung periods. Two of the greatest masters of the Southern Sung imperial painting academy were Ma Yuan and Hsia Kuei. Their styles, which became popular in Japan, are typically asymmetrical. All the landscape elements and human figures are placed to one corner; the empty remaining surfaces suggested an enveloping mist. Such masterpieces as Ma's "Springtime Premenade," painted between 1190 and 1225, and Hsia's "Chatting With a Guest by the Pine Cliff," which dates between 1180 and 1230, are typical examples of their work.

ruler said, "He will do. He is a true painter."

Ever since, the phrase "squatting down bare-backed" has become an expression that refers to the free and unshackled state of a painter at work.

Historical Notes
on Painting

Chinese painting blossomed during the Tang Dynasty (618-907 A.D.). The figure and horse paintings of that period were particularly exquisite. Few of them, however, have survived the centuries. The National Palace Museum has 65 paintings in its

Because of the short duration of the Yuan Dynasty, the number of paintings produced was relatively small. One Yuan-era painting in the National Palace collection is the masterpiece "Autumn Colors on the Chiao and Hua Mountains," dated 1295. It was executed by the famous scholar-painter Chao Meng-fu, a member of the Sung imperial family who had a profound influence on later generations of calligraphers and painters. The painting is supposed to represent the landscape of his friend's ancestral

Traditional paintings on Chinese fans above and at right, "Lotus in the Wind" by Feng Ta-yu (1127–1178) of the Sung Dynasty.

home in Shantung province. But it is more a display of Chao's knowledge of antique styles than it is an illustration of geographical features. There is an exaggerated disproportion between the elements, and spatial inconsistencies characteristic of work produced during the Six Dynasties period (420-589 A.D.). Such work marked a turning point in the history of the development of Chinese painting.

The Ming Dynasty saw the revitalizing of traditional Chinese institutions, including painting, after nearly a century of foreign domination. A Ming painting academy was formed by the government and artists were summoned to the court, commissioned to paint and even conferred official titles. Among the myriad notables were Wu Wei,

painters held government office.

The Ching period saw the flourishing of the so-called Individualists, including Chu Ta, Tao Chi, Kung Hsien, Kun Tsan and Hung Jen. A Jesuit priest named Giuseppe Castiglione, who went to China as a missionary and was called to the imperial court, also became famous as a painter of figures, flowers, birds and horses. Lang Shih-ning, as Castiglione was known to the Chinese, blended a European naturalism with Chinese composition and media.

The Painter as Calligrapher

It is perhaps impossible to discuss in general terms what it is that gives a painting life. The effect is a gestalt, a total impression

an ardent Taoist who so fully comprehended the mysteries of the Tao he came to be regarded as an immortal; Wen Cheng-ming, who excelled at images of old trees; and Tung Chi-chang, one of the most important artists of the late Ming period.

Chiu Ying, one of the Ming's four great masters, produced "A Ferry Scene in Autumn," a work that has adorned a Republic of China's postage stamp.

Although the leaders of the last imperial dynasty, the Ching, were originally from Manchuria, they held great respect for Chinese culture and adapted themselves to local forms and customs. Under the Manchus, officialdom remained opened to the native Chinese and many important Ching

that comes from a moment of genius. But although the whole may defy analysis, it is possible to examine the parts.

As has been noted, a Chinese painter was almost always a skilled calligrapher, a master of the subtleties of brushwork. And calligraphy is the supreme art of the line— of naked, unadorned and undisguised brushwork. The paintings' of the Chinese, far more than those of other traditions, are essentially based on linework. Their color is primarily symbolic and decorative. Tone is more important but plays a supporting role. It either fills the forms defined by line or provides definition where line would be too strong—in mist or in the far distance.

The strokes, by contrast, are so important

they have even been given labels. There are "hemp fiber" strokes, "big ax cut" strokes, "lotus leaf vein" strokes, "raveled rope" strokes and others. It is critical that every line, stroke or dot in a painting be alive and have a validity which plays a part in but can yet be separated from the painting as a whole. Each swish of the brush can thus be judged on its own merits, and a painting is "perfect in whole and in parts." This is quite unlike the West, where an individual mark contributes to a marvelous whole but can scarcely be subjected to a meaningful aesthetic appraisal in itself.

What is less obvious, but far more important in the sweep of history, is the debt of painting to calligraphy. The isolation of the strokes in any painting, with their self-

tree or a thick vine, there is an organic logic to the form and behavior of a line. Thus have the Chinese always used natural similes in aesthetic discussions of calligraphy. They talk of dragons coiling through the clouds, horses at full gallop, twisted vines.

Even in jest, the simile prevails. Su Tung-po and Huang Ting-chien, Sung dynasty contemporaries who were two of the greatest calligraphers China has produced, were close friends who jokingly criticized each other's styles. To Su, Huang's bony, energetic strokes looked like "a frog sitting under a stone." Huang described Su's fleshy strokes as "dead snakes hanging from a tree."

To quote Lao-tze, "The Tao that can be told is not the eternal Tao." In other words,

contained beauty and the many special qualities of the calligraphic line, stand as evidence.

Living lines have always been central to the Chinese painter's art. His years of training as a calligrapher made it difficult for him to make marks which did not exhibit their own beauty. What better way to achieve the harmony of the whole than to begin with elements that in themselves are harmonious? To capture the harmony of the parts brought the Chinese painter closer to achieving the harmony of the Tao.

The subtle art of Chinese calligraphy remains obscure to those who cannot see that a dot may be full of life and that a line may burst with energy. Like the branch of a

the Tao cannot be grasped, only evoked. So it is with Chinese painting and other cerebral pursuits. The Chinese artist evokes what cannot be told, creating magic that parallels the magic of nature.

It may be metaphoric to speak of a painting "possessing life." For that special quality of vibrancy found in the best paintings is life. It is the artist's genius to make the Tao manifest in his work, imparting life and vitality to his paintings in the same manner that it already exists in nature.

Above, a modern artist paints in the old style in a lotus pond. Right, "A Ferry Scene in Autumn" by Ming Dynasty master Chiu Ying. Following pages, the tao of a Taipei tile painting.

With so much to see and do in the Philippines, it will be a wonder if you have any time left for the rest of Asia.

The 7,107-some-odd islands that compose the Philippines are unique in their flora and fauna.

Here, you'll find the world's smallest deer and monkey, over 900 species of orchids, and the most expansive smiles in Asia.

Blessed by nature, the Philippines are also blessed by human nature. There's something for everyone — be he or she a beach-lover, back-packer, inveterate shopper, unabashed sightseer.

The following captions to the accompanying photographs will elucidate what we mean.

Nowhere in Asia will you find a more vibrant night-life than what Manila has to offer. Cabarets, discos, elaborate floorshows, intimate pubs — the city has it all.

Need anything be said? Our smiles will inflate your ego wherever you go.

Filipino cuisine is a cultural delight. A subtle blend of Spanish, Chinese, and Malay influences, it's a potpourri to tantalize every palate.

Fiestas abound t' year aroun One would almost thi that the provinc thrive on the

Yes, we have casinos. The table stakes are high, the atmosphere low-keyed.

Everything's righ

The "ubiquitous" jeepney is something of a cliché. But the fact remains that this gaudy mode of transportation is indispensable for most of the populace.

Paradise found! Pristine beaches, crystalline waters, and a myriad of wondrous undersea life.

The Philippines offer the last great shopping bargains in Asia. Take a long, long look and wish you were here.

Manila has more five-star hotels than any other metropolis in Asia. Each has garnered a world class status, and the rates are remarkably affordable.

Everything's right here on Philippine Airlines, too.

We were Asia's first airline, and we fly in the forefront to this day — to America, Australia, Europe, the Middle East, and, of course, the entire Asian circuit.

And the amenities we provide onboard, served with customary Filipino aplomb, are unequalled anywhere else on earth.

Or above it.

A wonder of the world, indeed! The Banaue rice terraces date back thousands of years and cover 100 square miles in area.

Philippine Airlines
Asia's first airline.

here in the Philippines.

INTERNATIONALLY HYATT.

Along with consistently outstanding service and fine cuisine, Hyatt hotels offer language translation, currency exchange, a business centre and other special services.

Our city centre hotels—like the elegantly expanded Hyatt Regency Singapore—make it easier to do business and communicate abroad. Our spectacular resorts, from the sapphire lagoons of Fiji to the colourful marketplaces of Tunisia, create unforgettable vacations.

Thanks to our instant worldwide reservations system, all these Hyatt touches are just one telephone call away. Hyatt helps take the guesswork out of international travel at over 120 hotels worldwide. Call us now for an international touch of Hyatt.

Don't you **WISH YOU WERE HERE**®

For group reservations at over 120 hotels worldwide call: Australia (008) 222 188, Bangkok (2) 541 1234, Hong Kong (3) 662 321, Kuala Lumpur (3) 248 2133, Tokyo (03) 345 1484, Singapore (65) 733 1188.

HYATT ✪ INTERNATIONAL HOTELS

GUIDE IN BRIEF

Traveling to Taiwan

By Air

Taiwan lies along one of the busiest air routes in Asia, and stopovers there may be included on any round-the-world or regional air tickets at no extra cost. Sixteen international airlines currently provide regular, scheduled air services to Taiwan: China Airlines (CI), Cathay Pacific (CX), Japan Asia Airways (EG), Korean Airlines (KE), Malaysian Airlines (MH), Northwest Orient (NW), Thai International (TG), Continental Airlines, Philippine Airlines (PR), Aloha Pacific Airlines, Singapore Airlines (SQ), Air Nauru, (ON), South African Airways (SA), Pan American World (PA) and KLM-Royal Dutch (KL).

Almost all international air traffic to and from Taiwan goes through the Chiang Kai-shek International Airport in Taoyuan, about 45 minutes drive from downtown Taipei. This is one of the safest, most well-designed airports in the Orient, fully equipped with the latest technology and passenger facilities to accommodate five million passengers and 200,000 metric tons of cargo annually. While you are here, it makes sense to visit the adjoining three-story Chung Cheng Aviation Museum. More than just a museum which exhibits models of aircraft (about 700 of those), it offers facilities for visitors to test their flying skills or experience the sensation of flying. Also housed within its premises are dioramas and close-circuit TV displays which trace aviation history from time of Icarus' plight to modern day space inquiries. The building is Asia's version of the National Aviation Museum in Washington, D.C.

At Kaohsiung in the south, Taiwan's other international airport, regular air services connect the island to Tokyo, Osaka, and Seoul. This route is served by China Airlines, Japan Asia Airways, and Singapore Airlines.

Check the Appendix for a listing of addresses and contact numbers of airline companies in Taiwan.

By Sea

Of the five international sea ports in Taiwan (Keelung, Taichung, Kaohsiung, Suao and Hwalien), the Kaohsiung and Keelung harbors are two of the largest and busiest at which a number of luxury sea liners call.

The Arimura Line of Okinawa operates a regular passenger ferry between Keelung and Okinawa. The ferry leaves Keelung on Monday at 8 a.m. and arrives in Okinawa on Tuesday at 7 a.m. The return trip departs Okinawa on Friday at 7 p.m. and arrives in Keelung on Saturday at 4 p.m. One-way fares for this trip are US$ 100 for Deluxe Class, US$ 85 for First-Class, and US$ 71 for Economy-Class. For further information and reservations contact Yung-An Maritime Co., Tel. 771-5911/8

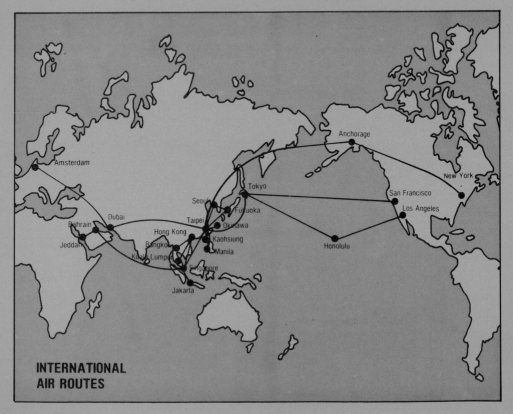

INTERNATIONAL AIR ROUTES

Travel Advisories

Visa Regulations

Visas for travel to Taiwan may be obtained at the various ROC embassies, consulates, and representative offices around the world. Refer to the Appendix for a listing of the overseas ROC embassies and consulates which represent Taiwan affairs in foreign countries. Five types of visas are issued: entry, tourist, transit, commercial, and student.

Entry. Entry visas are issued to those who wish to settle in Taiwan as residents. They are valid for six months from the date of issue and are good for a single journey to Taiwan. After arrival, foreigners holding entry visas are expected to apply for Resident Certificates at the Foreign Affairs Police Administration (台北市警察局外僑服務中心). Entry visas are usually issued to foreign businessmen working in Taiwan.

Tourist. Most travelers in Taiwan come on tourist visas, of which there are two types. Type "A" tourist visa is good for a one-month visit to Taiwan, and it may be extended locally once for a total of two months' stay. Type "B" tourist visa is good for two months in Taiwan, and it may be extended locally twice for a total of up to six months in Taiwan. Both types remain valid for six months from the date of issue. Extension, which usually takes three days or less, should be made at the nearest police headquarters. Be sure to have your passport with you.

Tourist groups of over 15 persons may be issued a single group visa, which remains valid for three months from the date of issue and is good for a single journey of no more than two weeks' duration. Group visas may not be extended or changed for other types in Taiwan, and every member of the group must enter and depart Taiwan by a same conveyance.

Transit. Transit visas remain valid for three months from the date of issue and are good for a single visit of two weeks' duration. They may not be' extended nor changed to any other types locally.

Commercial. Commercial visas are granted to foreign businessmen and technicians who come to Taiwan frequently on official business. They remain valid for six months from date of issue and are good for a single journey of up to two months' duration. They may be extended locally twice for a total stay of up to six months. Special multi-entry visas may be granted to representatives of foreign companies if more than US$ 1 million worth of Taiwan products have been imported during the previous year. This type of visa must be filed through diplomatic missions or trade consulars in the visitor's home country with accompanying documentary evidence. Foreigners who apply for commercial visas are required to present adequate supporting documents to establish their eligibility.

Student. Foreign students who wish to study in Taiwan may apply for student visas, which remain valid for six months from date of issue and are good for a single journey to Taiwan. On arrival, holders of student visas must apply for Resident Certificates.

Transit Without Visa. Taiwan currently does not permit international travelers who are not holding valid ROC visas to disembark in Taiwan. However, tourism authorities have been pressing the government recently to relax transit restrictions and permit passengers without pre-arranged visas to stop off in Taiwan for brief stays of two to five days. But until this proposal becomes law, travelers who intend to tour Taiwan must have some kind of valid visa upon arrival, otherwise they'll be turned away at the airport.

Some of the private, non-government organizations which handle Taiwan's affairs in foreign countries do not issue formal visas, but rather letters of recommendation. These letters may then be exchanged for visas either at ROC consular office in other countries, or upon arrival in Taiwan at either the Chiang Kai-shek or the Kaohsiung International Airport.

Extensions. To extend a tourist visa in Taipei, you must visit the Foreign Affairs Office of the Taipei Municipal Police Administration. It is located at the back of the Police Headquarters building on the corner of Wu-Chang Street and Chung-Hwa Road near the China Bazaar(中山堂 ‧ 台北市警察局外事室). Be sure to apply for extensions at least one to two days before your visa expires. For further information, call the Foreign Affairs Police at 361-0159 or 311-9940.

Health Regulations

Effective cholera and yellow fever inoculation certificates are required for passengers coming from certain countries or have stayed more than five days in infected areas. For certificates to be effective, they must be issued at least seven days prior to but not more than six months before arrival. Otherwise, health certificates are not normally required.

Airport Tax

All outbound passengers must pay an exit airport tax of NT$ 200. You must present the receipt when checking in.

Customs

Inbound Declaration.
All inbound passengers must fill a Customs Declaration form upon arrival in Taiwan. The following items must be clearly declared in writing if brought into Taiwan:

1) Items subject to duty, such as commercial samples, industrial accessories, expensive tools and instruments, etc.
2) Unaccompanied baggage which is to arrive after you.
3) Baggage to be left in bond until departure
4) Gold bars, ingots, or sheets
5) Gold and silver ornaments, jewelry and foreign currency which you intend to take out of Taiwan again within six months of arrival
6) Firearms and ammunition
7) Radioactive substances and X-ray apparatus

Duty-Free. All personal belongings such as clothing, jewelry, cosmetics, food, and similar items may be brought into Taiwan free of duty. Effects such as radio, TV sets and tape recorders, though also duty free, must be declared on arrival. Each passenger is also permitted to bring in duty-free one bottle (1 liter) of alcoholic beverage and one carton of tobacco (200 cigarettes, 25 cigars, or 1 pound of pipe tobacco).

Gold, Silver, and Currency. Travelers may bring unlimited amounts of gold, silver, and foreign currency into Taiwan, but they must be declared at Customs upon arrival. Gold in excess of 156 grams requires a special permit issued by the Ministry of Finance.

Taking bulk gold or silver out of Taiwan in any quantity is strictly prohibited by law. Therefore, inbound passengers who are carrying bulk gold or silver and intend to take it onward with them should declare it upon entry in Taiwan, seal it in a container, and leave it in custody of Customs until departure. Personal jewelry and ornaments such as watches, necklaces, bracelets, rings, and pins should be declared upon arrival, but need not be left in custody of Customs.

Although unlimited amounts of foreign currency may be brought into Taiwan, passengers who wish to take their excess foreign currency out again must declare the full amount upon arrival. Then unused balance may then be declared on the "Outbound Passenger Declaration" form upon departure. Otherwise, outbound passengers are limited to taking US$ 1,000 or the equivalent in other currencies out of Taiwan. No more than NT$ 8,000 per passenger in local currency may be brought into or out of Taiwan.

Prohibited Items. The following items are strictly prohibited from entry into Taiwan:
1) Counterfeit coins or bank notes
2) Gambling apparatus
3) Pornographic materials
4) Publications or articles promoting communism
5) Any articles produced in communist China, North Korea, Soviet Union, Vietnam, Cambodia, Laos, Albania, Romania, Bulgaria, or Cuba
6) Firearms and ammunition
7) Opium, *cannabis*, cocaine, and other illegal drugs
8) Toy guns
9) Items restricted by other laws such as fruits and vegetables, animals and pets, from infected areas, etc.

Outbound Declaration

The Outbound Passenger Declaration form must be completed when carrying any of the following items:
1) Foreign currency, local currency, gold and silver ornaments
2) Any unused foreign currency which was declared upon arrival
3) Commercial samples and personal effects such as cameras, calculators, recorders, etc., which you wish to bring back to Taiwan duty-free in the future

Passengers who have not declared gold, silver, and foreign currencies upon arrival and are discovered to be carrying these items in excess of the legally

designated quantities will have the excess amount confiscated by customs authorities. The designated legal limits are as follows:

1) Foreign Currency; US$ 1,000 or equivalent, in cash (excluding unused portion of currency declared upon arrival)
2) Taiwan Currency; NT$ 8,000 in banknotes and 20 coins
3) Gold Ornaments; 62.5 grams
4) Silver Ornaments, 625 grams
5) Gold and Silver Bullion, Ingots, and Coins; Strictly prohibited from export (except that which was declared upon arrival and left in custody of Customs)
6) Export Items; Articles valued at over US$ 500 per piece may not be taken out of Taiwan without an export permit.

For further information on Taiwan Customs regulations, you may contact the following offices:

Inspectorate General of Customs, 85 Hsin-Sheng S. Rd, Sec. 1, Taipei

Taipei Customs, Chang Kai-shek International Airport, Taoyuan

Kaohsiung Customs, 3, Je-Sing 1st St., Kaohsiung

A booklet giving complete customs regulations and hints has been published and your free copy may be obtained from any of these offices.

Remember. Outbound passengers must open their luggage for security inspection after checking in for their flights. This is done at the end of the check-in counters, and if you forget to do so, your bags may not be loaded onto the aircraft.

Currency and Exchange

Since the island-wide coinage change in 1981, more than 800 million new coins in denominations of 50 cents, NT$ 1, NT$ 5, and NT$ 10 (totalling to over NT$ 2.6 billion) have been reminted. Except for the 50-cent coin which has a plum blossom on it, all the others bear the profile of Chiang Kai-shek. The first of these new coins were being circulated beginning Dec. 8, 1981—a time when the old coins were still legal tender and in wide circulation, and so caused great confusion even among the residents at that time. However, they are almost completely phased out by now and it is rare to see one lying around. Bills come in units of NT$ 10, NT$ 50, NT$ 500, and NT$ 1,000.

In early 1984, the exchange rate was NT$ 40 to US$ 1. Foreign currencies can be easily exchanged for the local and vice versa at banks, hotels, most shops and all authorized money dealers. However, be sure to obtain receipts of all such transactions. You will find them saving you a lot of hassle with the customs authorities when you try to reconvert unused New Taiwan dollars upon departure.

Traveler's checks are also widely accepted at most hotels and other tourist-oriented establishments. This also applies to major credit cards such as American Express, Visa, Master Charge, Diner's Club, but the same cannot be said of personal checks which are difficult to cash, unless you are willing to wait for two or three weeks while they clear.

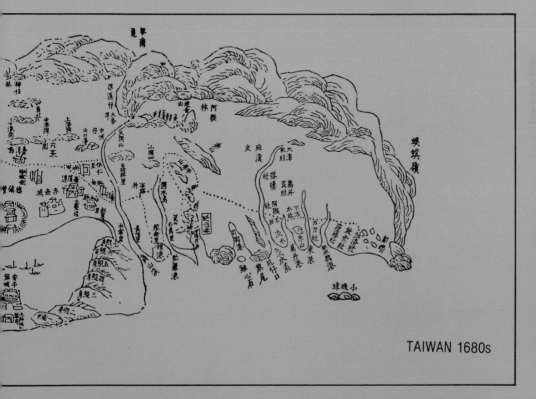

TAIWAN 1680s

Getting Acquainted

Government and Economy

"The island province of the Republic of China," as the Nationalist government officially refers to Taiwan, still marches to the battle cry of Dr Sun. Yat-sen who established a governing system "of the people, by the people and for the people" early in the 20th Century. The government adopted a constitution based on those principles in 1946. It incorporates five branches of government called Yuan under a President. The Executive Yuan resembles the cabinet of Western governments and includes eight ministries and other offices and departments. Lawmaking is the function of the Legislative Yuan which as of 1982 consisted of 392 members elected by direct suffrage. The 74-member Control Yuan has powers of consent, impeachment, censure and audit. Under the Judicial Yuan are the Courts, Council of Grand Justices and other offices that uphold and interpret the law. Finally, the Examination Yuan supervises the Ministries of Examination and Personnel.

Elections were suspended after the Communists took over mainland China and the government of the Republic moved its operations to Taiwan. But large scale elections were resumed in 1972. Essentially, the Kuomintang (KMT), or Nationalist Party, founded by Dr. Sun Yat-sen has remained the ruling party, but other parties include the Young China Party and the China Democratic Socialist Party. All are unquestionably opposed to communism and support reunification of Taiwan with the mainland under a free, democratic system of government.

In addition to the Nationalist government, the Taiwan Provincial Government and numerous county, city and aboriginal groups have freely elected representatives that participate in daily decision-making. The current president of the Republic is Chiang Ching-kuo, son of the longtime leader, Chiang Kai-shek.

In the economic sphere, the small island of Taiwan is one of Asia's giants. Taiwan's gross National Product grew at an annual rate of more than 10 percent in real terms between 1961 and 1981. It has slowed somewhat recently particularly during the recession that gripped the world in 1982. But total world trade was still expected to exceed more than US$ 45 billion in 1983, mostly with the United States and Japan. Major exports include fishery and farm products in the agricultural sector and manufactured items including electronics equipment, clothing, wood and metal products and footwear.

Despite setbacks in diplomatic and political foreign relations, foreign investors continue to demonstrate confidence in Taiwan's economic and political stability. Total foreign investment reached nearly US$ 400 million in 1981, a record amount.

The island's economic health has helped its people attain one of the highest living standards in Asia. Per capita income has surpassed US$ 2,500 and there are 96 refrigerators, 106 televisions, 96 telephones and nearly 10 automobiles for every 100 families in Taiwan.

Geography

Taiwan, essentially, comprises the main island of Taiwan, the Pescadores Archipelago (more commonly known as Peng-Hu) which is a make-up of 64 islands, and 13 other islands scattered on the circumferential waters of the main island. Together, these fill up about 35,981 square kilometers of the Pacific Ocean, with the main island alone occupying 98 percent of that area. Situated just off the southeastern coast of mainland China, Taiwan is bisected by the Tropic of Cancer.

Portuguese explorers first stumbled on the island in the late 16th Century, but it couldn't have been by chance that they named it "Ilha Formosa," which means "Beautiful Island"—surely a more fitting name they could not have thought of. Now called Taiwan, or Terraced Bay, the island is still as beautiful.

A central mountain range runs parallel to the length of the main island of Taiwan, virtually dividing it into the east and the west half. While the mountains descend steeply into the Pacific Ocean on the east coast, the highland levels off gradually on the western side. The terraced tablelands and alluvial coastal plains, thus formed on the west coast, become home to about 80 percent of Taiwan's 19 million population.

Scaling a magnificient 3,997 meters is Yu-Shan Taiwan's highest mountain, and within the mountainous area, numerous independent hills record an average height of 1,500 meters.

Climate

Overlying the tropics and subtropics zones, Taiwan sports the tropical climate in the southern and western flatlands and the subtropical climate in the north and the mountainous regions. Its location also subjects it to annual typhoons which pass through between the months of July and October, but most of these cause little more than strong winds and heavy rains over the island.

Taiwan's climate does not have four distinct seasons, but two: a hot season which lasts from May till October and a cold from December to March. The island remains excessively humid throughout the year and receives abundant rainfall; with the east (upland) receiving more than the west (lowlands). Except in the northern region where rainfall is more even, mean annual rainfall in other parts of the island range from 102 to 200 inches.

Temperature falls with altitude; snow falls on the summits of the Central Range in the cold season while lowland Taiwan remains frost free.

The most pleasant times of the year for travel in Taiwan are March through May and September through November, especially in Taipei. The following chart gives the average temperature and humidity in the Taipei area on a monthly basis:

	Temperature	Humidity
January	66°F (18°C)	84%
February	65°F (17°C)	84%
March	70°F (22°C)	84%
April	77°F (25°C)	83%
May	83°F (28°C)	82%
June	89°F (32°C)	81%
July	92°F (33°C)	78%
August	91°F (32°C)	78%
September	87°F (30°C)	80%
October	81°F (27°C)	81%
November	74°F (18°C)	81%
December	69°F (20°C)	83%

Clothing

During the hot season, appropriate clothing for Taiwan should include light cotton shirts and blouses, loose cotton skirts and trousers, casual sportswear, and comfortable walking shoes. Men need not wear jackets and ties, for even during office hours most Chinese businessmen prefer to wear leisure suits and open-collars to beat the heat in summer. You may want to bring along a lightweight jacket or dress for formal banquet and receptions, but otherwise such clothing is not necessary.

During the cold season, be sure to bring along some comfortable woolens to help protect you from the bone-chilling, moisture-laden airs of winter in Taiwan. Sweaters, woolen jackets and dresses, warm pants and socks will all come in handy during Taiwan winters, especially in Taipei. People in Taiwan tend to dress a bit more formally on winter evenings than in summer.

During both seasons it is advisable to bring along some sort of rain-gear, such as raincoats or umbrellas. As they say, "Taiwan's climate is like the mood of a woman," and it can burst out in thunderstorms at any moment without forewarning.

Time Zones

Taiwan Standard Time is eight hours ahead of Greenwich Meridian Time. There is no daylight savings here so Taiwan remains GMT +8 all year round. Aside from time variations made in certain countries during specific seasons, international time differences are staggered as follows: If it is 12 noon in Taiwan, it is

12 noon in Singapore and Hong Kong;
11 a.m. in Bangkok;
9.30 a.m. in New Delhi;
5 a.m. in Bonn and Paris;
4 a.m. in London;
11 p.m. yesterday in New York in summer;
8 p.m. yesterday in San Francisco in summer;
6 p.m. yesterday in Hawaii;
1.30 p.m. in Sydney; and
1 p.m. in Tokyo.

Tipping

Generally speaking, heavy tipping is not expected in Taiwan, although token gratuities are always appreciated. Hotels and restaurants automatically add 10 percent service charge to your bills but this money rarely gets distributed among the staff, so a small cash tip of five to 10 percent is always welcomed in restaurants.

Taiwan taxi drivers do not get upset if you do not tip them, but it is customary to let them "keep the change" in small coins when paying the fare. Taxis still cost far less in Taipei than most places but the cost of gas and maintainence here is quite high, so drivers appreciate even the smallest tips.

The only places in Taiwan where heavy tips are routinely expected are in wine-houses and dancehalls, where big tipping wins you "big face" and big favors from the ladies.

Etiquette

The Chinese, like the Koreans and Japanese, used to bow low and clasp their hands together when being introduced to someone new, but today the Western handshake has displaced that ancient custom. Nevertheless, the Chinese still shy away from overly boisterous greetings in public, such as hugs, kisses, and resounding slaps on the back. A firm handshake, friendly smile, and slight nod of the head are the most appropriate gestures of greeting.

In Chinese, a person's family surname precedes both his given personal names and his formal titles. For example, in the name "Li Wu-ping," *Li* is the surname and *Wu-ping* are the personal names. In the term "Li *jing-li*," *Li* is the surname and *jing-li* ("manager") is the title. Most Chinese names consist of three characters—one surname and two personal names—but many use only two. The majority of Chinese family names come from the "Old Hundred Names" (*Lao-Bai-Hsing*) first formulated over 3,000 years ago in feudal China. Among the most common are Li, Wang, Chen, Hwang, Chang, Yang, Liang, and Sun.

During formal introductions, the Chinese today usually exchange name cards, which has become the tradition throughout the Far East. In fact, many people don't even listen to oral introduction, but wait instead to read the person's card. It's a good idea to have some personal name cards printed up before traveling anywhere in the Orient. As the Chinese say, "When entering a new land, follow the local customs."

Some of the most common titles used in Chinese during introductions are listed below:

Hsien-sheng	"Mister,"	as in "Li hsien-sheng"
Tai-tai	"Mrs.,"	as in "Li tai-tai"
Hsiao-jye	"Miss,"	as in "Wang hsiao-jye"
Fu-ren	"Madame,"	as in "Chiang fu-ren"
Lao-ban	"Boss,"	as in "Chen lao-ban"
Jing-Li	"Manager,"	as in "Liang jing-li"

The Chinese term *ching-keh* （請客） literally means "inviting guests" and refers to the grand Chinese tradition of entertaining friends and associates with lavish generosity, usually at banquets. The Chinese are perplexed when they see Westerners call for their bills at restaurants, then pull out pocket calculators and proceed to figure out precisely how much each person at the table must contribute, right down to the last dime. The Chinese, on the contrary, almost get into fistfights while arguing for the privilege of paying the bill for the whole table. To the Chinese, "inviting guests" out for dinner and drinks is a delightful way to repay friends for favors or to cultivate new business relationships, and they do so often. For one thing, this is the type of gift which the giver may always share with the recipients. For another, the very moment you've paid a hefty dinner bill, everyone at the table is immediately obligated to invite you out as their guest sometime in the near future. This way, although the bill is high when it's your turn to "ching-keh," you only end up paying for one out of 12 banquets. In the final analysis, it all balances out, and everyone takes turns earning the "big face" that comes with being a generous host.

When toasted at dinner parties, it is well-mannered to raise your wine cup with both hands: one holding it and the other touching the base. The host would take his seat opposite (not beside) hi guest-of-honour and it is fitting to have his back to the door and his guest-of-honor's facing it.

Tea served at the end of a meal is your host's polite insinuation that the party is over and that it is time for you to leave. So don't overstay your welcome even though your host may insist. What is mere courtesy to the Chinese is often regarded as hypocrisy to Westerners. For example, even though it is late and the host would love to call it a day, he will gently persuade his guest to stay longer. In this case, it is up to the guest to detect from the host's tone what's the best thing to do. But this requires skill and good cultural sense. An experienced traveler once ventured, "The rule of the thumb is to do the exact opposite that your Chinese friend suggests," (!). Try it if you must but with discretion, please.

Chinese Weights and Measures

In both public markets and small shops throughout Taiwan, vendors still weigh and measure things with traditional Chinese units. If you're on your own with no interpeter to translate, the following conversion table may help you to figure out the unit price of whatever you're buying in terms more familiar to you.

Length: The Chinese "foot" is called a *"chir."*
1 *chir* (尺) = 11.9 inches or 0.99 feet
        = .30 meters
1 *jang* (丈) = 10 *chir*
Weight: The Chinese "pound" is called a "catty" or *"jin."*
1 *jin* (斤) = 1.32 pounds or 0.6 kilograms
        = 21.2 ounces or 600 grams
The Chinese "ounce" is called a*"liang."*
1 *liang* (兩) = 1.32 ounces or 37.5 grams
Area: The Chinese measure area in units of *"ping"* and *"jia."*
1 *ping* (坪) = 36 sq. feet (6' × 6')
1 *jia* (甲) = 2.40 acres

Banking and Business Hours

Official government business hours in Taiwan are 8.30 a.m.-12.30 p.m. and 1.30 p.m.-5.30 p.m. on Monday through Friday, and 8.30 a.m.-12 noon on Saturday, with Sunday closed. Check the Appendix of this section for a listing of foreign and local banks.

Banking hours are 9 a.m.-3.30 p.m. on Monday through Friday, and 9 a.m.-12 noon on Saturday, with Sunday closed.

Commercial business hours are 9 a.m.-12 noon and 1 p.m.-5 p.m. on Monday through Friday, and 9 a.m-12 noon on Saturday, with Sunday off.

Department stores and big shops stay open from 10 a.m. until 9.30 p.m. on Monday through Saturday, and usually close on Sunday. However, many smaller shops and stalls keep longer hours and stay open seven days a week.

Embassies and Consular Services

Since Taiwan's ouster from the United Nations 10 years ago, followed by the severance of formal diplomatic relations with the United States in 1978, many foreign embassies have closed their offices in Taipei and moved to Peking. However, this has not deterred Taiwan from maintaining friendly and active relations with her friends all over the world through private trade and cultural associations. Indeed, these private associations often handle international relations better than their official consular counterparts ever did. They are responsible for trade, travel and cultural exchanges between Taiwan and foreign countries. A number of them also offer passport and visa services. For a listing, refer to the Appendix of this section. It is advisable to telephone before calling over as most of them do not keep the normal business hours of Taiwan.

Tourist Information

Service and information centers for tourists are located at both the Chiang Kai-shek International Airport in Taoyuan and the Kaohsiung International Airport in Kaohsiung. Receptionists at these information counters speak English, and they can help you with transportation, accommodations, and other travel requirements.

There are two organizations in Taiwan 'which oversee and promote the tourism industry. The **Tourism Bureau,** a branch of the Ministry of Communications, is the official government organ responsible for tourism in Taiwan. The **Taiwan Visitors Association** is a private organization which promotes Taiwan tourism abroad and provides travel assistance to visitors in Taiwan. Since neither of these organizations is blessed with as generous a budget as their counterparts in Japan and Korea, the services and facilities they offer to travelers are limited. Nevertheless, they do their best to assist the inquiring traveler.

At the old Sung-Shan Domestic Airport in town, you'll find the **Travel Information Service Center.** This facility is designed primarily to provide information on foreign countries to the ever-growing volume of outbound Chinese travelers from Taiwan. However, in addition to audio-visual and printed information on 55 countries, the Center also offers a 25-minute audio-visual presentation on the most outstanding tourist attractions in Taiwan. You could also visit the Center to familiarize yourself with the culture and conditions of your next Asian destination. The Center is open from 8 a.m. until 8 p.m. daily, including Sundays and holidays. The Center's address is as follows:

Travel Information Service Center
Tourism Bureau
Ministry of Communications
Box 45-99
Taipei, Taiwan, ROC, Tel. 752-1212, ext. 471

If none of the above organizations is able to help you, you may direct further inquiries to the **Ministry of Foreign Affairs** or the **Government Information Office.**

Telephone numbers for the various tourist information centers in Taipei are as follows:

Tourist Service Center, CKS International Airport	(033) 834631
Taiwan Tourism Bureau	721-8541
Taiwan Visitors Association	594-3261
Ministry of Foreign Affairs	311-9292
Government Information Office	341-9211

In order to obtain information regarding tourism in Taiwan from abroad, write to the Tourism Bureau's head office in Taipei or to one of its overseas representatives. The addresses and contact numbers are included in the Appendix of the section.

Transportation

Domestic Air Travel

Regular scheduled domestic air service in Taiwan is provided by the international flag-carrier China Airlines and by Far East Air Transport (FAT), the main domestic carrier. These two airlines operate a total of 24 runs a day between Taipei and Kaohsiung (a 40-minute flight), 18 between Taipei and Hwalien (30-minute), six between Taipei and the Pescadores (40-minute), four between Taipei and Tainan (40-minute), and four between Taipei and Taitung (40-minute). In addition, they schedule flights which connect various cities in the South with each other and with the Pescadores. As of 1985, the one-way airfare between Taipei and Kaohsiung was set at NT$ 1,100, Taipei and Hwalien at NT$ 750, Taipei and Tainan at NT$960, and Taipei and Pescadores at NT$1,000.

In addition to the above, Taiwan Aviation Corporation (TAC) operates special flights from Taitung to Orchid Island and Green Island, and occasionally from Kaohsiung out to some of the smaller outer islands. Great China Airlines (GCA) operates a helicopter service from Taichung to Sun Moon Lake, Mt. Ali (more commonly known as Alishan), and Pear Mountain in central Taiwan. Yung-Sing Airlines (YSL) schedules flights from Kaohsiung to the Pescadores and other islands, and from Taitung to Orchid island and Green Island.

Strict security measures are enforced on all domestic flights within Taiwan, and foreign passengers are required to show their passports prior to boarding, so don't leave yours behind in Taipei when traveling down-island by air.

For bookings and other information, you may call your travel agent or the carriers directly.

Buses

Local City Buses: One of the first things you'll notice in Taipei is the incredible number of public buses on the streets. For budget-minded travelers, buses provide frequent and a very inexpensive means of trasportation to any point within or without the city limits. However, unless you are endowed with an extra measure of Oriental patience, it is advisable to avoid the buses during heavy rush hours, which fall between 7.30-9.30 a.m. and 5-7 p.m. During these hours, passengers on buses are packed in like sardines and traffic moves at a snail's pace. Outside these hours, buses provide a convenient and inexpensive mode of inter-city transport.

LOCATION 地區		CAL 中華	FAT 遠東	YSL 永興	TAC 台灣
Taipei (02)	台北	7113889	361-5431	531-6763	591-4156/8
Taichung (042)	台中	293961/3		314236	
Tainan (062)	台南	226-2181	225-8111		
Kaohsiung (C7)	高雄	231-5181/5	241-1181/8	8013369	8013793
Makung (069)	馬公	273866/8	274891-5	274541	272338
Hualien (038)	花蓮	322251/3	326191/5	327879	
Taitung (089)	台東		326107-3	326677	
Chi Mei	七美			971241	971274
Chiayi (052)	嘉義	230118-9			
Wonan	望安			991009	

There are two types of city buses: regular and air-conditioned. The regular bus costs NT$ 6 per ride, and the air-conditioned coach costs NT$ 8. Tickets and tokens should be purchased in advance at the little kiosks which you'll find at all bus-stops.

City bus service runs continuously from about 6 a.m. until 11.30 p.m. In order to signal the driver to stop at an upcoming station, simply pull the bell-cord. There are so many buses and bus-routes within metropolitan Taipei that it is best to ask a hotel clerk or local acquaintance for direction before venturing out on your own. All buses are designated by code numbers, which indicate their routes and final destinations. For example, 216, 217, and 218 take you from the Central Train Station, up Chung-Shan North Road, and all the way out to suburban Peitou. 301 runs from Chung-Shan North Road up to Yangming Mountain, and 210 takes you from downtown Taipei out to the National Palace Museum in the suburb of Wai-Shuang-Hsi. Once you know the numbers, it is quite easy to get around on buses.

Airport Shuttles: There are two types of shuttle buses which operate daily service between the old Sung-Shan domestic airport in downtown Taipei and the new Chiang Kai-shek International Airport in Taoyuan. The public Express Bus Line costs NT$ 32 one-way, but it has very little luggage space. It runs every 15 minutes in both directions between 6.30 a.m. and 10.40 p.m. The private Chung-Hsin Line costs NT$ 65 one-way, and it has ample space for luggage. It runs in both directions every five to 10 minutes between 6.35 a.m. and 8 p.m., then reduces

frequency to every 15 minutes until the last bus departs at 10.30 p.m. From the domestic Taipei Airport bus terminal you are only 10 minutes by cab from most major downtown hotels, many of which operate their own private airport shuttles. For further information on airport shuttles call 771-1330.

Highway Express Buses: A special fleet of deluxe highway express buses serves the Taipei/Kaohsiung and Taichung/Kaohsiung routes, using the new North/South Expressway. The one-way fare between Taipei and Kaohsiung is NT$ 363, and reserved-seat tickets for this route may be purchased up to two days in advance. These buses depart both Taipei and Kaohsiung every 20 minutes between 7 a.m. and midnight. This express bus-line is called "Kuo Kuang" (國光), and it departs daily from Taipei's West Bus Terminal, located within the main driveway of the Central Railway Station, across from the Hilton Hotel.

Other towns in Taiwan are served by the Chung Hsing Express Line (中興) and the Golden Horse Express Line (金馬). Chung Hsing Line's express buses have their terminals at all four of Taipei's bus terminals West Terminal, North Terminal, East Terminal, and Chung Lun Terminal. However, Golden Horse Line has its terminals at the North and East terminals only. The map below indicates the locations of these four express bus terminals in Taipei.

A few examples of one-way fares on express highway buses between various scenic points in Taiwan include:

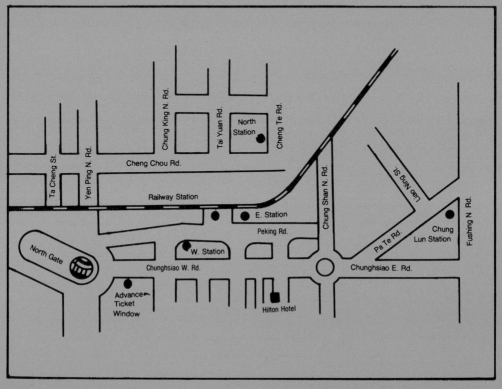

Hwalien/Tienhsiang Lodge	1½ hours	NT$	35
Taichung/Pear Mountain	3½ hours	$	90
Hwalien/Taichung	8 hours	$	195
Hwalien/Pear Mountain	4½ hours	$	105
Taichung/Hsitou	2 hours	$	55
Taichung/Sun Moon Lake	2 hours	$	60
Kaohsiung/Kenting National Park	4 hours	$	118

The best way to purchase reserved-seat bus tickets in advance is to go directly to the appropriate bus terminal and buy them one to two days prior to departure. Most hotel travel-desks and local travel agencies can make these arrangements on your behalf, if you prefer.

Railway

The Chinese Railway Administration maintains an extensive railroad network which connects various points of the island with Taipei and other major cities. In 1978, Taiwan's entire railway system was overhauled and many of the lines were fully electrified, increasing both the efficiency and the frequency of domestic rail services. For example, there are currently 24 daily departures scheduled from Taipei to Kaohsiung via Taichung and Tainan. Passenger carriages are impeccably clean and comfortable, and service includes such local amenities as complimentary cups of fragrant Taiwan tea kept hot throughout your journey with regular infusions of water, newspapers and magazines, and dampened hand towels to refresh your face and hands.

Taiwan's three major railway trunk lines and their intermediate stops are listed below:

Taipei to Kaohsuing Line

Taipei	台北	Changhwa	彰化
Panchiao	板橋	Touliu	斗六
Taoyuan	桃園	Chiayi	嘉義
Hsinchu	新竹	Hsinying	新營
Miaoli	苗栗	Tainan	台南
Taichung	台中	Kaohsiung	高雄

Taipei to Hwalien Line

Taipei	台北	Toucheng	頭城
Patu	八堵	Chiaohsi	礁溪
Juifang	瑞芳	Yilan	宜蘭
Houtung	候硐	Lotung	羅東
Santiaoling	三貂嶺	Suao	蘇澳
Hsuangshi	雙溪	Nan Shen-hu	南聖湖福隆
Fulung	福隆	Hwalien	花蓮

Hwalien to Taitung Line

Hwalien	花蓮	Fuli	富里
Fenglin	鳳林	Chihshang	池上
Kuangfu	光復	Kuanshan	關山
Tuanhui	端穗	Taitung	台東
Yuli	玉里		

The Railway Administration currently offers three types of services:

Chu Hsin (CH): Air-conditioned, limited express

Chu Kuang (CK): First-class, air-conditioned, express

Tsu Chiang (TC): Electrical Multiple Units, air-conditioned

Reservations for first-class express trains in Taiwan must be made at least one but no more than two days prior to scheduled departures. However, although you may purchase round-trip tickets in advance, reservations for return trips must be made upon arrival at your destination, also one to two days in advance. Even for local trains, it is highly advisable to purchase your tickets at least several hours, and preferably a full day, prior to departure. In Taipei, advance train tickets may be purchased directly at the Central Railway Station (台北火車站) by lining up before the appropriate window. Most hotels and travel agencies will also arrange advance train reservations on your behalf. To make first-class express train reservations by phone, call the following numbers:

Taipei; 312-2255 or 551-1131, ext. 2460
Taichung; 228-9608/9 ext. 246 or 346
Kaohsiung; 221-4721, 221-2376, ext. 253

A few sample one-way train fares, current as of 1985, are listed here:

Taipei/Taichung	TC	NT$259
	CK	$224
	CH	$188
Taipei/Tainan	TC	$500
	CK	$450
	CH	$380
Taipei/Kaohsiung	TC	$576
	CK	$496
	CH	$417
Taipei/Hwalien	TC	$300
	CK	$260
	CH	$218

Ferries and Boats

The Taiwan Car Ferry Co. operates daily service between Keelung and the scenic east coast town of Hwalien. It departs daily from Keelung at 9a.m. and arrives in Hwalien at 3p.m. Return trips depart Hwalien nightly at 10:30p.m. and arrive back in Keelung the following morning at 6a.m. The one-way fare is NT$ 350 per person, but special First-Class cabins (two beds plus TV) for two are available for about NT$ 600. Tickets are sold at 108 Chung-Shan North Road, Sec. 2, and at Pier 2, 16 Kang-Hsi Street in Keelung. For further information and reservations in Taipei contact Taiwan Car Ferry Co., Tel. 522-1215/7.

Perhaps the most pleasant boat ride of all in Taiwan is the journey from Kaohsiung to the Pescadore Islands. It departs daily from Pier 1 in Kaohsiung at 8a.m. and arrives in Makung (capital of the Pescadores) 4½ hours later. One-way fares range from NT$ 200-400, depending upon accommodations. You should reserve tickets for this trip at least one day in advance because it's quite popular and is often sold-out. For further information and reservations in Kaohsiung contact: Taiwan Navigation Corp. (Kaohsiung), Tel. 555825, 553730, 553866.

Taxis

Sometimes it seems as if there are as many taxis in Taipei as people. Usually all you have to do to get a cab in Taipei is stand on the curb and wave your arm in the street: within moments a taxi will glide to a halt by your feet, and the door will automatically swing open as the driver pulls a lever inside.

All taxi fares are calculated according to the meter. The basic fare starts at NT$24, and NT$6 is added for each additional half kilometer. Taxis in Taiwan do not expect heavy tips, but they appreciate it if you let them "keep the change" in small coins. Due to the distance and long waits between fares at the CKS International Airport in Taoyuan, taxis are permitted to charge an additional 50 percent of the amount on the meter when running passengers between the airport and town. Currently, this comes to about NT$ 850 (US$ 20) one-way. In small towns and villages down-island, taxis usually charge a set fee of about NT$ 40 to take you anywhere within town. If you wish to retain a taxi for a full-day, or for a long, round-trip excursion to a specific destination, ask a hotel clerk or local acquaintance to negotiate either a set fee for the whole day or a discount on the meter fare.

Be forewarned: although Taiwan's taxi drivers are almost uniformly friendly and polite, they tend to drive like maniacs. Many tourists have their wits scared out as their taxi drivers weave carelessly between speeding buses and trucks, narrowly missing pedestrians, run through red lights, careen through swarms of buzzing motorcycles, and screech blindly around corners. Unfortunately, this sort of driving is the rule rather than the exception in Taiwan, and very little can be done about it. Should you get a particularly reckless driver, have him pull over immediately, pay him the fare on the meter (with no tip!), and hail another cab. There is never a shortage of cabs anywhere in Taipei, day or night, rain or shine.

Very few taxi drivers in Taiwan speak or read English sufficiently well to follow directions given in English. So it's always a good idea to have your destination written out in Chinese before venturing out by cab. Hotel name cards, restaurant matchboxes, local advertisements, or simply the Chinese characters listed next to place-names in this book will also suffice to get you around town by taxi.

Car Rentals and Motoring Advisories

It's best to rely on public transportation such as buses, taxis, and tour-coaches to get around Taipei city. Trying to drive yourself around the city is a needless risk and a good way to spoil your day. But if you plan an extended tour down-island or along the northern coastline, then renting a private car is a fine way to go, for you'll see many more sights and enjoy the freedom to stop whenever and wherever you wish. The new North/South Expressway runs like a spinal column down the center of the island from tip to tip, giving quick, convenient access by car to cities and scenic sites along the way. From the highway, local roads lead out to mountains, mineral spas, temples, and other destinations along Taiwan's tourist trail.

The most convenient car rental agency for foreign tourists is Gordon's Rent-A-Car, where English is spoken and automobiles well maintained. Cars currently rent for NT$ 1,300–1,800 (US$ 31–41) per day, depending on the model. This does not include gas, which costs about NT$ 26 per liter, or US$ 3 per gallon. Gordon's is located at 1098 Cheng-Du

Rd., in Shih-Lin　(士林區，承德路，1098 號)　Tel. 881-9545, 881-6534. Other car rental agencies in Taipei include Hung-Ji Co., Tel. 596-6497/8; Hsing-Fu Co., Tel. 591-6859, 592-9339; Jian-Da Co., Tel. 591-6201, 591-5093; Ya-Tung Co., Tel. 731-2512, 781-8293/4.

If you'd like to splurge a bit and see the island in true comfort and convenience, the best way to see Taipei and all Taiwan is by air-conditioned (or heated) limousines driven by chauffeurs, who also act as personal guides and interpreters. Any hotel travel-desk or local travel agency can arrange a chauffeured limousine for you. The cost varies according to the type of car you specify. The minimum cost for such service is about NT$ 500 (US$ 12.50) per hour, including gas.

No matter how well you drive, Taiwan traffic bears the utmost attention. The Chinese have a strong faith in fate, and a big appetite for "face." The former factor makes them take incredible chances on the road, while the latter drives them to take up even the slightest challenge from other drivers. The road themselves are well maintained, however, and give convenient access to all of Taiwan's scenic treasures. With a little bit of luck, you should have no problems on the road if you bear in mind the following points:

* There are millions of motorcycles on the roads, and they constitute the single greatest hazard to automobile drivers. The most spine-chilling sight on the island is a husband and wife on a 90cc motobike with five or six infants hanging from the handlebars, gas-tank, fenders, and mother's shoulders, speeding through rainy streets among trucks and buses. Steer clear of these.

* Also steer clear of all military vehicles. Military drivers are notorious for their careless driving on public roads. Regardless of the circumstances, military vehicles always have the right of way, and they know it.

* Though roads down south are well marked, the directions are often in Chinese. So look for route numbers instead of place names, and match them with those on your maps. Route numbers are also inscribed on the stone mileage indicators set along the roadsides.

* Stop to ask directions when in doubt. The further south you drive, the friendlier the people become, and someone is always there to help. Don't attempt to pronounce place names in the countryside, because often people there don't understand Mandarin, at least not when it is spoken by foreigners. Show them the Chinese characters, and their eyes will light up with instant recognition, for these are universal symbols to Chinese the world over.

* Keep your gas-tank at least a third full at all times. In the more remote mountainous and coastal regions, gas stations are few and far between, and often closed at night.

Accommodations

Ever since the 1978 big boom in new hotels construction, the quality of hotel accommodations in Taiwan have been steadily improving. Today, travelers in Taiwan have a wide range of styles and prices to choose from when selecting a hotel, especially in Taipei. There are currently 139 tourist hotels operating on the island, 75 of them in metropolitan Taipei, with a total of 22,942 rooms available. Rates range from NT$ 800–2,200 for singles, NT$ 1,000–2,400 for doubles, and NT$ 1,500 up for suites. Ten percent service charge is added to all hotel bills.

Chinese hotels are renowned for attentive, gracious service rendered with a spirit of pride and a genuine desire to please. Visitors are treated as personal guests rather than anonymous patrons, and hospitality is approached more as an art than as an industry. However, Western travelers occasionally encounter frustrations. One reason is the ever-present language barrier: though uniformly trained in English, most Chinese hotel staff understand very little; yet to avoid "losing face" by admitting they don't understand your request, they'll sometimes nod and pretend to understand, then promptly forget about it. Another reason is cultural: Chinese priorities often differ from Western's, and what seems of vital importance to you such as punctuality, may seem trivial to the Chinese. Nevertheless, minor professional shortcomings in Taiwan's hotel industry are far outweighed by its notable strengths; its warmth, friendliness, and courtesy.

Tourist hotels in Taiwan are ranked in two categories: International Tourist and Regular Tourist. The former offers greater luxury and more varied facilities, while the latter offers lower rates and simpler services. In the Appendix, Taipei's "Top Ten" international tourist hotels are listed separately in arbitrary order (may be highly subjective), followed by the other hotels listed alphabetically by city and by category.

Hostels and Guest-Houses

If you're willing to sleep in dormitories, eat in cafeterias, and travel exclusively by bus, then you can actually tour Taiwan for as little as US$ 10 per day by utilizing facilities operated by the China Youth Corps (CYC). CYC operates a series of Youth Activity Centers and Youth Hostels around the island, and budget-minded travelers may avail themselves of these inexpensive facilities. Information and reservations for the 15 hotels and eight activity centers sponsored by CYC may be arranged by writing or calling CYC headquarters at 219 Sung-Kiang Road, Taipei, Tel. 543–5858.

Due to the popularity of these facilities, groups and individuals from overseas who wish to use them should make reservations well in advance. They usually remain fully booked from July through September and from January through February. If you have not made prior arrangements and wish to 'play it by ear' as you go, then at least be sure to call ahead to your next intended stop to make sure hostel accommodations are available.

Rates for room and board vary at different centers, but on the average three meals a day can be had for about US$ 4.50, dormitory accommodations for $3 a night, and local bus transport between various centers for about $2.50. Most of these establishments also offer private individual rooms at higher rates, and some even have spacious bungalows for families or small groups.

A list of Youth Hostels and Youth Activity Centers in Taiwan is given in the Appendix.

There are a number of "guest-houses" in the Taipei area which function as small hotels or inns and provide inexpensive accommodations. Weekly and monthly rates may be arranged as well. Some of the more popular guest-houses in the Taipei are included in the Appendix.

Communication

Despite Taiwan's exotic ambience and traditional culture, it is a modern, highly developed place with complete international postal and telecommunication services. You need never lose contact with the outside world while traveling in Taiwan, although many visitors prefer to do just that. Telecommunications link Taiwan with almost every country in the free world.

Postal Services

Taiwan boasts one of the fastest, most efficient postal services in the world. Mail is collected and delivered every day of the year, and all incoming mail is sorted and distributed within 24 hours of arrival. Many first-time residents have been astounded on seeing the local postmen trudging through driving rains and howling winds during a major typhoon to deliver a single letter to a remote hillside house. Letters mailed to the United States from Taiwan usually arrive at their destinations within five to seven days of posting. Local mail is delivered within 24 to 48 hours.

Taiwan's Central Post Office is located at the North Gate intersection (北門) two blocks west of the Hilton Hotel. This is the best place for foreigners to collect and post mail in Taipei. This office also provides inexpensive cartons and packing services for parcel posting. This and other post offices around town are open from 8a.m. until 6p.m. Monday through Friday, 8a.m. until 1p.m. on Saturdays. They are closed on Sundays.

Stamps may be purchased at the mail counter of any tourist hotel in Taiwan, and letters may be dropped in any hotel or public mail box, of which there are many in Taiwan. Local mail goes in the green boxes, and international airmail goes into the red boxes. Current rates for letters addressed to destinations in Europe and America are NT$ 18 for letters under 10 grams (plus NT$ 11 for each additional 10 grams), NT$ 9 for postcards, and NT$ 12 for aerograms. Postal rates change from time to time, so be sure to inquire before posting your cards and letters.

Taiwan's decorative and commemorative postage stamps are highly prized in the world of philately. Charming Chinese themes, such as landscape painting, porcelain, and calligraphy, are often incorporated into the design of stamps. If you or your friends back home collect stamps, be sure to take back a sampling from Taiwan.

Telephone, Telegraph, and Telex

Local city calls may be dialed from any public pay telephone, of which there are many in Taiwan. Local calls cost NT$ 1 for three minutes, after which the line is automatically cut off. For further conversation, drop in another coin and dial again. Public telephones take NT$ 1 coins for local calls, and have NT$ 5-coin slots for long-distance calls within Taiwan.

Long-distance calls within Taiwan can be dialed directly from private or public pay phones by using the following local area codes:

Taipei	02	Tainan	062
Keelung	032	Kaohsiung	07
Taoyuan	033	Hwalien	038
Taichung	042	Ilan	039
Hsinchu	035	Chiayi	052
Taitung	089	Pescadores	069

Overseas long-distance calls may be placed from private phones by dialing the overseas operator at 100. Both person-to-person and station-to-station calls are accepted. To place overseas calls from public facilities, you must visit an office of the International Telecommunications Administration (國際電信局). The main office is open 24 hours a day, seven days a week, and is located at 28 Hang-Chou South Road., Sec. 1 (杭州南路一段28號) Tel. 344-3781. Other ITA offices in Taipei and their hours of operation are listed below:

CKS International Airport	7a.m.—9p.m.
Taipei Domestic Airport	8a.m.—9p.m.
Tel. 771-6112	
23 Chung-Shan N. Rd.,	
Sec. 2, Tel. 541-7434	8a.m.—9:30p.m.
118 Chung-Hsiao W. Rd.,	
Sec. 1 (adjacent to Central	
Post Office) Tel. 344-3779	8a.m.—9:30p.m.

Both international and domestic telegrams may be sent from any of the ITA branch offices listed above, or from the mail counter of major international tourist hotels. ITA offers both "Urgent" (12 hours) and "Ordinary" (24 hours) telegram services. Visitors who wish to register local cable addresses in Taiwan should do so at ITA's main office.

Telex services are available at the main office of ITA, and at major international tourist hotels. ITA's main office also provides 24-hour facsimile service for transmitting documents and pictures to the following cities: New York, Washington DC, San Francisco, Singapore, and Bahrain.

News Media

Newspapers and Periodicals

Two English-language newspapers are published daily in Taiwan: *China Post* (morning) and *China News* (afternoon). In addition to international and regional news culled from major wire services, as well as local features written by their own staff, these newspapers carry financial news, entertainment sections, sports reports, and guides to English programs on TV and radio. Most hotel newsstands carry both. *The Asian Wall Street Journal* and the *International Herald Tribune* are also available at most bookstores and hotel newsstands, and some also carry the *South China Morning Post*.

The Government Information Office publishes an illustrated monthly magazine in English, *Free China Review,* which features articles on Chinese culture, travel in Taiwan, and other aspects of life in the Republic of China. Beyond this, the only English periodicals published locally are devoted exclusively to industrial and financial news.

Foreign periodicals available in Taiwan include *Time, Newsweek, Life,* and a varying assortment of fashion magazines, all of which are sold at English bookstores and hotel newsstands. All foreign publications brought into Taiwan are subject to official government censorship, so don't be surprised if you discover a page or two missing from your newspaper.

Radio and Television

There is only one radio station in Taiwan which broadcasts programs entirely in English. International Community Radio Taiwan (ICRT) broadcasts popular Western music and other programs in English 24 hours a day, with international news reports provided on the hour between 7a.m. and 11p.m. Tune your radio dial to 1550 AM or 100.1 and 100.9 FM to receive ICRT broadcasts. Chinese radio stations broadcast a wide variety of music, both Western and Chinese, so if you wish to listen to local tunes, fiddle with your radio dial until you hear something which pleases you.

There are three television stations which broadcast scheduled programs throughout Taiwan, where there is currently an average of one television set per household. The three stations are China Television Co. (CTV), Chinese Television Service (CTS), and Taiwan Television Enterprise (TTV). All three stations broadcast exclusively in Chinese, but they frequently schedule English-language films and programs from the West, which are shown with Chinese sub-titles. Check the local English-language newspapers for details regarding English films and programs on Chinese television.

Health and Emergencies

Although medical treatment and dental work cost far less in Taipei than in any Western country or Japan, the quality of medical facilities and services is excellent and up-to-date. It's such a good deal, in tact, that travel agents in Japan and Southeast Asia organize special "Medical Tours" to Taipei exclusively for medical treatments. The cost of a complete physical examination, for example, including three days room-and-board at a good hospital, comes to about NT$ 10,000 (US$ 260). Three-hour medical check-ups are available for NT$ 4500 (US$ 120). Major dental work also remains a bargain in Taipei, and residents of Hong Kong and Tokyo frequently fly to Taipei to have their regular dental work done. If you're interested in traditional Chinese therapy rather than modern Western forms, refer to the chapter on "The Magic of Chinese Medicine," which introduces the subject in detail and recommends an excellent traditional Chinese physician who speaks English.

Major Western-style hospitals and dental clinics in the Taipei area are listed in the Appendix.

Useful Telephone Numbers

Police

Emergency	110
Foreign Affairs Department of National Police Administration	321-8673
Foreign Affairs Department of Municipal Police Administration	311-9940
Foreign Affairs Police, Taichung	(042) 241141
Foreign Affairs Police, Kaohsiung	(07) 221-5796
Foreign Affairs Police, Tainan	(062) 229704
Foreign Affairs Police, Keelung	(032) 268181

Hospitals

Taiwan Adventist Hospital	771-8151
Mackay Memorial Hospital	543-3535
Country Hospital	771-3161
Veterans General Hospital	871-2121
Cheng Keng Memorial Hospital	713-5211

Fire — 119

Directory Assistance

Information, Chinese	104
Information, English	311-6796
Long Distance Information	105
Overseas Operator	100

Others

Tourism Bureau	721-8541
Taiwan Visitors Association	594-3261
China External Trade Development Council	752-2311, 715-1551
Board of Foreign Trade	351-0271
Ministry of Foreign Affairs	311-9292
Government Information Office	341-9211
American Institute in Taiwan	709-2000
Taiwan UFO Research Association	709-8285, 709-8290
ROC Golf Association	711-7482, 711-3046

Visa & Mountain Permits	321-3175
Extensions of visa, Resident Certificates, etc.	361-0159

Dining Out

Dining out remains the single greatest pleasure Taipei holds in store for the traveler. Whether you opt for Chinese or Western cuisine, Japanese *sushi* or Korean Barbecue, the restaurants of Taipei have something tasty for every palate. The happy marriage between China's highly sophisticated culinary arts and Taiwan's abundant supplies of the very best culinary products has given birth to a restaurant industry which never fails to delight even the most experienced epicure. Naturally, when in Taiwan it's best to do as the Chinese and go for gourmet Chinese cuisine, but if you prefer Western food, the restaurants listed in the Appendix will serve you a good meal with proper service. Due to the staggering number of restaurants operating in Taipei, it is advisable to select places included in this list, especially when opting for Western food. Though almost any Chinese eatery in Taipei serves good food, many of the so-called "Western restaurants" serve fare that looks and tastes like a careless melange of East and West.

All the restaurants listed are located in Taipei, where travelers generally spend most of their time and do most of their gourmet dining. Once you've mastered dining out in Taipei, you'll be able to make it on your own down-island, where the choice of restaurants and cuisines is far less confusing. When traveling down south, it's generally best to stick with Chinese food, for the demand for Western cuisine there is not yet sufficiently strong to support genuine gourmet Western restaurants. Good places to eat in southern towns are recommended in the appropriate chapters of the places section.

For details regarding the many regional varieties of Chinese food and the many delights of Taipei's nightlife, please refer to the chapters entitled "Tasting and Toasting, the Chinese Way" and "Nights of White Satin."

Northern Style

Recommended Dishes: Peking Duck（北平烤鴨）, Lamb and Leeks（蔥爆羊肉）, Hot and Sour Soup（酸辣湯）. Celery in Mustard Sauce（梨山芹菜）, Cold Shredded Chicken with Sauce（涼拌雞絲）, Sweet and Sour Yellow Fish（糖醋黃魚）. Steamed Vegetable Dumplings（素蒸餃）

Southern Style

Recommended Dishes: Roast Duck（燒鴨）, Poached Chicken with Onions and Oil（蔥油雞）, Greens with Oyster Sauce（蠔油芥蘭）, Steamed Whole Fish（清蒸全魚）, Assorted "Dim-Sum"（各種點心）, Roast Pigeon（燒鴿子）, Cabbage with Cream（奶油白菜）.

Eastern/Coastal Style

Recommended Dishes: West Lake Vinegar Fish
(西湖全魚), River Eel Sauteed with Leeks¹(韮黃鱔魚)
Fried Jumbo Prawns (乾燒明蝦), Braised Pork
Haunch (紅燒膀蹄), Sauteed Sweet-Pea Shoots
(炒豆苗), Drunken Chicken (醉雞), "Lion Head"
Meatballs (獅子頭), Steamed Crab (清蒸螃蟹),
Braised Beef Loin (紅燒牛腩).

Western/Central Style

Recommended Dishes: (Szechuan) Steam Pom-
fret (清蒸鯧魚), Chicken "Duke of Bao" (公保雞丁),
"Grandma's" Beancurd (麻婆豆腐), Fragrant Egg-
plant (魚香茄子), Whole Carp in Fermented Chili
Sauce (豆瓣魚), Duck Smoked in Camphor and Tea
(樟茶鴨), Twice-Cooked Pork (回鍋肉).
(Hunan) Frog Legs in Chili Sauce (麻辣田雞腿),
Honey Ham (蜜汁火腿), Beggar's Chicken (叫化雞),
Minced Pigeon in Bamboo Cup (竹節鴿盅), Steamed
Whole Fish (清蒸全魚).

Taiwanese Seafood

Recommended Dishes: Steamed Crab (清蒸螃蟹),
Poached Squid (墨魚), Fresh Poached Shrimp
(鹹水蝦), Shrimp Rolls (蝦卷), Grilled Eel
(烤鰻魚), *Sashimi,* or raw fish (生魚片), Grilled
Clams (烤蚵), Turtle Soup (鼈湯).

Chinese Vegetarian Cuisine

Recommended Dishes: Try the various types of
"beef," "pork," "chicken," etc., made entirely
from various forms of soy-bean curd, as well as fresh
crispy vegetables.

Chopsticks

There's nothing more Chinese than chopsticks.
The Chinese have been using two sticks to pick up a
single grain of rice and one stick to carry two buckets
of water ever since time began. Nothing ever appears
on the Chinese banquet table that cannot be
manipulated single-handedly with a simple pair of
chopsticks. Today, as the popularity of Chinese
cuisine spreads throughout the world, it is considered *de rigueur* to use chopsticks when eating
Chinese food. And in Taiwan you'll find abundant
opportunities to practice.
The Chinese only use forks and knives in the
kitchen—and when eating Western food. For their
own cuisine, they prefer to have everything cut,
sliced, diced, or otherwise prepared, in the kitchen
so that the food is in bite-sized pieces when it
appears on the table; ready to be eaten. As you'll no
doubt discover after a few banquets, those who wield
their chopsticks too slowly often miss the choicest
morsels whenever a new dish appears on the table.
Another advantage of using chopsticks to eat
Chinese food is that you leave most of the heavy oils
on the platters whenever reaching for a bite of food,
rather than scooping them into your mouth or onto

your rice with a spoon. Chopsticks can also be used
to select choice morsels from the best dishes for the
guest-of-honor or just for a friend at the table. The
polite way to do this is to turn the sticks around so
that you use the clean blunt ends to serve food to
others. Last but not least, using chopsticks makes
you a little more Chinese and a little less foreign in
Chinese eyes, and this always improves the pleasure
of traveling in Taiwan.

Here's how to handle chopsticks:

A. First, set one stick securely between the thumb
   and forefinger in the depression at the base of the
   thumb. Use the thumb to apply pressure inward
   on the stick, and the third finger to apply pressure
   outward, so that the stick is clamped securely.

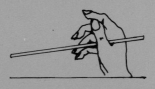

B. Place the second stick between the top of the
   thumb and the second and third fingers, and hold
   it like a pencil. Make sure the tips are even and
   the bottom stick is held securely.

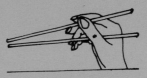

C. To manipulate the sticks, bend the second and
   third fingers slightly forward, until the tips come
   together around the desired morsel of food. Hold
   firmly, but avoid excess pressure, or the morsel
   may slip out. Guide gently to your bowl or mouth,
   adjust sticks, and repeat.

As a means of seeing the world cheaply and conveniently, group tours are very popular.

Unfortunately, with most of them you're tied to the group. So the opportunities of being treated like an individual are rare.

Thai's Royal Orchid Holidays, on the other hand, are uniquely different.

With us, you get all the benefits of group travel without having to travel in a group.

We give you the flexibility of travelling and staying where you want to, when you want to.

And, as we now have Royal Orchid Holidays in Europe as well as Asia, there's an even bigger selection for you to choose from.

See your travel agent for the brochures now.

And enjoy the advantages of group travel without the group.

You can get very lonely on our group holidays.

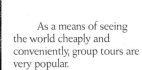

MNC&H/THA/6426

Apa Maps

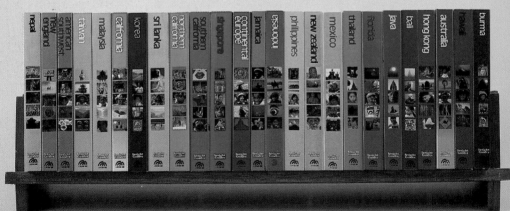

"No praise can be too high for Apa Productions' series of Insight Guides."
— Business Traveller, London

Since 1970, Insight Guides have established a milestone in travel-guide publishing. California or Korea, Mexico or Malaysia, each title in this fast-growing series will guide you with unprecedented style, inspiring as they inform.

And now a series of Apa maps which will eventually complement Insight Guides. Setting the highest standards in their fields, each map has a laminated cover that makes it ideal for rough handling.

Two unbeatable travel companions. Go to your nearest bookshop or write to us for further information:

APA PRODUCTIONS (PTE) LTD
5 Lengkong Satu Singapore 1441
Tel: 4450751 Cable: APAPRODUCT Telex: APASIN RS 36201

Insight Guides
FOR THE SOPHISTICATED TRAVELLER

Tours and Attractions

Five Taipei travel agencies operate daily bus-tours for travelers. All buses are air-conditioned, and all tours include bilingual guides. Tickets for these tours may be obtained through any hotel travel desk, or by contacting these five agencies directly:

Cathay Express, 306-5B Kuang-Fu S. Rd., Tel. 731-2355;

China Express, 100 Ren-Ai Rd., Sec. 3, Tel. 707-7777;

South East Travel Service, 58 Chung-Shan North Rd., Sec. 3, Tel. 571-3001;

Taiwan Coach Tours, 189 Hsing-Yi Rd., Sec 4, 7th Fl., Tel. 704-9461;

Wen-Bin Travel Agency, 575 Cheng-Teh Rd., Tel. 591-4133.

The 10 most popular city and island tours offered by these agencies are briefly introduced below:

Taipei City: This half-day city tour covers the National Palace Museum, Martyr's Shrine, other famous City Sights, and offers glimpses of contemporary Chinese urban life along the way. (NT$ 450 adults, NT$ 285 children)

CKS Memorial and Yangming Mountain Park: Tour begins at the grand-scale Chiang Kai-shek Memorial Hall downtown, then proceeds up to lovely Yangming Mountain Park with its colorful gardens and bucolic settings. On the way back,

you'll stop at the China Porcelain and Pottery factory (NT$ 500 adults, NT$ 250 children) to watch traditional Chinese ceramics in production.

Taipei by Night: An enduring favorite, this nocturnal tour commences with a traditional Mongolian Barbecue dinner, then proceeds to the famous Lung-Shan Temple and "Snake Alley" bazaar. It also gives you a taste of Chinese opera and glimpses of various night-markets. (NT$ 650 adults, NT$ 325 children)

Wu-Lai Aborigine Village: This is a half-day excursion to the colorful aborigine village at Wu-Lai, about an hour's drive out of Taipei. You'll see aborigine performances, hike through lush mountain terrain, and enjoy spectacular scenery. (NT$ 570 adults, NT$ 285 children)

The Northern Coast: A half-day tour of Taiwan's scenic northern coastline, this excursion takes you first to the port city of Keelung and the fantastic rock formations at Yeh-Liu, then proceeds down the northwest coast back to Taipei. (NT$ 570 adults, NT$ 285 children)

Taroko Gorge: Taroko Gorge is considered to be one of the "Seven Wonders of Asia" and it remains the single most popular tourist attraction outside of Taipei. Twelve miles of craggy canyon, enclosed by towering cliffs of marble which soar up to 3,000 feet high, Taroko Gorge is bisected by the eastern portion of the East-West Cross-Island Highway, with 38 tunnels cut into solid rock and several marble bridges. This tour flies you to Hwalien from Taipei early in the morning, then takes you up the Gorge for a 12-mile bus-tour of breathtaking

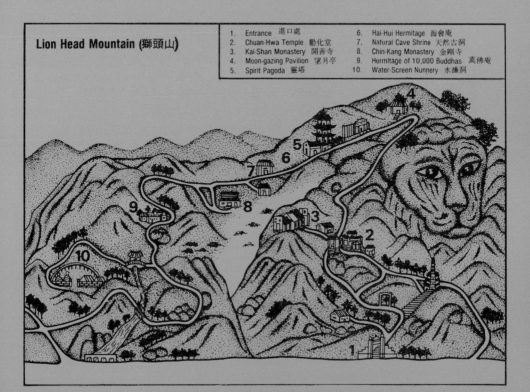

Lion Head Mountain (獅頭山)

1. Entrance 進口處
2. Chuan-Hwa Temple 勸化堂
3. Kai-Shan Monastery 開善寺
4. Moon-gazing Pavilion 望月亭
5. Spirit Pagoda 靈塔
6. Hai-Hui Hermitage 海會庵
7. Natural Cave Shrine 天然古洞
8. Chin-Kang Monastery 金剛寺
9. Hermitage of 10,000 Buddhas 高佛庵
10. Water-Screen Nunnery 水濂洞

beauty. Lunch is served in the alpine airs of the Tien-Hsiang Lodge, then your bus returns to Hwalien in time for aboriginal performances by the Ami tribe and a tour of Taiwan's biggest marble factory and showroom. The tour returns to Taipei by air around 5p.m. (NT$ 2,500 adults, NT$ 1,250 children)

Sun Moon Lake: This two-day tour takes you to bucolic Sun Moon Lake, Taiwan's favorite honeymoon resort, located 2,500 feet above sea level in Taiwan's only land-locked county. This all-year resort is famous for its landscape, hiking, temples, and pagodas. The tour departs Taipei by air-conditioned bus and arrives Taichung in time for lunch. You then proceed by bus to Sun Moon Lake, about an hour's drive from Taichung, passing through greening fields of sugar cane, tea, and vegetables, rice paddies, banana and pineapple plantations, and other lush scenery. After checking into a hotel, you'll go for a leisurely two-hour boat cruise on the lake. The second morning is free time, then after lunch the tour drives back to Taichung and entrains for Taipei, arriving back in town by nightfall. (NT$ 3,200 for double occupancy, NT$ 3,600 for single occupancy, NT$ 1,600 children)

East-West Cross-Island Highway and Sun Moon Lake: The 120-mile East-West Cross-Island Highway, a remarkable feat of engineering by any standards, is known in Taiwan as the "Rainbow of Treasure Island." The scenic wonders it unfolds are indeed as colorful as a rainbow. This three-day tour commences with a morning flight to Hwalien from Taipei, followed by a drive through spectacular Taroko Gorge and lunch at the Tien-Hsiang Lodge.

It then proceeds to scenic Pear Mountain (Li-Shan) for an overnight stay at the Li-Shan House. You'll spend the next morning sightseeing on Pear Mountain, then depart for Taichung, arriving in time for lunch and some city sightseeing. Next stop is Sun Moon Lake, where you'll spend the second night and tour the lake on the morning of the third day. The tour returns to Taichung by bus after lunch, then entrains for the trip back to Taipei. (NT$ 6,800 for double occupancy, NT$ 7,600 for single occupancy, NT$ 3,400 children)

Sun Moon Lake and Mt. Ali: This three-day tour features a visit to Mt. Ali (Ali-Shan), a magnificent range of 18 peaks which flanks the great Central Mountain Range in central Taiwan. A 45-mile narrow-gauge railway with diesel trains traverses 80 bridges and passes through 50 tunnels to bring you from the town of Chiayi up to Ali-Shan Village, which at 7,500 feet altitude is the highest railway station in the Orient. From a vantage point on Mt. Chu, you can catch one of the most spellbinding views in all Taiwan: the "Sea of Clouds" which swirls like water and fills the entire valley between Mt. Chu and 13,114-foot Mt. Morrison ("Jade Mountain") 25 miles away. The latter is the highest peak in Northeast Asia and a favorite destination for mountain climbers. This tour commences with an air-conditioned bus-ride from Taipei to Taichung, then up to Sun Moon Lake, where you'll spend the first night. After a morning tour of the lake and lunch at noon the following day, the tour proceeds by bus to Chiayi, where you'll board the mountain railway for the 3½-hour ride up to Mt. Ali. The second night is spent at the Ali-Shan Guest House,

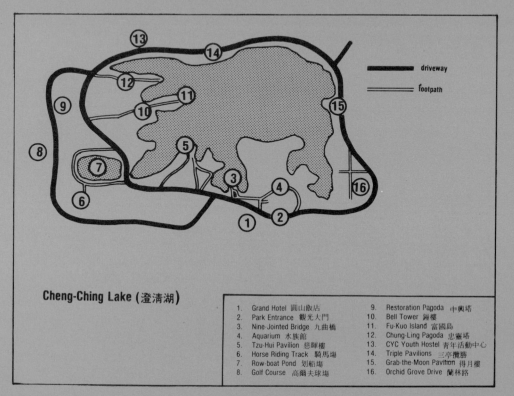

Cheng-Ching Lake (澄清湖)

1.	Grand Hotel 圓山飯店	9.	Restoration Pagoda 中興塔
2.	Park Entrance 觀光大門	10.	Bell Tower 鐘樓
3.	Nine-Jointed Bridge 九曲橋	11.	Fu-Kuo Island 富國島
4.	Aquarium 水族館	12.	Chung-Ling Pagoda 忠靈塔
5.	Tzu-Hui Pavilion 慈暉樓	13.	CYC Youth Hostel 青年活動中心
6.	Horse Riding Track 騎馬場	14.	Triple Pavilions 三亭攬勝
7.	Row-boat Pond 划船場	15.	Grab-the-Moon Pavilion 得月樓
8.	Golf Course 高爾夫球場	16.	Orchid Grove Drive 蘭林路

followed by a tour of the mountain the next morning and a return trip by rail to Chiayi after lunch. From there you'll board an express bus back to Taipei. (NT$ 7,000 for double occupancy, NT$ 7,600 for single occupancy, NT$ 3,500 children)

Round-the-Island Tour: This four-day tour is an extension of the Cross-Island Highway tour, with the addition of a visit to the southern seaport of Kaohsiung, Taiwan's second largest city. The first day is spent driving to and touring Sun Moon Lake, where you'll spend the first night. The second day returns you to Taichung, then on down to Kaohsiung by train, where you'll spend the second night. On the third day you'll visit various scenic sites around Kaohsiung, including lovely Cheng-Ching Lake and Long Life Mountain, then fly to Hwalien in the afternoon. After an overnight stay in Hwalien, you'll spend the fourth day driving up Taroko Gorge and have lunch at the Tien-Hsiang Lodge, then return to Hwalien for Ami aboriginal performances and a tour of the marble factory. The tour flies back to Taipei around 5p.m. (NT$ 8,500 for double occupancy, NT$ 9,700 for single occupancy, NT$ 4,250 children)

Cultural Activities

Museums and Cultural Centers

The rich and colorful history of the Chinese together with the pride they take in knowing and preserving their cultural roots have spawned many museums in Taiwan devoted to the procurement, care, study and display of objects of lasting value and interest. In Taipei alone, there are about a dozen of such institutions with the world-renowned **National Palace Museum** as the largest of them all. Itself a monument with 18 years of history behind it, the museum is home to some 620,250 priceless relics of bronze, porcelain, jade, lacquer, enamelware, paintings, portraits, tapestry and embroidery, rare books and documents. The museum is open daily throughout the year and admission charge is a mere NT$ 20 per person.

Just close by is the **Chinese Culture and Movie Center** whose main attractions are a wax museum and a 'Middle Kingdom Village.' The former displays wax models dressed in authentic Chinese costumes worn through the ages while the latter contains palaces, houses and inns architecturally similar to those found in the old Chinese Imperial and early Republican times. Many movie-makers have used this village as a shooting location and that probably explains why Chinese movie fans have found the setting in the background familiar in different movies. Admission into the center costs NT$ 30 and an addition NT$ 15 for each child you have with you.

Second in magnificence to the Palace Museum is the **National Museum of History** within which are exhibits reflecting more than 4,000 years of Chinese culture. The treasures found in this institution are not to be named nor listed; they have to be seen to be appreciated. Initially set up with public funds,

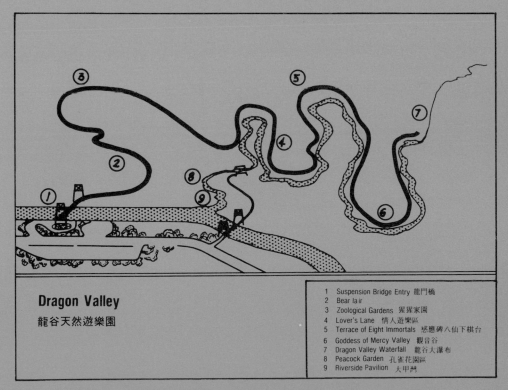

Dragon Valley

龍谷天然遊樂園

1 Suspension Bridge Entry 龍門橋
2 Bear lair
3 Zoological Gardens 冥冥家園
4 Lover's Lane 情人遊樂區
5 Terrace of Eight Immortals 感應碑八仙下棋台
6 Goddess of Mercy Valley 觀音谷
7 Dragon Valley Waterfall 龍谷大瀑布
8 Peacock Garden 孔雀花園區
9 Riverside Pavilion 大甲溪

the collection housed is being continuously enlarged by private individuals, mainly civic-conscious Chinese. Open daily, admission charge is NT$ 5.

In addition to these are special musuems like the **Postal Museum,** the **Children's Museum,** the **Butterfly Museum,** etc. Do not be deceived for although the names speak for themselves, visits to them while downtown are worthwhile. Refer to the Appendix for addresses and visiting hours.

Art Galleries

These galleries exhibit works of art by both established old masters and promising young artists. They display an impressive range of styles, from traditional Chinese landscape painting and calligraphy to contemporary Western abstracts and still-lifes, and the artists employ both Eastern and Western materials and methods. For further information on art and art exhibits in Taipei, contact the Taipei Art Guild（藝術家畫廊）at #7, Lane 728, Chung-Shan North Rd., Sec. 6 in Suburban Tien Mou, Tel. 871-8465. Some of the more interesting art galleries in Taipei are listed in the Appendix.

A spacious **Taipei Fine Arts Museum** has been opened recently at 181 Chung-Shan North Road, Sec. 3 (Tel. 595-7656) about 200 meters south of the Grand Hotel. This ultra-modern facility frequently sponsors exhibitions of arts and crafts by renowned international and local talents.

Chinese Opera

Taiwan is one of the best places in the world to attend the opera, Chinese style. From the bizarre melodies mouthed by magnificently-costumed performers to the exotic orchestral accompaniment to the astounding acrobatics and martial arts displays of the performers, a night at a Peking Opera will prove entertaining as well as educational.

There are two places in Taipei where Peking Opera is performed regularly. The **Armed Forces Cultrual Activities Center** (Tel. 331-5438), across from the Chinese Bazaar at #69 Chung Hwa Road （國軍文藝活動中心台北市中華路一段69號）has performances daily throughout the year that begin promptly at 7:30p.m. Many local fans arrive an hour late just to catch the features. The other venue is the **Sun Yat-sen Memorial Hall** （台北市仁愛路國父紀念館） ; Tel. 702-2411 which stages shows every Saturday and Sunday at 2 p.m.

For a preliminary taste of Peking or Taiwan Opera, try the television set. Live performances are broadcast almost every day. In the backalleys of Taipei and outside the big city, keep your eyes open for the traveling opera companies that set up and perform for several days.

Dance

There is a limited amount of traditional folk dancing in Taiwan, most performed by minority groups. Snippets of aboriginal dance can be viewed at the various aborigine tourism centers around the island. Other forms of dance are performed as part of the

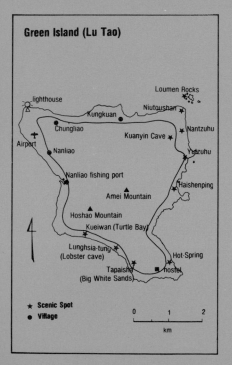

Chinese culture show staged daily at 10:30a.m., 2p.m. and 4p.m. in the first briefing room on the third floor of the **Dr. Sun Yat-sen** Memorial Hall.

On the other hand, modern dance has gained in popularity in Taiwan in the past decade. The Cloud Gate Dance Ensemble, led by Lin Hwaimin, has spearheaded the movement. It combines both Chinese and Western techniques and ideas choreographed to the music of contemporary Chinese composers. The group, internationally-acclaimed during a tour of Europe in 1981, holds regular performances in Taipei. Consult your hotel or the Taiwan Visitors Association (Tel. 594-2111/4) for the schedules of the Cloud Gate ensemble.

Music

Taiwan has produced numerous musicians of world class. Western classical music is regularly performed at various venues in Taipei by the Taiwan Provincial Symphony Orchestra and the Taipei Municipal Symphony Orchestra. Consult your hotel information desk or such organizations as the National Music Council and the Chinese Classical Music Association for information on scheduled performances. Traditional Chinese music has its roots in both special temple rituals and folk music. One good event at which to listen to temple music are the elaborate rituals held annually on September 28th to celebrate Confucius' birthday.

Handicraft Centers

If people were classified according to how good they are with their hands, you will definitely find the Taiwanese ranked among the top.

The Taiwanese take great pride in the things they can make with their hands; from lanterns and toys, handbags and baskets, bamboo and rattan crafts, rugs and carpets, to knitwear and embroideries, and so the list goes on. Their government shoved that pride one rung higher when it erected a four-storied air-conditioned building, housed in it a range of items which have undergone prior inspection for design and quality, named the building the **Handicraft Exhibition Hall** and opened it officially for public viewing in June 1977. Exhibits number more than 1,500 and are from all parts of Taiwan, some produced by cottage industry, and others by regular plants. The Hall, in Tsaotun, is situated on the highway running from Taichung to the Sun Moon Lake and the Chitou Forest Recreation Area. Open daily except Mondays, national and public holidays from 9a.m. to 12 noon and from 2p.m. to 5p.m., the hall is well worth a visit.

While in Tsaotun, also call at the **Taiwan Provincial Handicraft Institute** also operated by the Taiwan Provincial Government within which you will find a factory, a kiln and a research laboratory.

In Taipei, an excellent selection of local handicrafts are on display for sale at the Chinese Handicraft Mart at #1 Hsu Chou St., (徐州路 1 號), Tel. 321-7233. This is a good place to do your souvenir and gift shopping all in one trip.

Movies

Here is a fact which may surprise you: Taiwan residents view more films per year per capita than any other people in the world, including Americans. The average citizen of Taiwan sees about three full-length movies per week, and these include both local and foreign films. Taiwan is one of Hollywood's most lucrative markets, and all major Hollywood studios have permanent representatives here.

Most of the foreign films which come to Taiwan are from United States and they are always shown in English, with Chinese subtitles. This means that traveling movie fans need never fear a shortage of Western film entertainment when in Taiwan. On the other hand, since almost all Chinese films are shown with English subtitles, you may also enjoy local movies while in Taiwan. This is the place to see a *kung-fu* fighting movie, especially if you have never seen one before.

The daily *China Post* and *China News* carry information regarding English films currently playing in Taipei. There are usually three to five performances per day, with the last show beginning around 9p.m. Some of the most popular cinemas in Taipei are listed in the Appendix.

Festival

He makes a wise traveler who would take special note of the national holidays and festive seasons in the country he is visiting for in that way, he could plan his itinerary such as to avoid unnecessary frustration while at the same time creating ample opportunities to be part of the local festive scene.

In addition to ancient festivals such as Chinese Lunar New Year and the Mid Autumn Moon Festival, and national holidays such as Double-Ten and Dr. Sun Yat-sen's birthday, there are scores of local Taiwanese festivals known as *pai-pai* (pronounced 'bye-bye'), which are colorful celebrations held in honor of local city gods and deities. There are over 100 popular city gods in Taiwan, and not only are their birthdays commemorated; each of their 'death days' and 'deification days,' are also occasions for celebration. The sensible government therefore, only recognizes the major ones and declares these official public holidays during which most businesses and public offices are closed.

'Celebration' of *pai-pai* days begins with the faithful offering the best food and wine to the respective deities and ends with the devotees themselves gorging the offerings but not before they are sure that the deities have had their fill. This is usually the time taken for a joss-stick to burn out. Few Taiwanese remain entirely sober on these occasions, and everyone spends a lot of money to *ching-keh*, or "invite friends out." In recent years, the government has tried to dissuade the Taiwanese from indulging in such frequent and extravagant celebrations, branding the custom as "wasteful," but the colorful *pai-pai* tradition is too deeply ingrained in the island's culture to be abandoned. Besides, the relatively well-off people of Taiwan can afford it.

National holidays, which are of more recent origin, follow the Gregorian solar calendar used in the West but most festive dates still follow the lunar calendar thus, they vary from year to year. It is safest to check exact dates at the time of planning for your trip.

Brief descriptions of the major annual holidays follow:

NOTE: Only festivals marked with asteriks (*) are observed as national holidays.

January

* Foundation Day, (January 1)

On Jan. 1, 1912, Dr. Sun Yat-sen was inaugurated as the first President of the newly founded Republic of China. Also on that day, China officially switched from the lunar to the Gregorian calendar. This occasion is celebrated annually in Taipei with parades, dragon and lion dances, traditional music, patriotic speeches, and of course lots of firecrackers.

* Chinese Lunar New Year (First day of first lunar month, usually late-January to mid February)

Traditionally called the "Spring Festival," Chinese Lunar New Year remains the biggest celebration of the year in Taiwan, as it has for millenia in all Chinese communities. The festival is observed in various stages for a full month, from the 16th day of the 12th month until the 15th day of the first month although, today in Taiwan offices and shops generally close for only a week around New Year's Day.

Many ancient customs are associated with the Lunar New Year. For example, all outstanding debts must be paid off before New Year's Eve; failure to do so is a grave affront and an omen of bad luck for the coming year. Many wealthy Chinese businessmen in Taiwan keep running accounts in their favorite restaurants and clubs, paying their bills only once a year just before New Year's Eve. Another custom is exchanging gifts, especially little red envelopes (*hung-bao*) stuffed with "lucky money," the amount depending on the closeness of the relationship between giver and taker. Everyone dresses up in new clothes at New Year—from hats down to shoes—and this symbolizes renewal and a fresh start in life for the coming year. People visit family and friends and spend a lot of money on entertainment. Indeed, local banks are often plagued with cash shortages at this time of year. The dominant color is red, which is universally regarded as auspicious among the Chinese; red flowers, red clothing, red streamers, red cakes and candies, and the ubiquitous red envelopes appears everywhere.

At the stroke of the midnight on New Year's Eve, the entire island suddenly reverberates to the staccato explosions of millions of fire-crackers and sky-rockets, as every temple and household in Taiwan lights the fuses which will "frighten evil spirits" from their thresholds, insuring an auspicious start to the New Year. The Chinese invented gunpowder for this very purpose over 1,000 years ago—long before the West ever knew of it—and the fusillades which mark Chinese New Year make America's Fourth of July celebrations seem tame by comparison.

The stock phrase to offer all your friends and acquaintances whenever and wherever you encounter them during this period is *kung-hsi fa-tsai*

(pronounced "goong-shee fah-tsai"), which means "I wish you happiness and prosperity." The witty rhyming retort to this greeting is *hung-bao na-lai* ("hoong-bao nah-lai"), or "Hand over a red envelope!"

February

The Lantern Festival (Fifteenth day of first lunar month, usually mid to late-February)

The Lantern Festival, which falls on the first full moon of the lunar new year, marks the end of the Spring Festival. Celebrants appear at night in the streets, parks, and temples of Taiwan carrying colorful lanterns with auspicious phrases inscribed on them in elegant calligraphy. This tradition is supposed to insure against evil and illness in the coming year. The festival food associated with this event is a sweet dumpling of glutinous rice-paste stuffed with bean or date paste and called *yuan-hsiao* (元宵). Major temples are excellent places to observe the Lantern Festival in full color and pageantry. Prizes are awarded for the most beautiful and original lantern designs.

March

Birthday of Kuan-Yin, Goddess of Mercy (Nineteenth of second lunar month, usually late-March)

Kuan-Yin is one of the most popular Buddhist deities in Taiwan, Korea, and Japan. Known for her compassion and love for mankind, she is one of Taiwan's patron protective deities. Her birthday is celebrated with colorful *pai-pai* ceremonies in major temples throughout Taiwan.

* Youth Day, (March 29)

Originally called Revolutionary Martyr's Day, Youth Day commemorates the patriotic deaths of 72 young revolutionaries in China in 1911.

April

* Tomb-Sweeping Day, (April 5)

Traditionally calculated as the 105th day after the Winter Solstice and called the Ching-Ming ("clear and bright") Festival, Tomb-Sweeping Day in Taiwan is now celebrated annually on April 5, which coincides with the date of President Chiang Kai-shek's death in 1975. Therefore, April 5 is both a traditional Chinese festival and a contemporary national holiday in Taiwan. The evening of April 4, 1975, was a balmy Spring night in Taipei, with stars twinkling brightly in a cloudless sky. But at the moment of President Chiang's death, shortly after midnight, a violent thunderstorm suddenly gathered out of nowhere and burst out over Taipei, pelting the city with heavy rain and lightning for half an hour, before the skies abruptly clear again.

During this festival, entire families go out to their ancestral burial grounds to sweep accumulated dirt and debris from the tombs, place fresh flowers around the graves, and perhaps plant a few new trees or bushes in the area. Since 1975, formal memorial services for the late President have also been held on this day.

Buddha's Birthday, (April 8)

This day commemorates the birth of Sakyamuni (the historical Buddha) 2,500 years ago. The festival is marked in temples throughout the island with "Cleansing of Buddha" ceremonies, during which all statues of Buddha are ritually washed while monks recite the appropriate *sutra*. Many of the icons are then paraded through the streets to the beat of gongs and drums.

Birthday of Matsu, Goddess of the Sea (Twenty-third day of the third lunar month, usually late-April)

One of the biggest *pai-pai* of the year in Taiwan, this festival is dedicated to Matsu, Goddess of the Sea, patron saint of Taiwan, and guardian deity of the island's fishermen. It is celebrated with great fanfare in over 300 temples where Matsu is enshrined. The biggest festival takes place in central Taiwan at the Peikang Temple near Chiayi, but you can also get an eye and ear full at the famous Lung Shan ("Dragon Mountain") Temple in downtown Taipei, near Snake Alley. Sacrificial offerings of roast pigs and boiled chickens, billows of smoke from incense and burning paper money, undulating lion and dragon dances, colorful parades, and lavish feasting comprise some of the festivities dedicated to Matsu on her birthday.

May

* Dragon Boat Festival (Fifth day of fifth lunar month, usually late-May to mid June)

One of China's most ancient festivals, this event commemorates the death of Chu-Yuan, an accomplished poet and upright minister who plunged to his death in a river about 2,500 years ago to protest the corruption and misrule of his king, who had banished him from the court. According to the legend, upon hearing of his tragic death, the local people rowed their boats out on the river and dropped stuffed rice dumplings tightly wrapped in bamboo leaves into the water to supplicate and nourish his spirit. These dumplings, called *dzung-dze*（棕子）, remain this festival's major food item.

The occasion is celebrated with colorful "Dragon Boat Races," which in recent years have become a major sporting event in Taipei. Every year the government organizes the "Chiang Kai-shek Memorial Cup" Dragon Boat Race, which is held on the Tan-Shui River in West Taipei. Teams from all over the island, including several "foreigner teams" from the expatriate community, as well as teams from Hong Kong and Singapore compete for top honors in various divisions. The bows of the boats are carved into elaborate dragon-heads, and the crews row to the resounding beat of big drums placed at the back of each boat. During the last three Dragon Boat Races, several modern-minded teams appeared before the crowds on the banks of the river with their own pom-pommed, mini-skirted cheerleaders!

June

Birthday of Cheng Huang, the City God (Thirteenth day of fifth lunar month, usually mid June)

This *pai-pai* festival is celebrated with great pomp and ceremony at Taipei's famous City God Temple （城隍廟）at #61 Ti Hua St., Sec. 1（迪化街一段，61號）The worship of city gods is a practice that has been recorded in China as far back as the early Hsia Dynasty (ca. 2200 BC), and it remains one of Taiwan's liveliest celebrations. City gods are said to have the power to protect a city's inhabitants from both natural disasters and enemy intruders, and they also advice the Lord of Heaven and the King of Hell regarding appropriate rewards and punishments for the city's residents after death. No wonder the Chinese pay them such lavish homage!

Among this *pai-pai's* colorful and highly photogenic festivities are parades with icons of the City God held high upon pedestals, offerings of whole pigs and cows stretched on bamboo racks, processions of celebrants wearing stilts and colorful costumes, lion and dragon dances, lavish feasts, and much more.

July

Chinese Valentines Day (Seventh day of the seventh lunar month, usually late July)

Chinese Valentines Day is derived from the legend of the Herd-Boy and the Spinning-Girl. The Herd-Boy (a star formation in the constellation Aquila, west of the Milky Way) and the Spinning-Girl (the star Vega in the constellation Vyra, east of the Milky Way) appear closest together in the sky on this night, and all the magpies on earth are said to ascend to the sky to form a bridge across the Milk Way so that the lovers may cross over for their brief once-a-year tryst. This is a festival for young unmarried girls and for young lovers, who observe the romantic occasion by exchanging gifts, strolling in moonlit parks, and praying in temples for future matrimonial bliss.

August

The Ghost Festival (Fifteenth day of seventh lunar month, usually mid August)

The Chinese believe that on the first day of the 7th lunar month the gates of hell swing open, permitting the ghosts of deceased relatives to return to their earthly homes for a visit. In order to placate the spirits and discourage their mischief, trays of succulent foods are set out before each home as offerings to them, and Buddhist priests are invited to every neighborhood and alley to bless these offerings and supplicate the spirits with prayer. Incense is burned and bundles of paper "clothing" and "money" are set afire for use by the spirits in the other world. These offerings are also meant to prevent the ghosts of criminals and spirits with no living relatives from entering one's home and causing trouble. It is not an auspicious time for marriage or commencing important new ventures. Rites are held daily in all Buddhist temples during the Ghost Festival, which formally ends on the last day of the 7th month, when the spirits return to their underwold abode and the gates slam shut for another year.

September

Confucius' Birthday, (September 28)
This is an official national holiday, celebrated as "Teacher's Day," which commemorates the birth of the sage Confucius in 551 BC. Known as "China's greatest teacher," Confucius continues to exert profound influence on culture and society in Taiwan. Elaborate traditional ceremonies are held every year on this day at 6a.m. at Taipei's Confucius Temple (孔子廟) , complete with ancient musical instruments, formal court attire, ritual dances, and other Confucian rites as old as the sage himself. Tickets to attend this ceremony must be arranged in advance through local tourism authorities.

October

Mid Autumn Moon Festival (Fifteenth day of eighth lunar month, usually late September to mid October)
The Chinese believe that the "Harvest Moon" is the fullest, brightest moon of the year, and they celebrate its annual appearance by proceeding en masse to parks, hillsides, riverbanks, and seashores to gaze at "The Lady in the Moon," nibble on tasty snacks, and drink wine. According to Chinese legend, Chang-Eh, beautiful wife of the Tang emperor Ming-Huang, one day discovered a vial of the "Elixir of Immortality" specially prepared for her husband and decided to take a sip. But he caught her in the act, and in order to conceal the evidence, she quickly swallowed the entire potion. It took effect instantly and with such intensity that she immediately flew up from earth and landed on the moon. She's been there ever since, and on this night her beauty radiates at its very best.

The festival is celebrated by exchanging gifts of "Moon Cakes" (月餅) , which are large, round pastries stuffed with sweet bean paste, mashed dates, chopped nuts, minced dried fruits, and other fillings. Exchanging moon cakes also has patriotic overtones because during the successful overthrow of the Mongol Yuan Dynasty by the Chinese Ming, secret plans for the insurrection were concealed in moon cakes and distributed to patriots throughout the empire prior to the uprising.

Double-Ten National Day, (October 10)
"Double-Ten" refers to the 10th day of the 10th month and commemorates the overthrow of the Manchu Ching Dynasty, China's last, by revolutionary Chinese patriots on Oct. 10, 1911. It is by far the most important national holiday of the year in Taiwan, and it is celebrated with massive parades of military hardware and honor guards from all branches of the armed forces, aerial acrobatics by the Chinese Air Force's daring "Thunder Tigers," frogman landing demonstrations, patriotic speeches by top government leaders, and displays of folk dancing, sword-fighting, martial arts, and other cultural activities. Most of the action takes place in the huge plaza in front of the Presidential Mansion in downtown Taipei.

Hotels and restaurants in Taipei remain packed full throughout the week prior to Double-Ten Day, as tens of thousands of Overseas Chinese from all over the world pour into town for the festivities. Tourists who visit Taiwan at this time should make adequately early reservations for hotel and airline space.

Restoration Day, (October 25)
This national holiday celebrates the return of Taiwan to Nationalist Chinese rule after the defeat of Japan in 1945, thereby ending 55 years of Japanese colonial occupation. It is marked with several major athletic events, including regional competition in soccer and basketball for the Presidential Cup awards. Other festivities include lion and dragon dances and bountiful feasting at Taipei's many restaurants and hotels.

Birthday of Chiang Kai-shek, (October 31)
This is a national holiday celebrated annually in Taiwan to commemorate the birth of the late President Chiang Kai-shek in 1887.

November

Birthday of Dr. Sun Yat-sen, (November 12)
Sun Yat-sen, founder and first President of the Republic of China, is regarded as the "George Washington of China" by Chinese throughout the world, including the communist mainland. This holiday celebrates his birth in 1866 and is marked with solemn patriotic ceremonies and speeches.

December

*Constitution Day, (December 25)
This is an official national holiday which marks the day in 1947 on which the constitution of the Republic of China became effective. The government does not officially recognize Christmas as a holiday, but Christians throughout Taiwan observe Christmas Day with religious services, family gatherings, and other rituals similar to those in the West.

Below is the list of national holidays and major festival in Taiwan during the second and first half of 1983 and 1984 respectively:

1984

Jan. 1 — Foundation Day
Feb. 1 — Chinese Lunar New Year's Eve
Feb. 2 — Chinese Lunar New Year
Feb. 16 — Lantern Festival & Tourism Day
March 21 — Birthday of Kuan Yin, Goddess of Mercy
March 29 — Youth Day
April 5 — Tomb Sweeping Day, and death of President Chiang Kai-shek
April 23 — Birthday of Matsu, Goddess of the Sea
April 29 — Day commemorating the landing on Taiwan of the Ming Dynasty loyalist, Cheng Cheng-Kung (Koxinga) ousting the Dutch colonists who had occupied Taiwan for 37 years

June 4 — Dragon Boat Festival
June 12 — Birthday of Cheng Huang, City God of Taipei
July 28 — Month of the Ghosts
Aug. 10 — Cheng Cheng-Kung's Birthday (see April 29 above)
Sept. 28 — Confucius' Birthday or Teacher's Day
Oct. 10 — Double Tenth Day
Oct. 21 — Overseas Chinese Day
Oct. 25 — Taiwan Restoration Day
Oct. 31 — President Chiang Kai-shek's Birthday
Nov. 12 — Dr. Sun Yat-sen's Birthday
Dec. 25 — Constitution Day and Christmas Day

Sports

In recent years, sports activities have enjoyed increasing popularity in Taiwan, which hosts frequent international sports events and regularly sends teams to compete abroad. In international competitions, Taiwan's athletes have scored major victories in golf, soccer, and the martial arts, and Taiwan's hard-slugging Little League baseball teams have repeatedly made world headlines during the past decade by winning six world championships. Taiwan proudly boasts two Olympic Medalists: decathlon star C. K. Yang, Taiwan's "Man of Iron;" and runner Chi Chang, "Asia's Flying Antelope." The sports most easily accessible to tourists in Taiwan are golf, tennis, and swimming.

Golf: Golf is the oldest organized sport in Taiwan, and all 17 of Taiwan's golf clubs, nine of which are close to Taipei, are open to foreign visitors for guest memberships. The clubs are open all year round. The oldest club on the island is the **Taiwan Golf and Country Club** in Tan-Shui, which was built by the Japanese in 1919. The **Hwalien Golf Club** dates back to 1928. Taiwan's avid golfers garner frequent victories in competitions on the Asia Circuit.

Arrangements for guest privileges in Taiwan's golf clubs may be made through hotel travel-desks and local travel agencies, who will also arrange for regular club members to accompany or sponsor temporary guests in those clubs whose rules require it. Golf clubs, golf shoes, caddies, and food and beverage facilities are available at all of the clubs listed in the Appendix. Further inquiries regarding golf in Taiwan may be directed to **Golf Association of the Republic of China,** 71 Tun-Hwa S. Rd, Lane 369, Taipei, Taiwan, ROC, (Cable. GAROC, Tel. 711-7482, 711-3046)

Tennis: Tennis has been the fastest growing sport in Taiwan in recent years, and hundreds of new courts have been laid out around the island to meet the demand for tennis facilities. In Taipei, you'll find excellent facilities for tennis at public courts, private clubs, and several hotels. Check the Appendix for a listing.

Swimming: In addition to public beaches, there are numerous swimming pools at various hotels, clubs, and resorts around the island. Guests of the Grand Hotel have free access to the Olympic-sized pool at the adjacent **Yuan-Shan Club,** which is otherwise open only to members and their guests. For a nominal fee, you may enjoy a swim surrounded by green mountains at the **China Hotel** on Yangming Mountain. For a nominal fee, visitors may also use the outdoor pool at the **Mandarin Hotel** and the indoor pool at the **Ambassador Hotel.** The **American Club** and the **Yangming Mountain Country Club** both have large pools, but you must be accompanied by a member to use them. There are also several public pools in the Taipei area, but they're usually crowded and noisy.

Martial Arts: Traditionally, the Chinese have kept in shape by practicing various ancient forms of martial arts exercises, and in recent years these traditional forms have made a major come-back in Taipei. Every morning at dawn thousands of people pour into the parks and streets of Taipei to practice **tai-chi, martial arts, yoga, sword dances,** or simple **aerobics.** Visitors may also get a good work-out each morning by simply joining whatever group interests them and mimicking their gentle movements. The four most popular places in Taipei for early morning exercise sessions are **New Taipei Park** (near the Hilton), the landscaped grounds of the **Chiang Kai-shek Memorial Hall,** the compound of the **Sun Yat-sen Memorial Hall,** and the **hills around the Grand Hotel.** The reason that these exercise sessions always take place at the crack of dawn is that the Chinese believe the air is most densely impregnated with *chi* ("vital energy") at that time. Even if you don't participate, you should try to catch this scene at least once while in Taipei.

Mountain Climbing: Two-thirds of Taiwan is covered with lush evergreen mountains, and these rank among Taiwan's greatest attractions for mountain-climbers and trekkers. The two favorite climbs are to the 13,114-foot peak of **Jade Mountain** (Mt. Morrison), which is the highest in Taiwan and all Northeast Asia, and to the 12,743-foot summit of **Snow Mountain** (Mt. Sylvia), which is Taiwan's second highest peak. Both require prior arrangements by the Alpine Association of the ROC at 30 Lan-Chow St., 3rd Floor, Taipei (蘭州街30號3 樓). Mountain-climbing permits may be easily obtained at the Foreign Affairs Section of the Natonal Police Administration, located directly across the street from the Lai-Lai Sheraton Hotel, Tel. 321-3175 (警察局，忠孝東路一段，7號)

Climbers bound for Jade Mountain usually take the express train down to Chiayi, then switch to the alpine diesel train for the ride up to the Alishan Forest Recreation Area. From there they proceed 12 miles up to the Tungpu base-camp, where there is a hostel. The next morning they make the ascent up Jade Mountain where there is a second hostel located just 2,287 feet below the summit. You should allow four days for the trip from the Alishan Area to the summit of Jade Mountain and back. Snow Mountain is located north of Pear Mountain (Li-Shan), midway along the spectacular East-West Cross-Island Highway. You can get to Pear Mountain by driving in either from Taichung or Hwalien. From there, a bus takes you to Mt. Huan in the foothills of Snow Mountain, and a car carries you on up to the Wuling Farm at 5,777 feet altitude, where simple lodgings are available overnight. Climbers commence their ascent of Snow Mountain the following morning and should allow four days for the trip from Pear Mountain up to the summit of Snow Mountain and back.

For less formidable climbs, there are many scenic mountains located between Taipei and the northern coastline which require no prior arrangements nor police permits. **Seven Stars Mountain**(七星山)at 3,675 feet, is the tallest of these gentle northern peaks.

Skiing: For two months each year (January and February) enough snow falls on the slopes of Mt. Ho-Huan ("Harmonious Happiness Mountain") to permit skiing. Rising to an altitude of 11,208 feet in central Taiwan, Mt. Ho-Huan is easily reached by taking the Tayuling-Wushe branch of the East-West Cross-Island Highway. Its amenities include the cosy Pine-Snow Hostel, which accommodates 150 persons, a 400-meter ski-lift, ski instructors, and fabulous alpine scenery which is well worth viewing even if you do not ski. Since temperature there never rises above 60 degrees Fahrenheit (14°C), **Harmonious Happiness Mountain** also makes an excellent summer resort, especially for hiking and mineral baths.

Scuba and Skin Diving: An entirely new kingdom of colorful sealife unfolds for divers who plunge into the blue waters off Taiwan's coral coasts. Indeed, enormous colonies of live coral form one of the island's greatest underwater attractions, with colors in every conceivable shade of pink to purple. An astonishing variety of tropical and semi-tropical fish and molluscs; exquisitely shaped and colored conch, cone, cowrie, and other shells; brightly-plumed sea lilies; and other exotic underwater life inhabit these vast coral communities in Taiwan's off-shore waters.

The most spectacular diving in Taiwan is found near Oluanpi at the southermost tip of the island. The rocky, shallow shoreline here also permits excellent snorkeling. In the north, divers like to explore the underwater coral kingdoms off the coast of Yeh-Liu, which is famous for the bizarre formations of coral-rock protruding from its seaside promontory.

Air refilling facilities for divers are available in both northern and southern Taiwan, and several local diving clubs organize regular excursions to popular diving areas. For further information regarding scuba diving in Taiwan, equipment rental, and other details, contact the **China Diving Association** at Tel. 596-2341.

Trade with Taiwan

The China External Trade Development Council (CETDC) is designed to assist those who wish to do business with Taiwan, and it displays the full range of products manufactured here. It is an independent, non-profit organization supported by grants from both the government and local business associations. Its primary purpose is to promote Taiwan's growing two-way trade with other nations. It provides a wide variety of services and offers facilities to local and foreign businessmen, as well as to any visitor with an interest in Taiwan's industries.

CETDC operates an enormous Display Center and Export Mart at the Sung-Shan domestic airport in Taipei. Here you'll find 1,657 display booths exhibiting the full range of manufactured products available for export from Taiwan. Next to the Display Center is an Export Mart with 149 showrooms in which Taiwan's major exporters maintain permanent representatives to discuss any aspect of business and trade with interested foreign parties. At the Export Mart you may also purchase samples of various products at rock-bottom factory prices. The exhibits are changed constantly and kept completely up-to-date. The range and quality of the products on display there are impressive: watches and calculators; digital pen/watches and computer games; electronic components and audio-visual equipment; tools and machines; toys and sporting goods; jewelry and handicrafts; and much more. Even if you are not interested in business, it's well worth visiting CETDC's Display Center and Export Mart because it gives you a quick and vivid glance at Taiwan's ongoing economic miracles.

At CETDC's initiative, a major World Trade Center is currently being planned for Taipei, and it is slated to open in the mid 1980's. It will include a trade mart, exhibition halls, convention facilities, an international hotel, restaurants, shopping malls, and other related facilities, and is already destined to become the showcase of modern Taiwan.

The addresses and contact numbers of CETDC, as well as other related display centers and trade marts are listed in the Appendix.

On Relaxing Here

The Chinese are a sensual people given to creature comforts, and two of their favorite comforts are to relax in the pampered luxury of barber shops and bath houses. In Taiwan, bathing and grooming—like eating and drinking—are regarded as far more than mere necessities: they are approached as part of the grand art of living.

"Luxurious Tourist Barber Shops"(豪華觀光理髮廳) abound throughout Taipei and are easily identified by braces of electrified barber-poles spinning madly by their neon-lit entrances. Once you step inside the automatic doors, you will be greeted by a bevy of young barber-maids clad in long gowns. They will guide you to an empty chair, refresh you with a hot hand-towel, offer you hot tea and cigarettes, then proceed to groom you in a style to which you surely would like to become accustomed.

If you prefer to let your own barber do your hair-cutting and styling, then just go in for a shampoo, manicure, and massage. Taipei barber-maids shampoo your hair like nobody else, combining a stimulating scalp massage with the shampoo. While she's blow-drying and combing your hair, you may call for a manicure, pedicure, or whatever other grooming you require. Finally comes the massage—a curiously refreshing finger-pressure massage which covers scalp, neck, and spine and sends energy coursing through your nervous system. Those with the time and inclination may then stretch out in reclining position with a towel wrapped over their eyes and indulge in the great Chinese tradition of *hsiou-hsi* ("short rest"). Depending on which services you require and how long you stay, a visit to a "Luxurious Tourist Barber Shop" in Taipei will run between NT$ 300 and $600.

These barber shops cater exclusively to men, but women can get the same stimulating treatment at any Chinese beauty parlor (美容院), where shampoos, permanents, hair-styling, manicures, and massages are performed in the same luxurious comfort. Almost all international tourist hotels in Taipei have both barber-shops and beauty parlors, but these offer more contemporary Western style service and less Chinese flavor. To fully enjoy your grooming as the Chinese do, you should visit a typical barber shop or beauty parlor outside of your hotel. You'll find them in all the popular entertainment and shopping districts, especially on Chung-Shan North Road, Nanking East Road, the busy lanes off Lin-Sen North Road (between Min-Chuan East and Chang-An East roads), and the Teh-Hui/Shuang-Cheng street area.

Bath houses and saunas (浴室，三温暖) are about as numerous in Taipei as cafes in the West. The Chinese are fanatics about bathing and personal hygiene, and they devote much time to it, often spending hours scrubbing, soaking, and relaxing themselves in well appointed bath houses. Facilities vary from place to place, but generally they include showers, hot and cold pools, whirl-pools, saunas, professional massage, snack-bars, lockers and lounging areas. Many a multi-million-dollar deal in Taipei has been concluded by magnates lounging around bath houses in terri-cloth robes or lawyers soothing their weary bones in whirlpool-baths. It's a great way to relax, and it really gets the grit and grime of city air out of your hair and pores.

Remember that in an Oriental bath house you are always expected to thoroughly wash yourself with soap and water *before* stepping into any of the communal baths or whirlpools. Remember also that modesty is unnecessary, no matter what shape you're in, because the Chinese do not regard nakedness as obscene. Beyond that, simply play it by ear: plunge in and out of the hot and cold pools as the mood strikes you; bake yourself in the sauna; lose yourself in a swirling hot whirlpool; call for a massage and pedicure; relax in the lounge with a cool drink and magazine. A visit to a Taipei bath house will rejuvenate your body and spirit, all for only NT$ 400–800, depending on the services you request.

Almost all bath houses and saunas in Taipei have separate sections for men and women, and the facilities and services they provide are the same. A number of leading hotels in Taipei, such as the Hilton, Lai-Lai, and Imperial, have their own sauna and bath facilities. Others are located around town, including the following:

Hwa-Bin Sauna Bath, 21 Shuang-Cheng St., Lane 19, 7th Fl., Tel. 592-7728/9.

華賓三溫暖　雙城街，19巷，21號7樓

King Shanghai Sauna and Bath Center, 100 Chang-Chun Rd, Basement, Tel. 593-3847.

華皇上海三溫暖　長春路100路，地下樓

Yi Hsin Shanghai Bath, 181-7 Chung-Shan North Rd., Sec. 2, 2nd Fl., Tel. 591-8113.

一心上海浴池　中山北路二段181-7號，2樓

The Chinese Zodiac

Between mid 1976 and mid 1977, the number of births registered in Taiwan almost doubled overnight, before returning to its normal, well-disciplined level by the end of the year. Subsequently Taiwan's school system had to prepare for the flood of new students created by this brief baby boom by hiring 1,000 new elementary school teachers and building scores of new classrooms by 1982.

The reason for this sudden flurry of reproductive activity was the Chinese zodiac: 1976 was the Year of the Dragon. According to Chinese astrologers, seeds sown during the Dragon's cosmic ascendancy bear the strongest fruit of all. In 1988, the next Dragon year, Taiwan's birth-rate is expected to soar again.

Despite family planning programs, modern-birth control, industrialization, the ascendancy of scientific thought, and other pragmatic Western social influences in Taiwan, the Chinese continue to hold great faith in their age old cosmology. Prior to births, weddings, funerals, major business contracts, grand openings of new buildings, and other important events, most Chinese in Taiwan still consult their ancient almanacs and wizened old fortune-tellers for advice regarding auspicious days.

In fact the date of the wedding of this book's author to a Chinese bride in Taiwan was selected by her father, an advanced aircraft pilot scientifically trained in America, after lengthy consultations with a Chinese fortune-teller. Based on the harmonies and conflicts of the individual horoscopes, the fortune-teller selected a day with auspicious tendencies for both. So far, his choice has proven to be perfect.

The Chinese calendar was first devised during the reign of the Yellow Emperor around 2700 BC. It has been in continuous use ever since. Thus, the Chinese are currently living in the 48th century, not the 20th, which shows you just how old their culture is.

In the Chinese lunar calendar, which follows the cycles of the moon around the earth rather than the earth around the sun, each year is designated by its association with one of the Twelve Celestial Animals and one of the Five Cosmic Elements. The animals, in order of sequence, are the Rat, Ox, Tiger, Rabbit, Dragon, Snake, Horse, Sheep, Monkey, Chicken, Dog, and Pig. The Five Elements are

Metal, Wood, Earth, Water, and Fire. Since each of the animals is associated in turn with each of the Five Elements, a full cosmic cycle takes 60 years to complete. Then, the sequence repeats itself.

Like the Western solar calendar, the Chinese lunar calendar has 12 months, each consisting of 29 or 30 days. To adjust their calendar to the realities of solar time, the Chinese add an extra month every 30 months. Each month commences with the new moon, and the full moon always falls on the 15th day. Chinese Lunar New Year occurs sometime between January 21 and February 28, and remains the single biggest holiday of the year among Chinese all over the world.

The pervasive influence of the ancient Chinese zodiac and lunar calendar on contemporary Chinese life in Taiwan today is remarkable. Most major Chinese and all local Taiwanese festivals are still determined according to the lunar calendar, which means that every year they fall on a different day on the Western Gregorian calendar. If you ask a Chinese in Taiwan when his birthday is, he'll ask you whether you mean "sun calendar," Western, or "moon calendar," Chinese. Often he cannot tell you when his birthday falls on the Western calendar without first consulting an almanac. Dates for weddings and funerals in Taiwan are always set according to ancient Chinese cosmology. Many Chinese even refuse to travel or embark on new business ventures without first consulting a fortune-teller. Not to do so is considered an invitation to disaster.

When a modern new skyscraper goes up in Taiwan, the owners routinely consult a Chinese geomancer to determine the optimum position for the main entrance. Called *feng-shui* ("wind and water"), geomancy is the branch of classical cosmology which helps man build his dwellings in optimum harmony with the elements of his natural environment. Even if the building's owners don't really believe in *feng shui*, they will still follow the geomancer's advice because they know perfectly well that many prospective buyers and renters will consult their own geomancers about the building prior to moving in. Over the years, several major new buildings in downtown Taipei have remained unoccupied and their owners gone broke, because they failed to follow the dictates of Chinese geomancy during construction.

One Chinese restauranteur endured heavy financial losses for two years, despite excellent food and service and massive advertising campaigns. Finally, in sheer desperation, he consulted a geomancer, who cooly informed him that the position of his main entrance caused money to flow out rather than into his restaurant. He spent a small fortune to tear down and reconstruct the entrance according to the geomancer's instructions, and before long you couldn't find a seat in the place at night! Even the massive Chiang Kai-shek Memorial Hall in downtown Taipei, with its extensive gardens and numerous gates, was all laid out according to the laws of Chinese geomancy to provide maximum harmony with the elements and spirits of the cosmos.

The Chinese zodiac is a complex and subtle system which only fortune-tellers and scholars manage to master completely. But its basic tenets are applied daily in the lives of Chinese people everywhere. The most popular aspect of the zodiac today is the description of one's basic personality traits according to which animal dominates the year of birth. Professional match-makers still refuse to introduce prospective marriage partners whose signs conflict, and businessmen often attribute unfulfilled contracts, financial failure, and other problems to ill cosmology.

A favorite game among the Chinese is to guess the zodiacal identity of a new acquaintance according to his or her behavior. "Ah-ha, so you're a Rat!" or "Oh boy, another Dragon!" or "She must be a Rabbit!" are common remarks. You can find the Celestial Animal lurking in the hearts of friends and family by reviewing the following chart and brief descriptions of the zodiac.

Rat: Charming and attractive to the opposite sex. Hard-working, thrifty, and highly resourceful, with remarkable ability to see projects through to the end. Rats hoard their money and are loathe to lend it, but they like to spend lavishly on themselves. Only in love do they grow generous. Though timid and retiring, Rats are easily aroused to anger. Frank and honest, Rats also love to gossip.
Compatability: Ox, Dragon, Snake, Monkey
Conflict: Horse

Ox: Calm and quiet, the Ox inspires confidence and trust in others. Ill-tempered and volatile, the Ox tends to lose control when angry. Eloquent in speech, alert of mind, and dexterous of hand. The Ox is stubborn and not given to passion, which often causes problems with mates. The Ox tends to remain aloof from his family.
Compatability: Rat, Chicken, Snake
Conflict: Sheep

Tiger: Tigers are courageous and powerful, with strong will-power. They command respect from others and resent authority. Yet they are sensitive and thoughtful, with deep feelings and sympathy for their friends and loved ones. They are said to repel the three evils of thieves, fire, and ghosts.
Compatability: Pig, Dog, Horse
Conflict: Snake, Monkey

Rabbit: Talented and virtuous, Rabbits have conservative tendencies and display good taste. They are both clever and reliable in business, and are usually blessed with good luck. They are tender to those they love, yet often keep a distance from their families. Moody and sometimes arrogant, Rabbits tend to lead tranquil, fortunate lives.
Compatability: Pig, Dog, Sheep
Conflict: Chicken

Dragon: Energetic, healthy, and quick to react, Dragons are also stubborn and short-tempered. They are known for

honesty and courage, and they inspire trust and confidence in others. Though admired by all, Dragons often worry needlessly about affection. Dragons usually get what they want and are generally the most eccentric people in the zodiac.
Compatability: Rat, Chicken, Monkey
Conflict: Dog

Snake: Intense and introverted, Snakes are often distrusted by others and have trouble communicating effectively. They are wise and deep-thinking, but also tend to be vain and selfish. Still, they offer aid to those less fortunate than themselves. Money never seems to be a problem for Snakes, nor do they worry about it. They prefer their own judgement to the advice of others. Generally passionate and attractive, Snakes do not make the most faithful marriage partners.
Compatability: Ox, Rat, Chicken
Conflict: Tiger, Pig

Horse: Optimistic, perceptive, and self-confident, Horses are popular with others and rather talkative. Though good-looking and intelligent, they often find themselves at the mercy of the opposite sex. They manage money very well and are skillful in their work. Horses love freedom and tend to leave home early.
Compatability: Sheep, Tiger, Dog
Conflict: Rat

Sheep: Blessed with excellent dispositions, Sheep make fine marriage partners. They are upright, honest, and extremely generous, and show great sympathy for those struck by misfortune. They have excellent taste in fashion and are endowed with artistic talents. Gentle, compassionate, and rather shy, Sheep are sometimes puzzled by the vagaries of life.
Compatability: Ox, Pig, Tiger
Conflict: Horse, Dog

Monkey: Clever, inventive, and original, Monkeys can solve complex problems with ease. However, they are also cunning, inconsistent, and rather mischievous. They love to be the center of attention, but have little real respect for others. They succeed in almost anything they undertake, and are ingenious in handling money. Others respect them for their competence and ability to learn quickly, but their own enthusiasm for projects tends to fizzle out quickly.
Compatability: Rat, Dragon
Conflict: Snake, Pig, Tiger

Chicken: Outgoing, brave, and highly capable. Chickens early embark on many projects, many of which they

never complete. They are somewhat eccentric and self-righteous, with strong personal opinions. They tend to be moody, and are highly devoted to their work.
Compatability: Ox, Dragon, Snake
Conflict: Rat, Chicken, Dog, Rabbit

Dog: Dogs are honest, loyal, and easily trusted by others. They keep secrets very well and have a strong sense of justice. Though they don't possess great wealth, they rarely suffer for lack of funds. They tend to be somewhat cold, sarcastic, and erratic, but they are hard-working and devoted to their friends.
Compatability: Horse, Rabbit, Tiger
Conflict: Dragon, Sheep

Pig: Honest, polite, and devoted to their tasks, Pigs also place great value on friendship and are loyal. Though quick-tempered, they hate to argue and are affectionate to their mates. They have a tendency towards laziness and love to spend money.
Compatability: Rabbit, Sheep
Conflict: Monkey, Pig, Snake

Language

Chinese is at once the most complex written language and the simplest spoken language in the world. This may sound like a contradiction to Westerners, who are accustomed to alphabetic writing systems based on spoken sounds, but the Chinese system of writing operates wholly independently of the spoken language, and one can be easily learned without any knowledge of the other.

Chinese writing is based on ideograms, or "idea-pictures," which graphically depict ideas and objects with written characters derived directly from actual diagrams of the subject. The oldest recorded Chinese characters appear on oracle bones excavated this century in China and dating from the ancient Shang Dynasty (1766–1123 BC). At that time, questions of vital interest to the emperor were inscribed upon the dried shells of giant tortoises, which were then subjected to heat. The heat caused the shells to crack, and diviners then interpreted Heaven's answers to the emperor's questions by "reading" the cracks. The answers were then inscribed on the shells, and they were stored in the imperial archives. Based on the number and complexity of the characters inscribed on these oracle bones, Chinese historians have concluded that the Chinese written language was first invented during the reign of the Yellow Emperor around 2700 BC.

The written characters reached their current stage of development about 2,000 years ago during the Han Dynasty, and they have changed very little since then, which makes Chinese the oldest ongoing writing system in the world. The importance of China's unique written language cannot be overstated: it held together a vast and complex empire composed of many different ethnic groups, and due to its non-phonetic nature, it formed a written common denominator among China's various and sundry dialects. Once the symbols were learned, they gave the reader access to an enormous wealth of historical and literary writings accumulated in China over five millenia of continuous cultural development. Unlike Egyptian hieroglyphics, for example, which died with the Pharaohs, thereby cutting off subsequent Egyptian generations from their own roots, the Chinese written language evolved continuously from generation to generation, transmitting with it the accumulated treasures of Chinese culture right down to the present era. Small wonder that ancient traditions are so deeply ingrained in the Chinese mind. For example, the simple act of writing one's own surname in Chinese immediately recalls and identifies one with a host of great historical and literary heroes, spanning five millenia, who shared the same name.

A comprehensive study of Chinese characters is far beyond the scope of this book, but a few concrete examples should suffice to reveal their genius. Each character is denoted by a single monosyllabic sound, and each carries a basic, concrete meaning. Most words are then formed by combining two characters whose meanings describe the idea to be depicted. For example, 中 (pronounced "joong") —a box cut in half by a vertical line—means "central." Add to that the character 國 (pronounced "gwo")—an enclosed boundery 回 containing mouths 口 (i.e. population), protected by spears 戈 (i.e. defense), and hence meaning "country" or "nation" —and you have the Chinese word for China, 中國 , or literally, "Central Nation." 山 (pronounced) "shan")—three vertical lines ascending from a horizontal plane—depicts the word "mountain." Preceded by the character 金 (pronounced "jin"), which means "gold," it forms the word "Jin-Shan" ("Gold Mountain"), which is the Chinese designation for San Francisco, a place first settled by Chinese during the Gold Rush days. "Sun" is written 日 and "tree" is written 木 . Combine the two to form a new character 東 (pronounced "doong"), and you have the Chinese ideogram for "east," which depicts the sun rising through the trees on the eastern horizon. The word for "contradiction" is cleverly formed by combining the characters for "spear" and "shield." The permutations and combinations are endless and always interesting.

There are about 50,000 Chinese characters listed in Chinese dictionaries, but the vast majority are either obsolete or used only in the highly specialized branches of learning. Three thousand characters are required for basic literacy, such as reading newspapers and business documents, and about 5,000 are required for advanced literary studies. About 2,000 Chinese characters are still used in the written languages of Korea and Japan. Few scholars, however, are capable of using more than 6,000 characters without resorting to dictionaries. A sampling of 20 basic Chinese characters and their English meaning is shown below:

人	大	天	日	月
MAN	GREAT; BIG	HEAVEN; SKY	SUN; DAY	MOON; MONTH
木	山	門	雨	中
WOOD; TREE	MOUNTAIN	DOOR; GATE	RAIN	CENTRAL; MIDDLE
口	女	子	好	田
MOUTH; POPULACE	WOMAN	CHILD	GOOD	FIELD
明	龍	一	二	三
BRIGHT	DRAGON	ONE	TWO	THREE

The Spoken Language

There are only several hundred vocal sounds in the Chinese spoken language, which means that many written characters must share the same pronunciation. To somewhat clarify matters, the Chinese developed a tonal system which uses four distinctively different tones to pronounce each syllable. Even so, many characters share both common syllables and tones, and the only way to be really sure which words are meant when spoken is to consider the entire context of a statement, or demand a written explanation.

For example, 馬 ("horse") is pronounced "ma" in third tone, but so is 瑪 ("agate"). Nevertheless, when someone suggests "Let's go horseback riding," the listener is unlikely to confuse the word "ma" for agate. Similarly, if you ask someone what kind of stone is set in his ring, and he responds "ma" ("agate"), you probably will not think he meant "ma" ("horse").

Although Chinese has been called a monosyllabic language because each character has a single syllable sound, in effect it is polysyllabic because the vast majority of words are formed by combining two characters. This practice further reduces the linguistic confusion created by characters which share the same pronunciation. 民 (pronounced "min") means "the people," as in 民主 ("min-ju"), "democracy." So when someone says "min-ju" you are unlikely to mistake either the "min" or the "ju" for any of several dozen other characters which they denote.

Grammatically, spoken Chinese is so simple and direct that it makes other languages seem cumbersome, archaic, and unnecessarily complex by comparison. There are no conjugations, declensions, gender distinctions, tense changes, or other complicated grammatical rules to memorize. The spoken language consists of simple sounds strung together in simple sentence patterns, with the basic "subject/verb/object" construction common to most Western languages. Tones, while foreign to Western tongues, come naturally with usage and are not that difficult to master. Even within China, the various provinces give different tonal inflections to the various sounds. Proper word-order and correct context are all you need to know about Chinese grammar.

In Taiwan, the Mandarin dialect (known as *guo-yu*, "National Language") has been declared the official *lingua franca* by the government. Mandarin, which is based upon the pronunciations which prevailed in the old imperial capital of Peking, is by far the most melodious dialect of China.

In addition to Mandarin, there is a local dialect called "Taiwanese" which is derived from China's Fukien Province, ancestral home of the vast majority of Taiwan's Chinese populace. Taiwanese is commonly spoken among local people, especially in the rural regions, and one of Taiwan's major television stations broadcasts programs in that dialect for their benefit. The older generation still speaks some Japanese—a remnant influence of Japan's colonial occupation—and younger people tend to understand at least some basic English. But though English is a required subject for all Chinese students in Taiwan throughout middle and high school, it is spoken fluently by very few.

It helps immensely to learn a little spoken Chinese before traveling in Taiwan. Not only will it help you get around, it will also give you "big face" among the Chinese, who are always surprised and flattered to find a foreigner who has bothered to learn a bit of their language. The correct way to romanize Chinese sounds for foreigners has been a matter of dispute among linguists and sinologists for centuries, but this need not concern the layman, who simply requires a spelling system which at least approximates Chinese pronunciation. The so-called "pin-yin" system propagated in recent years by communist China is the most arbitrary and confusing system of all, with "x" used to denote "s" sounds, "c" for "ts," "zh" for "j," and other inexplicable anomalies. For the reader's convenience, the Chinese words, phrases, and sentence patterns introduced below are spelled according to the most common English pronunciations of the Roman alphabet.

Greeting and Address

Hello; how are you?	*Nee how-ma?*
Fine; very good	*Hun-how*
Not so good	*Boo-how*
Goodbye	*Dzai-jyen*
See you tommorrow	*Ming-tyen jyen*
Good morning	*Dzao-an*
Good evening	*Wan-an*
You; you (plural)	*Nee; nee-men*
I; we	*Wo; wo-men*
He, she, it; they	*Ta; ta-men*
Who?	*Shay?*
Mr. Lee	*Lee syen-sheng*
Miss Lee	*Lee shiao-jyeh*
Mrs. Lee	*Lee tai-tai*
Thank you	*Shyieh-shyieh*
You're welcome	*Boo keh-chee*

Time and Place

Where?	*Nah-lee?*
What time?	*Jee dyen joong?*
What day? (of the week)	*Lee-bai jee?*
Today	*Jin-tyen*
Tomorrow	*Ming-tyen*
Yesterday	*Dzuo-tyen*
One o'clock	*Ee dyen-joong*
Two o'clock	*Liang dyen-joong,*
Very far	*Hun yuan*
Very close	*Hun jin*

Food and Beverage

Restaurant	*Tsan-ting*
Bar	*Jiou-bah*
Let's eat; to eat	*Chir-fan*
Let's drink; to drink	*Huh-jiou*
Ice	*Bing*
Beer; cold bear	*Pee-jiou; bing pee-jiou*
Water; cold water	*Shway; bing-shway*
Soup	*Tang*
Fruit	*Shway-gwo*
Tea	*Cha*
Coffee	*Ka-fay*
Hot	*Reh*
Cold	*Lung*
Sugar	*Tang*
A little bit	*Ee-dyen*
A little bit more	*Dwo-ee-dyen*

A little bit less	*Shao-ee-dyen*
Bottoms up!	*Gahn-bay!*
Settle the bill	*Swan-jang*
Let me pay	*Wo ching-keh*

Numbers

One	*Ee*
Two	*Erh (liang)*
Three	*San*
Four	*Ssuh*
Five	*Wu*
Six	*Lyio*
Seven	*Chee*
Eight	*Bah*
Nine	*Jiou*
Ten	*Shir*
Eleven	*Shir-ee*
Twelve, etc.	*Shir-erh, etc.*
Twenty	*Erh-shir*
Thirty	*San-shir*
Forty, etc.	*Ssuh-shir*
Fifty-five	*Wu-shir-wu*
Seventy-six	*Chee-shir-lyio*
One hundred	*Ee-bai*
One hundred twenty-five	*Ee-bai erh-shir-wu*
Two hundred, etc.	*Liang-bai*
One thousand	*Ee-chyen*
One thousand three hundred fifty-two	*Ee-chyen san-bay wu-shir-erh*
Ten thousand	*Ee-wan*
Fifty Thousand	*Wu-wan*

Hotel and Transportation

Hotel	*fan-dyen*
Room	*fang-jyen*
Airport	*fay-jee-chang*
Bus	*Goong-goong chee-chuh*
Taxi	*Jee-cheng-chuh*
Telephone	*Dyen-hwah*
Telegram	*Dyen-bao*
Airplane	*Fay-jee*
Train	*Hwo-chuh*
Reservations	*Ding-way*
Key	*Yao-shir*
Clothing	*Ee-fu*
Luggage	*Shing-lee*

Shopping

How much?	*dwo-shao*
Too expensive	*Tai-gway*
Make it a bit cheaper	*Swan pyen-ee ee-dyen*
Money	*Chyen*
Credit card	*Shin-yoong kah*
Old	*Lao*
New	*Shin*
Big	*Dah*
Small	*Syiao*
Antique	*Goo-doong*
Red	*Hoong*
Green	*Lyu*
Yellow	*Hwang*
Black	*Hay*
White	*Bai*
Blue	*Lan*
Gold	*Jin*
Jade	*Yu*
Wood	*Mu*
Proprietor; shop-owner	*Lao-ban*
Wrap it up	*Bao-chee-lai*

Basic Sentence Patterns

I want ...	*Wo yao ...*
I don't want ...	*Wo boo-yao ...*
e.g. I want cigarettes	*Wo yao syahng-yen ... dzai nah-lee?*
Where is ...	
e.g. Where is the restaurant?	*Tsan-ting dzai nah-lee?*
Do you have ...?	*Nee yio may-yio ...?*
We don't have ...	*Wo-men may-yio ...*
e.g. Do you have beer?	*Nee yio may-yio pee-jiou?*
I like ...	*Wo shee-hwan ...*
I don't like ...	*Wo boo-shee-hwan ...*
e.g. I like you.	*Wo shee-hwan nee.*
I wish to go ...	*Wo yao choo ...*
e.g. I wish to go to the hotel.	*Wo yao choo fan-dyen.*

Appendix

Accommodations

TAIPEI
"Top Ten"

Hilton International Taipei （希爾頓大飯店）

Located directly across from Central Rail Station; 38 Chung-Hsiao W. Rd., Sec. 1; Cable: HIL-TELS; Telex: 11699, 22513; Tel: 311-5151.

500 rooms; polished, professional service in all departments; award-winning food & beverage facilities; lively disco; sauna.

The Ritz （亞都大飯店）

Located in northeast Taipei, near the nightlife area; 155 Min-Chuan E. Rd.; Cable: THERITZ; Telex: 27345; Tel: 597-1234.

220 rooms; small hotel with personalized service; "art-deco" decor; good European food & beverage facilities.

Lai-Lai Sheraton （來來大飯店）

Located three blocks from Hilton; 12 Chung-Hsaio E. Rd., Sec. 1; Cable: SHANTEL; Telex: 23939; Tel: 321-5511.

705 rooms; large hotel with many facilities including disco-club, health-club, and several restaurants.

Asia World Plaza Hotel

Located in the heart of the business district at 100 Tun Hwa North Road; Cable: ASIAWRDHTL; Telex 26299 ASIAWRD; Tel: 715-0077.

1,057 rooms; huge hotel with 57 bars and restaurants, cinemas, theater restaurant, fitness center, underground parking, convention facilities, a department stores, shopping mall with 500 boutiques and all major hotel amenities.

Howard Plaza

Central downtown location within walking distance of shopping and entertainment district; 160

Jen Ai Rd., Sec. 3
Telex: 10702 HOPLATEL. TAIPEI; Tel: 708-0505.
606 rooms; elegant decor; continental ambiance.

The Grand Hotel（圓山大飯店）

Located on top of Round Hill overlooking the city; 1 Chung-Shan N. Rd., Sec. 4; Cable: GRANDHOTEL; Telex: 11646, 11647; Tel. 596-5565.
575 rooms; classic Chinese palace architecture; exquisite traditional ambiance; extensive gardens and private recreation club.

The President Hotel（統一大飯店）

Located amid the most lively nightlife area; 9 Teh-Hui St.; Cable: PRESDENT; Telex: 11269; Tel: 595-1251.
469 rooms; popular among businessmen; convenient access to nightlife area; quick access to highway.

The Ambassador（國賓大飯店）

Located along Chung-Shan N. Rd, close to shopping area; 63 Chung-Shan N. Rd., Sec. 2; Cable: AMBASATEL; Telex: 11255, 11184; Tel. 551-1111.
481 rooms; indoor swimming pool; roof-top bar lounge with superb views; convenient access to shops.

The Imperial（華國大飯店）

Located near President Hotel; 600 Lin-Sen N. Rd.; Cable: IMPTEL; Telex: 11382, 11730, Tel: 596-5111, 596-3333.
380 rooms; convenient access to nightlife district; disco club; sauna.

Brother Hotel（兄弟大飯店）

Located in east Taipei; 255 Nanking E. Rd., Sec. 3; Cable: BROTHERTEL; Telex: 25977; Tel: 712-3456
304 rooms; excellent Cantonese "dim-sum" restaurant, roof-top lounge, well-maintained rooms.

Other International Tourist Hotels

Carlton Hotel（台華大飯店）

195 Min-Chuan E. Rd.; Cable: CARLTONTEL; Tel: 594-5271; 97 rooms.

Century Plaza（世紀）

132 Omei Street; Cable: CENPLATEL; Telex: 11609; Tel: 311-3131; 201 Rooms.

China Yangming Mountain Hotel（陽明山中國）

237 Ko-Chih Rd., Yangming Mountain; Cable: CHINATEL YMS; Telex: 21757 YMS; Tel: 861-6661; 50 rooms.

Emperor（國王）

118 Nanking E, Rd., Sec. 1; Cable: EMPEROR TEL; Telex: 21777; Tel: 581-1111; 97 rooms.

Gloria（華泰）

369 Lin-Shen N. Rd.; Cable: GLORIATL; Telex: 11192; Tel: 581-8111, 217 rooms.

Golden China Hotel（康華）

306 Sung-Kiang Rd.; Cable: GOLDNATL; Telex: 19550; Tel: 521-5151; 240 rooms.

Majestic Hotel（美琪）

2 Min-Chuan E. Rd.; Cable: MAJEHOTEL; Telex: 21828; Tel: 581-7111; 216 rooms.

Mandarin Hotel（中泰）

166 Tun-Hwa N. Rd.; Cable: MANDATEL; Telex: 11386; Tel: 712-1201; 351 rooms.

Royal Taipei Hotel

37-1 Chung Shan North Rd., Sec. 2, Tel: 542-3266

San Polo Hotel（三普）

172 Chung-Hsiao E. Rd., Sec. 4; Cable: SANPOHTL; Telex: 19794, 19795; Tel: 772-2121; 442 rooms.

Santos Hotel（三德）

439 Cheng-Teh Rd.; Cable: SANTEL; Telex: 27155; Tel: 596-3111; 304 rooms.

Taipei Miramar（美麗華）

420 Min-Chuan E. Rd.; Cable: TPMIRAMA; Telex: 19788; Tel: 531-3456; 584 rooms.

United Hotel（國聯）

200 Kuang-Fu S. Rd.; Cable: UNIHOTEL; Telex: 11679; Tel: 773-1515; 255 rooms.

Regular Tourist Hotels

Angel Hotel（天使）

199 Sung-Kiang Rd.; Cable: ANGELHOTEL; Telex: 21656; Tel: 511-9133; 146 rooms.

Astar Hotel（亞士都）

98 Lin-Sen N. Rd.; Cable: ASTARHOTEL; Tel; 551-3131; 40 rooms.

Cathay Hotel（光華）

36 Nanking E. Rd., Sec. 1; Cable: CATEL; Telex: 26246; Tel: 531-8326; 80 rooms.

China Hotel（中國）

14 Kuan-Chien Rd.; Cable: CHINAHOTEL; Telex: 21757; Tel: 331-9521; 155 rooms

Continental Hotel（中原）

73 Chung-Ching N. Rd.; Cable: CONTIHOTEL; Telex: 25523; Tel: 562-1166; 209 rooms.

Cosmos Hotel（天成）

43 Chung-Hsiao W. Rd., Sec. 1; Cable: COSMSHTL; Telex: 21887; Tel: 361-7856; 245 rooms.

East Dragon Hotel（東龍）

23 Han-Kow St., Sec. 2; Cable: EASTDRAGON; Telex: 19633; Tel: 311-6969; 90 rooms.

Eastern Asia Hotel（東亞）

23 Cheng-Du Rd.; Cable: EASIAHOTEL; Tel: 371-7261; 106 rooms.

Empress Hotel（帝后）

12 Teh-Hui St.; Cable: EMRESTEL; Telex: 11187; Tel: 591-3261; 68 rooms.

First Hotel（第一）

63 Nanking E. Rd., Sec. 1; Cable: FIRSTEL; Telex: 21533; Tel: 541-8231; 163 rooms.

Flowers Hotel（華華）

19 Han-Kow St., Sec. 1; Cable: FLOWERTEL; Tel: 312-3801; 200 rooms.

Frank Hotel（富國）

62 Min-Tsu W. Rd.; Cable: FRANKHOTEL; Telex: 23663; Tel: 592-1112; 91 rooms.

Gala Hotel（慶泰）

186 Sung-Kiang Rd.; Cable: GALATEL; Telex: 28453; Tel: 541-5511; 150 rooms.

Holiday Hotel（假期）

31 Chung-Hsiao E. Rd., Sec. 1; Cable: HOHOTEL; Telex: 25750; Tel: 391-2381; 140 rooms.

Kent Hotel（百利）

6 Chin-Hsi St.; Cable: KENTHOTEL; Tel: 511-7111; 71 rooms.

Kilin Hotel（麒麟）

103 Kang-Ding Rd.; Cable: KILINHOTEL; Telex: 28270; Tel: 314-9222; 173 rooms.

Leofoo Hotel（六福）

168 Chang-Chun Road; Cable: LEOFHOTEL; Telex: 11182; Tel: 581-3111; 238 rooms.

Merlin Court（華懋）

15 Chung-Shan N. Rd.; Sec. 1, Lane 83; Cable: MERLINCORT; Tel: 521-0222; 65 rooms.

Miramar（文華）

3 Nanking E. Rd., Sec. 2; Cable: MIRAMAR-TEL; Tel: 511-1241; 113 Rooms.

Modern City Hotel（名城）

1-1 Chung-Ching N. Rd., Sec. 1; Cable: MORN-TEL; Telex: 25549; Tel: 531-6101; 207 rooms.

National Grandee（國正）

646 Lin-Sen N. Rd.; Telex: 25761; Tel: 596-5161; 150 rooms.

New Asia Hotel（新亞）

139 Chung-Shan N. Rd., Sec. 2; Cable: NEWASIAT; Telex: 23394; Tel: 511-7181; 102 rooms.

New Taipei Hotel（新台北）

1 Sung-Kiang Rd., Lane 69; Cable: HOTELNTP; Telex: 11778; Tel: 551-3211; 66 rooms.

Olympic Hotel（奧林必克）

145 Chung-Shan N. Rd., Sec. 2; Cable: OLYMPICTEL; Telex: 21681; Tel: 511-5251; 195 rooms.

Orient Hotel（東方）

85 Han-Kow St., Sec. 1; Cable: ORIENTEL; Telex: 26504; Tel: 331-7211; 98 rooms.

Pacific Hotel（太平洋）

111 Kunming St.; Cable: PACIFICHTL; Telex: 26811; Tel: 311-3335; 102 rooms.

Palace Hotel（華園）

86 Hwai-Ning St.; Tel: 311-3888; 31 rooms.

Pan American Hotel（氾美）

88 Han-Kow St., Sec. 1; Cable: PANAMHOTEL; Tel: 314-7305; 57 rooms.

Park Hotel（國際）

150 Si-Ning S. St.; Cable: HOTELPARK; Tel: 331-3131; 52 rooms.

Peace Hotel（永安）

150 Chung-Hwa Rd., Sec. 1; Cable: PEACETEL; Tel: 331-3161; 119 rooms.

Phoenix Hotel（皇殿）

36 Wu-Chang St., Sec. 2; Cable: PHOENIXTEL; Tel: 311-9193; 83 rooms.

Plaza Hotel（華城）

68 Sung-Kiang Rd.; Cable: PLAZAHOTEL; Telex: 22307; Tel: 551-5251; 132 rooms.

Star Hotel（明星）

11 Hoping W. Rd.; Cable: STARHTEL; Telex: 28292; Tel: 394-3121; 105 rooms.

Sun Hotel（太陽）

92 Hwai-Ning St.; Cable: SUNHOTEL; Tel: 331-1551; 40 rooms.

Sun Star Hotel（日星）

7 Chung-Shan N. Rd., Sec. 2, Lane 65; Cable: SUNSTARTEL; Telex: 19034; Tel: 571-5281; 100 rooms.

666 Hotel（六六六）

6 Chin-Chou St., Lane 30; Tel: 562-1266; 80 rooms.

Taipei Paradise（一樂園）

24 Hsi-Ning S. Rd.; Cable: PARATEL; Telex: 26972; Tel: 314-2122; 208 rooms.

NORTHERN TAIWAN
PEITOU
Regular Hotels

I Tsun Inn（逸邨）
140 Wen-Chuan Rd.; Tel: 891-2121; 26 rooms.

Hilite Hotel（萬祥）
1 Chi-Yen Rd.; Cable: HTLHILTE; Tel: 891-3092; 170 rooms.

Whispering Pines Inn（吟松閣）
21 Yio-Ya Rd.; Tel: 891-2037; 891-2063; 24 rooms.

Sincere Hotel（新秀閣）
238 Kuang-Ming Rd.; Tel: 891-2166; 47 rooms.

TAOYUAN
International Hotels

Holiday Inn International Airport（桃園假期）
269 Da-shing Rd.; Cable: HOLIDAY INN, Telex: 31590; Tel: (032) 388021.

Shih-Men Sesame Hotel（石門芝蔴）
Shih-Men Reservoir; Lungtan Hsiang; Cable: SESEAMETL, Telex: 31256; Tel: Shih-Men 326, 246. Taipei 314-0346, 381-4844; 202 rooms.

Taoyuan Plaza Hotel（南華）
151 Fushin Rd.; Cable: PLAZATEL; Telex: 32150; Tel: (033) 372233.

Regular Hotels

Hawaii Hotel;（夏威夷）
20 Yu-leh St.; Cable: HAWAIIHOTEL; Tel: (033) 323131.

Today Hotel;（今日）
81 Fushing Rd.; Tel: (033) 324162; 100 rooms.

CENTRAL TAIWAN, CHIAYI

Regular Hotel

Gallant Hotel（嘉南大飯店）
257 Wen Hwa Rd.; Tel: (052) 223-5366.

EAST-WEST CROSS-ISLAND HIGHWAY
Regular Hotels

Dragon Valley Hotel（龍谷飯店）
Ku-Kuan; Tel: (045) 951225 & 931365. Taipei tel: 522-1291.

Li Shan Guest House（梨山賓館）
Pear Mountain; Tel: (045) 989501.

Wen-Shan Guest House（文山賓館）
Wen-Shan; Tel: (38) 691125.

Mount Lu Garden Guest House（蘆山園賓館）
Mount Lu; Tel: (049) 802369.

SUN MOON LAKE
International Hotels

Evergreen Hotel（涵碧樓）
142 Chung-Hsing Rd.; Sun Moon Lake; Cable: EVERGREEN: Tel: (049) 855311; 70 rooms.

Sun Moon Lake Hotel（日月潭）
23 Chung-Cheng Rd.; Sun Moon Lake; Cable: SOMOTEL; Tel: (049) 855351; Taipei Tel: 312-3645; 116 rooms.

TAICHUNG
International Hotels

National Hotel（全國）
257 Taichung Kang Rd., Sec. 1; Cable: NATIONALHTL; Telex: 51393; Tel: (042) 229-6011; 270 rooms.

Park Hotel（敬華）
17 Kong-Yuan Rd.; Cable: PARKTEL; Telex: 51525; Tel: (042) 220-5181; 124 rooms.

Regular Hotels

Apollo Hotel;（鴻賓）
14 Shih-Fu Rd.; Cable: APOTEL; Tel: 222-8041; 127 rooms.

Formosa Hotel; （寶島）
27 Chung-Shan Rd.; Cable: FORMOHOTEL;
Tel: 222-6701; 120 rooms.

Life Hotel; （名立）
1-23 Wu-Chuan Rd.; Cable: LIFEHOTEL; Tel:
229-4191; 89 rooms.

Paradise Hotel; （新天地）
15 Chung-Shan Rd.; Lane 175; Cable: PARA-
DISE; Telex: 51164; Tel: 223-1005; 62 rooms.

Taichung Hotel; （台中）
152 Tzu-Yio Rd.; Sec. 1; Cable: TCHOTEL;
Telex: 51134; Tel: 224-2121; 179 rooms.

Taichung Lucky Hotel; （吉祥）
68 Min-Chuan Rd.; Cable: TCLUCKYH; Telex:
51321; Tel: 229-5191; 113 rooms.

SOUTHERN TAIWAN
KANGSHAN
Regular Hotels

Kangshan Spa Hotel; （岡山溫家賓館）
Kangshan; Tel: (07) 631-3101.

KAOHSIUNG
International Hotels

Ambassador Hotel; （高雄國賓）
202 Min-Sheng 2nd Rd.; Tel: 211-5211; 457
rooms.

Grand Hotel;
Cheng-Ching Lake; Cable: GRANDHOTEL;
Telex: 71231; Tel: 383-5911; 108 rooms.

Holiday Inn （華園）
279 Liu-Ho 2nd Rd.; Cable: GARDEN; Telex:
89148; Tel: 241-0121; 313 rooms.

Kingdom Hotel; （華王）
32 Wu-Fu 4th Rd.; Telex: KINGDOMTEL;
Telex: 89138; Tel: 551-8211; 312 rooms.

King Wang Hotel; （京王）
329 Chi-Hsien 2nd Rd.; Cable: KINGWANG;
Telex: 72256; Tel: 221-9409.

Major Hotel; （名人）
7 Ta-Ren Rd.; Cable: MAJORTEL; Telex:
72121; Tel: 521-2266.

Summit Hotel; （皇統）
426 Chiu-Ru 1st Rd.; Cable: SUMMIHTL; Telex:
72423; Tel: 384-5526; 211 rooms.

Tourist Hotels

Buckingham Hotel; （白金漢）
394 Chi-Hsien 2nd Rd.; Cable: BUCAMTEL;
Telex: 71500; Tel: 282-2151; 144 rooms.

Empire Hotel; （帝國）
71 Chung-Shan 2nd Rd.; Cable: HOTEL-
EMPIRE; Tel: 221-6011; 60 rooms.

Grand China Hotel; （中華）
289 Chung-Shan 1st Rd.; Cable: GRANDCHI-
NA; Tel: 221-9941; 70 rooms.

Kennedy Hotel; （肯乃第）
67 Hsin-Hsing St.; Cable: KENNEDYHTL; Tel:
551-9251; 77 rooms.

Love River Hotel; （愛河）
8 Ho-Hsi Rd.; Cable: HOTELLR; Tel: 551-3271;
70 rooms.

Peach Hotel; （百騏）
65 Wu-Fu 4th Rd.; Cable: PEACHOTL; Telex:
71475; Tel: 551-8231; 115 rooms.

Prince Hotel; （王子）
26 Chi-Hsien 2nd Rd.; Tel: 231-7111; 90 rooms.

Royal Hotel; （皇都）
33 Chien-Kuo 3rd Rd.; Cable: HTLROYAL;
Telex: 71153; Tel: 251-0121; 131 rooms.

San Hwa Hotel; （三華）
91 Liu-Ho 1st Rd.; Cable: SANHUATEL;
TELEX: 72179; Tel: 231-8171; 125 rooms.

Southland Hotel; （南亞）
139 Chung-Cheng 4th Rd.; Cable: SOUTH-
HOTEL; Telex: 71469; Tel: 221-6036; 77 rooms.

Utopia Hotel; （桃源）
161 Pichung St.; Cable: HOTUTOPIA; Tel: 551-
8261; 105 rooms.

KENTING
Regular Hotel

Kenting House; （墾丁賓舘）
Kenting; Tel: (088) 861-301. Taipei: 311-6974,
381-0395; 72 rooms.

PESCADORES
Regular Hotels

Pao-Hwa Hotel; （寶華）
2 Chung-Cheng Rd., Makung; Tel: (069) 274881;
78 rooms.

Feng-Kuo Hotel; 12 Ren-Ai Rd., Makung.

Sheng-Kuo Hotel; 6 Shui-Yuan Rd.; Makung.

TAINAN
International Hotels

Redhill Hotel; （赤嵌大飯店）
46 Cheng-Kung Rd.; Telex: 73591; Tel: (062)
225-8121; 150 rooms.

Tainan Hotel; （台南）
1 Cheng-Kung Rd.; Cable: TANHOTEL
TAINAN: Telex: 71365; Tel: (062) 228-9101; 153
rooms.

Regular Hotels

Chengkung Hotel; 〈成功〉
11 Pei-Men Rd.; Tel: (062) 222-8151; 47 rooms.

Hwa Hsing Hotel; 〈華興〉
9 Min-Sheng Rd.; Lane 181; Tel: (062) 222-2104; 49 rooms.

Oriental Hotel; 〈華光〉
143 Min-Tsu Rd.; Cable: ORIENHOTEL; Tel: (062) 222-1131; 94 rooms.

CORAL LAKE
Regular Hotel

Kuo Min Hotel 〈國民旅舍〉
Coral Lake; Tel: (066) 983121.

EASTERN TAIWAN
HWALIEN
International Hotels

Astar Hotel; 〈亞士都〉
6-1 Min-Chuan Rd.; Cable: ASTAR; Telex: 22347; Tel: (038) 326111; 170 rooms.

CITC Hwalien Hotel; 〈中信〉
2 Yung-Hsing Rd.; Telex: 11144C; Tel: (038) 221171; 237 rooms.

Marshal Hotel; 〈統帥〉
36 Kung-Yuan Rd.; Cable: MARSHALHTL; Telex: c/o 21656 ANGELHTL; Tel: (038) 326123; 347 rooms.

Tourist Hotels

Northward Hotel; 〈朝北〉
361 Chung-Shan Rd.; Tel: (038) 325181; 81 rooms.

Toyo Hotel; 〈東洋〉
50 San-Min Rd.; Cable: TOYOHOTEL; Tel: (038) 326151; 70 rooms.

Tien-Hsiang Lodge, 30 Tien-Hsiang Rd., Hsui-lin, Hwalien County; Tel: (038) 691155. Taipei Reservations: 551-5933

TAITUNG
Tourist Hotel

Chih-Pen Hotel; 〈知本〉
5 Wen-Chuan Village; Pinan; Tel: (089) 512220. Taipei 331-1611; also P.O. Box 60, Taitung; 50 rooms.

Hostels

Teh-Chi Hostel
Teh-Chi Dam, East-West Cross-Island Highway
Sun Moon Lake Hostel
Sun Moon Lake, Yutsu, Nantou County
Hsi-Tou Hostel
Hsi-Tou Forest Recreation Area

Wushan-Tou Hostel
Wushan-Tou Reservoir, Tainan County
Tseng-Wen Hostel
Tseng-Wen Dam, Tainan County
Wuling Hostel
Wuling Farm, East-West Cross-Island Highway
Li-Shan Hostel (Pear Mountain)
Li-Shan, East-West Cross-Island Highway
Wu-She Hostel
Wu-She, East-West Cross-Island Highway
Ching-Shan Hostel
Ching-Shan, East-West Cross-Island Highway
Ali-Shan Hostel
Ali-Shan (Mt. Ali)
Mei-Shan Hostel (Plum Mountain)
Mei-Shan, South Cross-Island Highway
YMCA
19 Hsu-Chang St., Taipei, Tel: 311-3201
YMCA
7 Ching-Tao Rd., Taipei, Tel: 371-4993

Guest Houses

TAIPEI

Aloha Guest-House
10-1 Nung-An St.
〈農安街10-1號〉
Tel: 594-0292.

Chung-Shan Guest-House
26 Min-Tsu E. Rd.
〈民族東路26號〉
Tel: 593-1805.

Edward Mansion Guest-House
657 Lin-Sen N. Rd.
〈林森北路657號〉
Tel: 597-7261.

Lee Yuan Guest-House
26 Chiu-Chuan St.
〈酒泉街26號〉
Tel: 592-6486.

Rainbow Guest-House
91 Chung-Shan N. Rd., Sec. 3
〈中山北路三段91號〉
Tel: 596-5515.

Hai-Shan Guest-House
247 Chung-Shan N. Rd., Sec. 6—suburban Tien-Mu
〈天母, 中山北路六段247號〉
Tel: 831-4944.

Lan-Ya Guest-House
280 Chung-Shan N. Rd., Sec. 6—suburban Tien-Mu
〈天母, 中山北路六段280號〉
Tel: 831-5722.

Riverside Guest-House
71 Tien-Mu 3rd Rd.—suburban Tien-Mu
〈天母, 天母三路, 71號〉
Tel: 871-8771.

Yang-Ming Mountain Guest-House
12 Yang-Ming Rd., Sec. 1—suburban Yangming Mountain
（陽明路，一段，12號）
Tel: 861-6601.

EAST COAST

Wen-Shan Guest House,
Hwa-lien County, （文山賓舘）
Tel: (038) 691125.

Youth Activity Centers
Northern Taiwan

* Rate given are on daily basis.

Chien-Tan Youth Activity Center
16 Chung-Shan N. Rd., Sec. 4, Taipei; Tel: 596-2151.
(Accommodates 677 persons at NT$100 per dormitory, NT$600 per day for double rooms.)
Chin-Shan Beach Youth Activity Center
288 Huang-Kang Village, Chin-Shan; Tel: (032)982511.
(Accommodates 644 persons at NT$70 per dormitory, NT$400 per double room, NT$1,200 per bungalow.)
Taipei International Youth Activity Center
30 Hsin-Hai Rd., Sec. 3, Taipei; Tel: 708-3832/5.
(Accommodates 763 persons at NT$100 per dormitory, NT$300 per single room.)

Central Taiwan

Hsi-Tou Youth Activity Center
15 Shenlin Lane, Neifu Village, Lu-ku, Nantou County; Tel: (049)612161.
(Accommodates 380 persons at NT$100 per dormitory, NT$600 per double room.)
Sun Moon Lake Youth Activity Center
Sun Moon Lake, Yutsu, Nantou County; Tel: (049)855331.
(Accommodates 374 persons at NT$100 per dormitory, NT$600 per double room, NT$2,400 per bungalow.)

Southern Taiwan

Cheng-Ching Lake Youth Activity Center
10 Wen-Chien Rd., Wusung Village, Kaohsiung County; Tel: (07) 371-7182.
(Accommodates 500 persons at NT$100 per dormitory, NT$500 per room (three to four persons), NT$1,200 per bungalow.)
Tseng-Wen Youth Activity Center
70-1 Mi-Chih Village, Nanci, Tainan County; Tel: (062)226131.
(Accommodates 346 persons at NT$100 per dormitory, NT$300 per single room, NT$1,200 per bungalow.)

Eastern Taiwan

Tien-Hsiang Youth Activity Center
30 Tien-Hsiang Rd., Hsiu-lin, Hwalien County;

Tel: (038)691155.
(Accommodates 344 persons at NT$70-100 per dormitory, NT$600 per room (four persons), NT$360-1,200 per double room.

Airlines Serving Taiwan

Aloha Pacific Airlines, 162 Chang An East Rd., Sec. 2, Tel: 773-3534.
Cargolux Airlines, 751-1121.
Cathay Pacific Airways Ltd., 683 Min-Sheng E. Rd., Tel: 751-8228 (office), (033)832502 (airport).
China Airlines Ltd., 131 Nanking E. Rd., Sec. 3, Tel: 715-2626 (office), (033)832451 (airport).
Continental Airlines, Tel: 715-2766.
Japan Asia Airways, 125 Nanking E. Rd., Sec. 2, Tel: 551-9121 (office), (033)833761 (airport).
KLM-Royal Dutch Airlines, 216 Nanking E. Rd., Sec. 2, Tel: 536-4131.
Korean Airlines, 53 Nanking E. Rd., Sec. 2, Tel: 521-4242 (office), (033)833787 (airport).
Malaysian Airlines Systems, 95 Nanking E. Rd., Sec. 2, Tel: 561-1174 (office), · (033)834855 airport
Air Nauru, 2 Min Tzu E. Rd., Tel: 594-8116 (office).
Northwest Orient Airlines, 171 Chung-Shan N. Rd., Sec. 2, Tel: 596-5951 (office), (033)832473 (airport).
Pan American World Airways, 35 Kuang-Fu S. Rd., Tel: 767-3161.
Philippine Airlines, 46 Chung-Shan N. Rd., Sec. 2, Tel: 521-4101 (office), (033)832419 (airport).
Singapore Airlines, 148 Sung Kiang Rd., Tel: 531-4232 (office), (033)832247 (airport).
South African Airways, 131 Nanking E. Rd., Sec. 3. Tel: 772-2626 (office), (033)834131 (airport).
Thai Airways International Ltd., 100 Chang-Chun Rd., 3rd Flr., Tel: 521-5382 (office) (033)834131 (airport).

Off-Line Airline Offices

Alitalia
Tel: 341-5271
Varig Brazilian Airlines
Tel: 511-4157
British Airways
Tel: 542-3111
British Caledonian
Tel: 521-7252
Canadian Pacific
Tel: 581-4111
Delta Airlines
Tel: 700-1021
Eastern Airlines
Tel: 561-0273
Air France
Tel: 542-7345
Garuda Indonesian Airways
Tel: 551-0951
Air India
Tel: 541-1848
Air Lanka
Tel: 595-4201
Luftansa German Airlines
Tel: 581-4111

Air New Zealand
Tel: 521-2311
Qantas Airlines
Tel: 521-2311
Saudia Airlines
Tel: 511-3171
Scandinavian Airlines System
Tel: 551-7141
Swissair
Tel: 581-1122
Trans World Airlines
Tel: 341-5271
United Airlines
Tel: 700-1021
UTA French Airlines
561-0273
Western Airlines
542-3778
El Al Israel Airlines
563-1200
American Airlines
563-1200
Air Niugini
581-1133
Air Canada
581-1133
Sabena Belgian World Airlines
563-5121

Art Galleries

Alpha Art Gallery（太極藝廊）
101 Ren-Ai Rd, Sec. 4, 3rd Fl., Tel: 781-1714
Apollo Art Gallery（阿波羅畫廊）
218-6 Chung-Hsiao E. Rd, Sec. 4, 2nd Fl., Tel: 781-6596.
Avante Garde Art Gallery（尙雅畫廊）
572-1 Tun-Hwa S. Rd., Tel: 705-4221.
Cape of Good Hope Art Gallery（好望角畫廊）
99 Hoping E. Rd, Sec. 1, Tel: 321-4086.
Chang Liu Art Gallery（長流畫廊）
1-1 Hsin Yi Rd, Sec. 2, Lane 114, Tel: 321-8298.
James Art Gallery（精藝畫廊）
147 Sung-Kiang Rd., Tel: 551-6057.
Lung Men Art Gallery（龍門畫廊）
177 Chung-Hsiao E. Rd, Sec. 4, 2nd Fl., Tel: 781-3979.
Ming Sheng Art Gallery（明生畫廊）
145 Chung-Shan N. Rd, Sec. 1, Tel: 581-0858.
Printmakers Art Gallery（版畫家畫廊）
285 Fushing S. Rd, Sec. 1, 5th Fl., Tel: 707-9424
Spring Gallery（春之藝廊）
286B Kuang-Fu S. Rd., Tel: 781-6596
Sun Land Art Gallery（大地畫廊）
46 Tun-Hwa; S. Rd., Lane 390, Tel: 752-2575
Taipei Art Guild
#7, Lane 728, Chung-Shan North Rd., Sec 6, Tel: 871-8465
Taipei Fine Arts Museum
181 Chung-Shan North Rd., Sec. 3, Tel: 595-7656

Banks
Foreign Banks in Taipei

American Express Int'l., 214 Tun Hwa N. Rd., 2nd Floor, Tel: 715-1581.

Bank of America, 205 Tun-Hwa N. Rd., Tel: 715-4111.
Bangkok Bank Ltd., 125 Nanking E. Rd., Sec 2, Tel: 571-3275.
Bankers Trust Co., 205 Tun-Hwa N. Rd., 8th Fl., Tel: 715-2888.
Banque de Paris et des pays-bas (PARIBUS), 205 Tun-Hwa N. Rd., 11th Fl., Tel: 715-1980.
Chase Manhattan Bank, 72 Nanking E. Rd., Sec. 2, Tel: 521-3262.
Chemical Bank, 261 Nanking E. Rd., Sec. 3, Tel: 712-1181
Citibank, 742 Min-Sheng E. Rd., Tel: 715-5931.
Continental Bank, 62 Nanking E. Rd., Sec. 2, Tel: 521-0242.
Dai-Ichi Kangyo Bank Ltd., 23 Chang-An E. Rd., Sec. 1, Tel: 561-4371.
European Asian Bank, 180 Chung-Hsiao E. Rd., Sec. 4, Tel: 772-2580.
First Interstate Bank of California, 221 Nanking E. Rd., Sec. 3, Tel: 715-3572.
Grindlay's Bank, 123 Nanking E. Rd., Sec. 2, 2nd Fl., Tel: 542-7456.
Hbu Bank, 61-1 Sung-Kiang Rd., Tel: 581-8131.
International Bank of Singapore, 178 Nanking E. Rd., Sec. 2, Tel: 581-0531.
Irving Trust Co., 10 Chung-Ching S. Rd., Sec. 1, Tel: 311-4682.
Lloyds Bank International, 66 Nanking E. Rd., Sec. 2, Tel: 521-8521.
Metropolitan Bank and Trust Co., 52 Nanking E. Rd., Sec 1, Tel: 521-4191.
Rainier National Bank, 125 Sung-Kiang Rd., Tel: 536-3244.
Seattle First National Bank, 333 Nanking E. Rd., Sec. 3, Tel: 712-9131.
Societe Generale of France, 683 Min-Sheng E. Rd., Tel: 715-2161.
Toronto Dominion Bank, 20 Pa-Teh Rd., Sec. 3, Tel: 771-2161.
The Morgan Bank, 205 Tun-Hwa N. Rd., Tel: 712-2333.
United World Chinese Commercial Bank, 150 Po-Ai Rd., Tel: 381-8160.

Amsterdam-Rotterdam Bank, NV, 13th floor, World Wide House, 683 Min-Sheng East Rd., Tel: 713-0221.
Banque Nationale de Paris (BNP), 7th floor, 214 Tun-Hwa North Rd., Tel: 731-1167.
Credit Lyonnais Bank, 15th floor, Asia Trust Building, 116 Nanking East Rd., Sec 2, Tel: 562-9475.
Development Bank of Singapore, 214 Tun-Hwa North Rd., Tel: 713-7710.
First National Bank of Boston, 5th Floor, United Commercial Building, 137 Nanking East Rd., Sec 2, Tel: 563-3443.

Hong Kong & Shanghai Banking Corp, 205 Tun-Hwa North Rd., Tel: 713-0088.
Manufacturers Hanover Trust, 10th Floor, 62 Tun-Hwa North Rd., Tel: 721-3150.

Royal Bank of Canada, 8th floor, 214 Tun-Hwa North Rd., Tel: 713-0911.
Shanghai Commercial and Savings Bank, 28 Kuan-chien Rd., Tel: 311-0731.

Foreign Banks with representative offices only

Bank of California
Tel: 311-0551.
Bank of Canton of California
Tel: 312-3341.
Mellon Bank
Tel: 713-2792.
Republic Bank Dallas
Tel: 715-0745.
Security Pacific National Bank
Tel: 715-4237.

Local Banks in Taipei

Bank of Communications
91 Heng-Yang Rd., Tel: 331-3561.
Bank of Taiwan
120 Chung-Ching S. Rd., Sec. 1, Tel: 371-9111.
Central Bank of China
2 Roosevelt Rd., Sec. 1, Tel: 393-6161.
Chang Hwa Commercial Bank
57 Chung-Shan N. Rd., Sec. 2, Tel: 536-2951.
City Bank of Taipei
7 Ching-Tao W. Rd., Tel: 381-4755.
Cooperative Bank of Taiwan
30 Kung-Yuan Rd., Tel: 311-8811.
Farmers Bank of China
53 Huai-Ning St., Tel: 311-0681.
First Commercial Bank
15 Chung-Ching S. Rd., Sec. 1, Tel: 311-1111.
Hua Nan Commercial Bank
33 Kai-Feng St., Sec. 1, Tel: 361-9666.
International Commercial Bank of China
100 Chi-Lin Rd., Tel: 563-3156.
Land Bank of Taiwan
46 Kuan-Chien Rd., Tel: 331-3571.
Overseas Chinese Commercial Bank
8 Hsien-Yang Rd., Tel: 371-5181.
Shanghai Commercial and Savings Bank
28 Kuan-Chien Rd., Tel: 311-0731.
Taipei Business Bank
36 Nanking E. Rd., Sec. 3, Tel: 563-1212.
The Medium Business Bank of Taiwan
73 Chung-Ching S. Rd., Sec. 1, Tel: 371-9241.
United World Chinese Commercial Bank
150 Po-Ai Rd., Tel: 311-0681.

Dental Clinics

Adventist Hospital Dental Clinic; 424 Pa-Teh Rd., Sec. 2, Tel: 771–8739.
Dr. Chang Ta-tsai's Clinic; 29 Chung-Shan N. Rd., Sec. 3, 3rd Fl., Tel: 595-1588.
An-Hsin Dental Center; 21 Ren-Ai Rd., Sec. 4, Lane 12, Tel: 701-0470, 708-9618.
China Dental Clinic; 113 Sung-Kiang Rd., 2nd Fl., Tel: 561-9287.
Today's Dental Clinic; 72 Heng-Yang Rd., 6th Fl., Tel: 371-4398, 314-2481.

Foreign Embassies and Consulates

Bolivian Embassy
2nd floor, 15-2, Lane 31 Tien Mou 3rd Road, Tel: 836-9800.
Costa Rice Embassy
164 Chung-Shan N. Rd., Sec. 6, 2nd Fl., Tel: 832-0832.
Costa Rica Consulate General
66 Chung-Shan N. Rd., Sec. 2, 4th Fl., Tel: 551-3864.
Republic of Honduras Consulate
30 Chung-Shan N. Rd., Sec. 1, Tel: 371-5467.
Dominican Republic Embassy
54 Nanking E. Rd., Sec. 3, Tel. 541-7819, 561-7804.
El Salvador Embassy
12 Ming-Tsu E. Rd., 2nd Fl., Tel: 598-2794.
Republic of Paraguay Embassy
98 Fu-Kuo Rd, 2nd Fl., B5, Shih-Lin, Tel: 835-5340.
Guatemala Embassy
6 Chien-Kuo N. Rd., Lane 44, Tel: 561-7043.
Haiti Embassy
11, Tien Mou 2nd Rd., Tel: 871-4751.
Korean Embassy
345 Chung-Hsiao E. Rd., Sec. 4, Tel: 761-9361/5.
Nauru Consulate
2 Min-Tsu E. Rd., 1B. Tel: 598-1975.
Nicaragua Embassy
270 Chung-Shan N. Rd., Sec. 6, 3rd Fl., Tel: 832-1832.
Panama Embassy
614 Lin-Sen N. Rd., 4th Fl., Tel: 596-8563.
Saudi Arabia Embassy
11th floor, 550 Chung Hsiao East Rd., Sec. 4, Tel: 703-5855.
South Africa Embassy
205 Tun-Hwa N. Rd., 13th Fl., Tel: 715-3252.
Swaziland Consulate
127 Ren-Ai Rd., Sec. 3, 12th Fl., Tel: 751-8257.
Uruguay Embassy
16 Ming-Tsu E. Rd., 7th Fl., Tel: 596-4947.

Foreign Missions

Australia; Far East Trading Co., 71 Queens Rd., 7th Fl., Melbourne, Victoria 3004; Tel: 519-793.
Bahrain; Trade Mission of the ROC, Suite 202, Andalus Building, Salmaniya Rd., Manama; Tel: 713-070
Belgium; Centre Culturel Sun Yat-sen, Rue de la Loi 24, 1000—Bruxells, Belgique; Tel: 511-0887, 511-1528.
Brazil; Centro Comercial do Extremo-Oriente, Av. Paulista, 1.471-Conj 317, 01311 Sao Paulo, S.P. Brasil; Tel: 285-6194, 287-8328.
Colombia; Oficina Comercial del Lejano Oriente, Carrera 7, No. 79-75 Bogota; Tel: 235-4713, 255-4076.
France; Association Pour la Promation des Exchanges Commerciau et Touristiques avec Taiwan, 17, Ave. Matignon A.S.P.E.C.T. Time-Life Building, 75008 Paris; Tel: 256-3909, 256-2691.
Germany; Asia Trade Center.DreieichstraBe 59, 6000 Frankfurt/Main 70, Tel: (0611) 610743.
Great Britain; Free Chinese Center, 2nd Fl., National Bank House, 101 Baker Street, London WIM, 1 FD, England; Tel: 01-935-9339.

Holland; Far East Trade Service, Elandstraat 2, 2513 GR, The Hague; Tel: (070)469-438.

Hong Kong; Chung Hwa Travel Service, Room 1009, Takshing House, 20 Des Voeux Rd., Tel: 5-258315/8.

Indonesia: Chinese Chamber of Commerce, No. 4 JL, Banyumas, Jakarta; Tel: 351212/14.

Japan; Association of East Asian Relations, 2-4th Fl, Heiwado Boeki Honsha Bldg., No. 8-7, 1-chome Higashi Azabu, Minato-ku, Tokyo; Tel: 583-2171.

Luxembourg: Center Dr. Sun Yat-sen, 2 Alléé Léopold Goebel, Luxembourg-ville, Grande-Duche de Luxembourg, Tel: 444772/4.

Malaysia; Far East Trading and Tourism Center SDN, BHD, Room 907, 9th Fl., Fitzpatrick's Bldg., 86 Jalan Raja Chulan, Kuala Lumpur 05-10.

New Zealand; East Asia Trade Center, 7th Fl., IBM House, 155-161 The Terrace Alley, Wellington; Tel: 736474/5.

Norway; Taipei Trade Center, Ivar Aasensvei 19, Oslo 3; Tel: 143219.

Philippines; Pacific Economic and Cultural Center, 8th Fl., BF. Homes Condominium Bldg., Aduana St. Intramuros, Manila; Tel: 472261/65.

Singapore; Trade Mission of the ROC, Suite 1301, UIC Building, No. 5 Shenton Way, Singapore 0106 Tel: 222-4951/53.

Spain; Centro Sun Yat-sen, C/Zurbano, 92-60 Dcha, Madrid-3-, Espana; Tel: 44280-22, 44281-90.

Switzerland; Centre San Yat-sen, 54 Avenue de Bethusy 1012, lausanne, Suisse; Tel: (012 335005/6.

Thailand; Far East Trade office, 10th Fl., Kian Gwan Bldg., 140 Wit Thayu Rd., Bangkok; Tel: 251-9274/6

United States (WASHINGTON); Coordination Council for North American Affairs (CCNAA), Washington, 5161 River Road, Washington, DC 20016.

CCNAA Atlanta; Suite 1602 Peachtree Center, Cain Tower, 229 Peachtree St., N.E., Atlanta, Georgia 30303.

CCNAA Chicago; 20 North Clark St., 19th Fl., Chicago, Illinois 60602.

CCNAA Houston; 11 Green Way Plaza, Suite 2006, Houston, Texas 77046.

CCNAA Los Angeles; 3660 Wilshire Blvd., Suite 1050, Los Angeles, CA 90010.

CCNAA New York; 801 Second Ave., New York, NY 10017.

CCNAA San Francisco; 300 Montgomery St., Suite 535, San Francisco, CA 94104.

CCNAA Seattle; 401 Lyon Building, 607 Third Ave., Seattle, WA 98104.

CCNAA Honolulu; 2746 Pali Highway, Honolulu, Hawaii 96817.

Hospitals

Adventist Hospital; 424 Pa-Teh Rd., Sec. 2, Tel: 771-8151.

Air Force General Hospital; 1 Nanking E. Rd., Sec. 4, Alley 83, Lane 211, Tel: 764-2151.

Cathay General Hospital; 280 Ren-Ai Rd., Sec. 4, Tel: 708-2121.

Central Clinic; 77 Chung-Hsiao E. Rd., Sec. 4, Tel: 751-0221.

Cheng-Keng Memorial Hospital; 199 Tun-Hwa N. Rd., Tel: 713-5211.

Country Hospital; 1 Ren-Ai Rd., Sec. 4, Lane 71, Tel: 771-3161/5.

Mackay Memorial Hospital; 92 Chung-Shan N. Rd., Sec. 2, Tel: 543-3535.

Taipei Municipal Chung-Hsin Hospital; 145 Cheng-Chow Rd., Tel: 521-3801.

Taipei Municipal Hoping Hospital; 14 Kuang-Chow St., Tel: 311-4422/6.

Taipei Municipal Renai Hospital; 10 Ren-Ai Rd., Sec. 4, Tel: 707-3155.

Tri-Service General Hospital; 226 Ting Chow St., Tel: 311-7001.

Veterans General Hospital; 201 Shir-Pai Rd., Sec. 2, Tien-Mou, Tel: 871-2121, ext. 3530 (English information).

Museums
(Taipei)

Armed Forces Museum (國軍歷史文物館)
243 Kui-Yang St., Sec. 1
Hours: 8:30 a.m.—noon
1 p.m.—4 p.m.
(Closed Tuesdays)

Butterfly Museum (昆蟲科學博物館)
71 Chi-Nan Rd., Sec. 1
Tel: 321-6256
Hours: 9 a.m.—5 p.m.
(by appointment only)

Cathay Art Museum (國泰美術館)
1 Hsiang-Yang Rd.
Tel: 311-3575
Hours: 9 a.m.—5 p.m. daily

Children's Museum (兒童博物館)
Ho-Ping E. Rd.
Hours: 9 a.m.—5 p.m. daily

Chinese Culture and Movie Center (中國電影文化城)
34 Chih-Shan Rd., Wai-Shuang-Hsi, Shih-Lin
Tel: 881-2681
Hours: 8:30 a.m.—5:30 p.m. daily

Chung-Cheng Aviation Museum (中正航空科學館)
Chiang Kai-shek International Airport, Taoyuan
Hours: 9:30 a.m.—5 p.m.
(Closed Mondays)

Hwa-Kang Museum of Chinese (華岡博物館)
Culture University (Yangming Mountain)
6th Fl., Ta-Yi Building
Tel: 861-0511, ext. 266
Hours: 9 a.m.—4:30 p.m. daily

National Museum of History (國立歷史博物館)
49 Nan-Hai Rd (in New Taipei Park)
Tel: 361-0278
Hours: 9 a.m.—5 p.m. daily

National Palace Museum (國立故宮博物院)
Wai-Shuang-Hsi, Shir-Lin
Tel: 881-2021
Hours: 9 a.m.—5 p.m. daily

Postal Museum (郵政博物館)
17 Kuang-Ming St., Lane 142, Hsin-Tien
Tel: 911-1612

Hours: 9 a.m.—4:30 p.m.
(Closed Mondays)
Taipei Fine Arts Museum
181 Chung Shan North Rd., Sec. 3, Tel: 595-7656
Hours: 9 a.m.—5 p.m.
(Closed Mondays)
Taiwan Provincial Museum（台灣省立博物館）
2 Hsiang-Yang Rd.
Tel: 361-3925
Hours: 9 a.m.—5 p.m.
(Closed Mondays and Wednesdays)

Places of Worship
Taipei

Baha'i Center
149-13 Hsin-Sheng S. Rd., Sec. 1; Tel: 701-5091.
Calvary Baptist Church
21 Yang-Teh Ta-Tao, Sec. 2; Yangming Mountain; Tel: 831-3458.
Christian Science Services
10 Chang-An E. Rd., Sec. 2, Lane 201.
Church of Christ
3 Road 7, Lane 55, Tien-Mou; Tel: 321-4843 (Taipei), 871-4742 (Tien-Mou).
Church of the Good Shepherd
509 Chung-Cheng Rd., Shir-Lin; Tel: 882-3461.
English Vesper Service
3 Chung-Shan S. Rd (corner of Chi-Nan Rd).
Friendship Presbyterian Church
5 Roosevelt Rd., Sec. 3, Lane 269; Tel: 871-2452.
Mother of God Church (Catholic)
171 Chung Shan North Rd., Sec. 7, Tien Mou; Tel: 871-4397.
St. Christophers Church (Catholic)
51 Chung-Shan N. Rd., Sec. 3; Tel: 594-7914.
St. John's Cathedral (Anglican, Episcopal)
280 Fushing S. Rd., Sec. 2; Tel: 707-7740.
Sung Shan Seventh Day Adventist
424 Pa-Teh Rd., Sec. 2. Tel: 771-8151, ext. 14.
The Church of Jesus Christ of Latter-Day Saints
209 Fu-Lin Rd., Shih-Lin; Tel: 833-3709.
Taipei Grand Mosque
62 Hsin-Sheng S. Rd., Sec. 2; Tel: 392-7364.
Taipei International Church (Interdenominational)
Auditorium. Taipei American School, Shir-lin; Tel: 871-9067, 835-3314.
Taipei Jewish Community Center
#9, Lane 450 Chung Shan North Rd., Sec. 6, Tien Mou; Tel: 861-6303.

Taichung

St. James Church (Episcopal)
23 Wu-Chuan Rd.
St. Viator Chapel (Catholic)
242 Wei-Tao Rd.
Taichung Immanuel Baptist Church
241 Ta-Ya Rd.
Taichung Community Chapel
136-1 Shui-Nan Rd.

Kaohsiung

Wen-Hwa Baptist Church (Interdenominational)
146 Wen-Heng 2nd Rd.

Ren-Ai Christian Center
76 Yu-Feng St.
YMCA
Saint Mary's Church (Catholic)
113 Chien-Kuo 4th Rd.

Restaurants In Taipei
Northern Chinese

The Celestial Kitchen (Peking), 1 Nanking W. Rd., 3rd Floor, Tel: 563-2171.
天厨，南京西路１號３樓
The Happy Pavilion (Peking), 16 Chung-Hsiao E. Rd., Sec. 4, Alley 49, Lane 4, basement, Tel: 781-7738.
陶然亭，忠孝東路，四段，49巷，4弄，16號
The Happy Guest Pavillion (Peking), 43-47 Chung-Hsiao E. Rd., Sec. 1, Tel: 321-2801/5.
忠孝東路，一段，43－47號
Genghis Khan (Mongolian Barbecue), 176 Nanking E. Rd., Sec. 3, Tel: 711-4412.
成吉思汗蒙古烤肉，南京東路，三段，176號
Aristocrat (Mangolian Barbecue), 282 Lin-Sen N. Rd., 3rd Floor, Tel: 571-3869
貴都蒙古烤肉，林森北路282號，３樓

Southern Chinese

The Northern Garden (Cantonese seafood), 63-1 Chang-An E. Rd., Sec. 1, Tel: 561-6535, 581-9820, (reservations recommended).
北園，長安東路，一段，63－1號
Garden of Peaceful Happiness (Cantonese), 232 Tun-Hwa N. Rd., Tel: 715-4929.
安樂園，敦化北路，232號
Ruby Restaurant (Cantonese), 135 Chung-Shan N. Rd., Sec. 2, Tel: 562-0378.
紅寶石，中山北路，二段，135號
The Kowloon Restaurant (Cantonese), 99 Lin-Sen N. Rd., Tel: 571-1101.
九龍，林森北路，99號
Tiffany's (Dim-Sum), Taipei Hilton Hotel, 3rd Floor, Tel: 311-5151, (lunch only).
明皇廳，希爾頓大飯店
Phoenix Hall (Dim-Sum), Leofoo Hotel, 11th Floor, Tel: 581-3111, (beautiful roof-top views).
六福賓館，11樓
Plum Blossom Room (Dim-Sum), Brother Hotel, 2nd Floor, Tel: 712-3456.
梅花廳，兄弟飯店

Eastern Chinese

The Casual Garden (Chekiang), Lai-Lai Sheraton Hotel, basement, Tel: 321-5511.
隨園，來來大飯店
The Sunny Garden (Chekiang), 92 Nanking E. Rd., Sec. 1, Tel: 581-5541.
順利園，南京東路，一段，92號
A Sprig of Spring (Yang-Chou), 25 Hsin-Yi Rd., Sec. 4, 2nd Floor, Tel: 702-1564, 705-9377.
一枝春，信義路，四段，25號
The Good Fortune (Shanghai), 261 Nanking E. Rd., Sec. 3, Tel: 715-3145.
天吉樓，南京東路，三段，261號
The Country Restaurant (Shanghai), 65-67 Chung-Hsiao East Rd., Sec. 4, Tel: 781-0477.
家鄉樓，忠孝東路，四段，65－67號

The Soo-Hang Eatery (Kiangsu), 138 Chung-Hsiao E. Rd., Sec. 1. Tel: 392-9879, (good provincial style cooking).
蘇杭小館，忠孝東路，一段，138號

The Longevity Restaurant (Shanghai), 21 Shuang-Cheng St., Lane 19, Tel: 597-5700.
萬壽樓，雙城街，19巷，21號

Western Chinese

The Glorious Star (Szechuan), 45 Chi-Lin Rd., Tel: 521-5340.
榮星川菜，吉林路，45號

The Lucky Star (Szechuan), 160 Chung-Hsiao E. Rd., Sec. 4, Tel: 771-1755.
福星川菜，忠孝東路，四段，160號

The Angelica Garden (Szechuan), 96 Chung-Shan N. Rd., Sec. 2, Tel: 581-6636.
芷園川菜，中山北路，二段，96號

The China Restaurant (Szechuan), 26 Min-Sheng E. Rd., Tel: 551-5044, 551-5068.
中華川菜，民生東路，26號

The Grand Restaurant (Hunnan), 206 Nanking E. Rd., Sec. 2, 3rd Floor, Tel: 542-7676, 542-8844.
榮華堂，南京東路，二段，206號

The Golden China (Hunnan), Taipci Hilton Hotel, 3rd Floor, Tel: 311-5151, (award winning Chef, plush decor).
金華廳，希爾頓大飯店

Les Copains des Chines'' (Hunnan), Ritz Hotel, basement, Tel: 597-1234.
湘菜館，亞都大飯店

Treasure Hall (Hunnan), 152 Sung-Kiang Rd., 3rd Floor, Tel: 581-9151.
金玉滿堂，松江路152號3樓

Li-Hsiang Pavilion (Hunnan), Chung-Hsiao E. Rd., Sec. 4, # 295, Tel: 772-2304/8.
利湘樓，忠孝東路，四段，295號

Taiwan Seafood

Seafood of Tainan (Fresh Seafood), 31 Hwa-Hsi St. ("Snake Alley"), Tel: 382-1123, (best seafood in town).
台南担仔麵，華西街，31號

Sea King (Fresh Seafood), 7 Hsi-Ning N. Rd., Tel: 562-6345.
海霸王，西寧北路，7號

Sea Admiral (Fresh Seafood), 56 Chang-Chun Rd., 2nd Floor, Tel: 536-7510/2.
海將軍，長春路，56號，2樓

Country Vista Restaurant (Taiwanese Seafood and game specialities), Wai-Shuang-Hsi, Central District, River-side, Tel: 841-1050, (this restaurant straddles a rocky brook in a lovely outdoor countrysetting near the National Palace Museum).
望鄉餐廳，外雙溪，中央社區，河邊

Vegetarian

The Plum Grove 3 Lin-Sen N. Rd., 2nd Floor, Tel: 391-0723, 391-0833, (around the corner from Lai-Lai Sheraton Hotel).
梅林素菜，林森北路3號

Vegetarian House, 70 Hwai-Ning St., Tel: 314-2020. 素菜之家，懷寧街70號

The Bodhi Garden, 32 Min-Sheng E. Rd., Tel: 562-8568, 521-3163.
菩提園素菜，民生東路32號

Western Restaurants

Traders Grill (Continental), Taipei Hilton Hotel, 2nd Floor, Tel: 311-5151, (award winning restaurant, deluxe ambiance and service, expensive).
西餐廳，希爾頓大飯店

Paris 1930 (French), Ritz Hotel, 2nd Floor, Tel: 597-1234, (plush decor, attentive service, expensive).
法國餐廳，亞都大飯店

La Lune Vague (French), Tien Mou, Chung 14 Street, Lane 11, No. 1, Tel: 837-2214; (antique Chinese furnishings, authentic French cuisine and service).
（醉月，天母，中14街，11巷，1號）

Zum Fass (Swiss, German), 55 Lin-Sen N. Rd., Lane 119, Tel: 531-3815; (small, cosy restaurant with nice bar; Swiss-German chef; rotating menus on black-board.
香宜，林森北路，119巷，55號

Europa Haus (Swiss, German), 21 Chang-An E. Rd., Sec. 1, Tel: 563-6615; (bountiful buffets, attached delicatessen, Swiss chef).
香歐，長安東路一段21號

Chalet Swiss (Swiss, Continental), 47 Nanking E. Rd., Sec. 4, Tel: 715-2051, 715-2702; (Swiss specialities, fondue; cosy ambiance; Swiss chef).
瑞華南京東路四段，47號

Le Romantique (French), 158 Chung-Shan N. Rd., Sec. 2, Tel: 596-1695. 羅漫蒂，中山北路二段158號; and 353-15 Tun-Hwa S. Rd., Tel: 771-4344; (run by Saigon chefs).
敦化南路353-15號

Fellini's (Italian, Continental), Beverly Plaza Hotel, 2nd Floor, Tel: 708-2151; (trendy Hollywood decor, genuine brick pizza-oven).
西餐廳，碧爾邑大飯店

Mama Roma (Italian), 3 Chen-Kiang St., Lane 1, Tel: 392-2695; (gourmet pizzas and other Italian cuisine; kosher food; located in lane directly behind Lai-Lai Sheraton).
義大利餐廳，鎮江街一巷3號

La Cantina (Italian), 143 Tun-Hwa N. Rd., Tel: 713-0603; (plush decor, good food).
肯蒂娜，敦化北路143號

The Hope and Anchor (American), 16-3 Shuang-Cheng St., Tel: 596-2949
木匠西餐廳，雙城街16-3號

Ploughman's Cottage (English), 305 Nanking E. Rd., Sec. 3, Tel: 713-4942; (attached pub; English country cooking; warm atmosphere).
犁房，南京東路三段305號

Primacy Restaurant & Club (Steaks, Continental), 148 Sung-Kiang Rd., basement, Tel: 531-1577, 542-7341; (fancy decor and service; dance-club with live band).
統帥，松江路148號

Audio City (Steaks), 217 Nanking E. Rd., Sec. 3, Tel: 721-4740, 721-0430, (music club with live band).
音樂城，南京東路三段217號

Pepe El Mongol (Grilled Meats & Mongolian Barbecue), #8, Lane 460, Tun-Hwa S. Rd., Tel: 773-3268.
犛原餐廳，敦化南路 460 巷 8 號

Other Cuisines

Seoul Korean Barbeque (Korean Barbecue and Fire-Pot), 4 Chung-Shan N. Rd., Sec. 1, Lane 33, 2nd Floor, Tel: 511-2326, 511-3436.
漢城烤肉，中山北路一段33巷，4 號 2 樓

Korean Fragrance Pavilion (Korean Barbecue and Fire-Pot), 76 Nanking E. Rd., Sec. 2, basement, Tel: 531-0217/8.
韓香亭，南京東路二段76巷，地下樓

Exquisite Garden (Korean Barbecue and Taiwanese Seafood), 8 Lin-Sen N. Rd., Lane 107, Tel: 564-1393, 543-1722.
佳園韓國烤肉，林森北路107巷 8 號

Chinese Turkestan Shish Kebob (Chinese Moslem cuisine), 153 Tun-Hwa N. Rd., Tel: 711-9353, 721-4910.
新疆烤肉，敦化北路153號

Nakayama (traditional Japanese), Hotel Royal Taipei, 2nd floor, Tel: 542-3266, ext. 328.
幸亭，日本料理，南京東路一段11－3號

Longevity Restaurant (traditional Japanese). 152 Chung-Shan North Rd., Sec. 1. basement. Tel: 561-3883/5.
壽樂，中山北路一段，152號，地下樓

New Hama (Japanese Teppanyaki Steak), 10 Nung-An St., Tel: 596-9621.
新賓，農安街10號

Gaylord's (Indian), 328 Sung-Kiang Rd., Tel: 543-4003.
印度菜，松江路328號

Pondok Mutiara (Indonesian), 111 Sung-Kiang Rd., 2nd Floor, Tel: 541-0226, 581-2273.
印尼餐廳，松江路，111號，二樓

Sports Clubs
Golf

Abbreviations used—GF: Guest Fee; CF: Caddy Fee.

Chia-Kuang Group Club, Tel: (052) 230-823; GF: NT$250; CF: NT$80.

Chien-Hsin Garden Golf Club, Sheng-Keng (25 minutes by car from Taipei); Tel: (02) 662-1263; GF: NT$300 weekdays, NT$500 weekends and holidays; CF: NT$150.

Far Eastern Golf Club, Pan-Chiao (30 minutes by car from Taipei); Tel: (02) 961-9100; GF: NT$420 weekdays, NT$620 weekends and holidays; CF: NT$150.

Feng-Yuan Golf Club, Feng-Yuan (2½ hours by car from Taipei, ½ hour by car from Taichung); Tel: (045) 222-835; GF: NT$450 weekdays, NT$600 weekends and holidays; CF: NT$180.

Hsin-Chu Golf and Country Club, Hsin-Fong (60 minutes by car from Taipei); Tel: (035) 552-331; GF: NT$700 weekdays, NT$1,200 weekends and holidays; CF: NT$160.

Hwa-Lien Golf Club, Hwa-Lien (10 minutes by car from Hwa-Lien); Tel: (038) 323-693; GF: NT$441 weekdays, NT$630 weekends and holidays; CF: NT$140.

Kaohsiung Golf and Country Club, Cheng-Ching Lake (20 minutes by car from Kaohsiung); Tel: (07) 381-1101; GF: NT$823 weekdays, NT$1,264 weekends and holidays; CF: NT$140.

Lin-Kou International Golf and Country Club, Lin-Kou (40 minutes by car from Taipei); Tel: (02) 601-1211; GF: NT$850 weekdays; NT$1,250 weekends and holidays; CF: NT$140.

Lung-Tang Golf and Country Club, Lung-Tang (60 minutes by car from Taipei); Tel: (034) 792-955, Taipei office: 562-2613; GF: NT$600 weekdays, NT$800 weekends and holidays; CF: NT$200.

Nan-Tou Golf and Country Club, Nan-Tou (45 minutes from Taichung); Tel: (049) 22084; GF: NT$200 weekdays, NT$300 weekends and holidays; CF: NT$150.

New Tan-Shui Golf Club, Tan-Shui (40 minutes by car from Taipei); Tel: (02) 621-2466; GF: NT$780 weekdays; NT$1,032 weekends and holidays; CF: NT$170.

Peitou Kuo-Hwa Country Club, Peitou (35 minutes by car from Taipei); Tel: (02) 621-1281/3; GF: NT$950 weekdays, NT$1,350 weekends and holidays; CF: NT$180.

Tai-Feng Golf Club, Yuang-Lin; Tel: (048) 345-101; GF: NT$400 weekdays, NT$600 weekends and holidays; CF: NT$160.

Tainan Golf and Country Club, Hsin-Hwa (30 minutes by car from Tainan); Tel: (064) 983-161; GF: NT$420 weekdays, NT$600 weekends and holidays.

Taiwan Golf and Country Club, Tan-Shui (40 minutes by car from Taipei); Tel: (02) 621-2211/5; GF: NT$1,250; CF: NT$200.

Tao-Yuan Golf Club, Tao-Yuan (45 minutes by car from Taipei); Tel: (034) 794-444; GF: NT$450 weekdays, NT$680 weekends and holidays; CF: NT$300.

Ta-Tun Golf Club, Tan-Shui (35 minutes by car from Taipei); GF: NT$524 weekdays, NT$776 weekends and holidays; CF: NT$180-280.

Tennis

* denotes private clubs where visitors are only allowed entry if accompanied by member.

* American Club in China, 47 Pei-An Rd., Taipei; Tel: 594-8260/3; 2 outdoor hard courts, lights, 1 squash and 1 racquet-ball court.

* Chang-Rong Indoor Tennis Club; 31 Yu-Nung Rd., 3rd Fl., Shin-Lin; Tel: 834-7801; 2 indoor hard courts, lights, pro-shop; NT$150 per hour weekdays, NT$200 weekends and holidays.

* Evergreen Tennis Club; 150-1 Chung Yang N. Rd., Lane 130, Peitou; Tel: 892-4132/5; 3 clay courts, 4 hard courts, showers, pool, coffee shop, lights; NT$100 per hour weekdays, NT$150 per hour weekends and holidays, NT$150 per hour at night.

Foo Bin Tennis Club, 45-1 Ping-Chiang Rd., Lane 103; Tel: 521-4880; 4 hard courts, showers; NT$200 per hour.

Grand Hotel, 1 Chung-Shan N. Rd., Sec. 4; Tel: 596-5565.

* Green Lake Tennis Club; 150 Cheng-Kung Rd., Sec. 5, Nei-Hu; Tel: 764-8732; 6 outdoor hard courts, 3 indoor hard courts, lights, showers, coffee shop, pool, sauna; NT$250 per hour.

Leofoo Tennis Club, 150 Pai-Ling 5th Rd., Peitou; Tel: 893-2347; 4 clay courts, lights, showers, pro-shop; NT$100 per hour; NT$150 at night.

Mandarin Hotel, 166 Tun-Hwa N. Rd.; Tel: 712-1201.

* Olympic Country Club, 7-1 Chih-Hang Rd., Hsi-Chih; 4 outdoor hard courts, 3 indoor hard courts, lights, coffee shop, pool, sauna.

Sung-Kiang Tennis Club, 15 Ping-Chiang St., Alley 5, Lane 103; 4 hard courts, showers, snack-shop; NT$150 per hour weekdays; NT$200 weekends.

Taipei Tennis Club, 4 Nanking E. Rd., Sec. 4; Tel: 771-6557; 8 clay courts, lights, showers, pro-shop; NT$50 per hour; NT$100 at night.

Ta-Shin Tennis Club, 150-1 Huan Ho Rd., Hsin-Tien; Tel: 913-3840; 7 clay courts, lights, showers; NT$200 per hour.

* Yangming Mountain Country Club, 49 Kai-Hsuan Rd., Yangming Mountain; Tel: 861-0941; 6 outdoor hard courts, lights, showers, coffee shop.

Youth Park Tennis Club, 199 Shui-Yuan Rd.; Tel: 303-2451; 6 hard courts, lights, showers; NT$60 per hour; NT$140 at night.

* Yuan Shan Club (Grand Hotel), 1 Chung-Shan N. Rd., Sec. 4; Tel: 596-5565; 4 outdoor clay courts, lights, pool, snack-shop.

Theaters

Ambassador Theatre（國賓戲院）
88 Cheng-Du Rd., Tel: 361-1222.
Far East Theatre（遠東戲院）
155 Tai-Yuan Rd., Tel: 541-7263.
Great World Theatre（大世界戲院）
51 Cheng-Du Rd., Tel: 331-4665.
Happy Theatre（快樂戲院）
124/2 Wu-Chang St., Sec. 2, 4th Fl., Tel: 381-1085.
Hoover Theatre（豪華戲院）
91 Wu-Chang St., Sec. 2, Tel: 331-5077.
Hsin-Sheng Theatre（新聲戲院）
55 Chung-Hwa Rd., Tel: 331-4402.
Lux Theatre（樂聲戲院）
87 Wu-Chang St., Sec. 2, Tel: 381-1853.
Majestic Theatre（眞善美戲院）
116 Han-Chung St., 7th Fl., Tel: 331-2270.
New World Theatre（新世界戲院）
116 Han-Chung St., Tel: 331-2752.
Sun Theatre（日新戲院）
89 Wu-Chang St., Sec. 2, Tel: 361-0317.

Tourist Information Offices

Head Office:

Tourism Bureau, P.O. Box 1490, Taipei, Taiwan, ROC; Cable: ROCTB TAIPEI; Telex: 26408 ROCTB; Tel: 721-8541.

United States:

Travel Section, Coordination Council for North American Affair, 166 Geary Street, Suite 1605, San Francisco, CA 94108; Tel: (415) 989-8677, 989-8694.

Travel Section, Coordination Council for North American Affairs, 1 World Trade Center, Suite 8855, New York, N.Y. 10048; Tel: (212) 466-0691/2.

Travel Section, Coordination Council for North American Affairs, 3325 Wilshire Blvd., Suite 515, Los Angeles, CA 90010; Tel: (213) 739-8898/9.

Germany:

Asia Trade Center, Tourism Bureau, Dreieich-

Japan:

Taiwan Visitors Association, A-9, 5F, Imperial Tower, Imperial Hotel, Uchisaiwai-Cho 1-1-1-1, Chiyoda-Ku, Tokyo 100, Tel: (03) 501-3591/2.

Singapore:

Taiwan Visitors Association, 5 Shenton Way, 14-07, UIC Building, Singapore 0106; Tel: 2236546/7

Australia:

Far East Trading Co. Pty. Ltd. Suite 3503, 35th Floor, MLC Building, MLC Center, Sydney, NSW 2000, Tel: 231-6942, 231-6973

Trade and Cultural Organizations (in Taipei)

American Chamber of Commerce
Rm. 1012, Chia Hsin Building Annex, 96 Chung-Shan North Rd., Sec. 2, Tel: 551-2515, 551-5211, ext. 441, 475.
American Information and Culture Section
54 Nan-Hai Rd., Tel: 303-7231.
American Institute in Taiwan
7 Hsin-Yi Rd., Sec. 3, Lane 134, Tel: 709-2000.
American Trade Center
261 Nanking E. Rd., Sec. 2, Tel: 713-2571.
Anglo-Taiwan Trade Committee
36 Nanking E. Rd., Sec. 2, 11th Fl., Tel: 521-4116.
Asian Exchange Center (Philippines)
112 Chung Hsiao East Rd., Sec. 1, Tel: 341-3125.
Australian Commerce and Industry Office
148 Sung-Kiang Rd., 4th Fl., Tel: 542-7950.
Australia Free China Society
34 Ren-Ai Rd., Sec. 2, 10th Fl.
Austrian Trade Delegation
205 Tun-Hwa N. Rd., Room 806, Tel: 715-5221.
Belgian Trade Association
205 Tun-Hwa N. Rd., Room 806, Tel: 715-5221.
Belgian Trade Association
685 Min-Sheng East Rd., Suite 901, Tel: 715-1215.
CETDC Exhibition Complex
10th floor, 201 Tun-Hwa North Rd., Tel: 715-1551.
China Trade and Development Corp.
Showroom, 150 Nanking E. Rd., Sec. 2, 4th Fl., Tel: 551-3072.
Chinese Handicraft Mart of the Taiwan
(Handicraft Promotion Center), 1 Hsu-Chow Rd., Tel: 321-7233.
Chinese Products Promotion Center
285 Nanking E. Rd., Sec. 3, 6th Fl., Tel: 711-2888.
France Asia Trade Promotion Association
96 Chung-Shan N. Rd., Sec. 2, 10th Fl., Tel: 561-7043.
French Cultural and Scientific Center
213 Hsin-Yi Rd., Sec. 2, 10th Fl., Tel: 394-0850/1.

German Cultural Center
33 Chung-Hsiao W. Rd., Sec. 1, 5th Fl., Tel: 331-3741, 311-8681/2.
German Trade Office
1516-17 Jade Phoenix Hall, Grand Hotel, Tel: 596-5565, ext. 1516/17.
The Hellenic Organization for the
Promotion of Exports in Taiwan
125 Roosevelt Rd., Sec. 3, 6th Fl., Tel: 391-0597.
Interchange Association
43 Chi-Nan Rd., Sec. 2, Tel: 351-7250/4.
Jordanian Commercial Office
278 Chung-Shan N. Rd., Sec. 6, 2nd Fl., Tel: 833-0400.
Korea Trade Center
76 Nanking E. Rd., Sec. 2, 4th Fl., Tel: 581-3030/1.
Singapore Trade Representative
685 Min-Sheng E. Rd., Tel: 715-8852.
Spanish Chamber of Commerce
122-4 Chung-Hsiao E. Rd., Sec. 4, 5th Fl., Tel: 711-2402.
Taipei World Trade Center
Sung-Shan airport terminal, Tel: 752-2311.
Thai International Limited
Administration Office, 124 Nanking E. Rd., Sec. 2, 3rd Fl., Tel: 531-0364/5.
Commercial Office, Tel: 597-2723.
Trade Promotion Center of International
Trade Association of ROC, 215 Nanking E. Rd., Sec. 3, 7th Fl., Tel: 751-9720.

Further Reading

Ahern and Gates, editors, *The Anthropology of Taiwanese Society*, Stanford University Press, Stanford, 1981.

Carrington, George Williams, *Foreigners in Formosa, 1841-1874*; Chinese Materials Center, San Francisco, 1977.

Chen Cheng-siang, *Taiwan, An Economic and Social Geography*, Taipei, 1963.

Cheng, James, *Doing Business in Taiwan*, Cheng Cheng Law Offices, Taipei, 1982.

Clough, Ralph N., *Island China*, Harvard University Press, Cambridge, 1978.

Davidson, James W., *The Island of Formosa, Past and Present*, MacMillan & Co., London, 1903.

Goddard, William G., *Formosa*, China Publishing Co., Taipei, 1958.

Goddard, William G., *Formosa, A Study in Chinese History*, MacMillan & Co., London, 1966.

Ho, Samuel P.S., *Economic Development of Taiwan, 1860-1970,*; Yale University Press, New Haven, 1978.

Mackay, Rev. George Leslie, *From Far Formosa*, Fleming H. Revell Co., New York, 1895.

Silin, Robert H., *Leadership and Values: The Organization of Large-Scale Taiwanese Enterprises*, Harvard University Press, Cambridge, 1976.

Wei, Henry and Suzanne Coutanceau, *Wine for the Gods, an Account of the Religious Traditions of Taiwan*, Cheng Wen Publishing Co., Taipei, 1976.

Wolf, Margery, *Women and the Family in Rural Taiwan*, Stanford University Press, Stanford, 1972.

Yen, Sophia Yu-fei, *Taiwan in China's Foreign Relations, 1836-1874*, Shoe String Press, Hamden, Connecticut, 1965.

Yu Ju-chi, editor, *Taiwan: A Beautiful Island*, TTV Culture Enterprise, Taipei, 1981.

Gods, Ghosts and Ancestors: Folk Religion in a Taiwanese Village, University of California Press, Berkeley, 1966.

Republic of China: A Reference Book, United Pacific International, Taipei, 1983.

A Photographer's Sketchbook — Bill Wassman

"I had never been to Taiwan before. I don't read a word of Chinese, nor do I speak the language. Nonetheless, I accepted the challenge of photographing the island with the great enthusiasm with which I take on any challenging project. I allowed the immensity of the task to sink into my head — before leaving for Taiwan. There would be no time for that later, no time even to doubt my wisdom in taking on the job of filling an *Insight Guide* with photographs taken all over the island in a short period of time. I had nightmares about how I would have to be shooting during every waking moment in order to finish the assignment. But I packed my bag and went anyway . . .

"I made two trips to Taiwan and spent exactly 53 days moving non-stop around the island. During that time I took hundreds of shots. I photographed everything — from temples to zoos, from people to sunsets. It was 53 days of hard work — rising at 6 every morning and shooting until the sun set, and sometimes at night. I was driven around in a car, a definite advantage for serious photographic work. The driver was Taiwanese. He spoke little English. But at least his English was better than his driving. Luckily, the weather was good most of the time. Every shot I took turned out. I left Taiwan with my bags bulging with over 600 shots ready for selection by Apa's editorial team . . .

"Taiwan is an exotic haven for photographers. Its people are easy to photograph because they are warm and friendly. They tend to be shy at times, but they do not mind being photographed. Some request a 'tip' for their trouble, especially the aborigines who have made tourism their trade. People shots are generally best taken in the morning before 10 a.m. or in the late afternoon. At any time, you will have to contend with the problem of their own shadows falling over their faces. The same rule applies when photographing architecture in Taiwan. . .

"Beware of the signposts around the island that warn against taking photographs. They are particularly common along the coastline where there is concern for military security. Some of the signpost warnings can be ignored if you photograph discreetly. But most must be taken seriously if you do not wish to get into trouble with the law. Be especially careful on Orchid Island where military installations abound. Be guided by your own discretion. Its usually safe to follow the example of Chinese tourists who are toting cameras . . .

"Taiwan's weather is constantly changing. If you get a fairly good sky, take advantage of it. It is not likely to last very long. The light conditions at the Taroko Gorge, for example, change every minute. For a good shot of the cavernous, marble rich gorge, it is best to get there as early as possible. The gorge tends to get cloudy from mid-morning. My picture (pp 98–99) was taken very early in the morning . . .

"The photography business also involves a great deal of creativity and originally. When I was at the Wulai Village, for example, I was met by aborigines who were all too eager to have their photographs taken, because they each expected a 'tip' of about NT\$20 (U.S. 50 cents) for each photo I took. Two girls who came up to me are familiar faces that have appeared in dozens of tourist brochures. It was a challenge to photograph them in a new way. So I took them to another spot, pointed my camera at a special angle and lo and behold, I had a picture never done before (pp 90).

"The art of observation and the creation of a good photograph go together like Siamese twins. As a great photographer once said, 'the photographer's most important and, likewise, most difficult task . . . is learning to see photographically.' Although this involves a degree of professional training, it is also a matter of personal taste, feelings and close observation. Take a look at the images on pp 126-127 and pp 238. Both were taken in Taipei — within minutes of each other. When I arrived at the crucial spot, everything appeared ordinary. There was nothing worth pointing my camera at. I saw the shop pictured on pp 126-127 but there were no lights on and too many people would have been walking in front of the camera. But suddenly someone switched the lights on, the crowds parted and I saw an image that would certainly do justice to the display of hundreds of shoes on sale for half the price that they would cost anywhere else in the world. Then, on turning around, I caught sight of the two men trying to fit in the missing pieces of their giant movie poster puzzle on pp 238. I snapped the shot just before they had put it all together. Within moments, I had found myself facing two good shots — and I captured them before they vanished forever. Conditions change from one moment to the next. It requires a bit of close observation to see things which we don't normally see . . .

"In Taiwan, it is important to distinguish between a temple and a monastery. Although they can have interchangeable roles at times, the former is basically a place where the public gathers to pray while the latter is a home for monks or nuns and prayer services for the public are only held on special days. Outside those special hours, private ceremonial services are held and visitors, particularly photographers, may not be welcome . . .

"Make sure you are familiar with the camera you are using. Do not try out a new body or lens during a trip unless you have memorized its operations manual from cover to cover. If anything can go wrong, it will go wrong during crucial moments of your trip when priceless photographs manifest themselves . . .

"Carry as many rolls of film with you as possible. Although film and photographic accessories are readily available in Taiwan, they routinely cost more when you run out at an important site and have to buy more film at tourist shops situated near the attraction . . ."

"Carry your extra rolls of film in your shoulder bag for hand inspection to avoid being X-rayed at customs checkpoints in airports. Don't believe the signs that say the X-rays will not harm your film. They may not, but they may . . ."

"Although most people in Taiwan do not object to having their photographs taken, it is still polite and proper to ask first . . ."

"Finally, there are innumerable things to photograph when traveling. Instead of wildly shooting at anything that comes along, it helps to give yourself a theme each day. That way your photographs will tell a fascinating story when you show them off back home . . .

"Patience is another prerequisite for taking good pictures in Taiwan or anywhere. The adage that describes 'the patience of an angler' might have been better suited to describe the professional photographer. Sun Moon Lake was another much photographed attraction on my itinerary shopping list. I was a wee bit weary because I had seen so many shots of the place. The lake itself is a dull grey but with the right kind of blue in sky, it turns into a beautiful emerald-turquoise body of water. The golden rule applies, of course: 'Be there early, before 10 a.m.' Half the shots I had seen taken of this spot showed the lake fronted by the magnificent Wen-Wu Temple. I wanted something different. I searched and searched for a new angle and for an entirely new composition. The time spent searching proved fruitful as can be seen on pp 158-159 . . .

ART/PHOTO CREDITS

Continued from page 9

Taiwan, met with Reid in Taipei, and laid a firm groundwork for the book. A native of American's Pacific Northwest and a former newspaper reporter in Honolulu and Seattle, Anderson joined Apa in 1981 after completing the Gannett Fellowship program in Asian studies at the University of Hawaii. Since then, he has overseen the creation of several new titles, including *Burma, Nepal* and *Sri Lanka.*

Paul Zach took on the task of turning an assortment of words and pictures into a well-rounded *Insight Guide: Taiwan* after producing successful volumes on *Florida* and *Jamaica.* A native of Cleveland and a graduate of Ohio University, Zach has written extensively about Asia for the *Washington Post, International Herald Tribune, Los Angeles Times, Business Week* and *Asian Wall Street Journal,* among other prominent publications. Also a former Gannett Fellow in Asia studies, he lived in Jakarta, covering Indonesia for ABC Radio News, for three years prior to offering his help to this project.

Zach spent a month in Taiwan absorbing the atmosphere, mingling with people he found to be some of "the warmest in the world" and coordinating the work of Reid and other writers and photographers. Upon his return to Singapore, he and Anderson combined efforts to shape all text into final form.

The book was designed by publisher **Hans Hoefer,** the founder of Apa Productions in 1970 and still its guiding mind. Hoefer also supervised all photography and made final selections of graphics. German by birth, Hoefer now directs Apa's fortunes from his headquarters in the Southeast Asian island nation of Singapore. His concept of a culturally oriented guidebook, appealing to both the active and armchair traveler, grew out of his years of training in the Bauhaus school of printing, photography and design.

The principal photographer for this volume was **Bill Wassman,** a resident of New York whose work first attracted international attention in *Insight Guide: Nepal.* Wassman spent two months poking his Leicas into every part of Taiwan. A graduate of Indiana University in comparative literature and anthropology, Wassman worked as a full-time assistant to photographers Eric Meola and Pete Turner in 1973 and 1974 before establishing his own reputation.

Frank Salmoiraghi spent several weeks photographing Taiwan between assignments in Singapore, Malaysia and Indonesia. A resident of Hawaii's Big Island, his fine images also enhance the pages of *Insight Guide:*

Hawaii. Salmoiraghi teaches a course in photography at the Honolulu Community College.

Dan Rocovits is a relative newcomer to the art of photography, but, like Reid, is a long-time resident of Taiwan. He first steamed into Keelung Harbor in 1968 and settled in the island as a free-lance writer, but soon discovered it was more lucrative to market his stories along with photos. Rocovits speaks Mandarin fluently and lives near Reid in the seductive hills of Peitou.

An aspiring young Taiwan photographer, **Chyou Su-liang,** better known to her friends as "Smiley," has been fine-tuning her photographic techniques while holding down odd jobs in Taipei. She plans to begin studies toward a degree in photography at a university in the United States.

Unger Lee Loo

Other photographs in *Insight Guide: Taiwan* are the work of Taiwan's **Chi Feng Lin,** Germany's **Heidrun Guether,** Hawaii's **Allan Seiden,** The Netherlands' **Paul Van Riel,** France's **Pierre-Antoine Donnet,** England's **Nick Wheeler,** globetrotting Southeast Asia scholar **Eric M. Oey,** and **Kal Muller,** an American resident of Mexico.

Keith Stevens' exploration of Taiwan's "Realm of Temples and Deities" is an outgrowth of his long interest in Chinese folk religions. Born in England in 1926, he studied Chinese at universities in London and Hong Kong. After that, he spent nearly a quarter of a century in the Far East, first with the British Army and later with his country's Foreign and Commonwealth Office.

Stevens first became interested in the Chinese pantheon of gods when he bought a large collection of images in 1948. His quest for further information about his collection took him to temples and god carvers in every Far Eastern country in which Chinese folk religion thrives. Stevens has been working on a definitive guide to the gods of China for nearly 20 years. He is also completing books on the gods that adorn the altars of Hong Kong and Macau.

Andy Unger penned this volume's introduction to Places and "The Tao of Chinese Art." He studied the psychology of language at Harvard and painting in Florence and London before moving to Taiwan to pursue a long-standing interest in Chinese calligraphy. Since then, he has played an active part in Taipei's contemporary gallery scene and has exhibited his own work in Taiwan and the United States. Unger was a contributing editor for the Republic of China's official yearbook. He presently edits a Taipei business journal and is Taiwan correspondent for a Hong Kong architectural magazine.

Jon-Claire Lee, a graduate of New York University's Department of Drama, contributed his insights to the piece on "The Taiwan Talent and Variety Show." He returned to his native Taiwan to take up a position as a faculty member of the Chinese Cultural University after working as a professional director

Smiley   Stevens

and actor in New York and Washington, D.C. Lee has played starring roles in Taiwan television dramas and was assistant director of the triumphant Taipei theatrical production of Pai Hsien-yung's *Wandering in the Garden/Working for a Dream*. His wife, Jeamin, a concert pianist and composer who collaborates with him in the musical aspects of his projects, also collaborated on the *Insight Guide* story. Despite his busy schedule, Lee also writes for Taiwan's two English-language newspapers and is the movie critic for *The Economic News*.

Assistant Editor **Vivien Loo** joined the Apa crew in 1982. Since then, her talent and drive have helped keep Apa's editorial factory in Singapore moving forward. Loo is in charge of coordinating work on the annual revisions of all *Insight Guides*. A resident of Singapore, she helped expand and improve *Insight Guides* on *Singapore, Hong Kong* and *Malaysia* before working on final preparation of the Taiwan book.

In addition to the main selection of color maps produced by cartographers under the direction of **Gunter Nelles** in West Germany, additional maps and charts were drawn by **Yong Sock Ming. Justine Rajoo** and **Frances Yap** also provided invaluable production assistance.

Also helping to make this book possible were Yu Wei, Chou Chung-Ying and Watt Ju of the Tourism Bureau of the Republic of China's Ministry of Communications,

Michael T.C. Chen of the Government Information Office's Division of Information and Protocol, Richard C.T. Wang and his staff at the National Palace Museum, C. Shen of the City of Tainan's Office of the Secretary and the staff of the Tainan Historical Museum at Koxinga's Shrine and Taiwan's Central News Agency (CNA). Special thanks to Dick T.K. Chen of the Singapore office of the Taiwan Visitors Association who proofread Chinese characters used in the text.

Apa is also grateful for assistance from Joseph Lue and May M.Y. Hwang of the Taipei Hilton International, Johnny Wu of The Whispering Pines Inn (In-Song-Ger) in Peitou, David Low of the Taipei Lai Lai Sheraton, driver Huang Lu-tang, Yang Kuang, Lee Pei-ling, Jenny Jin, Milo Chang, Mac S.F. Wang, Tony Lim Tow Long, Eric Oey, Kathy McClure, and to the proprietors of the Sunshine City Restaurant and Queen's Restaurant.

Apa's executive marketing director Yvan Van Outrive, also deserve a tip of the hat. To everyone else who contributed in some way to the production of this book as well as to the warm people of Taiwan, a hearty *Sheh sheh ni*.

— Apa Productions